AFRICAN HISTORICAL DICTIONARIES
Edited by Jon Woronoff

60. *Rwanda,* by Learthen Dorsey. 1994.
61. *Benin,* 3rd ed., by Samuel Decalo. 1995.
62. *Republic of Cape Verde,* 3rd ed., by Richard Lobban and Marlene Lopes. 1995.
63. *Ghana,* 2nd ed., by David Owusu-Ansah and Daniel Miles McFarland. 1995.
64. *Uganda,* by M. Louise Pirouet. 1995.
65. *Senegal,* 2nd ed., by Andrew F. Clark and Lucie Colvin Phillips. 1994.
66. *Algeria,* 2nd ed., by Phillip Chiviges Naylor and Alf Andrew Heggoy. 1994.
67. *Egypt,* 2nd ed., by Arthur Goldschmidt, Jr. 1994.
68. *Mauritania,* 2nd ed., by Anthony G. Pazzanita. 1996.
69. *Congo,* 3rd ed., by Samuel Decalo, Virginia Thompson, and Richard Adloff. 1996.
70. *Botswana,* 3rd ed., by Jeff Ramsay, Barry Morton, and Fred Morton. 1996.
71. *Morocco,* 2nd ed., by Thomas K. Park. 1996.

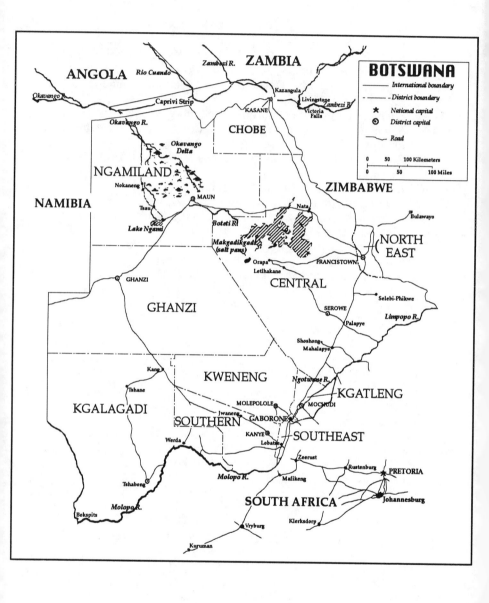

Historical Dictionary of Botswana

Third Edition

Jeff Ramsay
Barry Morton
and
Fred Morton

African Historical Dictionaries, No. 70

The Scarecrow Press, Inc.
Lanham, Md., & London
1996

SCARECROW PRESS, INC.

Published in the United States of America
by Scarecrow Press, Inc.
4720 Boston Way
Lanham, Maryland 20706

4 Pleydell Gardens, Folkestone
Kent CT20 2DN, England

Copyright © 1996 by Jeff Ramsay, Barry Morton, and Fred Morton

British Cataloguing-in-Publication Information Available

Library of Congress Cataloging-in-Publication Data
Ramsay, Jeff.
Historical dictionary of Botswana / Jeff Ramsay, Barry Morton, and
Fred Morton. — 3rd ed.
p.   cm. — (African historical dictionaries series ; no. 70)
Fred Morton's name appears first on the earlier eds.
Includes bibliographical references.
1. Botswana—History—Dictionaries. I. Morton, Barry.
II. Morton, Fred, 1939– . III. Title. IV. Series: African
historical dictionaries ; no. 70.
DT2434.R36 1996   968.83′003—dc20   96-5457   CIP

ISBN 0-8108-3143-0 (alk. paper)

Contents

Editor's Foreword

When independence arrived in 1966, Botswana's prospects were not very bright. Poor, arid, and landlocked, Botswana had been one of Africa's most neglected colonies. Its people were among the poorest in the world. Moreover, it was not "free" in the way that other emerging states were, with friendly and sympathetic neighbors. Botswana had to contend with the white regimes almost completely surrounding it, in colonial Rhodesia, South African-controlled Namibia, and South Africa itself. Yet Botswana has managed to overcome many difficulties and remain at peace with the other countries in the region. Also remarkably, it has successfully expanded its economy and cultivated an indigenous democracy within a modern bureaucratic state.

How Botswana managed to overcome such adversities is a major story in itself. It is only the latest chapter in a much longer development that stretches back into colonial and precolonial times. Moreover, having been confronted by forces operating in the southern African region rather than by a powerful colonial state, Botswana's people and their institutions have historically assumed much responsibility for dealing with many of their own problems. Consequently, indigenous roots are much stronger here than elsewhere and external influences are less decisive. The authors have taken meticulous care to describe these antecedents and to explain the present situation.

The third edition of the *Historical Dictionary of Botswana* results from the cooperation of three scholars with very close ties to Botswana. Fred Morton, who led the team, is professor of history at Loras College, Iowa, and past senior lecturer at the University of Botswana. Jeff Ramsey teaches at Legae Academy, Gaborone, and writes a column on Botswana affairs and history in the local press. Barry Morton has recently completed his doctoral degree in African history at Indiana University; he wrote his dissertation on colonial Ngamiland. This considerably expanded and updated volume should prove extremely useful for all who want to know more about a very special part of Africa.

Jon Woronoff
Series Editor

Acknowledgments

The authors are grateful to the Department of History, Loras College, for their support in seeing this volume to a conclusion. We wish also to thank Mrs. Gladys Fitzpatrick of Loras College for her assistance with the bibliography.

Note on African Languages and Glossary[1]

In this Dictionary, entries of Africans are usually listed by the first name (e.g., Seretse Khama, rather than Khama, Seretse). If commonly known by a western name or set of initials, the last or surname is listed (e.g., Masire, Quett; Motsete, K.T.)

With the exception of **Khoisan** languages, spoken by roughly 5 percent of the population, all other indigenous languages of Botswana are members of the Bantu family of African languages. Of these the only one in common use is SeTswana, a branch of the Sotho-Tswana group. SeTswana is, along with English, an official national language used in the government press, radio broadcasts, and public meetings, and is taught as part of the primary and secondary school syllabi.[2] Other Bantu languages spoken by significant numbers are SeKgalagadi (a separate dialect of Sotho), Ikalanga (of the Shona group), OtjiHerero, SiNdebele (of the Nguni group), and SiYei.

The following SeTswana terms, which appear in the entries, are widely understood by residents of Botswana.

BaTswana	The people of Botswana.
Bogosi	The title, power, authority, and institution of the **Kgosi.**
Bogwera	**Initiation** for young men.
Bolata	Status of permanent inferiority, sometimes giving way to servitude, slavery. Similar to botlhanka.
Dikgosana	"Little diKgosi," properly applied to royal de-

---

[1] Each reference to a dictionary entry appears in boldface.
[2] Bantu names appear in this Dictionary in their proper form, i.e., with prefixes. For example the people of Botswana are referred to as BaTswana, a citizen of that country as a MoTswana, and the language, SeTswana. To make it easier for those unfamiliar with Bantu languages, the prefix is always indicated by capitalizing the first letter of the root term that follows it and by alphabetizing entries according to the root, rather than the prefix (e.g., *See* Tswana).

	scendants of the paternal line who often served as leading councilors and assistants of the **Kgosi.**
DiKgosi	Plural of **Kgosi.**
Dingaka	Traditional doctors, singular mungaka. *See* Health.
Kgosi	Often mistranslated as "chief," a Kgosi is a leader who inherits his position among SeTswana-speaking people but is usually installed and able to exercise authority only after his succession is approved by his subjects at large.
Kgotla	A public place in a traditional town ward or center where meetings are held to discuss group matters and customary legal cases are heard and decided.
Mafisa	Cattle loaned to others for draught use and/or milking in return for their proper care. Mafisa is also a way to disperse heifers for lowering risks of reproductive failure.
Masimo	The land used strictly for the raising of grain, fruits, and vegetables. It may also refer to the rural, as opposed to the town, residence of a family.
Merafe	*See* Morafe.
Mfecane	An Nguni word referring to the upheavals of the early nineteenth century. The Sotho equivalent is **Difaqane.**
Mohumagadi	Matriarchal title most often applied to the wife or mother of the present or future Kgosi.
Morafe	The people who accept the authority of the Kgosi, thereby constituting a SeTswana polity. Often mistranslated as "tribe." Plural: merafe.
Moraka	The "cattle post" where, traditionally, a man kept his herd during one of the seasons, but which, with the spread of boreholes, is now used year-round.
MoTswana	A person of Botswana; modern usage, "citizen." Plural: BaTswana.

Acronyms

The acronyms below appear in various entries. Boldface is used to indicate those with their own entry; *See* [term] is used for terms that form part of another entry.

AAPC   African Auxiliary Pioneer Corps. *See* World War II.

ANC   **African National Congress.**

BBP   Bechuanaland Border Police. *See* Police.

BDF   **Botswana Defence Force.**

BDP   **Bechuanaland/Botswana Democratic Party.** *See* Democratic Party.

BIP   **Botswana Independence Party.** *See* Independence Party.

BNF   **Botswana National Front.** *See* National Front.

BPP   **Bechuanaland/Botswana People's Party.** *See* People's Party.

BPWU   Bechuanaland Protectorate Workers' Union. *See* Trade Unions.

BSACO   **British South Africa Company.**

BWCCO   British West Charterland Company.

DRC   **Dutch Reformed Church.**

JAC   Joint Advisory Council. *See* Councils.

LEGCO   Legislative Council. *See* Councils.

LMS   **London Missionary Society.**

MP   Member of parliament (i.e., of the National Assembly).

SADC   **Southern African Development Community.**

SADCC   **Southern African Development Coordination Conference.**

SAR   South African Republic.

UCCSA   United Congregational Church of Southern Africa. *See* London Missionary Society.

ZCC   **Zion Christian Church.**

Chronology

23,000 BC	Stone Age; **rock art** in the region.
200 BC	Evidence of livestock keeping in northern Botswana.
on or before 1000 AD	Ancestors of Ba**Kalanga** and Sotho-Tswana speakers in Botswana; evidence of permanent settlements.
ca. 1400	Further migrations of ancestors of modern Ba**Kgalagadi** into Botswana; Ba**Yei** present in Ngamiland.
ca. 1450	Rise of the Ba**Kalanga** kingdom of **Butwa** under the Chibundule dynasty.
ca. 1500	Further colonization of Botswana by ancestors of modern Ba**Tswana**; Bekuhane (BaSubiya); Ba**Birwa**; Ba**Pedi**.
ca. 1650	Ba**Kwena** occupy southeastern Botswana.
ca. 1680	Nichasike overthrow Chibundule dynasty to rule **Butwa**. His "Rozwi" defeat the Portuguese in Zimbabwe.
ca. 1730	Ba**Ngwaketse** break from Ba**Kwena**.
ca. 1750	Ba**Ngwato** break from Ba**Kwena**.
ca. 1790	Ba**Tawana** split from Ba**Ngwato**.
1825	Ba**Kololo** of Sebetwane invade Botswana, defeat Ba**Kwena**, Ba**Ngwaketse**, **Mmanaana Kgatla**, and begin fifteen-year migration through eastern and northern Botswana.
1826	Ba**Ngwaketse** ruler **Sebego I** defeats Ba**Kololo** at **Dithubaruba**, resulting in their migration northward.
ca. 1828	Ba**Kalanga** (**Butwa**) defeat Ba**Ngwato** at Matopos.
1832	Ama**Ndebele** of Mzilikazi move to western Transvaal and send tribute collectors into Botswana.

1834	Sebego's BaNgwaketse defeat AmaNdebele at Dutlwe.
1837–1840	AmaNdebele migrate through eastern and northern Botswana, settle permanently in western Zimbabwe.
1841	David Livingstone begins missionary work in Botswana.
1842	AmaNdebele raid BaKwena, Kgafela Kgatla, BaNgwato.
1844	BaNgwato use guns in defeating AmaNdebele at Shoshong.
1847	David Livingstone establishes mission at Kolobeng.
1852–1853	BaTswana-Boer War. BaTswana of Botswana preserve their independence. BaTlokwa, BaLete, BaHurutshe, Mmanaana Kgatla, BaRolong migrate into Botswana.
1857	BaTswana-Transvaal Boer relations improve, Lutheran missionaries arrive.
1863	BaNgwato defeat AmaNdebele for the second time, at Shoshong.
1864	BaKwena, BaNgwaketse, and BaRolong threaten South African Republic with renewed war if Transvaal Boers seize BaHurutshe land; SAR backs down.
1867	German explorer Karl Mauch finds gold at Tati.
1871	Missionary Joseph Ludorf drafts constitution for "United Barolong, Batlhaping, and Bangwaketse Nation"; BaKwena subsequently join union, but constitution lapses.
1883	BaRolong, BaNgwaketse, BaKwena, and Kgafela Kgatla renew defensive alliance in face of Boer aggression against the BaRolong.
1884	BaTawana defeat AmaNdebele at Khutiyabasadi.
1885	British proclaim the Bechuanaland Protectorate.
1889	Most BaTswana diKgosi object to colonial rule at Kopong Conference.
1890	Over local objections, British grant themselves right to exercise colonial control

through the **Foreign Jurisdictions Act**; the "pioneer column" of the **BSACO** passes through Botswana en route to **Zimbabwe**.

1891   **Order-in-Council** gives the **high commissioner** wide-ranging administrative powers.

1893   Bechuanaland Border Police and Ba-**Ngwato** help the **BSACO** destroy the Ama-Ndebele kingdom in **Zimbabwe**.

1895   **Bathoen I, Khama III**, and **Sechele I** travel to Britain to oppose the transfer of their territories to **BSACO**'s administrative control.

1896   **Jameson Raid** ends threat of transfer; **rinderpest** destroys most livestock.

1897   Mafikeng-Bulawayo railroad built.

1899   The **boundaries** of major BaTswana "reserves" demarcated; hut tax introduced.

1899–1902   BaTswana fight in the **South African War**.

1901   *Koranta ea Becoana*, the first **newspaper** owned and run by BaTswana, appears.

1903–1905   Thousands of Ova**Herero** and **Nama** flee to Botswana to escape German oppression in **Namibia**.

1906   British depose **Sekgoma Letsholathebe**, Kgosi of the Ba**Tawana**.

1908–1910   BaTswana campaign against **incorporation** into the Union of South Africa commences.

1912   Native Recruiting Corporation begins systematic recruitment of **migrant labor** for the mines. BaTswana delegation attends opening conference of **African National Congress**.

1914–1918   **World War I** in which BaTswana soldiers serve in France, East Africa, and Namibia.

1919   Native (later African) Advisory Council established, begins history of **councils**.

1920   Ba**Birwa** of Malema forced from the **Tuli Block**.

1924   **South Africa** begins fifteen-year ban on **cattle** exported to the Union from the Protectorate.

1926   **Tsekedi Khama** begins eventful reign as BaNgwato regent.

1931	British depose **Sebele II**, Kgosi of the Ba-Kwena, and exile him to Ghanzi.
1933	**Tshekedi Khama** briefly suspended as Ba-Ngwato regent after having a European flogged in the Serowe **kgotla** for misconduct; British threaten to bomb Mosopa, forcing Kgosi **Gobuamang** to surrender.
1934	Resident Commissioner **Charles Rey** issues "Native Proclamations," resisted by Tshekedi and other diKgosi; Witwatersrand Native Labour Association begins recruiting mining laborers north of twenty-two degrees latitude.
1936	**Molefi** of the **Kgafela Kgatla** suspended as Kgosi.
1938	Tribal treasuries introduced.
1939–1945	**World War II,** in which more than 10,000 BaTswana serve in Europe, the Middle East, and North Africa.
1943	DiKgosi accept revised "Native Administration" proclamations.
1947	Village of followers of **John Nswazwi** stormed by BaNgwato in presence of Protectorate police.
1946–1949	BaTswana soldiers stationed in Middle East.
1949	**Seretse Khama** banished from Bangwato Reserve; **Tshekedi Khama** suspended.
1950	The multiracial Joint Advisory Council established.
1952	At Serowe, three police officers killed in protest against Seretse's banishment.
1954	**Abattoir** opened in **Lobatse.**
1956	**Seretse Khama** returns to Botswana.
1957	Elected local **councils** introduced.
1959	**Leetile Raditladi** establishes the **Federal Party.**
1960	**People's Party (BPP)** founded.
1961	First meeting of the Legislative Council; **Democratic Party (BDP)** founded.
1962	BPP splits; **Philip Matante** and **K.T. Motsete** attack **Motsamai Mpho** and "ANC influence" in Botswana.
1963	Independence talks lead to agreement

based on one person, one vote constitution; construction of new capital at **Gaborone.**

1965   **BDP** wins by a landslide in first National Assembly election; **Seretse Khama** becomes prime minister.

1966   **Independence; Seretse Khama** becomes Botswana president.

1967   Discovery of **diamonds** announced.

1970   First diamond mine opened at Orapa.

1974   Production of **copper** begins at Selebi Phikwe.

1976   Pula becomes national **currency**, replacing the South African Rand.

1977   **Botswana Defence Force** formed.

1980   **Seretse Khama** dies; **Quett Masire** becomes president.

1980–1987   In spite of severe, prolonged **drought**, nutritional standards improve.

1982   Second diamond mine opens at Jwaneng.

1985   Twelve Gaborone residents murdered during a night raid by the South African Defence Force.

1986   Sir Seretse Khama Memorial International Airport opens in Gaborone.

1987   Morupule Electric Power Station begins operation.

1988   Four Gaborone residents die in a night raid by the South African Defence Force.

1991   Sowa Soda Ash Works begins production; Botswana's **population** doubles over previous twenty years, passes the one million mark.

1992   Botswana placed among "upper middle income" national economies in the world.

1994   Botswana conducts seventh free and fair national election; Quett Masire reelected to third term as president.

Introduction

The Country

The Republic of Botswana covers 224,710 square miles, making it the equivalent in size of Kenya, the Iberian Peninsula, or the old Northwest Territory (Illinois, Indiana, Michigan, Ohio, and Wisconsin). Botswana stands in the center of southern Africa, bordering Namibia on the west and north, South Africa on the south and southeast, and Zimbabwe on the northeast. For a few miles, Botswana's northernmost border touches Zambia.

Botswana (literally, "the country of the Tswana") is a former British **protectorate** known as the Bechuanaland Protectorate (1885–1966).

Geographically, most the country is part of the ancient Kalahari Basin and is dominated by the Kalahari Sands, which stretch from the northern Cape of South Africa to Zaire. The Kalahari Basin is one of Africa's principle semiarid zones. The Kalahari Sands region is, nevertheless, a passageway for major rivers. The Molopo, along the southern border of Botswana, flows west into the Orange River. The Chobe, along the northern border, flows east into the Zambezi. But in the case of the Okavango, which is the only large river to penetrate Botswana, the Kalahari stands in its way. The Okavango flows south into northwestern Botswana from Angola and soon fans out to form one of the world's largest inland deltas (5,000 square miles). Emptying enormous amounts of water into the desert, the **Okavango Delta** is a huge oasis, supporting all forms of life. Typical of oases, this vast water source simply evaporates and contributes nothing to the semiarid country surrounding it.

Apart from the Delta, most of Botswana's surface is unsuitable for permanent settlement. The great majority of Botswana's population is concentrated on a narrow strip straddling the railway line along its eastern borders with **South Africa** and **Zimbabwe**. This territory is situated outside the Kalahari Sands and inside an area where rainfall tends to be heavier and more reliable. Nevertheless, arable land amounts to only about 5

1

percent of Botswana's total area, and even here **water** is a constant concern. Botswana is subject to regular cycles in which sufficient rainfall occurs over a ten-year period, followed by ten years of below-average rainfall often accompanied by severe **drought**. Apart from the peak years of the wet cycle, rain is often highly localized, irregular in amounts, and otherwise unpredictable.

Though characteristically dry, Botswana supports an abundance of stock and game. The typical cover for much of the Kalahari Sands is shrub or tree savanna, which for generations has proved ideal for hunting and grazing. Except during periods of extreme drought, herds of wildebeest, gemsbok, and other ungulates migrate seasonally into most parts of the Kalahari. Through the use of shafted wells (boreholes), cattle can be ranged there permanently.

Botswana is for the most part a tableland, averaging heights of little more than 3,000 feet above sea level and having few significant depressions or elevations. Its altitude and straddling of the Tropic of Capricorn account for Botswana's subtropical climate. Temperatures range from a daytime high of above 100 degrees Fahrenheit during the summer months (December through February) to a nighttime low below freezing in winter (June through August). Greater extremes of temperature are experienced in the Kalahari and in the south than in other parts of Botswana. Throughout the country, rain is most likely to fall between November and March and least likely to occur between June and August. Seasonal changes can be marked by great turbulence, with winds and duststorms during August and September and thunderstorms between October and December.

The People

The most recent **census** (1991) of Botswana's population reported a total of 1,327,000, of whom 1,258,837 were resident citizens and 29,557 were resident non-citizens. Average population density, though up to 5.9 per square mile from 4.3 in 1981 (a 37% increase), is still among the lowest in the world. Botswana's population growth continues, though birth rates are down from 3.5% in 1981 to 2.8% in 1991. Population increase is, in part, testimony to Botswana's success in improving the **health** of its people, attested to by the increase in the average life expectancy over the same period from 58 to 62.6 years, the subcontinent's highest. The most recent estimate of Botswana's population (1993) was 1,444,000.

Most of Botswana's people are rural dwellers, though the number living in **towns** is increasing dramatically. In 1991, 24.4% of the population lived in one of eight urban districts, up from 15% in 1981, and an additional 21.4% lived in rural towns with populations of 5,000 or more. Urban and town migration has been stimulated by economic growth in these sectors, as well as the government's investment in infrastructure and provision of social services. During the drought-stricken 1980s, many migrated from the countryside to the towns. Botswana's fastest-growing city—the capital of **Gaborone**—is also its largest. With 133,463 residents in 1991, it was growing at a rate of 10.3% annually.

Botswana's people are quite heterogeneous and representative of the southern African region as a whole. Linguistically, the Bantu family is by far the most common, and the Sotho-Tswana group predominates within it. **SeTswana** is the first language of most of the indigenous population and is known by the vast majority. It is also one official language, the second being English. Other Bantu languages spoken in Botswana are SeKgalagadi, SeLozi, SePedi, Ikalanga, OtjiHerero, IsiNdebele, SiMbukushu, and SiYei. Apart from Bantu, eleven languages loosely grouped as **Khoisan** are spoken by approximately 60,000 persons. More recent permanent settlers speak Afrikaans, English, IsiXhosa, and Gujerati.

The major social groups, known as *merafe* (sing. *morafe*; sometimes mistranslated as "tribes"), are also extremely heterogeneous. The largest of these are the BaKgatla, BaKwena, BaNgwaketse, BaNgwato, and BaTawana, each of which consists of many wards with varied ethnic, totemic, and linguistic origins. Merafe members were historically united through a hierarchical legal and political system and the use of the SeTswana language. Each *morafe* has its capital town, the population of which can exceed 30,000. In the past the merafe also controlled many subject people who were not recognized as having their own wards and who were not absorbed culturally.

Botswana's people utilize a wide range of resources. The traditional rural economy is mixed, with **agriculture**, herding, hunting, and gathering providing important dietary inputs. The most important crops have been millet, sorghum, cowpeas, beans, melons, and corn (maize), which are planted as early as November and harvested as late as June. Cattle, sheep, and goats are ranged in nearly all parts of the country, though **cattle** are by far the most numerous, totalling 2,844,000 in 1991. Cattle are kept at posts *(meraka)* away from the major rural towns, though oxen are kept in the towns or taken to the fields for draught purposes. Traditionally, the men and boys of a cattle-holding family spent months away at the cattleposts, whereas the women, girls, and young children lived away from the town next to the cultivated fields. Hunting game and drying meat *(biltong)* supplemented the family diet, as did gathering of wild fruits and vegetables (at independence, game meat accounted for more than half the protein consumed in the country). In and around the Okavango Delta, where the **tsetse** fly is prevalent, fishing plays an important role, as does farming in the fingers of the delta swamp when the seasonal flood recedes.

The modern national **economy**, which began to emerge in the late colonial period, revolves around exporting minerals and importing food and manufactured goods. Botswana's **mining** industry produces **diamonds, copper,** nickel, coal, salt, soda ash, and potash, which together constitute nearly 95% of the nation's exports. In 1993, the export value of diamonds was $4.37 billion, amounting to 88.2% of the nation's exports. Botswana also exports frozen beef (4.4%). Foreign credit has been used for the building of Botswana's infrastructure, which was virtually nonexistent at independence, and export revenues have covered recurrent expenditures and the import of manufactured and processed goods. In excess of 80 percent of the food consumed in Botswana is grown outside the country, mostly in South Africa, on which Botswana is also dependent for **railroad** and trunk road outlets, investment capital, **customs union** revenues, fuel imports, vehicles, spare parts, pharmaceuticals, electrical goods and appliances, and items such as paper, pencils, and chalk. In terms of **employment,** approximately 22,000 citizens of Botswana held jobs in South Africa in 1991.

Botswana's mineral revenues have made possible a major expansion of social and public facilities. Universal free primary and secondary **education** has been achieved, and all towns of 5,000 or more have been provided with water, schools, health clinics, and in many cases electricity and telephone communication. Permanent roads, which totaled three miles at independence, covered more than 2,000 miles in 1992. Large-scale projects include a national electricity grid, dam construction, urban planning and development, irrigated farming, international **air transportation** and satellite telecommunications, and university and technical education.

The hub of Botswana is its capital city **Gaborone.** In addition to being the site of the National Assembly and Office of the President, Gaborone is the headquarters of the National Bank and of all government ministries, departments, and **parastatals**. The main offices of the country's largest company Debswana, and its subsidiary Botswana Diamond Valuing Company (BDVC), are also located there, as are many companies and commercial houses operating in Botswana. The other important commercial centers are **Francistown** in the northeast, Selebi Phikwe in the east, and **Lobatse** in the south. Lobatse is also Botswana's principal meat-packing center, and Selebi Phikwe is important for copper-nickel mining. The small towns of Jwaneng and Orapa are located next to Botswana's two largest diamond mines. Mahalapye is the headquarters of the new Botswana Railways, and Palapye is located near the Morupule coal fields and national power station. **Maun**, located next to the Okavango Delta in the northwest, is the center of Botswana's **tourism**.

History

Botswana has always been an integral part of southern Africa. Early Iron Age sites reveal connections with **Zimbabwe, South Africa, Namibia**, the **Caprivi Strip**, Angola, and **Zambia**, and interaction with them has continued to the present. Most notable in this respect have been the past two-and-a-half centuries, when people from surrounding areas entered Botswana and greatly influenced its modern history. In the north the BaYei colonized the Okavango Delta and BaKalanga were disturbed by the Ama-Ndebele and then dominated by the BaNgwato. In the central and southern Kalahari, the BaKwena, BaNgwaketse, BaNgwato, and BaTawana encroached upon the BaKgalagadi and Khoe.

In the nineteenth century, upheavals and displacements in southern Africa had their impact in Botswana. During the **mfec-ane**, the BaKololo and AmaNdebele passed through Botswana raiding cattle; after trekking into the Transvaal, the **Boers** attempted to invade Botswana in the 1850s. White conquest in southern Africa created refugees who resettled in Botswana, such as the **Kgafela Kgatla, BaLete, BaRolong, BaTlokwa**, and **BaHurutshe**. BaKalanga migrated toward the Kalahari away from AmaNdebele and Rhodesian rule, as did the BaBirwa. The Ova-**Herero** and **Nama** fled the Germans occupying Namibia (South-west Africa). Botswana has for generations provided a haven for **refugees**. In the twentieth century, persecuted groups and individuals from surrounding colonies have relocated here, including (Ba)Hurutshe from the Transvaal, **Vapostori** from Rhodesia, Ha**Mbukushu** from Angola, AmaXhosa from the Cape, BaSotho and BaTswana from the Orange Free State and Lesotho, **coloureds** from the northern Cape and Namibia, and members of all the liberation groups in southern Africa.

During the nineteenth century, as well, the people of Botswana developed new trade and diplomatic connections throughout the region. Kalahari game trophies, which were marketed in Europe via Grahamstown, Durban, and Walvis Bay, attracted hunters and **traders**, gave rise to long-distance wagon trails, spread western technology and manufactured goods, and opened Botswana to missionaries, in particular those of the **London Missionary Society** and of the Hermannsburg **Lutherans**. Many Tswana towns grew as commercial centers, such as **Molepolole**, and the head (**Kgosi**) of each assumed importance as supervisors of trade and traders, dispensers of **concessions**, negotiators with white governments, patrons of black and white missionaries, and regulators of westernization. Such nineteenth-century diKgosi as **Sechele I**, **Khama III**, and **Linchwe I**, played important roles in shaping modern Botswana. Following the discovery of diamonds in Kimberley and gold on the Witwatersrand, Botswana became part of the region coveted by Cape settlers, Transvaal Boers, and the British. The greatest potential harm to Botswana was posed by the **British South Africa Company (BSACO)**, headed by Cecil Rhodes.

The colonial period began in 1885 with the **Warren Expedition** proclaiming the land north of the Molopo River and south of twenty-one-degree latitude as the Bechuanaland Protectorate of Great Britain. The borders of the **Protectorate** were later altered to constitute the shape of present Botswana, and the **reserves** demarcated by the Protectorate government correspond closely to Botswana's present-day **districts**. For years, Britain regarded the Protectorate as an orphan rather than its own creation. In 1895 the Protectorate was almost handed over to the BSACO, and in 1909 Britain provided for its transfer to the Union of South Africa. **Incorporation**, which was resisted for years by nearly all BaTswana, was never carried out by the British. The Protectorate remained free from the control of the white settler governments surrounding it, and diKgosi, who were relied on to raise taxes, uphold customary law, and control their subjects, exercised considerable power at the local level. Major events in the colonial period often centered around diKgosi with forceful personalities, such as **Tshekedi Khama**, **Bathoen II**, and **Kgari Sechele**, who were as likely to be in conflict with the colonial administration as their own subjects.

In terms of economic development, Britain neglected the Protectorate, except as a labor reserve for South Africa's mines. Apart from failed efforts of the **Resident Commissioner Charles Rey** in the 1930s, the British waited until the 1950s to invest in the country's development. Even then, such responsibilities fell primarily to the diKgosi and to missionary churches. When **independence** arrived in 1966 amidst a serious drought, president **Seretse Khama** led a nation that ranked among the very poorest in the world.

Since independence, thanks to the discovery of high quality diamond deposits, Botswana has rapidly developed its infrastructure, its ability to provide social and physical services to rural and town populations, and its foreign reserves. In spite of considerable regional stress surrounding the liberation of Zimbabwe, Namibia, and South Africa, Botswana has remained peaceful, stable, and non-racial in its political and public affairs, while playing an active diplomatic role among independent nations in the region. In its first thirty years, Botswana has held six peaceful and fair **elections**, maintained a system of **economic planning**, established an independent **currency**, sustained a coherent policy of **external relations**, and created a **defence** force to patrol its extensive **boundaries**. Serious problems remain. Significant income differences between a wealthy few and the rest of the population have emerged, urban populations are growing rapidly, and Botswana has especially suffered from the spread of **AIDS**.

The Dictionary

A

ABATTOIR. Botswana's abattoirs, located in Lobatse, Maun, and Francistown, serve as the linchpin in the nation's successful beef industry. The first abattoir was built in 1931 at Lobatse by the Imperial Cold Storage and Supply Company, but it was closed six years later after intermittently processing only 21,000 head. South African protectionism, competition from the smuggled live export trade, and the refusal of the colonial government to subsidize the infant industry were crippling handicaps.

In the early 1950s, after South Africa lifted its ban on the import of beef from the Protectorate, the abattoir was largely rebuilt by the Colonial Development Corporation (CDC) and opened in 1954. The Bechuanaland Abattoirs Limited (BAL) was set up to manage the Lobatse plant. Prices paid to cattle owners were subsidized to match those paid in Johannesburg, thus making cross-border cattle smuggling less attractive. The government went even further in its support of the abattoir by ensuring that all cattle had to go south to Lobatse for processing. This latter measure was very unpopular with northern cattle farmers, who were forced to pay higher rail costs and accept prices lower than would have been the case had they been allowed to market their cattle in the Rhodesias. They campaigned for a northern abattoir but had to wait until 1983 before a second plant was built at Maun.

At independence the BAL became the Botswana Meat Commission (BMC). In theory the abattoir was a nationalized concern, but in practice the BMC operated as a parastatal corporation governed by directors appointed by and responsible to the President alone. In the 1970s the Lobatse abattoir was modernized in order to qualify for subsidized quotas in the European Economic Community (EEC) market, into which Botswana beef has since been allowed on a 10 percent tariff basis. Altogether, the three BMC abattoirs are designed to

9

process up to 300,000 cattle per annum. In 1992, a total peak of 214,000 cattle were slaughtered. *See also* Agriculture; Cattle; Colonial Development Corporation; Drought; Economy; Rey, Charles; Zambia.

ADMINISTRATION. During colonial rule, central government business was conducted by a few officials exercising power in concert with traditional authorities (diKgosi). Since independence, the central government has steadily transferred power from traditional authorities to its own magistrates and executive officials.

Formal colonial administration originated with the Orders-in-Council of 1890 and 1891, which authorized the high commissioner of South Africa to enact laws, establish a court system, raise revenues, and in other ways create an administration for the Protectorate. The administrative system was nevertheless rudimentary, for until 1895 the assumption was that the Protectorate was to be handed over to the British South Africa Company and, for a number of years after 1901, to South Africa. As a consequence, no internal administrative headquarters were developed. Instead, offices of the resident commissioner (the high commissioner's principal deputy) were maintained in the Northern Cape, at Vryburg from 1885 and, after 1895, in the Imperial Reserve at Mafikeng. The high commissioner of the Protectorate, who retained his designation of British high commissioner for South Africa and stayed in Cape Town or Pretoria, issued laws for the Protectorate, as well as for the High Commission Territories of Swaziland and Basutoland.

Inside the Protectorate two small administrative centers cum police camps were established in 1890, one at Gaberones and the other at Palapye (in 1904 moved to Francistown), under assistant commissioners (AC) for the South and North, respectively. Until the 1920s, when they were phased out, the ACs also served as Resident Magistrates, presiding over appeals from assistant magistrates stationed in Kanye, Molepolole, Serowe, and Maun, as well as cases involving persons from outside the Protectorate and disputes between reserves. In matters pertaining to Europeans, Indians, and Africans from outside the Protectorate, the AC could claim sole jurisdiction or intervene when their interests clashed with those of Protectorate Africans. The same was true of matters coming to his attention directly and from outside the reserves.

Within the reserves, official policy stated that the diKgosi would "rule their own people much as at present" without interference from her Majesty's officials (Chamberlain 1895). In brief, the high commissioner, who appointed all officials, stood atop two systems of administration, one operated by his own officials for the Protectorate as a whole, another by the "chiefs" (diKgosi) for the people of the respective reserves. Lord Hailey referred to this dual administrative structure as one of "parallel rule."

In practice, the two levels frequently overlapped, particularly in matters pertaining to authority within the reserves. Well into the 1920s various diKgosi obstructed the activities of local traders licensed by Protectorate officials and combined to oppose official policies, just as officials took sides in internal disputes involving diKgosi and in some instances set up councils to limit their authority. The smooth conduct of parallel administration depended on diKgosi accepting a subordinate position in the hierarchy. The diKgosi who remained autonomous and undisturbed administrators within their respective reserves, such as **Khama III** and **Linchwe I**, had convincingly demonstrated their loyalty to the Protectorate and rendered it valuable service.

Under the system of parallel rule, all diKgosi gained authority in the sense that officials depended on them for tax collection, maintenance of peace, the hearing of nearly all cases, the promulgation of laws suitable to changing times, and mobilizing labor for public works. In the large reserves, too, diKgosi were able to expand their authority by establishing administrations in outlying districts and placing them under hand-picked loyalists from the reserve capital. Methods by the Kgosi's governors firmly subordinated many non-Tswana and *bafaladi* groups and made their resources available for developments of the Kgosi's own choosing. The many abuses resulting from this system rarely led to official action.

In the 1930s the Protectorate began the revamping of its administrative structure through a series of "Native Administration" Proclamations (1934, 1938, and 1943). In theory, the parallel structure was to be replaced with a hierarchical one based on "Indirect Rule" principles that had evolved in other parts of British-controlled Africa over the previous decades. The earmarks of this system were the creation of local councils, treasuries, and tribunals, which while incorporating traditional authorities (i.e., the diKgosi) were to be filled by traditional ward heads. The new system was in fact an attempt to reduce the Kgosi's authority within the reserve and increase the control of the resident commissioner. Parallel to this development was the creation of district colonial administration, which placed district commissioners in each of the reserves and accorded them a range of newly-created tasks and authority to review the activities of local councils, treasuries, tribunals, and diKgosi. In the 1930s officials also deposed two diKgosi, **Sebele II** and **Molefi**, for insubordination, and installed more pliant men in their place.

By and large the Proclamations merely enlarged the local government bureaucracy. Because of the Great Depression and World War II which followed, the financial resources available to the Protectorate remained limited, and diKgosi continued to be indispensable to overall administration and recruitment of labor. Officials were most unhappy where a Kgosi was weak and councils were left to fill the vacuum and least so where the Kgosi was strong and councils were prepared to let the Kgosi run things single-handedly. DiKgosi, too, tended to rely increasingly on official support to deal with internal discontent. The result was that diKgosi of the 1930s, 1940s, and 1950s were capable of exercising even greater authority than they had been before the Protectorate attempted to reduce their powers. DiKgosi dominated most of the new councils or defied them, and more often than not, district commissioners supported diKgosi in controlling their reserves, suppressing dissent, banishing opponents, and in other ways becoming authoritarians.

From 1956 to 1957, elected tribal and other local councils with real administrative duties were created, but by independence only a few were functioning effectively. With independence, however, administrative councils were carried forward throughout the Republic and given increasing authority over local matters. As they normally included the diKgosi as key members, however, the councils tended to reflect the division of power carried over from the colonial period. Since the mid-1970s, the central government has given increasing authority in most local matters to district administrations with the effect that diKgosi, apart from heading customary courts, have been relegated to a largely ceremonial role, and local councils have become dependent on budgets rebated from Gaborone. By the 1980s the centralization of administration for the country as a whole, a process that began in 1891, was more or less complete.

Today, administration in the Republic is apportioned among the various ministries and departments based in Gaborone, with district administration directed by the Ministry of Local Government and Lands, which also exercises authority over all town councils and the city council of Gaborone. *See also* Boundaries; British South Africa Company; Concessions; Constitution; Councils; Districts; Flogging Incident; High Commissioners; High Commission Territories; Incorporation; Indirect Rule; Kgosi; Orders-in-Council; Orders-in-Council, 1890 and 1891; Proclamation; Protectorate; Reserves; Resident Commissioners; Rey, Charles; Three Kings in London.

AFRICAN AUXILIARY PIONEER CORPS. *See* World War II.

AFRICAN METHODIST EPISCOPAL CHURCH ("ETHIOPIAN CHURCH"). With approximately 2,000 members in 25 congregations in 1994, the AME was begun by Richard Allen of Philadelphia, Pennsylvania (U.S.A.), who became its first bishop in 1816. Established as a black breakaway church, its missionaries operated in the Cape in the 1890s, and in 1896 the AME incorporated Rev. Mangena Maake Mokone's Ethiopian Church, which had broken from the Wesleyan Mission in 1892. The AME was brought into Botswana by Rev. Marcus Gabashane, who while rebuffed by the leading diKgosi, founded congregations in the Tati area and in Lobatse. By 1903, his church had spread to Lehututu and Hukuntsi. The AME later absorbed the Ethiopian Church of **Mothowagae Motlogelwa**. *See also* Religion.

AFRICAN NATIONAL CONGRESS (ANC). Botswana's connection to the struggle for equal rights in South Africa is as old as the movement itself. Tshidi BaRolong, BaKgatla, BaKwena, and BaNgwaketse were involved in many of the activities as well as the discussions that led to the 1912 inaugural convention of the South African Native National Congress (SANNC), renamed the African National Congress (ANC) in 1923. Acting Kgosi Lekoko of the Tshidi BaRolong and Kgosi **Linchwe I** of the BaKgatla were among the first honorary Vice Presidents elected by the SANNC. Linchwe's brother, Kgari Pilane, was a founding member and Treasurer of the Transvaal African Congress and became a founding SANNC member and one of its treasurers. Richard Sidzumo, **Sechele II**'s secretary, was a founder of the Bechuanaland and Griqualand Provincial Congress of the SANNC, serving as its first General Secretary. The fight against the incorporation of the Protectorate into South Africa provided much of the motivation. Notably,

Khama III of the BaNgwato refused to have anything to do with the ANC, and his position was later adopted by all other Protectorate diKgosi. They concluded that direct involvement in South African politics would make incorporation more likely, rather than less so. At the popular level, however, particularly among BaTswana working in South Africa, many individuals joined the ANC, attended their meetings, and took part in their boycotts and strikes. **Motsamai Mpho** and **N. T. "Fish" Keitseng** were ANC treason trialists in the 1950s, and **Michael Dingake** was tried for treason and jailed ten years on Robben Island.

After South Africa banned the ANC in 1960, the Protectorate became a temporary haven for many ANC refugees, including Nelson Mandela, as well as an alternate meeting site for ANC leaders. In June 1961 the ANC's internal and external wings met at Lobatse. The conference endorsed a call to engage in armed struggle against the apartheid regime, and Umkhonto we Sizwe was formed as the armed wing of the movement. The Protectorate government, like the post-independence Republic, did not ban the ANC but refused to allow Botswana to become a base for its armed attacks against South Africa. In 1966 and 1967, the ANC launched armed attacks against Rhodesia from Botswana, but the Botswana government then apprehended many of these ANC soldiers, including Chris Hani (who joined the 1967 attack), and jailed them for several years. From the 1960s, the ANC maintained a small Botswana cell, which operated under the leadership of N.T. Keitseng. *See also* Refugees; Sidzumo, Peter; Wankie Campaign.

AFRIKANERS (BOERS). Beginning in the 1840s, and possibly earlier, Dutch-speaking traders and hunters from the Cape and the Transvaal entered eastern Botswana, some settling in **Molepolole** by the mid-nineteenth century. Following the establishment of the Protectorate, hundreds of Afrikaners settled in the several freehold areas opened to white farmers and became the predominant element. Within the small white population of the Protectorate as a whole, they constituted the majority. Many of these Boer settlers, including those long resident in places like Molepolole, left the Protectorate on the eve of Botswana's independence. *See also* Dorsland Trek; Ghanzi Farms; Land Tenure; Slave Trade; South Africa; Van Zyl, Hendrik; Viljoen, Jan; White Slaves.

AGRICULTURE. Suitable soils and adequate rainfall for crop growing converge on only 5% of Botswana's land surface, principally on its eastern perimeter. The country has a great deal of grassland suitable for stock keeping, but there being almost no surface water, stock keeping can be extremely precarious, even for large and heavily capitalized owners. When the plough was introduced in the mid-nineteenth century, the acreage under tillage increased along with food production, and the population grew. Agricultural techniques remained the "risk-aversion" type, because of the unreliability of rainfall. The "lands" (*masimo*) of each family and ward were scattered and usually located away from cattle posts (*meraka*). Manure fertilizer was not used, nor were crops rotated. Fields were ploughed with oxen, and sown with mixed seeds by broadcasting, thus taking advantage of each rain storm for different rates of germination. Women and children remained on the lands, weeded by hoe, and scared birds away. Harvests of greatly mixed quality could only be selectively cropped. The more common crops were traditional varieties of sorghum, millet, beans, and melons (and later maize, which arrived in Botswana no earlier than the 1850s, becoming widespread in the twentieth century). As of 1993, 105,819, or 61%, of Botswana's households were raising at least one food crop. Of these households, 83% planted sorghum and 69% planted maize, followed by beans (57%), melons (40%), millet (25%), sweet reeds (12%), groundnuts (3%), and pumpkins (2%). The number of hectares in crops at any one time can vary depending on patterns of rainfall. In 1991, 189,000 hectares were planted, but in 1992, a dry year, only 84,000, a decline of 55.6%.

As much as by climate and soils, Botswana's agriculture was depressed by the country's transformation into a labor reserve. Colonial tax and labor policies increased labor migration to South Africa and other neighboring colonies and withdrew male and female labor essential to plough and hoe cultivation. Wages of migrant laborers went into government taxes and helped those at home purchase food and other items from local stores. Colonial agricultural policy was limited to stock disease control and the drilling of boreholes until 1935, when the Department of Agriculture was established. Thereafter, pilot attempts were made, such as through the Master Farmer scheme, to introduce new seeds and tractor-based techniques, but the impact was limited to a few. Since the 1930s Botswana has been, with few exceptions, an annual net food importer, increasingly so during periodic droughts. At independence, the total acreage under cultivation was less than it had been when the Department of Agriculture was created.

Throughout the colonial period and since independence, the lion's share of funds for the development of food production has gone into beef, almost entirely for its export. In 1965 the parastatal Botswana Meat Commission (BMC) was established to manage the abattoir and market the national beef product. In the early 1970s the BMC secured very favorable terms for beef exports to the European Economic Community at four times the world market price. Not until 1978 was beef surpassed by diamonds as the nation's leading export earner.

Government concern for crop agriculture has steadily increased in recent years. In 1974 the Botswana Agricultural Marketing Board (BAMB) was established to centralize storage, distribution, and marketing mainly of grain production, as well as sell seeds and fertilizers at low cost, but it has been underfinanced and poorly managed. Cooperatives for farmers have sprung up in many towns and villages for the same purpose, but overall they are even shorter on qualified staff and government support. In 1981 the Arable Lands Development Policy (ALDEP) was implemented to achieve national self-sufficiency in grain, reduce poverty in rural areas, and narrow the economic gap between the wealthy few and the rest of the population that has been widening since independence. ALDEP has supplied draught power, fencing, and agricultural implements to the poorest farmers, those with no cattle. The drought of the 1980s has nevertheless made self-sufficiency impossible, and rural inequalities have continued to increase. The farmers able to benefit from ALDEP are those with salaried jobs, having the means to supplement its inputs, and therefore tend to be, at minimum, owners of small cattle herds.

In the 1980s independent market gardening increased in response to urban demand. The tonnage in sorghum production increased nine fold between 1982 and 1991, reaching a high of ninety-four tons in 1988, while other crops declined or stagnated. Nevertheless, agricultural self-sufficiency in Botswana remains a remote possibility, even though political pressures on the government will probably force continued financial support for food production in spite of past failures. In the 1992–93 season, Botswana imported 200,000 tons of grain alone. Although all southern African countries imported grain in that drought period, Botswana's food production per capita was the region's lowest.

By the same token, employment in Botswana's agricultural sector has declined, from 5.6% of the total private labor force in 1985 to 3.9% in September 1992. *See also* Abattoir; Cattle; Cooperatives; Drought; Migrant Labor; Water; Women.

AIDS. According to Dr. Mathsediso Moeti of Botswana's national AIDS control program, the spread of AIDS in Botswana is "among the swiftest in the world." Since 1985, when the first case of Acquired Immune Deficiency Syndrome (AIDS) was reported in the country, Botswana has quickly found itself faced with the threat of an AIDS epidemic. According to the Ministry of Health, as of early 1993 estimates of HIV-positive residents were as high as 70,000, or 5.4% of the total population. Projections for the HIV group of the year 2,000 are between 90,000 and 242,000. Most disturbingly, the highest rates of infection are recently found among women ages 20–29. In a 1991 sample of 1,936 pregnant women in Gaborone, Francistown, and Maun, 351, or 18.1%, tested HIV-positive.

Since 1987 the Botswana Ministry of Health's National AIDS Control Programme has conducted a public campaign for AIDS awareness among all age groups through radio, clinics, school classrooms, billboards, public notices, newspapers, the *AIDS News* publication, symposia, workshops, and free literature and condoms in an effort to increase safe sexual behavior. More than four million condoms were distributed between November 1992 and March 1993 alone. Their efforts have been supplemented by non-government organizations, such as the Botswana Christian Council, AIDS Action Trust, and the Botswana Red Cross. Nevertheless, the most optimistic expectations are that by the end of the century health costs alone will approach $300,000,000 and the infected population will exceed 6%. *See also* Health.

AIR TRANSPORTION. The national parastatal airline, Air Botswana, is based in Gaborone and provides scheduled internal service to Francistown, Ghanzi, Kasane, Jwaneng, Maun, Orapa, and Selebi Phikwe and external flights to Dar es Salaam, Harare, Johannesburg, Lusaka, Maseru, Manzini, Nairobi, and Windhoek. In the late 1980s internal and external services were added and jet aircraft purchased for some of the external connections, but since 1990 indebtedness has plagued the airline and forced cutbacks. Other airlines from southern and eastern Africa, England, and Europe fly wide-bodied jet aircraft into Sir Seretse Khama International Airport, Gaborone, which opened in December 1984. *See also* Rey, Charles.

ALCOHOL. Intoxicating drink has long been the preferred beverage of BaTswana men. In pre-colonial days traditional beer (*bojalwa*, nowadays also a term for alcohol in general) was made from sorghum and consumed at all-night vigils hosted by women, who brewed on a rotating basis. *Khadi*, made from fermented roots and berries, appeared in the late eighteenth or early nineteenth century and is often used today as a term for fortified drinks, not necessarily alcoholic.

After 1850, when active trade with the Cape got underway, a cheap and potent form of South African brandy, "Cape Smoke," became popular. As the consumption of Cape Smoke increased, an indigenous prohibition movement arose. After 1875 official prohibition was declared by **Khama III** of the BaNgwato, was lifted in 1895, and in the 1920s was reinstated by his son, **Tshekedi Khama**. Another prohibitionist was **Bathoen I** of the BaNgkwaketse, who, along with **Sekgoma Letsholathebe** of the BaTawana, banned alcohol consumption in the early 1890s. Prohibition was very unpopular and was evaded at the risk of severe floggings. A number of political disputes arose over the issue. The colonial authorities supported BaNgwato temperance and banned the sale of hard liquor to "natives" as a means of maintaining "tribal" cohesion and warding off "modern" influences.

During the colonial era, when sugar was increasingly used to brew khadi, women increasingly came to dominate khadi brewing, which largely replaced bojalwa. Khadi was by far the more potent of the two varieties. Its sales were an important way for women to earn cash. A few brewed on a full-time basis, but in most neighborhoods each household took turns on a rotating basis.

After independence the South African Breweries, operating under the Botswana-registered Kgalagadi Breweries (Gaborone), monopolized bottled and tinned beer production throughout the country. Along with traditional and modern beer, imported wine and spirits are popular in Botswana today and available at numerous, privately-operated "bottle stores."

ANGLICANS. The Anglican Church's 7,575 members are found in 17 parishes, the principal ones in Gaborone, Molepolole, Tonota, and the Northeast District. As early as 1888 the Anglican bishop of Bloemfontein, George Knight-Bruce, toured the Bechuanaland Protectorate, but the Anglicans made no serious efforts to establish a permanent presence in the territory until 1907. In that year, the Rev. James Toy began mission work in the Tati area. His most notable early convert was Rauwe, Kgosi of the BaKhurutshe. In 1900 the Church of the Province in South Africa incorporated a segment of the

Ethiopian Church as an autonomous Order of Ethiopia, under the leadership of the Rev. James Dwane. Products of this association were instrumental in establishing Anglicanism in the Kweneng under the patronage of Lena Rauwe, wife of **Sechele II** and for the first time breaking the religious monopoly of the **London Missionary Society** among the western Ba-Tswana. Moreover, in 1917 the Church took what was then the unprecedented step of giving its blessing to the revival of bogwera (though several years later this policy was reversed). Around 1919, a dissatisfied group broke from the Anglicans and established the African Mission Church in Tlokweng.

The Diocese of Botswana was established in 1972, with headquarters in Gaborone. Its first bishop was the Rt. Rev. Charles Shannon Mallory. *See also* Initiation; Mashwe, George; Religion.

ARCHAEOLOGY AND PREHISTORY. Contrary to its image as the home of surviving ancient hunter-gatherers ("Bushmen"), Botswana has been a land of stockkeepers and farmers for at least the past 1,500 years. Largely through the archaeological work of James Denbow, who examined more than 250 sites from 1975 to 1985 and whose work has been paralleled by geographers and other archaeologists, it is clear that as early as 500 A.D. people living in present-day Botswana were practicing fully-developed pastoralism, extensive grain agriculture, and iron-working. Judging by the glass beads and marine shells dating from 800 A.D., they appear also to have been connected to East African-Indian Ocean trade routes. By 1,000 A.D., well before the Normans invaded England, centralized cattle-keeping chiefdoms were present in the eastern Kgalagadi. These states, which predate Great Zimbabwe, appear to have collapsed early in the thirteenth century, possibly because of overgrazing and drought. *See also* BaKalanga; BaTswana; Butwa; Sarwa; Toutswe.

ARCHIVES. The Botswana National Archives, located in the government circle in Gaborone, is the main national repository of records. It has jurisdiction over all government records and has supplemented its collection through acquisition of privately-held records as well as copies from governmental repositories outside the country. It also seeks to collate all material on Botswana published and unpublished.

Most surviving official records of the colonial period are in the new, modern National Archives building and form a rich collection of historical data. They form but a fraction of the total colonial records: fires, deliberate destruction of records before independence, and the predations of insects have each taken their toll. In 1958, for example, after an inventory of district records had been taken, 80 percent were destroyed. The remaining 20 percent were sent to Salisbury (Harare), from which they were retrieved in 1967. Since independence the destruction of valuable documents has continued despite efforts of the archivists.

Important archives located outside Gaborone include Khama III Memorial Museum, Serowe (Khama family and Bessie Head papers), Moeding College (Tiger Kloof and Z.K. Matthews papers), and the Phuthadikobo Museum, Mochudi (BaKgatla Tribal papers and the Isang Pilane papers). Outside Botswana, important bodies of material are housed in government archives in South Africa, Britain, and Zimbabwe, and notable collections include Rhodes House, Oxford; School of Oriental and African Studies (University of London); Selly Oak Colleges, Birmingham; University of Witwatersrand; the DRC archives, Cape Town; and the Anglican archives, London. *See also* Bakgatla National School; Isang Pilane; Khama III; Matthews, Z.K.; Serowe; Tiger Kloof.

ARDEN-CLARKE, SIR CHARLES (1898–1962). Resident commissioner, 1937–1942. By establishing good working relations with such BaTswana leaders as **Tshekedi Khama**, who earlier had been obstructive to British policy, Arden-Clarke paved the way for the implementation of important reforms, in particular the introduction of Tribal Treasuries and the Native Proclamations of 1943. He later became governor of Ghana. *See also* Proclamation; Resident Commissioner.

ARMY. *See* Botswana Defence Force.

ASIANS. The first Asians to settle in Botswana entered the Protectorate from South Africa during the 1880s and opened trading stores in **Molepolole**, Mosopa, and **Ramotswa**. Before 1910 relatives of the early settlers immigrated directly from India and established stores in other villages in the southeast, including **Kanye**, Mogoditshane, Thamaga, and Magobane. About the same time Asians from Southern Rhodesia opened trading stores in **Francistown**. Curbs on Asian immigration into the territory were introduced during World War II and pressure was applied by European traders to limit the number of trading licenses granted to Asian traders. At independence, however, nearly all the general dealers' stores in the southern Protectorate were Asian-owned, and **Lobatse** was the most important Asian business center.

Most of the Asians who settled in Botswana during the colonial period were Indian Muslims. They included the Chand, Moorad, Hussain, Sayyed, and Khan families from the Gujerat district; the Desai, Abdullah, Mohideen, Kablay, and Jalal families from the Cochin and Bombay districts; and the Ada, Arbi, and Ebrahim families from the Kathiawar district. Their first organization, the Protectorate British Indian Mohammedan Society, was formed in the 1920s, and the first school for Muslims was opened in 1963 in Lobatse, where the first mosque in the country was built in 1967. Other mosques were built in Kanye (19??), **Gaborone** (1980), Francistown (1983), and Molepolole (1991). *See also* Chand, Abdul Rahim; Hindus; Islam; Traders.

B

BAHAIS. The Bahai faith was introduced to Botswana in 1965 by a Canadian couple, John and Audrey Roberts. In 1970 the Spiritual Assembly of Bahais of Botswana was formed. The Bahais have enjoyed relatively rapid growth and constitute Botswana's largest adherents to a non-Christian world religion, with 5,000 members active in over 200 communities. *See also* Religion.

BAKGATLA NATIONAL SCHOOL. Opened in 1923 as the Mochudi National School, it was built by regimental labor and paid for by the **Kgafela Kgatla** under Regent **Isang Pilane**. Situated atop Phuthadikobo Hill in **Mochudi**, it was the largest building in the Protectorate until after the Second World War. Apart from the years 1939–1941 and 1958–1963, when the school offered a junior secondary course, only primary schooling to Standard 6 was offered until its closure in 1975. The building was renovated and in 1977 reopened as the Phuthadikobo Museum under the direction of Sandy Grant. The Museum, which contains many artifacts related to Kgafela Kgatla culture and history, is also used as a civic, educational, and crafts center. *See also* Archives; Education.

BALLINGER-BARNES TOUR. In 1931 William Ballinger, Margaret Hodgson (later Mrs. Ballinger), and Leonard Barnes,

prominent South African liberal activists, toured the Bechuanaland Protectorate while gathering evidence of British neglect
of the **High Commission Territories**. Beforehand they had already come into contact with the leading BaNgwato dissidents
Simon Ratshosa, K.T. Motsete, and **Moanaphuti Segolodi**. In
subsequent articles and books they attacked British policy and
the autocratic rule of diKgosi and opposed incorporation of the
territory into South Africa. Their arguments reinforced the
recommendations of Alan Pim and Resident Commissioner
Charles Rey and administrative reform of the Protectorate. *See
also* Incorporation; Tshekedi Khama.

BAPTISTS. Small as Christian groups go in Botswana, the Baptists' connection is, however, among the oldest. American
Baptist missionaries were briefly active among the BaTswana
and AmaNdebele of the western Transvaal from 1835 to 1837,
but their mission ended with the Boer–BaRolong attack on
Mosega in 1837. Baptists did not enter Botswana again until
1868, when misionaries based in Zimbabwe introduced the
church. The Baptist Mission of Botswana is under the authority
of the Southern Baptist convention of the United States of
America, and it is active in medical and social work as well
as evangelism. Baptist tenets may be found in many of the
independent **Pentecostal** churches. *See also* Religion.

BARATANI HILL. "Hill of Lovers," a familiar landmark near
Otse and west of the Lobatse-Gaborone road. According to
tradition, two young lovers fled there after they were forbidden
to see one another. They disappeared, and ever since the hill
has been said to be haunted.

BAROLONG FARMS. Individual African land tenure was largely
prohibited in the days of the Protectorate, with the exception
of Barolong Farms, located on the southern boundary. Soon
after the establishment of the Bechuanaland Protectorate, the
Tshidi Ba**Rolong** of Mafikeng and the BaNgwaketse of Kanye
disputed one another's claim to the territory standing between
them. In his attempts to win the claim, Montshiwa argued that
disputed land should be held by Africans in individual tenure,
rather than in communal ownership, in order to keep it out of
the hands of land-hungry whites. In 1892 the British awarded
this territory of 432 square miles to the BaRolong, and in 1895,
after the territory had been surveyed and divided into forty-
one farms, Kgosi **Montshiwa** alloted four of them to himself and

leased the remainder to royals, headmen, and other influential individual BaRolong. Certificates of occupation were restricted to BaRolong and were made non-transferrable to whites. Over time, all but three of the farms registered with the original certificates of occupation, regarded by the recipients or their descendants as title deeds entitling them to full ownership and control, were eventually recognized in republican courts. Three of the farms retained by Montshiwa remained attached to the chieftainship and were passed on to his successors.

Since World War II the tenure system at Barolong Farms facilitated commercialized farming in the area. Farms were leased to non-BaRolong, including whites, and for some time Barolong Farms has ceased to be an ethnic area, although it remains BaRolong-owned. Since the mid-1970s a sizeable proportion of Botswana's maize crop has come from the farms. Their productivity has been used to support attempts for modifying communal tenure elsewhere in Botswana.

BARUTI KGOSIDINTSI (1842–1922). Son of Kgosidintsi of the BaKwena, from whom he inherited a substantial malata population. Between 1900 and 1916 he led the opposition against **Sebele I** and **Sechele II** as a spokesman for a powerful group of diKgosana who usually enjoyed the support of the **London Missionary Society.** In 1916 he was tried for impregnating the divorced wife of Sechele II and found guilty. Baruti was sentenced to exile and, though the sentence was not carried out, his influence waned. *See also* Neale Sechele.

BATHOEN I (1845–1910). Son of **Gaseitsiwe,** whom he succeeded as Kgosi of the BaNgwaketse, 1889–1910. Bathoen married **Gagoangwe,** one-eyed daughter of **Sechele I,** and was succeeded by their eldest son, **Seepapitso II.** Bathoen was a member of the Ma-Isantwa regiment, as was his later political rival, **Mothowagae Motlogelwa.**

Bathoen played an important role in the transition to colonial rule, often acting as mediator among diKgosi. During the first years of his reign Bathoen joined with other southern Protectorate diKgosi in limiting the extent of colonial interference, culminating in his trip to London in 1895 as part of a BaTswana delegation. Later he resisted British attempts to demarcate boundaries in the southern Protectorate. In 1908 he helped lead the BaTswana protest against incorporation into South Africa and contributed to discussions that led to the formation of the South African Native National Congress (later the **African National Congress**) in 1912. He also helped in financing the first independent SeTswana newspapers.

Within the BaNgwaketse Reserve he was the principal champion of Christianity and established the LMS as the national church of the BaNgwaketse. He abolished many traditional practices, notably *bogwera*. In 1902, in collaboration with the LMS, he imposed an educational levy which led to the formation of one of the first school committees in the Protectorate.

Known affectionately as RraLesego ("Lucky"), Bathoen was an avid hunter and was remembered as a smart dresser who preferred black on most occasions. *See also* Concessions; Kopong Conference; Three Kings in London.

BATHOEN II (1909–1990). Son of **Seepapitso II**, Kgosi of the BaNgwaketse (1928–1969), and thereafter a leading opposition politician. Married Esther Mmatani Ntsieng of the Thaba Nchu BaRolong. Known popularly as "B-2" and "Seheretlhane," Bathoen was part of a generation of young diKgosi who came to power after World War II and took a critical attitude toward colonial rule. He was educated at **Tiger Kloof** and Lovedale, where as a student he was called to take over bogosi from his aunt, **Ntebogang**, who had served as his regent.

Under the influence of his uncle, **Tshekedi Khama**, Bathoen established strong rule over his people and played a prominent role in Protectorate affairs. In 1936, by which time he was already the leading ruler in the Southern Protectorate, Bathoen joined Tshekedi in challenging the legality of Resident Commissioner **Charles Rey**'s administrative reforms. He served as chairman of the Native (later African) Advisory Council from 1937 until 1950, when he became the leading MoTswana member of the Joint Advisory Council and then the African Council and Legislative Council. In 1965 he served as the first chairman of the House of Chiefs, but in 1969, having recognized the House's impotence, he abdicated as Kgosi, gained an elected seat in the National Assembly, and became the leader of the **National Front**. In 1985 he retired from active politics to become the first president of the Customary Court of Appeal.

Bathoen's energetic leadership as BaNgwaketse Kgosi extended to many fields of activity: he promoted the improvement of agriculture and public health, the building of schools, the organization of sports, and the preservation of customary law. During his long and extraordinary career he had an influence on almost every aspect of development in Bechaualand/Botswana. Among his many honors Bathoen was named a

Commander, Order of the British Empire. *See also* Councils; Gobuamang; Health; Kgampu Kamodi; Kgari Sechele; Ngwaketse; Proclamation; Seepapitso II; Sports; Tshosa Sebego.

BATSWANA-BOER WAR OF 1852–1853. A six-month conflict that marks the emergence of unity among BaTswana merafe in southern Bechuanaland and the birth of modern Botswana. The Boers of the infant republic in the Transvaal, having tenuously established their military supremacy, entered a pact with the British government at the Cape in January 1852, known as the Sand River Convention, which bound the British to prohibit the sale of guns and ammunition to Africans outside Boer territory. With legal access to modern weaponry cut off to Africans along the "road to the north" stretching into Bechuanaland, the Boers set out to disarm their African neighbors to the west, take their cattle, seize their women and children, and establish hegemony over the BaTswana in these areas in much the same fashion as they had over the BaTswana of the Transvaal. They were also eager to drive out members of the **London Missionary Society**, which they held responsible for supplying arms to Africans and arousing anti-Boer sentiments.

Their campaign began in July 1852, when a commando of 430 Boers and 600 African auxiliaries was mobilized by Commandant Piet Scholtz against the BaNgwaketse, Ba**Kwena**, and **Mmanaana Kgatla**. Members of the force included young Paul Kruger, future Transvaal president, and **Jan Viljoen**, Marico district field-cornet and trader, with whom the BaTswana were already familiar. On 17 August Scholtz's force advanced on Manwaane, the capital of the BagaMmanaana. Kgosi Mosielele then retreated with most of his people to the BaKwena settlement at Dimawe. The Boers sacked Manwaane, its LMS mission site, killed ninety BaTswana, and enslaved between 200 and 400 women and children. On the 28th the commando arrived at Dimawe, where they fought an inconclusive battle against a combined force of BaKwena, BaNgwaketse, Baga-Mmanaana, and BaKaa, led by **Sechele I**. Following the **Battle of Dimawe**, Sechele regrouped his forces at **Dithubaruba,** while many of the BaNgwaketse redeployed at Kanye's Kgwakwe hill. Scholtz divided his forces in pursuit of both. The segment following the BaNgwaketse sacked the LMS station at Kolobeng, built by the then-absent **David Livingstone**, attacked Kgwakwe, and were repulsed. Scholtz's Boers then refused to attack Dithubaruba, whereupon on 3 September, his commando returned to the Transvaal with 143 captive women and children and a large number of captured cattle. Additional property, belonging to the BaKwena to English **traders**, was also seized and later auctioned. On their retreat, Scholtz's commando was harassed by BaTswana in several hit-and-run attacks.

The failed Boer invasion, which resulted in thirty-six Boers and eighty-nine BaTswana killed, succeeded in uniting BaTswana and igniting a series of retaliatory raids into the Marico district bordering Bechuanaland. Sechele's alliance was augmented by the BaTlhaping and BaNgwato. In November 1852, Boers began abandoning their farms in fear, and by January 1853 the entire Marico district, including Swartruggens, had been evacuated. A defensive line, running between Potchefstroom and Rustenburg, ultimately held. A number of subject African groups in the Transvaal, persuaded of Sechele's power over and against the Boers, migrated into his territory and were given refuge. The Ba**Lete**, Ba**Hurutse**, BaTlhako, BaRakologadi, and some **Griqua**, were among them. Others, such as the **Kgafela Kgatla** fled to Sechele's BaKwena in later years.

The BaTswana-Boer war ended in February 1853. As one of the first official acts of the newly-named South African Republic, President Andries Pretorious offered, at the encouragement of Jan Viljoen and other Marico doves, an armistice to Sechele, who accepted. Nevertheless, tensions remained high until 1857, when further negotiations normalized relations. *See also* Afrikaners; Slave Trade; Traders.

BATSWANA-BOER WAR OF 1881–1884. A war of resistance fought mainly by the BaTlhaping and Ba**Rolong** in the northern Cape, this conflict was a major factor leading to the commencement of British colonial rule over the Bechuanaland Protectorate in 1885. Fighting began in 1881, when the BaRolong of **Montshiwa** and the BaTlhaping of Mankurwane were attacked by white British and Boer mercenaries (then labeled "filibusters"). Intent on grabbing land, the filibusters cloaked their design with the claim that they fought on behalf of BaTswana to the east who had already accepted Boer overrule. Mankurwane, who hired white mercenaries himself, ultimately became one of their victims. In 1882 the interlopers set up two small, self-styled "republics," Stellaland and Goshen on BaTlhaping and BaRolong land. The prospect of Boer influence in these areas, which lay across the "road to the north," was too much for Cape-based expansionists, led by Cecil Rhodes, who raised the cry of British intervention in a chorus that included local missionaries and traders. They complained that the republicans were disrupting the flow of goods north and that of mine labor south (to Kimberley) between the Cape Colony and Bechuanaland. Their arguments became more persuasive in England after April 1884, when the Germans, with whom the Boers were friendly, occupied the Namibian coast. Visions of Stellaland and Goshen providing the land link between South West Africa and the South African Republic (Transvaal) encouraged Whitehall to act. **John Mackenzie**, missionary of the **London Missionary Society** and British agent, was authorized to negotiate with the Stellalanders for the purpose of establishing a Protectorate south of the Molopo river. The agreement proved unworkable until Mackenzie's replacement, Cecil Rhodes, granted most of the BaTlhaping's land to the Stellalanders.

The Goshenites met stiff resistance from the BaRolong, who were backed by the BaNgwaketse of **Gaseitsiwe** and the **Kgafela Kgatla** of **Linchwe I**. Following a BaRolong attack on Rooigrond on 12 May 1884, the Goshenites retaliated by raiding BaRolong and BaNgwaketse cattle posts inside present Botswana, setting up the final showdown. On 1 August 1884, near **Mafikeng**, a combined BaNgwaketse-BaRolong force intercepted the Goshenites, defeated them, and drove them into the Transvaal for good. Killed in this final battle were some 50 Boers, 181 BaTswana, and two of their white sympathizers. In September when SAR President Kruger falsely claimed that Montshiwa had accepted Transvaal's protection, the British sent a 4,000-strong force under Charles Warren to secure the area. Then, in March 1885, Warren was instructed to proceed north of the Molopo and extend British "protection" over southern Bechuanaland. *See also* British Bechuanaland; Warren Expedition.

BATTLE OF DERDEPOORT (25 NOVEMBER 1899). One of the most controversial battles in the **South African War of 1899–1902**, supposedly a "white man's war," in which armed African troops from the Protectorate attacked a fixed Boer position inside the Transvaal. Under the cover of darkness, **Kgafela Kgatla** regiments led by **Ramono** forded the Madikwe river near the town of Sikwane and at daybreak initiated a three-hour attack on the commando laagered next to the small town of Derdepoort. The British troops accompanying the Kgatla withdrew minutes after the opening shots. The South

African Republic raised a diplomatic outcry in Europe over the use of armed Africans against their white troops and accused the BaKgatla of committing atrocities. The BaKgatla suffered fourteen dead and many casualties, the Boers, under the command of J.T. Kirsten, six dead and four casualties. *See also* Linchwe I; River Villages; Segale.

BATTLE OF DIMAWE (30 AUGUST 1852). The most important engagement of the **BaTswana-Boer War of 1852–53,** Dimawe was the first major BaTswana defense against Boer attack and a seminal event in Botswana's history. On Saturday, 28 August 1852, Scholtz's commando of 430 Boers and 600 African auxiliaries arrived at Dimawe, a fortified settlement of Sechele's **BaKwena.** Under Sechele's leadership as well were the **Ba-Ngwaketse, Mmanaana Kgatla,** and **BaKaa.** When Scholtz demanded that Sechele surrender the Mmanaana Kgosi, Moseilele, and "enter into an arrangement" with the Transvaal Boers, Sechele refused. During a two-day truce for negotiations, Boers were given free passage to the waters of the Kolobeng river, and some attended the BaTswana's Sunday prayer services led by the MoTswana LMS preacher, Mebalwe. On Monday, when Sechele and Scholtz met and failed to reach an agreement, the battle commenced. The Boers stormed Dimawe's hillside entrenchments, shielding themselves with their African hostages and forcing the dug-in BaTswana to hold their fire. In six hours, the Boers managed to burn down Dimawe village and overrun the BaNgwaketse and BagaMmanaana positions, but by sunset the core of defenders under Sechele held their positions atop Botswelakgosi hill. At nightfall Scholtz ordered a retreat, giving Sechele time to regroup at Dithubaruba. Thirty-six Boers and at least eighty-nine BaTswana died during the battle and related skirmishes. Sechele himself was credited with killing five Boers while avoiding capture among the rocks as one of his wives loaded his rifles. Scholtz's Boer commando left with 3,000 head of cattle and other BaKwena property, as well as roughly 200 women and 400 children for use on Boer farms as *inboekelinge* (so-called "apprentices"). *See also* Battle of Dithubaruba; Slave Trade.

BATTLE OF DITHUBARUBA (28 AUGUST 1826). A decisive battle in the **mfecane** that led to the withdrawal of the Ba**Kololo** from southern Botswana. In 1823 the BaKololo had aggrandized the area, driven the BaNgwaketse from **Dithubaruba,** and launched raids on BaTswana cattle. In response Kgosi **Sebego**

I raised a 4,000-man force, including some **Mmanaana Kgatla**,1,000 armed men of unknown provenance from Kang, and two British traders (Bains and Biddulph) and their Griqua and BaTlhaping assistants. At dawn on the 28th of August, Sebego's force launched a surprise attack on the BaKololo, seized Dithubaruba, inflicted heavy casualties on the BaKololo, and captured most of their cattle. The BaKololo regrouped at **Mochudi**, spent the 1826–1827 growing season recuperating, then moved into northern Botswana, where after coming into conflict with the **BaTawana** among others, they eventually settled in western **Zambia**.

BATTLE OF DUTLWE (ca. 1834). During the **mfecane** Dutlwe represents an important BaTswana victory over the **AmaNdebele**, who were then based at Mosega in the western Transvaal. Under their *inkosi enkhulu*, Mzilikazi, the AmaNdebele had moved their kingdom into the western Transvaal from 1832 to 1834, and began demanding tribute from BaTswana in the area. When Mzilikazi's tribute collectors approached **Sebego I** of the BaNgwaketse, Sebego had them killed. Immediately Mzilikazi attempted to retaliate, sending an expeditionary force against Sebego's people. Sebego skillfully retreated into the Kgalagadi Desert, drawing the AmaNdebele in pursuit. Unfamiliar with the harsh environment, Mzilikazi's force soon weakened. At Dutlwe, Sebego's regiments annihilated the AmaNdebele, none of whom, it is alleged, returned to Mzilikazi. Descendants of the few known survivors may be found among the **BaKgalagadi**.

BATTLE OF MATOPOS (ca. 1828). A battle during the **mfecane** in which the BaNyayi-BaKalanga of the **Butwa** kingdom defeated the BaNgwato of **Kgari I**. Around 1828, during a severe drought and following losses at the hands of the BaKololo, the BaNgwato invaded the **BaKalanga** to the north. The BaNgwato invaders, remembered in Ikalanga traditions as "Barwa" (literally, southerners), initially met little resistance, but after pushing deeper into BaKalanga territory, they were ambushed in the Matopos, an extensive rock outcrop in present western Zimbabwe. Kgari, along with "half" of his regimental force, was killed. The BaKalanga, nevertheless, were seriously weakened by this engagement. In some BaKalanga accounts, the subsequent fall of the Butwa is attributed to the failure of the BaNyayi royals to give appropriate thanks to their God **Mwali** for the victory. *See also* Nyayi.

BATTLE OF NGWAPA [SELEKA] (MAY 1887). An example of "sub-imperialism" in the Bechuanaland Protectorate. In February 1887 the BaNgwato Kgosi **Khama III** sought to impose his authority over the aged, blind Ba**Seleka** ruler, Kobe. Khama's regiments first tried intimidation, by burning the BaSeleka's crops, but the BaSeleka mounted armed resistance. Protectorate officials then gave Khama permission to attack with force. In May 1887 Kobe's capital of Ngwapa (old Seleka) was surrounded by a BaNgwato army of approximately 4,000 men, accompanied by a small detachment of Bechuanaland Border Police (BBP). Lieut. Bates, BBP commander, called on Kobe to surrender or face destruction. When Kobe refused, many BaSeleka fled into the Transvaal leaving about eighty, including Kobe's son Seleka, to stand with the recalcitrant ancient. The battle, which lasted several hours, left at least seven BaNgwato and thirteen BaSeleka dead. Seleka escaped, Kobe was captured, and Khama, content with resistance at an end, allowed Kobe to rejoin his people exiled in the Transvaal.

BATTLES OF SHOSHONG (1842, 1844, 1863). During the nineteenth century the Shoshong hills were the site of three important engagements between the Ba**Ngwato** and Ama**Ndebele.** In 1842 the BaNgwato under **Sekgoma I** repulsed an AmaNdebele raiding party, leading to a larger attack in 1844. The large quantity of muskets the BaNgwato purchased from the trader Gordon Cumming contributed to this victory. In 1863 after two decades of truce, the AmaNdebele launched their final attack, which was repulsed by Sekgoma's son, **Khama III.**

BECHUANALAND. An early nineteenth-century English corruption of "the BaTswana's land," referring loosely to territories immediately north of the Cape Colony where SeTswana-speaking peoples were found. *See also* the Introduction; Boundaries; British Bechuanaland; Protectorate.

BECHUANALAND/BOTSWANA DEMOCRATIC PARTY (BDP). *See* Democratic Party.

BECHUANALAND/BOTSWANA PEOPLE'S PARTY (BPP). *See* People's Party.

BESELE WESSELS. Kgosi of the Tshidi BaRolong, 1896–1903. In 1895 he represented his father, Kgosi **Montshiwa**, and attempted to join **Bathoen I**, **Khama III**, and **Sebele I** on their trip to London, where Besele wished to lodge a protest against the incorporation of British Bechuanaland into Cape Colony. Besele was turned back by British authorities in Cape Town. After his failed mission Besele took over his father's position and became an English loyalist. During the **South African War**, he played a key role in the Anglo-Rolong defense of **Mafikeng**, which the Boers besieged from November 1899 to May 1900. Besele died in office. *See also* Three Kings in London.

BIRWA (BABIRWA). A people, many of whom became subject to the BaNgwato and whose traditional territory straddles the common borders of eastern Botswana, southwestern Zimbabwe, and the northern Transvaal. Their name derives from a legendary ruler, Mmirwa. Relations with the BaNgwato date from the rule of Kgari (ca. 1817–1826), but they were not fully incorporated into the BaNgwato state until the second reign of **Khama III**. During the 1920s those BaBirwa living in the BaNgwato Reserve and the **Tuli block** were forcibly removed to Bobonong village. One group, under Malema, resisted and subsequently settled at Molalatau. *See also* Villagization.

BOBJWALE (BOYALE). Second wife of **Kgari I** and mother of **Macheng** by Sedimo, brother of Kgari (according to the levirate custom). After Sedimo's death and several BaNgwato battles against the BaKololo, she aspired to bogosi. When she failed, a large faction of the BaNgwato seceded with her and they lived for a time near Victoria Falls. Her group later returned, whereupon she and Macheng lived in the Kweneng. In 1842 the AmaNdebele raided the Kweneng and took her son captive.

BOERS. *See* Afrikaners.

BOLATA. Sometimes used synonymously with *botlhanka*, *bolata* is the SeTswana form of servitude that in the past often degenerated into slavery. In southern Botswana, a *mothlanka* translates roughly as a subordinate, though in northern Botswana it may be used to refer to a person living in enforced servitude. *Lelata* (pl. *malata*) is a person who more closely resembles a permanent inferior owned or controlled by another.

The institution of *bolata* may have begun generations ago when groups of BaKgalagadi conquered **Bushmen** in the Kgalagadi and kept them as servants, herders, and hunters. All the large BaTswana merafe adopted *bolata* prior to the **mfecane**, usually enslaving BaSarwa, BaKgalagadi, and war captives. In the ivory hunting era (1840–1880), BaTswana states expanded and vastly increased *bolata*. Groups such as the BaYei and HaMbukushu were especially affected. Slaves (*malata*) hunted, herded, and paid tribute to their masters, while women performed domestic labor and worked in fields. After 1880 male malata were increasingly used in cattle production.

Malata were the absolute property of their owners, who regarded them as sub-human animals. They were denied property and legal rights and assigned child status, though in some areas the men were allowed to undergo **initiation**. A common misconception is that *malata* were not liable to be sold. In fact *malata* changed hands among BaTswana owners and some were sold to outsiders, black and white. *Malata* families were inherited and often split between heirs.

The British did little to end slavery. In 1924 Resident Commissioner **Jules Ellenberger** informed a League of Nations inquiry that "slavery is not known to exist in the Bechuanaland Protectorate" (resident commissioner to high commissioner, telegram, 14 May 1924, s. 43/7, Botswana National Archives). Two years later High Commissioner Lord Athlone stated that "the Government will not allow any tribe to demand compulsory service from another . . . Any Masarwa who wish to leave their masters and live independently of them . . . are free to do so." (high commissioner to secretary of state for the colonies and dominions, 13 August 1926, s. 43/7, Botswana National Archives). The Athlone Declaration, as it became known, was nevertheless legally enforceable. In 1931 an official commission of inquiry, led by E.S.B. Tagart, recommended that the BaSarwa be incorporated into the BaNgwato by being granted the same rights and obligations as the rest of the "tribe." Tagart's recommendations were implemented during the mid-1930s, but the BaSarwa were not provided with alternative means of earning a livelihood and remained servants of the BaNgwato. In the same year, a proclamation made slavery illegal and required that all "native labourers" be paid in cash or kind, but no minimum wage was laid down, making the proclamation meaningless.

Desertions of *malata* did more to diminish *bolata* than did legal edicts. Around 1920 they began to leave their masters and avoided further dealings with them, a process that steadily increased. Nevertheless, *bolata* still exists in some remote areas. *See also* Slave Trade.

BONEWAMANG PADI SECHELE (1926–1978). Tribal Authority for the Kweneng District (1970–1978) and pretender to the BaKwena throne. Son of Padi (d. 1929), son of Sechele II. Bonewamang was educated at **Tiger Kloof**, where he was a very poor student. When Padi's elder brother **Sebele II** was removed from bogosi and confined to exile in 1931, the British bypassed Bonewamang and appointed **Kgari Sechele**, Bonewamang's junior uncle. After Kgari's death, Bonewamang's claim to bogosi was challenged by Sebele II's son **Moruakgomo**. In 1963 the judge of an inquiry recognized the legitimacy and seniority of both claimants while ruling that **Neale Sechele** should succeed. In 1970 the Botswana Government forced Neale to abdicate and appointed Bonewamang as Tribal Authority.

BOTETI RIVER. This river, which is fed by the overflow from the **Okavango Delta**, flows south-east into the desert and empties into the Makgadikgadi Pans. Prior to the nineteenth century, the few inhabitants alongside its banks included BaKhurutshe, Deti-khoe, and BaKalanga. In the ivory hunting era Boteti's large elephant herds were exterminated and the BaTawana and BaNgwato migrated into the Boteti area, increasing and diversifying its population. The BaKwena also used the area until 1904. In 1894 most of the Boteti was awarded to the BaNgwato through intruiging by **Khama III**. In the twentieth century, large cattle owners moved their herds into the area. Commercial cattle trading in the area was dominated by the R.A. Bailey firm, which trekked cattle from Ngamiland and moved thousands of them slowly south through a series of way stations to the rail line for transport to the Union or to the **Tuli block** for smuggling across the South Africa border.

The name Boteti is commonly associated with witchcraft, especially ritual murder. *See also* Deti.

BOTLHANKA. *See* Bolata.

BOTSWANA DEFENCE FORCE (BDF). Botswana's national army was formed in 1977, largely in response to the security problems posed along its northeastern and eastern borders by the Rhodesian civil war. Initially its officers and men were drawn from the **Police**, including its first commander, Major-General Mompati Merafhe. In the 1980s the BDF was stationed primarily along the South African and Namibian borders, where a number of violations of Botswana's borders occurred.

The BDF failed to repel South African commando raids on sites in and around Gaborone in 1984 and 1986. By 1986 the BDF had 3,000 troops and a modest airwing. In 1992, following Namibian independence and the beginning of negotiations toward democracy in South Africa, the BDF had 7,000 in uniform and received 16 percent of Botswana's annual budget, much of it committed to a large new airforce base (Project Eagle) near Molepolole being built by a French company and South African sub-contractors at an estimated cost of $250 million. The BDF officer corps has received its training largely in the United States and Great Britain. As of 1996 the BDF was commanded by Brigadier General S.K. Ian Khama, eldest son of the late Sir **Seretse Khama**. *See also* Military, Traditional.

BOTSWANA DEMOCRATIC PARTY (BDP). *See* Democratic Party.

BOTSWANA INDEPENDENCE PARTY (BIP). *See* Indpendence Party.

BOTSWANA NATIONAL FRONT (BNF). *See* National Front.

BOTSWANA PEOPLE'S PARTY (BPP). *See* People's Party.

BOTSWANA SOCIETY. A society which states as its aims the "encouragement of interest in the research and scholarship on subjects in the fields of the Natural Sciences, the Social Sciences, the Humanities and the Arts, especially where such subjects are related to Botswana." From its offices (Box 71, Gaborone) in the National Museum and Art Gallery, the Society publishes an annual journal, (*Botswana Notes and Records*), as well as selected monographs, diaries, bibliographies, and symposia proceedings. It also organizes symposia, field trips, public lectures, films, and varied fund-raising activities. Membership is open to the public.

BOUNDARIES. *Internal.* In the pre-colonial era, frontier wells marked where the various peoples within Botswana met and exchanged goods and divided their access to farm land, pasturage, game, water, and trade routes. Competition for resources was a major cause of boundary clashes, notably during the **Civil Wars** beginning in the 1870s, and in 1880 the British

Administration in the Transvaal was used to arbitrate the settlement of the BaKwena-BaNgwaketse border.

When the Bechuanaland Protectorate was proclaimed by the **Warren Expedition** of 1885, Warren submitted, with his plan for the future administration of the territory, a map showing boundaries of "tribal reserves" and "crown lands," based on his interpretation of the territorial claims and offers made by **Khama III**, **Sechele I**, and **Gaseitsiwe**. Warren's plan was rejected, and his map was shelved. Administration began, therefore, without official policy on internal boundaries.

Between 1885 and 1899, Protectorate officials were frequently involved in boundary matters, notably the BaKwena-BaNgwato dispute over the Lephephe wells, the extent of southern Ngamiland, the BaKwena-BaKgatla and BaLete-Ba-Ngwaketse boundaries, and the BaNgwato-BaKgatla dispute over the Serurume valley. No general demarcation took place, however, and in 1895, when Chamberlain was poised to hand over the Protectorate administration to the **British South Africa Company** (BSACO), Warren's map was dusted off and used to determine which "tribal reserves" would remain under British protection. The BSACO plan was scrapped following the abortive **Jameson Raid**, whereupon the Protectorate began its own boundaries survey, which in 1899 culminated in the creation of five "reserves" (named Bangwaketse, Bakwena, Bamangwato, Bakgatla, and Batawana) and surrounding "crown lands." Later, portions of the crown lands were sold as freehold blocks, some reserve boundaries were adjusted, and two additional reserves were created (Tati Native and Bamalete).

External. Nearly all of Botswana's boundaries came into existence before or after, rather than with, the declaration of the Protectorate. Agreement on the southeastern boundary began in 1857 with the opening of peaceful relations between **Sechele I** of the BaKwena and M.W. Pretorius of the South African Republic (SAR), and the line separating their spheres was adjusted to define the limits of the SAR by the Keate Award of 1871, the Pretoria Convention of 1881, and the London Convention of 1884. The southern border originates with the September 1885 proclamation, which separated the Bechuanaland Protectorate from the protectorate of British Bechuanaland "south of the Molopo River." In 1895, when **British Bechuanaland** was transferred to the Cape Colony, the border was adjusted by moving a section north of the Molopo to the Ramatlabama spruit so as to place the town of **Mafikeng** in the Cape and south of the Bechuanaland Protectorate. By

then the Gordonia region had been transferred to the Cape
Colony. The northern border, which in 1885 stood at the
twenty-second parallel south longitude, was finally extended
north of the Zambezi, west of Matebeleland (western Zimbabwe) and east of German territory, by the 1890 Order-in-
Council. The present northeastern, Botswana-Zimbabwe border was largely set in 1895 by Chamberlain during the visit of
Khama III, Bathoen I, and **Sebele I** and was confirmed in
1899. The western, or Botswana-Namibia border, was likewise
determined in Europe by the Anglo-German agreements of
1884 and 1890. Ngamiland was added to the Protectorate
despite German attempts to annex it. Britain's claim was
recognized because of the Nicolls-Hicks Concession signed by
the BaTawana in 1888 and 1889. *See also* Limpopo River.

BOYNE, HENRY (d. 1898). Irish-born trader and confidant of
BaKwena diKgosi. He married into the **BaKwena** and became
the most important trader in nineteenth-century Kweneng.
Boyne obtained breech-loading rifles for the BaKwena during
the **Civil Wars** and abducted an AmaNdebele princess, Kholoma, for **Sechele I.** On the journey to Molepolole, Kholoma
spurned Boyne's offer of brandy, declaring that Lobengula
gave her champagne. In 1895, after being caught smuggling
brandy in violation of Protectorate laws, Boyne was exiled to
an area that later became the Gaberones block. There he built
a store on a farm granted to him by Sechele I and **Sebele I,**
though the latter claimed that the farm was for Boyne's use,
not ownership. The government nevertheless gave Boyne title
to the farm. *See also* Race Relations; Traders.

BRAMESTONE MEMORANDUM. The Colonial Office document that defined the limits of British authority in the Bechuanaland Protectorate and that was applied to other British protectorates in Africa. Officially titled "Memorandum as to the
Jurisdiction and Administrative Powers of a European State
holding Protectorates in Africa," it was drafted in February
1891 by John Bramestone, Undersecretary of State for the
Colonies. Bramestone's memorandum was designed to sweep
away legal arguments by various BaTswana diKgosi that they
remained the "sovereigns of the soil" under British protection.
Bramestone ruled that sovereignty was ultimately indivisible
and rested with the British Government. He defined the Protectorate as "an uncivilized territory to which Europeans resort
in greater or less numbers, and where, in as much the native

rulers of the territory are incapable of maintaining peace, order and good government among Europeans, the protecting Power maintains courts, police and other institutions for the control, safety and benefit of its own subjects and of the natives." According to the memorandum, sovereignty in an "uncivilized African territory [could be] exercised by the same methods as if the ruler had ceded his whole country to her Majesty."

Britain's claim of right to rule the Bechuanaland Protectorate was based not on any perceived need to protect BaTswana from the Boers or any other threat, but rather to protect whites from BaTswana. On the basis of the Bramestone Memorandum, a second document, known as the **Order-in-Council of May 1891** authorized the **high commissioner** to enact laws, to establish a court system, to levy taxes, and to take additional steps to maintain "peace, order and good government of all persons" within the Bechuanaland Protectorate. *See also* Protectorate.

BRIGADES. A non-government vocational training movement for boys and girls initiated by **Patrick van Rensburg**. The term "brigade" derives from post-independence Ghana, but the brigades of Botswana gained some of their inspiration and character from the indigenous age-regiment system. The first brigade was founded in **Serowe** in March 1965 for training young builders and for contributing to other work skills useful to the community. The training content of this Builders Brigade, and its work-for-profit services, set it apart from the traditional self-help development projects carried out by age-regiments formed during **initiation**. As other brigades were established, young men and women were trained in such skills as carpentry, auto mechanics, welding, and printing. By the early 1970s brigades were operating in rural towns throughout Botswana and were supported by international donors.

During the late 1970s, however, external interference and internal dissension weakened the movement; the Botswana government sought to cut some brigades and convert others into vocational training schools for the purpose of responding to the needs of the market rather than of the local community, thereby undermining the brigades' ability to cover their costs and remain self-sufficient. Serious financial problems and a loss of direction further hampered the brigade movement into the 1980s. The brigades have since recovered under a new arrangement that places each of them under Botswana's trust laws as a brigades development trust, governed by an elected board of trustees. As of 1992 there were twenty-seven registered autonomous brigade centers in twenty-six towns and villages. They are affiliated with other non-government organizations and cooperate with the Botswana Ministry of Education through the Brigades Development Center (BRIDEC), Gaborone.

BRITISH BECHUANALAND. Sometimes confused with the Bechuanaland Protectorate (later renamed Botswana), British Bechuanaland was formed earlier and became part of the Cape Colony. In February 1884, following the London Convention, Britain declared a Protectorate over British Bechuanaland, the territory west of the recognized boundary of the Transvaal. British Bechuanaland, which contained the erstwhile Boer "republics" of Stellaland and Goshen, was created to forestall Boer expansion and keep open the "missionary road" (or "the road to the North") and to advance British interests. Cape land speculators, who had elbowed their way into the diamond fields and the territories around Kimberley, were particularly keen to see the British control this important avenue, which connected the Cape with the trade and mineral potential of Zimbabwe.

British Bechuanaland rapidly became the scene of a struggle between Boer and British land grabbers, Cape colonialists, British humanitarians, and the Africans (mainly BaTlhaping and BaRolong) caught in between. **John Mackenzie** of the **London Missionary Society** was appointed the first deputy commissioner of **British Bechuanaland**, but within months Hercules Robinson, British high commissioner at the Cape, replaced him with a Cape man of large political and economic ambitions, Cecil John Rhodes. Rhodes proved unable to bring calm to the Protectorate, and South African Republic President Paul Kruger declared a freebooter republic at Rooigrond, near **Mafikeng,** as part of the Transvaal.

British authority was not firmly established until early 1885, when Sir Charles Warren led a military expedition into the area and met Kruger at Fourteen Streams. Warren created a strong police force (the Bechuanaland Border **Police**—the BBP), and the British authorized the establishment of administrative camps at Vryburg, Taungs, Mafikeng, and Kuruman.

With the **Warren Expedition**, British Bechuanaland became an important staging ground for further penetration of the interior. In May 1885, Warren, together with his advisor, John Mackenzie, and a small military party traveled to Kanye,

Molepolole, Mochudi, and Shoshong, there declaring the territory north of the Molopo River to be the "Bechuanaland Protectorate." Separation took place on 30 September 1885, known for years as "Protectorate Day" (the same day and month were chosen for Botswana's "Independence Day" eighty-one years later). The new Protectorate and British Bechuanaland were administered together from Vryburg, where **Sidney Shippard** wore the two hats of deputy commissioner (for British Bechuanaland) and resident commissioner (for the Bechuanaland Protectorate). Shippard's office also became the vantage point for Rhodes's **British South Africa Company (BSACO)**, founded in 1889, which British administrators and police helped to become a power in the region.

Between 1885 and 1895, Mafikeng became the main BBP depot and the commercial center of the region connecting the Cape, the Transvaal, and Namibia with the "road to the north." The BSACO's Leander Starr Jameson recruited BBP men in Mafikeng in preparation for his abortive 1895 raid into the Transvaal. In the same year British Bechuanaland ceased to exist, when British authority was transferred to the Cape Colony government, a move opposed by Africans, who preferred British to Cape rule. *See also* BaTswana-Boer War of 1881–1884; Jameson Raid.

BRITISH SOUTH AFRICA COMPANY (BSACO). After receiving its royal charter in 1889, Cecil Rhodes's BSACO became a major influence in the Bechuanaland Protectorate. The primary objective of the BSACO was to take control of the gold fields of Zimbabwe in the name of Britain, but its plans necessarily included the Protectorate, which fell within the boundaries of the 1889 charter. Rhodes received valuable assistance from Protectorate officials and members of the Bechuanaland Border **Police** (BBP), many of whom Rhodes rewarded with shares in his company. Protectorate officials helped negotiate treaties with Lobengula, obstruct company competitors, keep open the lines of communication, and collect police at key points. Many of the BBP's men joined the BSACO's "Pioneer Column" which invaded Zimbabwe in 1890, and several BBP companies, together with 1,700 BaNgwato, took part in the BSACO's war against Lobengula's AmaNdebele from 1893 to 1894.

During this war, the BSACO prepared to take over the full authority for the administration of the Bechuanaland Protectorate from Britain. In 1893 a Concessions Commission was set up to eliminate all competing commercial concessions made in the Protectorate since the BSACO charter came into effect and thereby clear the way for transfer. In September 1895 three diKgosi went to London with petitions opposing a BSACO takeover, but the Secretary of State for the colonies, Joseph Chamberlain, disallowed their case except for assurances that a part of their respective territories would be exempt from Company rule. Soon thereafter, the **Jameson Raid**, which was launched from Pitsani Potlhogo inside the Protectorate, ruined the BSACO's reputation and forestalled the transfer indefinitely. The agreements signed by diKgosi **Montshiwa** and Ikaneng giving the BSACO control of their lands inside the Protectorate were also revoked.

The BSACO presence nevertheless remained. The Company continued to operate the telegraph line it had erected in 1890, and in 1896 it received land for the construction of the Mafikeng-Bulawayo railroad, completed the following year. In 1898 the Protectorate ceded more land to the BSACO, which in 1905 it formed into the Lobatse, Gaberones, and Tuli Blocks and in turn sold portions of block land to white farmers from the Union. BaHurutshe, BaLete, BaTlokwa, and BaBirwa lost land as a result, and the BaTlokwa under **Gaborone** remained subject to BSACO authority until 1932. Along the rail line, Rhodesian railway by-laws segregating the races were enforced by Company police and helped to make **Lobatse** and **Francistown**, the Protectorate's key rail points, white settler towns. *See also* Concessions; Ghanzi Farms; Grobler Affair; Seleka; Three Kings in London; Tuli Block.

BUBI (d. 1849). During the 1830s and 1840s Bubi was the leader of the Tshosa and Maunatlala wards, a large section of which had become independent of the BaKwena under Kgosi **Sechele I**. In order to reunite his morafe, Sechele I sent Bubi a gift of gunpowder as an inducement to make common cause against the Boers. According to tradition, Bubi suspected the powder to have been bewitched and had a flame passed over it to remove any curse. The powder exploded and killed him. Shortly thereafter Bubi's followers surrendered to Sechele.

BUDDHISTS. Since 1974 a small but growing, largely expatriate, community of believers, the Buddhists numbered 150 adherents in 1994 with congregations in Gaborone, Francistown, Lobatse, and Keanye. The Botswana Buddhist Society was formed in 1990.

BUSANG, VICTOR (1922–). Trade union organizer in Lobatse in the early 1960s. After involvement in nationalist politics in South Africa, Busang became the leader of what was then the most active branch of the Bechuanaland Protectorate African Workers' Union. In 1961 he launched a campaign of selective boycotts and strikes against employers practicing racial discrimination. However, the union's efforts were eclipsed by the activities of the **People's Party.** By 1965 Busang had joined this party and was its candidate for the Gaborone seat in the first general election. He lost. Later, after entering private business, he became a member of the **National Front** and became their 1994 candidate in Molepolole. *See also* Trade Unions.

BUSHMEN. Anglicized from old Dutch terms such as *Bosjesmans* or *Bosjesman Hottentot*, (literally "bush people"). The term is popularly, and mistakenly, used as a racial type for Khoisan-speaking, nomadic, hunter-gatherers organized into small bands and having such assumed physical characteristics as peppercorn hair, small stature, yellowish skin, naturally erect penises, and steatopygia. Such definitions are inadequate in almost every respect. Historical and archaeological evidence demonstrates that distinct racial types are fictitious (as does genetic and other scientific evidence) and that no mode of economic organization and production has remained exclusive to any particular southern African community over time.

People referred to as Bushmen in Botswana have for generations, just as have all other groups in the region, engaged in such varied pursuits as cattle keeping, fishing, agriculture, mining, and migrant labor, as well as hunting and gathering. Moreover, no such thing as a distinct Bushman language exists.

The term Bushman first appeared in the 1680s, when it was used by Dutch settlers to describe Cape Khoe speakers who had not succumbed to their overrule in the aftermath of the 1673–1677 Dutch-Khoe war. These people were said to lack livestock and land, as well as chiefs. Boers labelled them "bandits," commonly shot them on sight, and enslaved their women and children. In the nineteenth century, a small external market also existed for "Wild Bushmen," who were exported from South Africa as commodities for the amusement of circus and freak show visitors in Europe and the United States. Beginning with Saartji Baartman's captivity in Paris as the "Hottentot Venus" (1809–1915), to the "Missing Link" exhibitions in America organized by the "Great Farini" (aka Leonard Hunt, of **Lost City of the Kalahari** fame), Bushmen became identified in the European and American public's mind as throwbacks to the Stone Age. These popularized "Bushman" notions have persisted into modern times, as attested in Laurens van der Post's *Lost World of the Kalahari*, in Jamie Uys's cinematic box office hit, *The Gods Must Be Crazy*, and in many twentieth-century anthropological studies of the **Khoisan**. *See also* Bolata; Khoe; Sarwa; Slave Trade.

BUTWA. Perhaps the largest state on record in pre-colonial southern Africa. Butwa was a Ba**Kalanga** state, located in modern-day western Zimbabwe/northeastern Botswana, that existed ca. 1450 to 1840. Initially Butwa was controlled by what the Portuguese called the Torwa dynasty, in Ikalanga oral traditions recalled as the reign of "Chibundule" (ca. 1450–1680). The Chibundule were overthrown by the Nichasike ("Lord Cha the creator," Portuguese: Changamire). The Nichasike period is sometimes referred to as the Rozwi confederacy, derived from the royal Moyo-Varozwi clan.

Butwa monarchs from both dynasties took the title of Mambo and respected **Mwali** as a state god. During the Chibundule period, the Mambos were chosen from the Ba**Lilima** line; whereas under the Nichasike, the Moyo-Varozwi (known as Ba**Nyayi**) provided the Mambo. Under the Chibundule and Nichasike, the Mambos and their regional representatives ruled from (d)zimbabwes, large stone walled structures still architecturally impressive. During the later Nichasike period, the kingdom's chief tribute collector, Tumbale, emerged as an autonomous power.

In many accounts Butwa is incorrectly identified as a "Shona" state. Our knowledge of Butwa is somewhat sketchy, but it controlled much of the regional trade in gold, ivory, and salt. Butwa ruins reach across northeastern Botswana into the Kalahari as far as the Makgadikgadi Pans.

BUYS, COENRAAD ("DIPHAFHA") (1761–1831). A white outlaw and cattle rustler from the Cape Colony who drifted into the Kalahari region before settling in the northern Transvaal. After 1815 he operated as a bandit and cattle raider in the southern Kalahari, occasionally in the employ of various di-Kgosi. For a time he lived with the BaNgwaketse and in 1820 he worked for **Kgari I** of the Ba**Ngwato**, before moving to the Transvaal. Descendants of Buys followed his lead as slave traders and ivory hunters. *See also* Race Relations.

C

CAPRIVI STRIP. Control of this thin strip of territory, which lies between the northern border of Botswana west of the Zambezi river and the southern border of Angola, has long been in dispute. It originated in 1890 as the recognized extension of German South West Africa and was named after the then Chancellor of Germany, Count Leo von Caprivi. Though not occupied by the Germans until 1909, the Strip accorded them access to the Zambezi and kept alive their hopes of linking their South West and East African colonies; these plans bore no fruit. Previously it had been under the control of the BuLozi state and had been occupied by a variety of peoples, including Bekuhane (Ba**Subiya**) and Ha**Mbukushu** who extended into northern Botswana. Until 1909, the Strip remained "lawless," and its effective control was contested by the Ba**Tawana** and BaLozi. In 1893 its western portion was conquered by BaTawana regiments in a brutal campaign. BaTawana diKgosi maintained de facto control over the area until 1912, despite nominal German control from 1909. The Strip lay beyond their effective colonial administration and was a popular poaching spot for white hunters. BaTawana and BaLozi tax collectors operated uncontested in the area, and some British officials patrolled and hunted there unchallenged.

From 1909 a small German detachment operated in the eastern Caprivi under British supervision until 1914 when with the onset of World War I the Strip was occupied by police from Southern Rhodesia and the Bechuanaland Protectorate and placed under the administrative control of the Protectorate's resident commissioner. These arrangements were formalized in accordance with the League of Nations Mandate of SWA 1922.

In 1930, at the insistence of the Union of South Africa, the Strip was placed under the Union's Southwest Africa administration in Windhoek. But control proved illusory, which Windhoek admitted in 1936, and in 1939 the Caprivi was made part of Transvaal province, which administered it until 1980. Until the 1950s, Protectorate police assisted the South Africans in maintaining law and order in the Caprivi. In 1962, LEGCO politicians **Tsheko Tsheko** and **Quett Masire** called for the Caprivi's reincorporation into the Bechuanaland Protectorate, but the issue was dropped. Border demarcation for the Strip west of the Chobe was accepted by the self-governing Protectorate in 1965 on the eve of Botswana's independence. The Caprivi remained under the control of Pretoria until Namibian independence in 1990, though the Strip was a war zone in the struggle between South Africa and the South West Africa People's Organization (SWAPO).

CATTLE. Cattle have been part of the economy of what is now Botswana since at least 1 A.D., when it is estimated that the ancestors of the Khoikhoi acquired cattle in the **Okavango Delta** area before migrating south to the Cape. From 500 A.D. until 1200 A.D. cattle-keeping was associated in eastern Botswana with centralized and stratified states, which thereafter became integrated within the political economy of states on the Zimbabwean plateau. After 1800 a series of BaTswana states arose in which cattle "feudalism" became important. Such patron-client relationships as *mafisa* bound men and their families to large cattle holders. BaTawana and BaNgwato chiefs lent cattle to commoners as *kgamelo*, a relationship that bound the borrower to absolute obedience to the Kgosi. After 1850 the largest cattle herds were located in Ngamiland and GammaNgwato.

The 1896–97 **rinderpest** was accompanied by drought, disease, locusts, disappearance of game, and famine and eliminated most of the country's cattle population and increased what was already considerable human suffering. For the first time, many men entered South Africa as migrant laborers. The recovery of cattle herds, more or less complete by the 1920s, failed to revive the economy, because in 1924 the Union government imposed weight restrictions which blocked Protectorate beef from reaching the lucrative Rand market. An active cattle smuggling business developed, but only with World War II and the reopening of the Lobatse abattoir in 1954 did a beef industry become possible.

Until 1978 beef exports were Botswana's leading money earner and since then have been outdistanced by the mining industry. As of 1993, beef made up only 4.4 percent of Botswana's export earnings, most of the income going to the largest cattle owners. According to the 1991 census the number of cattle in the country totaled 2,844,000, with 124,541 or 45 percent of all households owning cattle.

Botswana is excellent cattle country with an abundance of tsetse-free pasture. Historically, cattle herds have been a major protection against drought in a land characterized by light, localized, and erratic rainfall. The traditional male life cycle revolved around the keeping and accumulation of stock, with responsibilities at the cattle post learned at an early age.

Pasture traditionally is communal, but increasing commercialization and the threat of overstocking have resulted in rigorous attempts on the part of government to demarcate grazing areas through such programs as the Tribal Grazing Land Policy. Still, overgrazing threatens extensive areas, including the Okavango Delta. *See also* Abattoir; Archaeology and Prehistory; Deti; Toutswe; Tsetse; Water; Zambia.

CENSUS. The colonial government produced population statistics based on tax returns and other rough forms of estimates in 1904, 1911, 1921, 1936, 1946, and 1956. The first enumerated census was conducted in 1964, followed by others in 1971, 1981, and 1991. The Government Central Statistics Office in Gaborone produces annual estimates of population by district, village, and town. As of 1994, the estimated population of Botswana stood at 1,444,000. The projected population for 2001, the year of the next census, is 1,890,727.

CHAND, ABDUL RAHIM (1916–1988). Political leader of the Asian community, representing its interest in LEGCO, 1961–1964. An active sympathizer in the anti-apartheid struggle, Chand harbored **refugees** and was barred from South Africa after 1961. He participated in the constitutional talks of 1963. *See also* Asians; Councils.

CHIEF. *See* Kgosi.

CHIEPE, GAOSITSWE K.T. (1920–). Born in Serowe. Prominent educator, diplomat, and politician. The daughter of Tibe Chiepe, an LMS teacher of BaKalanga origin, she was educated at Khama Memorial School, and in 1939 on a government bursary she attended **Tiger Kloof**, where she became the school's best student and head prefect. In 1944 she attended Fort Hare College. She was the first Protectorate woman to obtain a university degree (1947) and subsequently the first to be awarded a higher degree (MA in 1959). From 1948 to 1970 she played an important role in educational administration, serving as education officer at Serowe in the mid-1950s. In 1970 she was appointed high commissioner to the United Kingdom, and in 1974 she was specially elected as MP and became the first woman in the National Assembly. Since 1979 she has represented the Serowe South constituency. She has filled several cabinet posts. From 1984 to 1994 she was minister for External Affairs, and since October 1994 has been minister of Education.

CHILUME, OBED (1934–). MP for Nkange since 1965.

CIVIL WARS. Beginning in the early 1870s, a series of armed clashes involving the major BaTswana *merafe* seriously disturbed the region. These civil wars, which continued into the early 1880s, disrupted trade, lowered agricultural production, resulted in the loss of thousands of cattle, and led to the deaths of thousands of people. During this period, the far-flung BaKwena trading state began to break up, a strong BaNgwato state developed under Khama III, and new *merafe* emerged in the South: the BaKgatla of **Linchwe I**, the BaTlokwa of Matlapeng, and the BaLete of **Mokgosi I**. By the time the British proclaimed their Protectorate in 1885, the entire area had only just completed a major transformation.

Prior to the wars, the BaKwena of **Sechele I** had dominated much of the region by controlling the Kgalagadi trade, amassing large herds of cattle and hundreds of servile herders to move them about, and maintaining their independence from the Boer republics to the east. In addition to attracting refugees from the Boer-controlled Transvaal to his capital, Sechele's strength was apparent in his meddling in the affairs of his African neighbors, particularly the BaNgwato of Shoshong to his north. Sechele's position declined steadily after 1875. In that year, **Khama III** began to consolidate his position in Shoshong and build his own trading state independent of Sechele's interference. The BaKgatla at Mochudi, refugees from the Transvaal who had lived as Sechele's guests since 1872, refused him tribute and repulsed a force sent from Molepolole to attack them. A bitter, protracted struggle for the control of the water of the Madikwe and Ngotwane rivers then began, with the BaKgatla emerging as victors seven years later. During the war, the BaTlokwa and BaLete joined against the BaKwena, who had also been their former masters. The BaKwena also lost authority over the Mmanaana Kgatla, who moved from Thamaga and settled at Mosopa, recognizing the nominal authority of the BaNgwaketse. The latter, under **Gaseitsiwe**, attempted to extract subservience from the BaLete, who had moved away from Sechele and settled in their territory at Ramotswa, but Gaseitsiwe's forces were repulsed with great loss in a battle fought near the BaLete capital in 1881.

Conflict in the region came to an end in 1882, when an

appeal for peace and unity came from **Montshiwa** of the Tshidi BaRolong at Mafikeng, then under threat of a takeover by white filibusters and land speculators. The focus of the leaders shifted quickly away from local quarrels toward the south, from whence the Boer and British threat to BaTswana independence was forthcoming. The effects of the previous decade, however, prevented any unified response and undercut the ability of any one BaTswana state to alter the trend of events. As a result, the coming British were met with a mixed, though peaceful, reception. *See also* Kgafela Kgatla.

COLONIAL DEVELOPMENT CORPORATION (CDC). The CDC was a British development agency formed in 1948 to initiate, finance, and operate agricultural and veterinary projects in British colonies. In 1963 it was renamed the Commonwealth Development Corporation. Before Botswana's independence, the CDC set up a viable export abattoir at Lobatse and established an effective beef export monopoly. It was less successful in promoting ranching and farming schemes: the Pandamatenga, Nata, and Bushman Pits projects in the northern state lands, as well as projects in the south along the Molopo river, all suffered serious financial losses. After independence, the CDC continued to contribute significant aid to the Botswana Meat Commission and other parastatals, including the Botswana Housing Corporation and the Botswana Power Corporation. *See also* Abattoir.

COLOUREDS. In Southern Africa, a racial category often used to denote Afrikaans-speaking peoples of "mixed racial origin." Often derogatory in connotation (as is the SeTswana "Masetedi"), it was also used in Protectorate days for various groups including **Griqua,** "Basters," Cape Coloureds," and "Hottentots," as well as the offspring of unions between Africans and Europeans or Asians. *See also* Nama; Race Relations; Riley, Charles.

COMMUNICATIONS. *See* Air Transportation; Radio; Railways; Roads; Telecommunications.

COMMUNIST PARTY OF SOUTH AFRICA (CPSA). Formed in 1921 out of the amalgamation of the International Socialist League and other Marxist groups. From the beginning the party had a non-racial policy, but not until 1924, with J.B.M. Hertzog's prime ministry, did BaTswana and other Africans join in large numbers. In 1928 the party formed an alliance with the Lekgotla la Bafo, a Lesotho-based movement, and supported the latter group's call for a League of Protectorates. DiKgosi in the Bechuanaland Protectorate rejected these overtures, however, and remained reluctant to identify with this and other political movements in South Africa for fear of increasing the chances of incorporation. The CPSA and its weekly *South African Worker* denounced the British for deposing **Sebele II** and suspending **Tshekedi Khama** as BaNgwato regent. It also encouraged BaTswana to struggle for political independence. Copies of the paper, which were confiscated by Protectorate post office officials, were smuggled into the territory inside the staid *Sunday Times*.

CONCESSIONS. The earliest concession affecting Botswana was the Tati gold-prospecting concession of 1880 made by the AmaNdebele inkosi, Lobengula, to the Northern Light Company. In 1888 Northern Light sold it to the Tati Concession Mining and Exploration Company, the second in a long line of companies recognized as Tati-owners by the British. In 1885, **Khama III** made his "magnificent offer" of land for use by British settlers to Sir Charles Warren, and his lead was followed by **Sechele I** and **Gaseitsiwe**. Thereafter BaTswana diKgosi made a series of concessions to government and private individuals and groups, and by 1893 a total of forty-five concession claims in the Protectorate were reviewed by a Concession Commission (see below). In general, concessions subsequent to 1885 granted rights for prospecting, mining, wood cutting, trading, and construction of railways, telegraph lines, and similar undertakings. Two post-1885 concessions granted by as yet uncolonized BaTswana were the 1888 and 1889 Nicholls-Hicks Concessions for general prospecting and mining rights signed over by the BaTawana.

DiKgosi served economic ends in signing these concessions. The larger concession yielded substantial cash revenues. From the Kanya Concessions Ltd., for example, **Bathoen I** received an annual payment of £900 (which he deposited in the Standard Bank of Mafikeng as a state treasury). From their respective concessions Sechele I (and his successor **Sebele I**) received at least £700, and **Linchwe I**, £400. Trade concessions were also used by Khama III and Linchwe I to monopolize trading stores within their territories and exclude traders licensed by the Protectorate.

Concessions were also used to pursue political objectives.

By granting concessions diKgosi asserted their powers of jurisdiction over or against that of the Protectorate or other diKgosi. From late 1889, when the **British South Africa Company (BSACO)** received its charter entitling it, among other things, to proceed with the building of telegraph and rail communications in the Protectorate, Bathoen I, Sechele I, and Linchwe I granted railway and other concessions to non-BSACO syndicates in an attempt to block the path of Company progress. Corrupt officials constituted the Concession Commission of 1893 to clear away these concessions and other obstacles and prepare for handing over the Protectorate to Company rule. For this reason the Commission was unpopular among diKgosi, and some of its decisions were challenged by concession lawyers in London.

In some instances, concessions were obtained through deceit and were intended to remove the authority of a Kgosi over the land of his People. In 1894, the BSACO representative to Ngamiland, I. J. Bosman, got **Sekgoma Letsholathebe** to sign a concession granting the Company virtually sole rights over the control and sale of Ngamiland. The concession was later repudiated. In the large majority of cases, however, Botswana diKgosi granted concessions to men they knew and understood.

After the BSACO threat disappeared following the **Jameson Raid**, widespread interest in concessions lapsed. Several of the older concessions were renegotiated, however, primarily for regulating mineral prospecting, and were maintained for decades. The Protectorate continued to recognize the authority of "chiefs" to enter into agreements with mining companies for the development of "tribal" land on behalf of their people. Through concessions, asbestos mining was carried on in the BaNgwaketse Reserve, gold and diamond prospecting in the BaKgatla Reserve, and the Bamangwato Concessions Limited (BCL) was established as a subsidiary of Roan Selections trust in 1959 for **copper** development in the Central District. After independence, the ownership of the BCL concession was transferred from the tribal treasury to the central government as were authority and control over mineral rights throughout the country. *See also* Boundaries; Diamonds; Jameson Raid; Riley, Charles; Tati Concession; Warren Expedition.

CONSTITUTION. At least two constitutions have operated in Botswana, though since independence BaTswana are governed almost entirely by one. The original constitution was a body of

laws and practices by which peoples subject to various Ba-
Tswana diKgosi were governed at the time colonial rule was
established. The BaTswana constitution increased in importance during the early colonial period when a number of non-
BaTswana came under the direct authority of diKgosi, and for
decades it persisted in a robust form in many parts of the
Protectorate. Principle elements of this constitution, as observed by Schapera in the 1930s, are discussed in his *Handbook of Tswana Law and Custom*. Colonial rule excised certain
portions of the traditional constitution from the outset and
challenged other features over the years, particularly in areas
related to the diKgosi's authority. Currently much of the
traditional constitution has lapsed, that which survives being
mainly legal precedents for the settlement of individual disputes. Calls for its codification have been made, but the di-
Kgosi responsible for administering customary law are not
united on the issue.

The second constitution, dating from 1965, is that by which
the Republic is presently governed. Its history dates back to
1959, when Britain was preparing to quit Africa as a colonial
power. A Constitutional Committee of the Joint Advisory
Council drew up the Protectorate's first formal constitution,
which came into operation in 1960. It provided for an Executive Council of three ex-officio and six appointed members
and a Legislative Council of thirty-two (seven officials, four
nominated, one Asian directly elected, ten Europeans also
directly elected, and ten Africans indirectly elected by the
African council).

In 1963 consultations began at Lobatse to prepare a second
constitution, one which would confer internal self-government.
The new constitution, under which elections were held in 1965,
was closely modeled on the Westminster system of parliamentary democracy: a unicameral legislature of thirty-eight seats
(thirty-two directly elected by universal adult suffrage, four
chosen by elected MPs, and two officials); a prime minister
and cabinet of five ministers responsible to the legislature; a
Declaration of Fundamental Rights; and a House of Chiefs
with consultative powers only.

When Botswana attained full independence in 1966, the
prime minister was replaced by a president elected by the
legislature (renamed the National Assembly) and vested with
executive powers. Since 1965 the Constitution has been
amended to increase the number of elected members to thirty-
two after 1974, to thirty-four after 1984, and to forty after

1989; the only other major changes have been in the area of citizenship law and modifications to the Declaration of Fundamental Rights. *See also* Councils.

COOPER (KOPPER), SIMON. *See* Nama-German War of 1904–1909.

COOPERATIVES. The marketing cooperative movement in Botswana was established only in the 1960s with the aid and encouragement of the colonial administration, in particular from Resident Commissioner **Peter Fawcus**, who saw it as a means of "localizing" the market place. In 1962, in one of its first measures, the Legislative Council passed the Cooperatives Societies Act, and in 1964 a Department of Cooperative Societies was formed.

In 1974 the Botswana Cooperative Bank was established to provide capital and the Botswana Cooperative Union created to act as wholesale supplier to cooperative consumer shops. By and large, cooperatives have taken the form of cattle producers' marketing societies and retail outlets. By the early 1980s cooperatives controlled 20 percent of the cattle trade and 30 percent of the retail trade in basic commodities. Among the most successful is the Etsha Co-Operative, the members of which consist largely of **HaMbukushu** refugees resident in northern Ngamiland.

COPPER. Copper was mined in Botswana as early as 650 A.D., but attempts to develop a copper mining industry did not begin until the early twentieth century. Small-scale copper mining was carried on after World War II, but large-scale mining did not begin until 1967, when major copper-nickel deposits were discovered in the Central District. The new copper mining town of Selebi Phikwe became the core of the ambitious Shashe Project, the objective of which was to turn **Francistown** and its hinterland into a center for mining and industrial development.

Mining at Selebi Phikwe was financed mainly by German and South African capital and run by the Bamangwato Concessions Limited (BCL), 15 percent of which is owned by the Government, the rest by Botswana Roan Selection Trust (backed in part by American Metal Climax [AMAX] and Anglo-American Corporation). Copper and nickel production began in 1974. Due to generally low prices on the world market and declining recovery of ore grades, the three Selebi Phikwe mines have been unprofitable. In 1992, in spite of a record 3.49 million tons of ore milled, spurred by the opening of a fourth mine, the volume of metal sales declined, as did earnings from copper. In 1991 copper generated 7.5 percent of Botswana's total export earnings. At the end of 1992, the company's deficit stood at approximately one billion U.S. dollars. The copper mines have been supported by the government and aid donors as a job-creating scheme. AMAX pulled out in 1993. *See also* Mining; Nama.

COUNCILS. Until the late 1950s Protectorate officials created an assortment of councils to listen to white and black opinion and use it when they saw fit. With the approach of independence, however, new councils were established to develop representative government at local, district, and national levels.

Advisory Councils. In 1920 the government created the Native Advisory Council (NAC) for discussion of the use of the recently-established "Native Fund" and to "enable the chiefs and councilors to consult together and to advise government on native affairs generally." The NAC was a purely advisory body, but it became a forum for discussing issues of general importance and a platform for opposing unpopular ones, such as incorporation. The NAC normally met once a year. It was dominated by diKgosi, who chose most of the delegates apart from themselves. At first the BaTawana and BaNgwato did not take part, joining in 1931 and 1940, respectively. In the latter year, the council became known as the African Advisory Council (AAC). By 1944 the AAC members totaled thirty-five, with eight from BaNgwato, four each from BaNgwaketse and BaKwena, three each from BaTlokwa, BaRolong, BaKgatla, BaLete, and BaTawana, and two each from Kgalagadi and Francistown Districts. The AAC was dissolved in 1960, though its role was partly continued by the African Council (see below).

The European Advisory Council (EAC) was established in 1921 for the small white settler community concentrated primarily on freehold farms in the Tati and in the respective blocks. White traders in the various reserves were also represented. The EAC began with four members, increased to six in 1929, and in 1948 to eight. Its members were the principal advocates for **incorporation** into the Union and/or Rhodesia. In its final years, however, more of its members began to regard the Protectorate as a black man's country and participated in the Joint Advisory Council (JAC) and, after the EAC was dissolved in 1960, in the Legislative Council (LEGCO).

The Joint Advisory Council was formed in 1950 for the purpose of uniting representatives from the AAC and EAC in discussing the development of the Protectorate as a whole. It was made up of eight representatives from each council, as well as eight officials. Though without any powers and of little influence before 1958, it became instrumental in the formation of the Legislative Council and in bringing together future leaders of the territory.

The Legislative Council (LEGCO). In the 1950s calls to form a legislative council came from members of the various advisory councils, most notably **Tshekedi Khama** and **Bathoen II**. Once it decided not to link the future of the territory with that of the Union of South Africa or the Central African Federation in 1958, the government allowed the JAC to form a Constitutional Committee to review the LEGCO question. The Committee's recommendations for the creation of a LEGCO were accepted in full, and with the Order-in-Council of 21 December 1960 the Bechuanaland Protectorate Legislative Council came into being. The older councils were dissolved, but an African Council was established to continue the AAC's functions and to serve as an electoral college for the African members of LEGCO. The first session of LEGCO was held in June 1961.

LEGCO consisted of twenty-one elected members, three ex-officios, seven nominated officials, and up to four nominated non-officials. One of the ex-officios was the resident commissioner, who served as LEGCO president and nominated the officials and non-officials. Only the European and Asian communities were entitled to direct elections (excluding South African citizens who after 1961 ceased to be citizens of the British Empire). The African Council selected the African members, five each from the Southern and Northern divisions.

Local and District Councils. Representative local and district councils were introduced in the late 1950s. Before then, traditional headmen's and advisers' councils functioned in many of the reserves, but their usefulness depended on cooperation with the respective diKgosi. On occasion the colonial government attempted, and failed, to control diKgosi through such councils, as was the case in the Kweneng during the reigns of **Sechele II** and **Sebele II**, and in the Kgatleng in the time of **Molefi**. Unsuccessful efforts to impose them in Ngamiland and Gammangwato were also made. During the 1930s, Resident

Commissioner **Charles Rey**, in an attempt to strip chiefs of their powers, introduced proclamations which established tribunals and councils beyond the chiefs' control. Opposition to Rey's new system of "Native Administration" prevented these bodies from taking root. Rey's plan was overridden by the Native Proclamations of 1943, which provided for tribunals and tribal councils appointed by diKgosi.

In the early 1950s, when the colonial government was confronted by African demands for greater representation at the national level in the form of a legislative council, the government countered by demanding that diKgosi cooperate first in establishing representative local and district governments. The government was also concerned about the continued suppression of subordinate groups, such as the BaYei in Ngamiland and the BaKalanga in the Bangwato Reserve, who had been demanding representation. Government feared them and the outspoken young, educated men whose numbers were growing in many parts of the Protectorate. Between 1956 and 1960 "Tribal Councils" were introduced in all reserves. They consisted of popularly-elected representatives and hereditary/appointed traditional authorities. In "nontribal" areas, such as Kgalagadi, District Councils were created. When the African Council was established alongside LEGCO, District and Tribal Councils elected members to the African Council, which in turn elected African members to LEGCO.

In 1965, the Local Government Act established new District Councils, which replaced the old tribal councils and required that all members be elected by ballot, with the exception of the Kgosi who acted as ex-officio (i.e., nonvoting) chair. Popularly-elected town councils were introduced at the same time in Francistown, Lobatse, and Gaborone (and later in Selebi Phikwe, Orapa, and Jwaneng).

Since independence district councils have assumed the nonjudicial powers of diKgosi and have themselves come increasingly under the authority of central government through the Ministry of Local Government and Lands. Since 1970 some of their functions have been subdivided and transferred to land boards, development committees, village committees, and central government bodies operating at the local level. As of 1973, district committee staff have been employed by the central government under Unified Local Government Service. *See also* Proclamation.

CRAFTS. Botswana produces a variety of crafts for the local and international markets. They were first displayed at the 1869

World's Fair in Dublin. Botswana is best known for hand-woven baskets, most of which are made by the women of Ngamiland and for which the National Museum and Art Gallery holds an annual exhibit and sale. Other indigenous crafts include gameskin karosses, ostrich shell items, leather clothing, and "bushman" implements (bows, quivers, arrows, sticks, hunting bags, jewelry). Craft growth centers around several weaving industries, which import dyes and produce high quality wool blankets, rugs, wall-hangings, and stuffed objects destined mainly for the export market. Other craft industries, which produce goods primarily for local markets are pottery, leather products, wood and horn carvings, etched and stamped copper decorations, clothing, furniture, and batiks.

The craft industry has been developed primarily for income creation in rural areas, particularly among women, and capitalized through donor agencies such as Norwegian Agency for International Development, and smaller supporting agencies such as missions. Botswanacraft Marketing Company, which links individual craft producers with urban and overseas buyers, is a government parastatal.

CURRENCY. Since 1976 the basic unit has been the Pula, equal to 100 Thebe. Between 1961 and 1976 Botswana was a member of the Rand Monetary Area, and the South African Rand was its legal tender. Since its appearance, over the objections of the International Monetary Fund, the Pula has reflected Botswana's growing economic strength and has enabled the country to prevent South Africa from using Botswana's healthy foreign reserves to strengthen its own economy. Nevertheless, the value of the Pula is determined by a floating basket of currencies in which the Rand predominates at 70 percent, thus keeping Botswana's economy closely tied to South Africa's and obliging it in recent years to import South Africa's high inflation.

The Pula is denominated in a 1P coin and notes of P2, P5, P10, P20, P50, and P100.

CUSTOMS UNION. Since 1910 Botswana has been a member of the Southern African Custom Union (SACU), together with South Africa, Swaziland, Lesotho, and (since 1990), Namibia. Under periodically renegotiated distribution arrangements, respective members receive proportions of the import duty revenues into the customs area, and members other than South

Africa (the BNLS countries list above) receive percentage remissions for goods purchased in South Africa.

As of 1992 the BNLS countries received 38 percent of total SACU import revenues and used its own considerable export surpluses to purchase South African merchandise. In that year BNLS countries purchased 40 percent of South Africa's total exports, and 70 percent of South Africa's exports to Africa. *See also* External Economic Relations; External Relations.

D

DAMBE, AMOS M. (1911–1991). Nationalist politician; born in Nswazwi village. Married Grace Ratshosa. A product of K.T. Motsete's Tati Training Institution and Adams College, Natal, Dambe served in the High Commission Territories Corps in the Middle East (1946–1949) after World War II and achieved the rank of sergeant major. After his return Dambe became president of the BaKalanga Students' Association. In the 1950s under the nom-de-plume "Push and Pull" he penned several articles in the newspaper *Naledi ya Batswana* relating to the position of the BaKalanga in the Protectorate. At the time, Dambe was a schoolteacher in the Tati area and became the treasurer of the Bechuanaland Protectorate Teachers' Association. In 1955 he quit teaching and worked in Francistown for **L.D. Raditladi**, who founded the Bechuanaland Protectorate **Federal Party** in 1959. Dambe then became involved in politics. He was a founding member of the Bechuanaland **Democratic Party (BDP)** (1961) and its most prominent politician in the IKalanga-speaking areas of northeastern Botswana. In 1965 he was elected MP for Mmadinare and entered the cabinet, where he served for many years. He held portfolios as minister of Mines, Commerce and Industry (1965–1966), minister of Home Affairs (1966–1969), minister of Works and Communications (1969–1970), and minister of Agriculture (1970–1972). He was also Botswana's ambassador to the United States of America, from 1972 to 1976. *See also* Motsete, Kgaleman; Newspapers.

DEFENSE. *See* Botswana Defence Force.

DEMOCRATIC PARTY. The Bechuanaland (later Botswana) Democratic Party (BDP) was founded in 1961 in Lobatse by northern members of LEGCO around **Seretse Khama** and his followers in Serowe. Shortly thereafter **Quett Masire** was recruited as the party's principle organizer in the south. The **People's Party** had alienated many of the territory's educated elite, particularly in the rural areas. The BDP sold itself as the party of moderation; it had the sympathy, if not active support, of the colonial government and was willing to cooperate with the British in a peaceful transition to self-rule. The real strength of the BDP, colloquially known as "Domkrag" (Afrikaans) because of its symbol of the jacklift, was in its capacity to garner support in the traditional towns and rural areas throughout the territory. In the general election of 1965 the party won twenty-eight out of the thirty-one seats in the National Assembly and in the 1969, 1974, 1979, 1984, and 1989 elections won similarly overwhelming majorities. In 1989, the BDP held thirty-one of the thirty-four seats. In the 1994 election, however, its margin slipped markedly. Of the votes cast in 1994, the BDP garnered but 54.3 percent, down from 64.7 percent in the 1989 election, and won twenty-seven of the forty seats, or two-thirds. *See also* Chiepe, Gaositswe; Constitution; Dambe, Amos; Elections; Haskins, James; Kgaboeselem, John; Lenyeletse Seretse; Mosinyi, Goareng; Nwako, Moutlakgola; Reokwaeng, Eyes; Steinberg, Benjamin; Thema, Benjamin; Tsheko Tsheko; Tsoebebe, Archelaus.

DETI. A Khoe-speaking group that gave its name to the **Boteti River**. Traditions relate that they migrated from northwest Zimbabwe in the distant past. They are credited with introducing the exotic Sengologa cattle breed—a skinny, hardy beast with long horns. Sengologa cattle enjoyed a big reputation in the pre-**rinderpest** era, when they were traded in huge numbers to southern Botswana and the northern Cape. After 1840 the Deti lost their sovereignty and many cattle to the BaTawana. They continue to reside on the Boteti and have a mixed economy. *See also* Cattle; Khoe; Sarwa.

DIAMONDS. In 1967 diamonds were discovered at Orapa in the Central District. At the time the new find was the world's second largest diamond pipe; its exploitation was financed by DeBeers, a subsidiary of Anglo American of South Africa, which also provided loans to government for the building of a new mining township at Orapa. Open-cast mining began in July 1971 at a rate of 2.4 million carats per annum. Output steadily increased during the 1970s, and new mines were opened at Letlhakane in 1977 and Jwaneng in 1982. In 1984 nearly 13 million carats were produced with an estimated value of almost

P900 million. Although the Botswana government owns 50 percent of the equity of DeBeers Botswana (Debswana) and has exercised full control since 1992, its diamonds are marketed through the DeBeers-controlled Central Selling Organisation (CSO) in London, under a contract that expires in 1996. As of 1991 Botswana was the only diamond producer in the world selling all of its stock to the CSO.

Diamond mining's contribution to the economy has been by far larger than any other sector. Between 1981 and 1984, diamonds accounted for 91 percent of Botswana's export growth, and as of 1991 more than 88 percent of Botswana's export earnings came from diamond sales. In 1993, Botswana produced 14.7 million carats at a value of $4.37 billion.

Botswana's dependence on diamonds has meant that in recent years, as world prices have declined and quota restrictions have increased on its share of CSO sales, government budgets have had to resort to deficit financing for the first time since independence, though in 1993 a modest surplus came as a surprise. *See also* Economic Planning; Economy; Mining.

DIFAQANE. A SeSotho term for the tumultuous period in southern Africa occurring in the early nineteenth century when drought, famine, war, migration, and cattle and slave raiding disrupted many African societies. In this dictionary, the IsiXhosa/IsiZulu term **mfecane** is used as an equivalent.

DINGAKE, MICHAEL (1928–). Once a prominent member of the **African National Congress**, Dingake has become a prominent political figure in Botswana in the 1990s. His involvement with the ANC's liberation struggle resulted in his arrest and imprisonment on Robben Island in 1965, where he remained for fifteen years. After his release he worked for many years at the University of Botswana while playing an active role in community development projects. In 1992 he became an active politician, was elected vice president of the **National Front** in 1994, and won a seat in the National Assembly.

DISTRICTS. There are ten districts in which tribal administrations and district councils perform administrative and judicial duties alongside a district commissioner, who represents the central government.

District	Headquarters	Population (1991)
Central	Serowe	412,970
Chobe	Kasane	14,126

Ghanzi	Ghanzi	23,725
Kgalagadi	Kang	31,134
Kgatleng	Mochudi	57,770
Kweneng	Molepolole	170,437
Ngamiland[1]	Maun	94,534
Northeast[2]	Francistown	43,354
Southeast[3]	Ramotswa	43,584
Southern[4]	Kanye	147,389

[1] including Chobe
[2] excluding Francistown (108,598)
[3] excluding Gaborone, Lobatse (203,104 combined)
[4] including Barolong Farms (18,400)

DITHAPO MENO (1840[?]–1918). Cousin of **Moremi II** and **Sekgoma Letsholathebe** of the BaTawana. In 1864 he led in the massacre of Kololo refugees under Leshage. He acted as regent to Moremi from 1875 to 1876 and subsequently was the guardian of Sekgoma. Dithapo was a wealthy cattle and slave owner and the headman of Meno ward. Following Moremi's death in 1890 he acted as Sekgoma's regent. After the latter's accession in 1891 Dithapo was one of the few dikgosana to support Sekgoma Letsholathebe's right to bogosi in the face of the claim of Moremi's son, **Mathiba**. In 1905, Dithapo withdrew his support for Sekgoma when the Kgosi had several witnesses lie in divorce court about adultery between Dithapo's son, Weshootsile, and Sekgoma's wife. With Dithapo in charge of the pro-Mathiba conspiracy, Sekgoma was deposed several months later, whereupon Dithapo served for the third time as acting chief. His grandson Dibolayang later served as regent.

DITHUBARUBA. From approximately 1824 to 1826 this site, located in the Ditajwane hills, was occupied by the BaKololo until they were defeated by the BaNgkwaketse under **Sebego**. Following the **Battle of Dimawe** in 1852, the Bakwena made it their capital (1853–1863), building a fortified settlement there. When the threat of war subsided, the Bakwena moved to Molepolole in the plains below. The ruins of Dithubaruba, a few minutes drive from the chief's office at Molepolole, are well-preserved and include a series of stone walls. *See also* Battle of Dithubaruba; Kwena; Lutheran Church.

DORSLAND TREK. The Dorsland ("thirst land," i.e., Kgalagadi Desert) trekkers were Transvaal Boers of the Dopper sect who entered northern Botswana in the 1870s in search of the "Promised Land." In 1875 they assembled along the Limpopo River and asked permission of **Khama III** to cross BaNgwato territory. Khama allowed small groups to pass through Gammangwato, and one of these settled temporarily in Ghanzi. In 1877, a larger group under Louwrens du Plessis also asked permission from Khama, who feared a Boer invasion and asked the British to prevent them from entering his territory, but the British refused. Khama then allowed in du Plessis and his party of 500 trekkers. They subsequently attempted to cross the Kgalagadi without guides. They lost many of their cattle and upon reaching Ngamiland plundered game for meat, leading to hostility with BaSarwa and BaTawana. By 1878, at least 200 of the trekkers had died of disease, hunger, and thirst. Some of the survivors trekked into Angola, and some settled in Molepolole. *See also* Ghanzi Farms.

DROUGHT. Drought periodically afflicts arable and pastoral farming in parts or all of Botswana. Over the past century, drought has tended to occur in cycles of several successive years, as happened in the late 1840s, late 1870s, late 1890s, early 1920s, early 1930s, late 1940s, early 1960s, and the 1980s. Drought was often associated with war and disease, which compounded the effects. The worst drought occurred during the years 1856–1860, when large herds of stock perished, and starvation was widespread. In the 1870s, drought coincided with widespread **civil wars** and led to serious famine in southern Botswana. In the 1890s drought and **rinderpest** destroyed nearly all **cattle** and brought famine to the entire territory. Colonial rule prevented people from using their traditional strategy of migrating away from drought-affected areas, but it began centralized food relief distribution, which by the 1930s was having some effect. Since the 1960s, Botswana has been able to avert starvation and limit malnutrition during drought years through international food relief donations, government-purchased grain imports, a school feeding program, and a system of food distribution and monthly stipends to destitute persons. Toward the end of the most recent drought, Botswana was providing food rations directly to more than 150,000 persons, or roughly 12 percent of the population. Most of these were children. Government has also helped rural areas after droughts with grants for ploughing and free seed. During the 1980–1987 period, particularly hard-hit by drought, the nutritional levels of BaTswana in fact increased; credit for which went to President **Quett Masire**, who received the Hunger Project Leadership Prize (1989). *See also* Water.

DUKURI (d. 1858). Mid-nineteenth-century **Naro-Khoe** leader. Dukuri built up his wealth and power by raiding cattle from the BaTawana, with whom the Naro were in constant conflict. After years of failing to capture Dukuri, Kgosi **Letsholathebe I** lured him and his men with an offer of peace, had them put to death, and made the other Naro subjects of the BaTawana. *See also* Bolata.

DUTCH REFORMED CHURCH (DRC). The DRC is largely confined to the Kgatleng district, where until the 1940s it was the only established church among the **Kgafela Kgatla**. The Nederduitse Gereformeerde Kerk, as it is known, has its headquarters in the western Cape, from which mission work north of the Vaal river began in 1857. A Swiss minister, Henry Gonin, started a mission in 1864 at Welgevallen, north of Rustenburg, and in 1866 he moved to nearby Saulspoort and established the DRC mission among the Kgafela Kgatla of **Kgamanyane**. After Kgamanyane fled the Boers, Gonin's colleague Pieter Brink (1844–1886) opened a DRC mission in Mochudi in 1877. After B. Beyer converted and baptized **Linchwe I** in 1892, the church grew rapidly until about 10 percent of the BaKgatla had become members. The mission has spawned many BaKgatla teachers and evangelists, the first being Leoke Mariri, who in 1884 started work in Sikwane and there created, together with **Thomas Phiri**, the largest DRC congregation in the Protectorate. In the 1920s the DRC began medical work and later opened hospitals in Mochudi (1932) and Sikwane (1949). The mission also established a Homecrafts Center (1945), which was rebuilt and expanded in 1969 and includes the first school for blind children in the country.

DRC congregations were also established in the 1920s among the "Coloureds" of Mogopeetsane Ward, Molepolole, and, after independence, among the urbanizing BaKgatla community in Gaborone.

In 1979, the Botswana DRC congregations broke away from the South African church and became self-governing, though South African pastors continued to play an important role in the Botswana church. As of 1994 the DRC maintained ten congregations in the country, with 4,479 members. *See also* Mochudi; Retief, Deborah; Reyneke, Johan; River Villages; Segale.

E

ECONOMIC PLANNING. Prior to World War II, economic planning consisted of balancing the budget for the forthcoming financial year. In 1946 multi-planning techniques were introduced, and in 1956 the first development plan was drawn up, based on the recommendations of the Symon Commission of 1954. The plan was essentially a shopping list of development schemes, each to be funded by separate grants from the Colonial and Welfare Fund. Symon had suggested that the livestock industry should be the focus of development, thus the bulk of the budget was earmarked for the upgrading of water supplies in order to expand the cattle herds.

The 1963–1968 Development Plan was a radical departure from previous plans. It was the brainchild of Resident Commissioner **Robert Peter Fawcus,** who introduced a central planning process. The Fawcus plan was drawn up by members of LEGCO and British "experts" in order to "equip the territory for early independence." Its priorities—administrative development, urban infrastructure, and stimulation of the private sector—have to a large extent been adopted in most development plans since. Once the date of independence was moved from 1968 up to 1966, the Fawcus plan was effectively merged with Botswana's new Ministry of Finance.

The Transitional Plan for Social and Economic Development (1966–1968) extended the Fawcus plan in style and content. One addition was the ill-fated Shashe Complex, a project which became a focus of planners' attention for the next decade. On its heels came National Development Plan 1 (1968–1973), the first comprehensive five-year plan. Its architect was **Quett Masire,** head of the Ministry of Development (in 1970 it merged with the Ministry of Finance to become the Ministry of Finance and Development Planning, headed by Masire). Though its content differed little from previous plans—60 percent of capital expenditure was to go into physical infrastructure—it was imbued with the rhetoric of social justice and announced that "the greatest challenge" was rural development. NDP 2, for 1970–1975, put forward a "trickle-down" strategy in which income from the export of diamonds, copper, and beef were to be invested in "education and training, promoting agriculture and labor-intensive manufacturing, and improving services in the rural areas." The bulk of capital expenditure was allocated to infrastructural projects which made only an indirect contribution to rural development.

The Accelerated Rural Development Programme and the Tribal Grazing Lands Policy, both introduced in the mid-1970s, originated outside the mainstream of the planning process, and they received little support in terms of development finance. With NDP 4 (1976–1981), the Ministry of Finance and Development Planning introduced a rhetorical theme to rival rural development: employment generation. A package of fiscal incentives for employers and new business investment, known as the Financial Assistance Policy (FAP) was the result. NDP 5 for 1979–1985 accepted that the revenues from mining development had reached a plateau and looked to private enterprise to generate growth and employment opportunities.

The current NDP 7 (1991–1997) reflects the concerns of Assistant Minister **Festus Mogae** about the limits of using diamond revenues and public sector expansion as engines of growth. Its stated goal is to build on past plans "but greater emphasis has been given to establishing a sustainable development path and improving the participation of BaTswana in both the process and benefits of development . . . Creating a more conducive environment for private sector activities is an essential task of Government. Stable democratic institutions, prudent fiscal policy and sound monetary management are essential ingredients for promoting private sector development." In fact, much of NDP 7 is still a shopping list with a good deal of "pork." NDP 7 mid-term review provides the Ministry of Finance and Development with an opportunity to restrain ranking government officials who favor continued large expenditures. In the ministry's words, "The diamond boom has lasted so long that many Batswana have come to take it for granted. That boom appears to be ending. It is likely that the time will soon come when Government can no longer continue to expand the network of government services at the rapid pace of the last fifteen years. As was stated in NDP 7, the current Plan period is one of transition between a period of exceptional economic growth and one of slow economic growth."

National Development Plans

NDP 1	1968–1973
NDP 2	1970–1975
NDP 3	1973–1978
NDP 4	1976–1981
NDP 5	1979–1987

NDP 6   1986–1991
NDP 7   1991–1997

See also Diamonds; Economy.

ECONOMY. *Pre-colonial.* Archaeological evidence points to the existence of centralized communities based on cattle-keeping as early as 500 A.D. The BaTswana states which expanded into the Kgalagadi from the southeast during the eighteenth and early nineteenth centuries were cattle-based economies using subjugated BaKgalagadi and BaSarwa inhabitants as herders and servants. In the nineteenth century, the BaNgwaketse, BaKwena, BaNgwato, and BaTawana strengthened themselves by participating in the Cape-based trade in hunting goods (mainly ivory, skins, and feathers). This trade gave BaTswana access to horses, wagons, and guns, which increased the ability of their leaders to control large areas, increase their cattle holdings, and subordinate additional groups of servile "malata."

Colonial. With colonial rule, cash-earnings from migrant labor assumed importance. Following the collapse of the hunting trade in the 1880s, BaTswana suffered additional reverses to their traditional sources of wealth. In 1897 the Mafikeng-Bulawayo railway displaced the wagon trade upon which the growth of BaTswana states had been built, and the 1896–1897 **rinderpest** epizootic killed 90 percent or more of the cattle in the Protectorate. In 1899 the hut tax was imposed. For many BaTswana, signing mining labor contracts provided the means of paying it. In the 1920s, by which time cattle herds had recovered, South Africa imposed weight restrictions and export embargoes that prevented even large Protectorate cattle-owners from marketing their stock legally.

Until the Great Depression, the Protectorate government confined itself to maintaining law and order, extracting revenues from adult males through hut and other forms of tax, and allowing revenues to determine the level of expenditures, the bulk of which went to the salaries of officials and their upkeep. The doctrine of the balanced budget was challenged after Dominions' secretary Leopold Amery toured the Protectorate in 1927, and **Charles Rey** was appointed resident commissioner in 1930. The Pim Report of 1933 argued that the protectorate should be developed somewhat and then transferred together with perhaps Rhodesia to South Africa as English-controlled territory so as to counter rising Afrikaner power in the Union. Rey thus requested grants-in-aid to help in building dams, sinking boreholes, and erecting a small abattoir, along with other projects in the protectorate. The Depression rendered the Pim report irrelevant and deafened London to Rey's requests. The onset of World War II further postponed development efforts.

After the war, grants-in-aid resumed only in 1954, in spite of the Protectorate's major contribution to the war effort. The building of a new **abattoir** at Lobatse in that year marks the beginning of a long-term commitment to the economy's development. From 1954 development expenditures steadily increased, from £123,000 to £550,000 in 1956–1957 to £1,800,000 in 1964–1965. The bulk of British aid was spent on projects, notably the building of an internal administrative headquarters and capital at Gaborone, which merely up-graded the machinery of government to a minimal level in time for independence. Nevertheless, Botswana achieved its independence as one of the five poorest nations in the world, with a per capita income of U.S. $35. Wage employment within the country was virtually non-existent. On the eve of independence only 73,000 out of a total population of 580,000 held formal employment, and most were working in South Africa, Rhodesia, and South West Africa.

Post-colonial. As a result of the discovery of several major diamond deposits in the late 1960s, Botswana's economy has grown at remarkable rates, particularly since the early 1970s. Following the opening of Orapa mine in 1971, per capita Gross National Product rose to $910 in 1984 and to $2,790 in 1991, exceeding that of South Africa and placing Botswana in the category of "upper-middle income" economies (though some argue that in terms of "real" per capita GNP, factoring in cost of living and consumer purchasing power, Botswana is less well-off than South Africa). Over those two decades, Botswana's GNP expanded at a rate faster than that of any other country in the world, reaching an annual average rate of 14.5% in the 1970s and 9.8% in the 1980s, a decade beset by drought. These rates of increase have since declined, largely due to a weak diamond market, but as recently as 1993 the GNP increase stood at 5.8%. Much of the GNP increase came from mining revenues, though manufacturing, construction, transport, banking and insurance, and agriculture all posted gains during this period. As of 1992, total GNP was P7,810 million ($ 3.1 billion), from mining (36.8%), government (19.9%), trade, hotels, and restaurants (15.3%), manufacturing (5.7%), agriculture (5.2%), banks and insurance (5.2%), construction (5%), and misc. (6.9%).

Handsome export earnings, mainly from the sale of uncut diamonds, have enabled Botswana to import foodstuffs and a wide array of consumer goods and invest heavily in its infrastructure while maintaining a favorable balance of trade, though this formula for success remains dependent on the diamond market. In 1992, for example, Botswana purchased $1.588 billion in imported goods, led by machinery and electrical equipment (18.8%), food, beverages, and tobacco (18.7%), vehicles and equipment (10%), and chemicals and rubber products (9.4%). The same year, when diamond prices remained relatively depressed, export revenues reached only $1.35 billion (of which 86.1% came from diamonds and copper-nickel). Still, for the fiscal year 1992–93, the Botswana government incurred a relatively small deficit based on its budgeted development and recurrent expenditures at $1.69 billion, a shortfall of $40 million. As of 1994 Botswana's foreign exchange reserves stood at $4.097 billion (from which it derives income through investments abroad) and its national debt at $400 million.

With overall growth has come much greater formal employment within the country, increasingly from the private sector. In contrast to many other African countries, which have been dominated by the public sector, as of 1993 Botswana's private sector accounted for 62% of formal employment, followed by 26% by the central government, and 6% each by local governments and parastatals. Whereas close to 70,000 BaTswana worked as migrant mine workers before independence, only 12,755 were so employed in South Africa at the end of 1993. Underemployment within Botswana remains a problem, however, with rates hovering around 14% since the late 1980s and productivity levels of employed workers hindered by lack of skills and the low status associated with wage employment.

The high volume of import/export trade has generated much commercial activity and employment. Since the early 1980s employment in commerce has led all other single categories, except government employment. As of 1992, 40,000 or 30% of total private sector employment was in commerce. Relatively little of the surplus generated from trade is invested in the country. At the end of 1993 the leading commercial banks, Barclays Bank of Botswana, Standard Chartered Bank Botswana, and several lesser banks, had combined deposits of $809 million and credits of $615 million.

Botswana's private investment opportunities remain largely limited to property, though since June 1989 a thriving shares market has emerged. In 1991 the Botswana Stock Market (BSM) listed nine companies with a total value of new and rights issues of $15.6 million; as of late 1993, twelve companies were listed with total capitalization of $267 million, rising to $326 million in 1994. In Pula terms, the market has performed extremely well (on average 24% per share in 1991, including dividends of 6.3%), though less so in U.S. dollar terms.

Since the mid-1980s inflation has fluctuated between 10% and 17.7%, reflecting continued high levels of imported goods; low individual savings rates; state-subsidized credits for private housing and automobiles; a wide array of government entitlements, including free education from primary through university (subject after junior secondary to entrance qualifications); health; water; as well as government outlays for dealing with concurrent crises in the region, namely drought, disinvestment and boycotts relative to pre-democratic South Africa and South West Africa, and poaching and border violations. *See also* Agriculture; Air Transportation; Bolata; Cattle; Colonial Development Corporation; Copper; Currency; Customs Union; Diamonds; Economic Planning; Education; Employment; Energy; External Economic Relations; External Relations; Health; Land Tenure; Manufacturing; Migrant Labor; Mining; Railways; Roads; Tourism; Trade Unions; Water.

EDUCATION. In the colonial period, responsibility for developing education was for the most part left to the BaTswana merafe and missionaries. Real achievements were made at the primary level, but parents remained dependent on secondary schools in South Africa and Rhodesia. At independence, Botswana had only one government secondary school (Gaborone Secondary School, built in 1965) and was a decade away from building its own university college.

The first school in Botswana was built at Kolobeng in 1847 by the BaKwena and **David Livingstone** of the **London Missionary Society**. Cooperation between merafe and missionaries set the tone during the nineteenth century, but in 1902 dissatisfaction with mission education led BaTswana into attempts at setting up secular "national schools" and introducing English and other practical subjects into the curriculum. In a number of Tswana capitals, education levies were imposed by diKgosi, and school committees were formed to administer the funds. Some missions adapted to and assisted with these changes, whereas the government, apart from recognizing the school committees, remained indifferent even though the 1908 Sargent

Report recommended it play a much greater role. In 1919 the government regularized grants to mission and secular schools through a Native Fund, fed by an education levy on adult males, but the grants were inadequate for educational development. The only successful national school prior to the 1930s was the **Bakgatla National School**, built on a self-help basis in 1923. In 1937 reformed Tribal Treasuries initiated a second phase of primary school construction.

Until 1944, when the Roman Catholic mission built St. Joseph's College at Khale, students able to attend secondary school did so outside the territory at such places as Lovedale in the eastern Cape, **Tiger Kloof** in the northern Cape, Adams College in Natal, and St. Matthews in the Transvaal. The Tati Training Institution, a primary-cum-secondary school built by **K.T. Motsete** in 1932 at Tsesebe, was closed down in 1941. Government indifference to secondary schooling persisted after World War II, but missions, BaTswana, and outside donors began to commit the necessary resources. Before independence seven non-government secondary schools were built: St. Joseph's (1944), Moeng (1949), Seepapitso II (1950), Mochudi (1951), Kgari Sechele (1956), Moeding (1962), and Swaneng Hill (1963).

Since independence, universal primary education has been the goal of every development plan, and since 1985 the percentage of school-age children attending schools has remained around eighty-five. Since 1987, the government guaranteed universal access to nine years of schooling (a tenth year may be added soon), and in January 1988 school and uniform fees for all primary and secondary school students were abolished.

As of 1992, the government supported 301,482 primary students and 75,873 secondary students. Botswana operates 167 secondary schools, 4 teacher training colleges for training primary school teachers, 31 vocational and technical institutions, 2 colleges of education, and a national university, with the main campus in Gaborone and branches at Maun, Selebi Phikwe, Francistown, and a College of Agriculture at Sebele, near Gaborone. In terms of the national expenditures for educational development budgeted in the current NDP 7 (*see* Economic Planning), 39.2% is earmarked for secondary education, university/colleges and primary schools each receiving approximately 18%, 17.1% for vocational training, and 5% for primary teachers (known as "Teacher Training").

Tertiary education in Botswana began in 1964 with the establishment of the University of Basutoland, Bechuanaland

and Swaziland, subsequently University of Botswana, Lesotho and Swaziland (UBLS), with its campus at Roma. Following the breakup of UBLS in late 1975, Botswana and Swaziland established the University of Botswana and Swaziland (UBS) and built university colleges in Gaborone and Kwaluseni. In 1983, UBS was dissolved, and the University of Botswana (UB) came into being (as did the University of Swaziland). UB consists of the seven faculties of Agriculture, Accounting and Management Studies, Education, Humanities, Law, Science, and Social Sciences. UB offers certificates, diplomas, and undergraduate and graduate degrees to a student body of 3,976 (1992). Colleges of Education at Molepolole and Tonota provide post-secondary diplomas in education for teachers in Botswana's junior secondary schools. Teacher shortages remain acute. As of 1992, 45% of the teachers in secondary schools and 31% in the community junior secondary schools were expatriates.

Admission into all senior secondary and tertiary institutions is through competitive examination and earns BaTswana students a full government bursary (though in recent years the bursary has not been guaranteed), but the percentages of students who can be accommodated within the government school system at this competitive level remains very low. In 1991, for example, approximately 25% of Botswana's students were admitted into senior secondary school, while the number of university students represented 4.3% of the total number of students in senior secondary schools. In 1992, university students represented 1% of students in all schools (i.e., primary, secondary, technical/vocational, and teacher training colleges). Adding an additional year to non-competitive junior secondary and increasing the teaching of vocational and other employable skills within the existing curriculum is under consideration, because a substantial majority of "school-leavers" (i.e., failed examinees) have been entering the ranks of the unemployed.

The Government has established the Department of Non-Formal Education to increase literacy and extend education to adult learners throughout the country, and it has established a range of training institutions for primary school teachers, technicians, nurses, mechanics, civil servants, and white collar employees in the private sector.

Botswana provides perhaps greater opportunities for education proportionate to its citizenry than any other country in Africa and many other countries in the world. In 1990, according to the United Nations, Botswana's literacy stood at 73.8%.

ELECTIONS. Since 1965, Botswana has held seven successive multi-party, one-person/one-vote elections. In all cases most neutral observers have judged the balloting to have been free and fair. Technical irregularities have occasioned revoting in single constituencies in 1984 and 1989. Opposition parties have complained that the minimum voting age of twenty-one years is too high and that no provisions have been made for voters absent from the country. They have advocated, too, that an independent election commission replace the Office of the President as the responsible administrator.

Though the **Democratic Party (BDP)** has won all the national elections with substantial majorities, the trend in recent years has been toward a two-party contest between the BDP and the **National Front (BNF)**, with the smaller **People's Party (BPP)** and **Independence Party (BIP)** retaining strong support in the Northeast and Northwest districts, respectively.

National election results since 1965, by percentage of votes won and by seats won to the National Assembly:

Year	BDP	BPP	BIP	BNF
1965	80.4 (28)	14.2 (3)	4.6 (0)	—
1969	68.3 (24)	12.1 (3)	6.0 (1)	13.5 (3)
1974	76.6 (27)	6.6 (2)	4.8 (1)	11.5 (2)
1979	75.2 (29)	7.4 (1)	4.3 (0)	12.9 (2)
1984	67.9 (28)	6.6 (1)	3.0 (0)	20.5 (5)
1989	64.7 (31)	4.3 (0)	2.4 (0)	26.9 (3)
1994	54.3 (27)	4.0 (0)	3.0 (0)	37.7 (13)

ELLENBERGER, JULES (1871–1973). Colonial official, 1890–1927. Born in a Lesotho cave, son of Alsatian missionary and historian Rev. D.F. Ellenberger of the Paris Missionary Society mission in Lesotho, Jules proved invaluable to the Protectorate administration because of his deep knowledge of SeTswana and SeSotho language and culture. Well known to BaTswana (who dubbed him "Ramaeba," literally father of doves), he was an early collector of oral history. From 1902 to 1916 he was assistant commissioner of the Southern Protectorate, thereafter rising to become government secretary (1916–1923) and resident commissioner (1923–1927). His son Vivien Frederick Ellenberger also served in the Protectorate civil service.

EMPLOYMENT. Formal sector wage employment within Botswana has grown at a rate of 10% from independence until 1985 and since 1985 until 1992 at 14% to reach a total of 238,205 employees, at an average monthly wage of $264 ($3,168 per annum). This remarkable rate of growth derives in part from a very low base—there were few formal sector jobs within the territory during the colonial era. Government remains Botswana's leading employer, though in percentage terms its proportion of the total workforce is declining. In 1992, 27.6% of all wage earners were government employees, followed by employees in commerce (17.8%), construction (13.6%), manufacturing (9.8%), finance and business (8%), local government (6.9%), transport (4.4%), mining (3.7%), community and personal services (3.7%), and agriculture (2.5%). As of 1993 Botswana's private sector accounted for 62% of formal employment, followed by the central government (26%), and by local governments and parastatals (6% each). Whereas close to 70,000 BaTswana worked as migrant mine workers before independence, only 12,755 were so employed in South Africa at the end of 1993. In 1991, the unemployment rate stood at 13.7%, with Gaborone having the lowest (10.6%) among Botswana's urban centers, and Kgalagadi North having the highest (24.3%) among Botswana's rural districts. In contrast to many other African countries, Botswana's unemployment rates are higher on average in urban districts (15%) than in rural districts (12.1%).

In many respects, these official figures conceal significant underemployment if not unemployment, especially in rural areas. Of the so-listed ''economically active population,'' only 54% had formal sector jobs in 1991. *See also* Economy; Migrant Labor; Trade Unions.

ENERGY. For the vast majority of the population the most important source of energy has been and still is firewood, though as in other parts of Africa it is a resource that is rapidly being depleted. Urban dwellers depend increasingly on kerosene, electricity, containerized gas, and coal. Botswana's resources in coal are stunning—10% of the world's recoverable deposits—and though its best quality is only medium calorific bituminous, coal has made possible the development of a $195 million electric generation plant at Morupule which since 1990 has met the nation's needs, though for the time being at a cost well above that of South Africa, its previous source. The electrification of rural towns and centers has been a government priority since the early 1980s and with water accounted for an estimated 8.6% of the total government development expenditures. *See also* Economy.

ENGLAND, SIR RUSSELL (1890 [?]–1970). Leading white politician, Lobatse rancher, and businessman, of probable Polish origins. Russell served as chair of the Joint Advisory Council and European Advisory Council during the 1950s and a member of LEGCO, including its Executive Council, 1961–1964. England played a significant role in reconciling white and African interests during the transition to independence. He was knighted in 1965. A slightly shadowy figure, he was murdered in 1970 in highly unusual circumstances. *See also* Councils.

EXTERNAL ECONOMIC RELATIONS. In 1891 the Bechuanaland Protectorate joined the Cape Colony/Orange Free State/Transvaal Customs Union, which was extended to include Southern Rhodesia and Swaziland in 1903–1904. In 1910 renegotiations resulted in the South African Customs Union (SACU). The Protectorate's customs revenue was averaged out from the three previous (depressed) years and fixed at .27622% of the annual customs revenue. In 1966 Britain raised Botswana's percentage to .30971%, at the expense of Basutoland's share. In 1969 a new agreement was negotiated on the basis of recorded annual trade, rather than fixed percentages. As a result, customs and excise revenue increased from 1.4 million Rands in 1969–1970 to R12.5 million in 1972–1973, equal to 45% of total domestic revenues. The importance of SACU revenues has declined proportionately as Botswana's diamond-driven economy has boomed, but as of 1992, SACU receipts still constituted 25% of Botswana's total domestic revenues.

In the late 1970s, as the regional crisis intensified and as sanctions against South Africa became more likely, Botswana reviewed its membership in SACU and took an active role in the founding of the **Southern African Development Coordination Conference (SADDC)**, which was designed to build up multilateral economic relations among the non-apartheid states of Southern Africa and to reduce their economic dependence on South Africa. Nevertheless from then until South African independence, and since, Botswana has remained in the Customs Union because of the considerable benefits it derives as an importer within the region. As of 1992 Botswana received 85% of its imports from SACU countries, whereas 85.1% of the value of its total product was exported to Europe. *See also* Customs Union; Economy; External Relations.

EXTERNAL RELATIONS. Since its independence and until 1994 when **South Africa** held its first non-racial democratic elections,

Botswana has been committed mainly to assisting in the spread of democracy in Southern Africa in opposition to white regimes and reducing where possible its economic dependence on South Africa. In 1966, Botswana was surrounded almost entirely by South Africa, Namibia, and Rhodesia, each of which was controlled by its white minority. Botswana established close ties with **Zambia**, entered the Organisation of African Unity (OAU), and established embassies in Lusaka, London, and Washington.

From the beginning, and especially after 1969, Botswana consistently denounced apartheid and colonial rule in Southern Africa and opened its borders to political refugees (but prohibited the use of its territory for attacks on its neighbors). In 1969 Botswana demurred from signing the OAU Lusaka manifesto enjoining sanctions against Rhodesia and South Africa as economically suicidal for itself, and for the same reason it opposed sanctions against South Africa until the early 1980s, whereupon it began to encourage sanctions while exempting itself.

In 1974 Botswana, Tanzania, Mozambique, Angola, and Zambia formed the "Front Line States" (FLS) to assist the struggle for the liberation of **Zimbabwe**. Botswana accommodated as many as 17,000 Zimbabwean refugees prior to 1980. Though unwilling to allow its country to be used by them as a springboard for the guerrilla war, Botswana helped to unite the Zimbabwe African Peoples Union and Zimbabwe African National Union parties under the Patriotic Front and prevented Rhodesia from receiving military supplies by rail through Botswana.

Similarly, its relations with apartheid South Africa remained restricted to matters arising from its membership in the customs union and to incidents arising from border infractions. Botswana refused to recognize any of the so-called independent homelands (and frustrated repeated attempts by the now defunct Bophuthatswana on Botswana's southern border to achieve diplomatic recognition from Gaborone), to enter a South African constellation of states, or to sign an Nkomati-type nonaggression pact with South Africa.

After Zimbabwe joined in 1980, the FLS became the leading coordinator of African political support for the liberation of Namibia and South Africa, as well as for the defense of its own members threatened by South African-backed armed resistance groups. Botswana played a leading role in developing an economic strategy among independent states to supplement the political goals of FLS. In 1979 the **South African Development**

Coordinating Conference (SADCC) brought together the FLS with Lesotho, Malawi, and Swaziland for the purpose of reducing dependence on South Africa in manufacturing, communications, rails and roads, port facilities, and markets. Botswana served as chair of the annual SADCC conference, and in 1982 SADCC headquarters were located in Gaborone.

Botswana has, nevertheless, at times been regarded with suspicion by its neighbors, whether independent or not. During the 1980s Botswana's open door policy for political refugees aroused hostility from South Africa, which launched raids into Botswana, including two separate strikes into suburbs of the capital. South Africa claimed in its defense that Botswana knowingly harbored ANC activists, which Botswana denied. During the 1980s, when Botswana supported a pro-sanctions stand against South Africa, Zimbabwe accused it of assisting South Africa in sanctions-busting by putting Botswana labels on South African textiles and marketing them in Zimbabwe.

Following South Africa's withdrawal of troops from Angola, its grant of independence to Namibia, the removal of South African support for Renamo resistance in Mozambique, and its own democratization, Botswana has normalized its relations with all countries in the region. Botswana maintains high commission offices in Windhoek and Pretoria, while the diplomatic representatives of South Africa and Namibia sit in Gaborone. In anticipation of Namibian control of Walvis Bay, which was accomplished in 1994, Botswana developed all-weather road links to the Namibian border near Gobabis.

Blessed with internal economic prosperity and political stability, Botswana has in the recent prevailing calm in the region enlarged its presence in Africa and on the world scene. Botswana has contributed to peace-keeping efforts in Somalia and Rwanda, where its troops were highly praised, worked to moderate disputes in Lesotho and Mozambique, and expanded its diplomatic presence in Africa, Europe, and Asia. On 1 January 1995 Botswana became for the first time a member of the United Nations Security Council, for a two-year term, and in January 1996, its ambassador, Joseph Legwaila, became Security Council chairman. *See also* Caprivi Strip; Customs Union; External Economic Relations; Refugees.

F

FAMILY. Isaac Schapera's pioneering anthropological studies of family life made during the 1930s provided the first evidence of the "breakdown" of the nuclear family, caused mainly by **migrant labor**. Since then, considerable damage has also been caused by war, urbanization, illegitimacy, disease, and sexual discrimination, although the desire for children and social obligations toward dependents within the context of the extended family remains strong in Botswana. Reliable statistics are unavailable, but it is estimated that anywhere from 30% to 50% of all households in Botswana are headed by women. According to the 1991 census, of males above the age of 12 only 113,422 (28.5%) have ever married, and only 153,950 (33.8%) females in the same age group. However, 457,165 females were mothers.

The high incidence of failure of fathers either to marry or support the mothers of their children is a major national problem. Though females predominate among primary school students, their presence in secondary school and university tapers off, often due to pregnancy. In 1991 nearly 11,000 children were born to girls 14 years or under, and 23,465 to mothers between the ages of 15 and 19. The result is a disproportionate number of single, often young, mothers trying to compete in the unskilled labor market, where opportunities are fewer than for men. Unsupported mothers with inadequate personal incomes are liable to depend on parents, in-laws, and friends, attempt new liaisons, and/or resort to prostitution. The government provides no direct support to broken or single parent families as such, although all children are entitled to free health care and education, including free meals during school term. Rates of juvenile crime and vagrancy in the urban areas, however, indicate that the number of broken families is on the increase. *See also* Census; Women.

FAWCUS, ROBERT PETER (1915–). As government secretary (1954–1959) and resident commissioner (1959–1965), Fawcus presided over the process of decolonization in Bechuanaland. He encouraged the growth of national politics and in 1963 presented the constitutional reforms which led to Botswana's independence three years later. Fawcus also took advantage of increased colonial expenditure in the Protectorate after 1954 to implement wide-ranging programs for economic development which in turn laid the infrastructural groundwork for independence. *See also* Constitution; Councils; Economy; Gaborone (city of).

FEDERAL PARTY. The Bechuanaland Protectorate Federal Party (sometimes called the Liberal Party) was founded in

April 1959 by **Leetile Raditladi**. Raditladi and his followers were concerned about the upcoming negotiations to determine the nature of LEGCO and also about **Tshekedi Khama**, then reemerging as the dominant figure in BaNgwato politics. Raditladi's Federal Party feared that LEGCO would be dominated by Europeans and a pro-Tshekedi faction. The Federal Party called for liberal democratic reforms at both the local and national level. Federalism was put forward as a means of achieving national unity among the merafe. Its members included several future national party founders, including **P.G. Matante, A.M. Tsoebebe,** and **K.T. Motsete**. The party established branches in the protectorate as well as among migrant workers in South Africa. In 1960 it was eclipsed by the Bechuanaland **People's Party (BPP)** and was finally dissolved in 1962, when its leading members joined the BPP. *See also* Councils.

FLEMING, GEORGE (1800 [?]–1880[?]). African-American who became **David Livingstone**'s partner in exploring northern Botswana and central Africa. A former, probably escaped, slave, Fleming assumed a "West Indian" identity while living in Cape Town. In 1849 he joined Livingstone, Oswell, Murray, and Wilson in their journey to "discover" Lake Ngami, Fleming serving as the expedition's cook. In 1851 he joined Livingstone and Oswell on their visit to the BaKololo. With financial backing from Howson Rutherford, a prosperous Cape Town merchant who also served as a South African director of the **London Missionary Society**, Fleming established himself as a trader in the interior. In January 1853 he and Livingstone set out from **Dithubaruba** for the BaKololo. After exploring the Zambezi together they split up in November 1853. In the following months, Fleming may have been the first outsider to visit Mosiwatunya (what David Livingstone later renamed Victoria Falls), before returning to Grahamstown with a profitable load of ivory and other goods. In June 1856 he was hired by the LMS to sail with supplies to Quelimane, Mozambique, from where he was to "proceed in quest of" Livingstone. Fleming met the missionary-doctor, however, on arrival at the port. At this point, Fleming's story disappears into mystery. In the 1870s he is said to have been an impoverished old man living at the Cape.

While a genuine bond of friendship appears to have existed between him and Livingstone, the missionary's obsession with gaining sole credit for his own African "discoveries" played its own part in obscuring the contributions of this uncelebrated black man. *See also* Traders.

FLOGGING INCIDENT. In 1933 **Tshekedi Khama** ordered the flogging of Phinehas MacIntosh, a white youth, for assaulting a MoNgwato man jealous of MacIntosh's affair with a Mo-Ngwato woman. MacIntosh, a local lad, had been warned on previous occasions for breaking customary law. Resident Commissioner **Charles Rey** claimed that Tshekedi had no jurisdiction over Europeans (though MacIntosh accepted the punishment and made no complaint) and used the incident as a pretext for dethroning Tshekedi, who had angered Rey by foiling his administrative reforms. In a show of power, Rey called in from the Cape a crew of British sailors under Admiral Evans and conducted a kangaroo court in Serowe. The court found Tshekedi guilty and banished him to Francistown. Within weeks, Rey and Evans reinstated Tshekedi due to overwhelming popular support he received from British and South Africans abroad, though Rey and Evans asserted they had so acted because Tshekedi had apologized. *See also* Administration.

FOREIGN JURISDICTION ACT, 1890. The legal source of British jurisdiction in the Bechuanaland Protectorate. All colonial orders-in-council and proclamations were enacted through its authority. The Act authorized jurisdiction over British subjects in foreign territories and over foreign persons either by agreement with their governments or simply by "usage, sufferance, or other lawful means." Thus, although most diKgosi, apart from **Khama III**, did not agree to allow the British jurisdiction over their subjects, a liberal interpretation of the Act made such agreement unnecessary. Following the Foreign Jurisdiction Act of 1890 (which was in fact the latest version of an act which had first been passed in 1843 and which was to be amended again in 1913), the Order-in-Council of 1891 authorized the high commissioner to provide "for the administration of justice, the raising of revenue, and generally for the order and good government of all persons" in the Protectorate. In effect, this clause was used by later colonial administrators to claim unlimited power over BaTswana. *See also* Bramestone Memorandum; Orders-in-Council; Proclamation; Protectorate.

FOREIGN RELATIONS. *See* External Relations.

FRANCISTOWN. Francistown (1991 population: 65,244) has existed as a place of human settlement for centuries. Archaeological studies confirm that gold was mined in the region by the BaKalanga's ancestors as early as 1,100 A.D. The town's modern history began in 1880, when the AmaNdebele Inkosi Lobengula ceded mining rights in the area to a group of white speculators. Ownership of these rights eventually devolved to the Tati Company (its legal title varied slightly over the years). During the colonial era this company retained control over much of the Northeast District as a private concession. It owned most of Francistown's municipal land, ran its utilities, planned urban expansion, and taxed local blacks.

Named after one of the Company's directors, Daniel Francis, the settlement was established in 1897 to serve as a depot for miners, being the place where the road from the old Monarch Mine crossed the recently-constructed Mafikeng-Bulawayo railway. In August 1897 the Tati Company auctioned off 300 freehold stands for the then considerable sum of about £400 each. These stands were laid out on a square grid, east of the railway line, that was divided by eight "avenues" running east and west and eight "streets" running north and south. Each of these roads was wide enough to allow an ox wagon to turn around. In the middle of the town was a large "Market Square." Commercial establishments were originally lined up along 1st Street.

Until independence Francistown remained a Rhodesian-style settlement characterized by strict racial segregation. The main town was reserved as a white residential area, while Satellite Township was established for Coloureds. Blacks were initially settled in the area west of the railway and east of the Tati River. In 1957, however, the black township was removed to Tatitown on the west bank of the river in order to make way for the creation of the industrial area adjacent to the railway. Two years earlier the Company had been bought by Johannesburg speculators who were determined to increase profits by selling more land to white farmers, while raising rents and fees on blacks.

By the late 1950s resentment against the color bar and the squalid living conditions of the townships gave birth to nationalist politics, civil rights activism, and revived trade unionism. From 1961, these sentiments found a home in the **People's Party (BPP)**. Under the threat of consumer boycotts most of the town's businesses were forced to desegregate, while the colonial regime was belatedly made aware of the combustible nature of the long-suffering townships. The political temperature was further raised by an influx of refugees from other areas of white oppression, and the nefarious activities of Rhodesian and South African agents.

After independence, blatant racism continued to pervade much of Francistown's economic and social life, and in 1970 the Government took measures to combat it. In an address that drew strong non-partisan support, then Vice President **Quett Masire** warned leading members of the white community of tougher measures unless they began to honor the country's non-racial principles. The subsequent easing of racial tensions provided a stimulus to Francistown's growth. By the mid-1980s, new light industries, in such areas as textiles, chemicals, and leather goods, were expanding at annual rates in excess of 75 percent. The commercial retail sector, which catered to newly-independent Zimbabwe, also expanded rapidly. Since this boom period, however, Francistown has experienced economic stagnation. *See also* Race Relations; Railways; Tati Concession; Towns.

G

GABORONE (1820[?]–1932). Kgosi of the BaTlokwa, 1880–1932. He led his people from Tshwene-Tshwene in the Transvaal to the protectorate in 1887, settled at Moshwaneng on the Ngotwane River, and acknowledged the overlordship of the BaKwena. In 1905 the Moshwaneng area, known as Tlokweng to the BaTlokwa and as Gaberones to the British, was transferred to the **British South Africa Company (BSACO)** and arrangements were made to move Gaborone and his people into the BaKwena Reserve. The BSACO agreed to postpone the move, however, until the Kgosi, then advanced in age, had died. Gaborone waited another quarter of a century before deciding to comply with BSACO expectations and expire, at the age of 112, in 1932. The same year, the British acquired the land from the company and turned it into the BaTlokwa Reserve. *See also* Gaborone (City); Tlokwa.

GABORONE (CITY). Gaborone was built from 1964 to 1965 as Botswana's capital and chartered as Botswana's first city in 1986. Unlike other African countries under colonial rule, Botswana was administered from outside its own boundaries and at independence had the advantage of creating its own administrative headquarters. From 1895 to 1965, the Bechuanaland Protectorate was administered from the Imperial Reserve at Mafikeng, Northern Cape, South Africa. The name Gaborone is associated with the colonial administrative site of Fort "Gaberones," which was founded in 1887 adjacent to the BaTlokwa village of Kgosi **Gaborone**. From 1891 the fort became the administrative headquarters of the Assistant Resident Commissioner for the Southern Protectorate, and in 1897 a railway station was built nearby. The **Jameson Raid** was allegedly planned in a small hotel in "Gaberones" camp—possibly the building which belongs to the National Museum and stands adjacent to the Gaborone Club in the present "Village" section of the city. In one of the first actions of LEGCO in 1961, Gaborone was chosen as the new capital site because it possessed plentiful Government land between the camp and station as well as an adequate dam site. Construction began in 1964.

Gaborone has since become one of the fastest-growing cities in Africa. In the 1970s, its growth rate was approximately 25 percent annually, which has tapered to 10 percent in recent years. In 1991, one out of every ten people in the country lived in Gaborone, the population of which stood at 133,463. An additional 26,747 people reside in the suburbs of Tlokweng (12,501) and Mogoditshane (14,246).

Gaborone is the nation's administrative and commercial center, with all government ministries headquartered in the government sector to the north of the town's central mall. The head offices of most commercial, construction, small manufacturing, transportation, and banking firms are found here, as is the national university, the national stadium, Seretse Khama International Airport, the National **Archives**, and the headquarters of the government-owned diamond company Debswana.

GAGOANGWE (1845[?]–1924). The "one-eyed Queen." Daughter of **Sechele I** of the BaKwena and successively wife to the Kgosi of the **Mmanaana Kgatla** and the Kgosi of the BaNgwaketse. As a child she once put out the eye of a servant. Her father used this occasion to invoke the biblical judgment of "an eye for an eye, a tooth for a tooth" by allowing the injured servant to blind his own daughter, establishing thereby as well a degree of legal equality among his subjects. In 1875 she deserted her husband Kgosi Pilane of the Mmanaana Kgatla and eloped with **Bathoen I**, heir to the BaNgwaketse throne. The event strengthened the BaNgwaketse-BaKwena alliance at a time when control of their territories was being challenged by refugee groups from the Transvaal, in particular the BaLete and **Kgafela Kgatla**. Gagoangwe was an enthusiastic Christian and influenced the pro-LMS policy of her husband. Following the assassination of her son **Seepapitso II** in 1916, she became the dominant political force among the BaNgwaketse, eventually seizing control of the regency in 1923 on behalf of her grandson **Bathoen II**. *See also* Civil Wars; Ntebogang Ratshosa; Regency; Tshosa Sebego.

GAGOMAKWE K. SECHELE (1910–). Widow of Kgari **Sechele II**. Since the 1920s she has played an important role, and as of 1994 was still active, in community affairs. During and after the reign of her husband she has had significant political influence behind the scenes. She attended **Tiger Kloof** in the 1930s. Gagomakwe helped found the Scouting movement in Bechuanaland and is a leading farmer in the Kweneng.

GAME PARKS. *See* Parks/Game Reserves.

GARVEY, MARCUS. *See* Universal Negro Improvement Association.

GASEITSIWE (1829[?]–1889). Kgosi of the BaNgwaketse during the crucial period of colonial takeover. Installed perhaps as early as 1846 but effectively Kgosi only after the **BaTswana-Boer War of 1852–1853**, Gaseitsiwe reigned until 1889. He became Kgosi after a period of turmoil that began with the death of his grandfather **Makaba II**, and within a decade he succeeded in reuniting the morafe. During the 1860s the BaNgwaketse gained access to the trans-Kgalagadi trade and expanded westward. During the 1870s Gaseitsiwe and **Sechele I** established the present boundary between BaNgwaketse and Kweneng and became close allies. The alliance failed to make these two groups dominant powers, and in 1881 the BaLete under Ikaneng handed a major defeat to the BaNgwaketse regiments attacking Ramoutswa. The South African Republic (SAR) then demanded reparation from the BaNgwaketse, who had raided BaLete cattle in the Transvaal. The SAR captured Gaseitsiwe under a flag of truce and later ransomed him. Thereafter affairs of the morafe came increasingly under the sway of **Bathoen I**, Gaseitsiwe's son. In 1884 the Boer threat reemerged when the Tshidi Rolong under **Montshiwa** fled the filibusters of the Goshen Republic and took refuge with the BaNgwaketse, then temporarily settled at Moshaneng. Mission work in BaNgwaketse was begun in 1848 by Sebobi, evangelist of the **London Missionary Society (LMS)**. A formal LMS mission was not established in Kanye until 1871. Gaseitsiwe, who was taught to read by Sebobi, never converted to Christianity.

In 1885 Gaseitsiwe hosted the **Warren Expedition**, and he followed the lead of **Khama III** and Sechele I in accepting the declaration of the Protectorate. *See also* Mmanaana Kgatla; Sebego I; Senthufe.

GASETSHWARWE. Son of **Sekgoma II** and a contender to succeed after his father's death in 1925. Gasetshwarwe was regarded as the product of an irregular marriage, and **Tshekedi Khama** was chosen to act as BaNgwato regent until Sekgoma's recognized heir, **Seretse Khama**, grew to maturity. In 1930, claims to bogosi were revived on Gasetshwarwe's behalf by a group then opposed to Tshekedi. The regent received strong backing from the Administration, which imprisoned Gasetshwarwe for sedition.

GERRANS, J. Early Mafikeng trader, friend of BaRolong and Bangwaketse royals (and a champion of their causes), and an acquaintance of journalist Solomon Plaatje. Possibly of mixed, or coloured, parentage, Gerrans acted as an agent for the southern Protectorate diKgosi in 1909 during his trip to London, where he voiced their opposition to the proposed **incorporation** of the Protectorate into the planned Union of South Africa.

GHANZI FARMS. A group of freehold farms in the northwestern corner of the Ghanzi district. In 1877 the area was briefly settled by a few members of the **Dorsland Trek** at a time when it was recognized as part of the BaTawana state of **Moremi II**. In 1897 Moremi's successor **Sekgoma Letsholathebe** was maneuvered into ceding this area to the **British South Africa Company (BSACO),** and in 1898 another group of Boer farmers, who had been attracted by earlier advertisements placed by the BSACO in the Dutch South African press about large farms in the "vicinity of Lake Ngami," arrived to settle in the new crown lands. By 1899 the British had allocated them forty-one farms. In the process the **Nharo-Khoe** had their lands alienated. Although most of the original Boer settlers were disappointed and soon left, a small number of farmers, relying on BaSarwa laborers, remained and gradually established a permanent community. In the 1950s, with the opening of the Lobatse abattoir and the drilling of boreholes, some of them became large-scale commercial ranchers. Since independence, the government has increased the number of commercial farms in the area. The town of Ghanzi will soon be linked to southern Botswana by a Trans-Kalahari road, ending a century of difficult communications. *See also* Abattoir; Afrikaners.

GLOVER, LOUIS. *See* South African Native Labour Contingent.

GOBUAMANG (1845–1940). Regent (1889–1897, 1899–1912) and Kgosi (1916–1940) of the **Mmanaana Kgatla.** Gobuamang championed the autonomy of his people within the Bangwaketse Reserve. In 1930 such pretensions strained relations with the proud young **Bathoen II,** who with British backing tried to depose Gobuamang. A period of severe crises in the Protectorate followed. On several occasions the Mmanaana Kgatla resisted BaNgwaketse and British attempts to remove their leader. In April 1933, Resident Commissioner **Charles Rey** declared the area to be in a state of rebellion, sought external military assistance from Southern Rhodesia and South Africa, and proposed the aerial bombardment of Mosopa, Gobuamang's town. London vetoed Rey's request for airplanes, but Rey placed Mosopa under siege and mobilized Southern Rhodesian police. In order to avert bloodshed, Gobuamang surrendered unconditionally. After serving a brief prison sentence, the aged Gobuamang, then nearly ninety, settled at Thamaga just inside the BaKwena Reserve, north of Mosopa. In 1935 about half of the Mosopa population joined him. *See also* Letlole Mosielele; Mothowagae Motlogelwa.

GOOLD-ADAMS, SIR HAMILTON JOHN (1858–1920). An early Protectorate official who initiated the work of demarcating the Bangwato, Bakwena, Bangwaketse, Batawana and Bakgatla reserves. For most of his Botswana career, Goold-Adams was a senior officer in the Bechuanaland Border Police (BBP). In 1893 he led a combined BBP force against the AmaNdebele in support of the **British South Africa Company (BSACO)** forces in Rhodesia (Zimbabwe). During this campaign, in two separate incidents, his men were responsible for the deaths of emissaries sent by Lobengula to the **high commissioner** in a desperate attempt to avert the fighting. In 1895, while on leave in England, Goold-Adams served as an advisor to Colonial Secretary Chamberlain during the visit of **Bathoen I, Khama III,** and **Sebele I.** Chamberlain then commissioned Goold-Adams to demarcate internal boundaries in the Protectorate in a manner that would favor the BSACO. Goold-Adams, for many years a pawn of Cecil Rhodes and from whom he received BSACO shares and other benefits, needed little encouragement. However, his plan to divide the reserves into small, unsustainable locations along the lines of those in South Africa was abandoned following the abortive **Jameson Raid**. From 1897–1901 he served as the Protectorate's **resident commissioner** and then became the governor of the Orange River Sovereignty. *See also* Reserves; Three Kings in London.

GREAT THIRST. White travelers often used this name with reference to the Kgalagadi Desert. A "thirst" measured the distance between two watering points.

GRIQUA. One of the old Khoe clans (Charigri-khoe), the Griqua dominated the dagga (marijuana) trade in southern Botswana before 1800. After 1790 they acquired guns and horses, traded into the interior, and thereby connected the southern BaTswana to the Cape. They also raided for cattle and slaves in the same areas. The resulting violence and instability contributed to the **mfecane**. They converted to Christianity at the beginning of the nineteenth century through the **London Missionary Society (LMS),** which then came into contact with the southern BaTswana. Based in settlements in the Orange River valley in the Kimberley area and led by members of the Kok and Barends families, they were prominent in the Kalahari hunting trade of the 1840s and 1850s, linking that region with the markets in Grahamstown; one Griqua party came close to reaching Ngamiland in 1848 but halted in Nharo territory. Another small Griqua group under Raseme Adam Kok joined Sechele and settled at Kumakwane, where some of their descendants remain to this day. The Griqua of the Kimberley area remained independent until the diamond discoveries led to the alienation of their territory as "Griqualand West" in 1871. *See also* Bolata; Marijuana; Naro; Slave Trade.

GROBLER AFFAIR. An 1888 incident that accelerated Britain's involvement in Zimbabwe. Piet Grobler was a Boer trader in Matabeleland, where he was also consul of the South African Republic (SAR). In July 1887 he successfully renegotiated a friendship treaty with Lobengula, Inkosi of the AmaNdebele. The terms of the treaty included a mutual defense pact and a guarantee that the subjects of the SAR in Matabeleland would be under the authority of the consul. Grobler's activities upset the British in Bechuanaland and also **Khama III** of the Ba-Ngwato, who was contending with Lobengula over the mineral rights of the territory that lay between their two states.

In July 1888 when Grobler passed through this disputed territory en route to Matabeleland, his party was waylaid by Khama's men, who claimed to be searching for two English traders who had violated an agreement with Khama. Shooting erupted, resulting in the death of Grobler (sixteen days later—from a wound probably inflicted by one of his own party). An official inquiry was held by Resident Commissioner **Sidney Shippard**, although Shippard's authority did not extend to the site of the incident, which occurred north of the then Protectorate boundary of twenty-two degrees latitude. The inquiry was attended by German military advisors as well as officials of the SAR. After the inquiry, Shippard traveled to Bulawayo, persuaded Lobengula to renounce the Grobler Treaty, and laid the groundwork for Lobengula's signing of the Rudd Concession, which was later used by Cecil Rhodes to claim that Lobengula had granted ultimate control of Zimbabwe to the **British South Africa Company (BSACO)**.

Shippard's formal exoneration of the BaNgwato who attacked Grobler's party was rejected by the Colonial Office and the SAR, and the Protectorate was committed to paying an annual pension to Grobler's widow. *See also* Kopong Conference; Ndebele.

/GWI. A Khoe-speaking group concentrated in the Ghanzi District. By the early twentieth century many /Gwi paid tribute to the **BaKwena** while others worked as laborers on white-owned farms. George Silberbauer, bushman survey officer of the Bechuanaland Protectorate, described them as among the last of the "wild Bushmen," whereupon the British in the early 1960s established the Central Kalahari Game Reserve largely as a place where the /Gwi and related //Ganna could continue to practice their supposed hunter-gatherer way of life. By the 1980s, however, the Botswana government came under international conservationist pressures to remove the people from the reserve. *See also* Ghanzi Farms; Khoe; Sarwa.

H

HASKINS, JAMES GEORGE (1914–1990). Prominent businessman and politician, born in Bulawayo. His father was Bristol-born James Haskins ("Pompong," literally mosquito), who arrived in Tati in 1897 and ran a boarding house and coffee house near the Monarch Mine. In 1907 he initiated a trading store chain that eventually extended into the present Central District. J. Haskins & Sons, with headquarters in Francistown, is still in operation. J.G. Haskins, James's second son, entered politics in 1948 as a member of the European Advisory Council. In the 1950s he served on the Joint Advisory Council and from 1961–1964 on LEGCO, by which time he was a leading member of the Bechuanaland Democratic Party. As a leading spokesperson of the white community in northern Botswana, he played a key role in the accommodation of white settler opinion to independence. In 1966 he entered the first National Assembly as specially-elected MP. The same year he became minister of Commerce, Industry and Water Affairs, and later of Finance, of Agriculture, and of Works and Communications (1970–1979). In 1979 Haskins retired from politics and returned to trading, where he also made important contributions. From 1980 until 1989 he served as Speaker of the National Assembly. *See also* Councils; Democratic Party.

HEAD, BESSIE (1937–1986). Novelist and historian. Born in a South African mental hospital to a white mother, who soon died, and a black father she never knew, Bessie Head arrived in Botswana as a political refugee in 1963. She became one of Africa's most widely read novelists. All her books are set in Botswana, particularly in the Central District and Serowe, where she lived. Her novels are *Where Rain Clouds Gather* (1969), which deals with the transition to independence in Botswana from a local perspective; *Maru* (1971), which attacks discrimination against BaSarwa by BaTswana and is probably her best-known work; *A Question of Power* (1973), a feminist novel about mental instability; *The Collector of Treasures and Other Botswana Village Tales* (1977); *Serowe: Village of the Rainwind* (1981); and *A Bewitched Crossroad: An African Saga* (1984), an historical novel of nineteenth-century Gammangwato. In 1991 a collection of her correspondence was published posthumously (*A Gesture of Belonging: Letters from Bessie Head, 1965–1979*). Her private papers are reposed with the Khama III Memorial Museum, Serowe.

HEALTH. Before independence, health care was primarily the responsibility of the merafe and the missions, and centered around hospital care and traditional medicine. Western-type medicine and medical doctors rivalled but never replaced indigenous medicine and its practitioners, and in modern Botswana the two traditions co-exist and overlap.

After the turn of the century, diKgosi became increasingly committed to the introduction of western medical services. In 1909 a doctor was stationed in Serowe by the **London Missionary Society (LMS)**, and from 1914 one served Molepolole and Kanye. Shortly after World War I, hospitals were established in the same three towns, in Serowe by the LMS, in Molepolole by the United Free Church of Scotland, and in Kanye by the Seventh Day Adventist Church. By independence (1966), hospitals had been built in Gaborone, Mochudi, Francistown, Maun, Ramotswa, and Lobatse.

Since independence, the Government has initiated a policy of decentralization of health care by building a network of health posts and clinics. In 1981, 80% of the population lived within 15 km. of a government health facility, at which treatment is available for a nominal payment. As of 1992, the government maintained 185 clinics throughout the country, 68 of which had beds. The Ministry of Health obtains most of its doctors and specialists from abroad and depends on the National Health Institute to train its nursing and paramedical staff. In 1992, the Ministry employed a total of 7,565 health workers, including 257 doctors and 2,807 nurses.

The government has also attempted to improve health through providing piped water, sinking drop toilets in urban areas, using government media to encourage disease prevention, placing health in the primary school curriculum, and providing primary school children with nutritious meals at no cost under the famine relief scheme.

Botswana has been able to lower significantly its infant mortality rate, from 102.1 per 1,000 births in 1971 to 68.4 in 1981 and 45.1 in 1986. The overall death rate declined over the same period from 13.7 per 1,000 to 12.95 in 1981, and 11.4 in 1991. In 1986 the average life expectancy in Botswana was 62.6 years, the highest of southern African countries, apart from South Africa. The incidence of tuberculosis, which once accounted for as many as 25% of institutional deaths, has also been considerably reduced, though TB is making a comeback recently. Major causes of death in Botswana are infectious and parasitic diseases, followed by circulatory disease, perinatal conditions, neoplasms, and respiratory diseases. Improvements in health care have also been a factor in the growing birth rate, which in 1981 stood at 48.7 per 1,000, representing a rate of natural increase of 3.5%. Figures have declined recently (in 1991: 38.7 births per 1,000, 2.8% natural increase).

The current challenges to the health system are the remergence of malaria in the north, and the spread of HIV throughout the country (as of early 1993, possibly in excess of 5% of the population was HIV-positive). *See also* Aids; Merriweather, Alfred M.; Religion.

HERERO (OVAHERERO). A people, comprised of two main clans (Mbanderu and Herero), who originate in **Namibia**. Early Mbanderu immigrants into Botswana arrived in the mid-1890s. In 1904 **Samuel Maharero**, son of Kamaherero, revolted against German rule in Namibia. The Germans responded by exterminating nearly 70 percent of his people. Roughly 6,000 to 8,000 OvaHerero fled to the Protectorate, where **Sekgoma Letshola-thebe** of the BaTawana gave them refuge. A large group under Kahaka settled at Nxau Nxau near the Namibian border, and another group, the Mbanderu under **Kahememua Nikodemus**, settled at Nokaneng; many others, including Samuel Maharero, scattered across the Protectorate and Transvaal, eventually concentrating at Mahalapye after 1922. Samuel Maharero died in 1923 and was succeeded by his son Frederick. In Ngamiland and in Mahalapye, the OvaHerero rebuilt their herds through a combination of migrant labor, clientship, systematic cattle theft, and good herding. By 1930 they had emerged as leading pastoralists.

In 1946 a section of the OvaHerero petitioned the British and South African governments to be allowed to return to Namibia. The petition was a response to the Pretoria declaration that South Africa planned to incorporate Namibia into the Union (the OvaHerero wished to return in order to vote against incorporation in a referendum). Pretoria refused their request on the grounds that there was insufficient land to absorb them. In 1957 a second petition was refused by South Africa.

Since Botswana's independence, the OvaHerero have prospered as renowned pastoralists. Though they maintain ties with their relatives in Namibia and meet every August to commemorate Samuel Maharero's death, few desire to return permanently to Namibia. Since 1990, when Namibia gained its independence, fewer than 2,000 OvaHerero have returned with their cattle to their original homeland. See also Keheranju, Monjuku; Nama-German War; Refugees.

HIGH COMMISSION TERRITORIES. Basutoland, the Bechuanaland Protectorate, and Swaziland constituted the three

Southern African dependencies of Great Britain prior to their gaining independence in 1966 (Swaziland in 1968), during which time they fell under the jurisdiction of the **high commissioner** in South Africa. Britain enjoined each of these territories on different terms. Sovereignty over Basutoland was proclaimed in 1884, Protectorate status was declared for Bechuanaland in 1885, and right of Jurisdiction over Swaziland was transferred from the Transvaal in 1906. The High Commission Territories, along with the Union of South Africa and Southern Rhodesia, fell under the authority of the Colonial Office until 1924, when they were transferred to the new Dominions Office (later the Commonwealth Relations Office). Each of the three territories was governed by proclamations from the office of the high commissioner, whose powers were based on the United Kingdom **Foreign Jurisdiction Act of 1890** and the **Order-in-Council of 1891** derived from the former. The proclamations were executed in each Territory by a **resident commissioner**, who headed the local administration.

The principal assumption underlying this arrangement was that the three territories would eventually become part of a British South Africa, the "grand illusion" which persisted until after World War II and which indirectly affected Bechuanaland in three important ways. First, for the first half-century of its existence, colonial administration was supervisory, rather than creative, and depended on diKgosi for the day-to-day running of affairs. Second, the Protectorate administration was staffed, not by British colonial civil servants, but mainly by English-speaking South Africans, who admired locally-bred heroes such as Cecil Rhodes and distrusted British rulers from overseas as much as they did the local Boers. The high commissioner, who was posted to South Africa from the privileged classes of Great Britain, was not a man they cared to drink with, tea or otherwise. Third, administrative headquarters lay outside the territory, either in Cape Town or Pretoria in the case of the high commissioner and in Mafikeng (Northern Cape) for the resident commissioner. The absence of an internal, regulatory hub preserved decentralized administration until independence and made possible the creation of a central government through popular participation.

Still, the Territories' common relationship with Great Britain and their shared problems with South Africa, as with the threat of **incorporation**, created loose, symbolic ties and occasionally cooperation. Following **World War II**, a combined volunteer force from the High Commission Territories served in the

Middle East, and as each of these Territories approached independence, they pooled their resources to establish the University of Bechuanaland, Basutoland, and Swaziland (UBBS), precursor to the national universities in Botswana (1980), Lesotho, and Swaziland. The campus of UBBS (UBLS from 1966 to 1976) was located at Roma, Lesotho. *See also* Administration; Education.

HIGH COMMISSIONER. The British office of high commissioner was originally attached to the office of governor of the Cape Colony in 1867 and assumed administrative authority over Bechuanaland Protectorate in 1891. In 1910, the office of high commissioner was attached to that of governor general of the Union of South Africa. The Statute of Westminster of 1931 separated the governor general from the office of the high commissioner for the Union of South Africa and the High Commission Territories, which applied until South Africa declared itself a republic and withdrew from the Commonwealth in 1961. Between 1961 and 1964, Britain's representative to South Africa became an ambassador, who held as well the office of high commissioner of the three Territories. The latter office was abolished in 1964, when the resident commissioners were designated "Queen's Commissioners" with the responsibility of guiding their respective territories to independence.

List of High Commissioners

High Commissioner and Governor of Cape Colony (Cape Town)

1881–1889   Sir Hercules G.R. Robinson
1889–1894   Sir Henry Loch
1894–1997   Sir Hercules G.R. Robinson
1897–1901   Sir Alfred Milner

High Commissioner (separate from office of Governor) (Johannesburg)

1901–1905   Sir Alfred Milner
1905–1910   William Waldegrave Palmer, Earl of Selborne

High Commissioner and Governor General of the Union of South Africa (Cape Town, Pretoria)

1910–1914   Viscount Herbert John Gladstone
1914–1920   Sydney Charles Buxton, Earl of Buxton

1920–1923   Arthur Frederick Patrick Albert, Duke of
             Connaught
1924–1930   Alexander Augustus Cambridge, Earl of Athlone

High Commissioner (to South Africa and for the High Commission Territories) (Cape Town, Pretoria)

1931–1935   Sir Herbert James Stanley
1935–1940   William Henry Clark
1940–1941   Walter Clarence Huggard
1941–1944   William George Arthur Ormsby-Gore, Baron
             Harlech
1944   Walter Clarence Huggard
1944–1951   Sir Evelyn Baring
1951–1955   Sir John Helier le Rougetel
1955–1958   Sir Percivale Lisching
1959–1960   Sir John Primatt Ratcliffe Maud

High Commissioner and Ambassador to the Republic of South Africa (Pretoria)

1960–1963   Sir John Primatt Ratcliffe Maud
1963–1964   Sir Hugh Southern Stephenson

See also High Commission Territories; Resident Commissioner; Tautona.

HINDUS. Hinduism in Botswana dates back at least to the 1890s, but until recently its adherents have been few. No more than 100 or so lived in Botswana at independence. Since the Botswana Hindu Society was formed in 1979, its members have grown to 2,000, belonging to nine communities. *See also* Asians.

HIRSCHFELDT, MAX LUIS ("RAPHALANE") (d. 1935). The leading businessman in the Kweneng at the time of his death. Hirschfeldt, of Latvian Jewish origin, settled in Molepolole in 1895 along with his elder brother, Adolph ("Ranko") Hirschfeldt. Both Hirschfeldt brothers married into the BaKwena. Max's business included the finishing and export of game skins and furs on the world market. The British were suspicious of his ties to BaKwena diKgosi, but in the 1930s they sought his assistance in the collection of hut tax among the BaKgalagadi. The Hirschfeldt descendants have been prominent civil servants, particularly in law enforcement. Adolph Hirschfeldt was chief of police intelligence until his retirement in the early 1990s, and Simon Hirschfeldt was near retirement as chief of police in 1994.

HOTTENTOT. Apparently from an old German or Dutch expression, "hotteren-totteren" (to stammer, stutter), Hottentot was used by early white visitors to the Cape to describe the Khoe-speaking Khoikhoi of the western Cape, whose "click" language was exceptionally odd to their ears. The designation carried then, and has ever since, the connotation of inferiority and savagery. In early southern Africa this term was also eventually used to refer to Khoe who became servants in the Cape Colony, as well as to powerful Khoe-speaking groups living in the interior, such as the **Nama**. *See also* Khoe.

HUME, DAVID ("TAUTE") (1796–1863). A trader, an "1820 settler," who achieved great significance at the beginning of Botswana's ivory-hunting era. He arrived in Bechuanaland in 1825, moved to Mzilikazi's in 1829, shifted to Gammangwato and GaNgwaketse in 1832 and 1834, respectively, and then set up a trading post in Kuruman in 1838. Until 1863 his agents went around the southern Kalahari buying up ivory and ostrich feathers. The hunting trade of southern Botswana was largely in his hands, and he enabled the BaTswana to evade Boer trading restrictions. He made annual trading trips to Grahamstown where his spectacular troves drew enormous crowds. In 1843 he arrived there with a ton of ivory and 200 pounds of ostrich feathers. *See also* Traders.

HURUTSHE (BAHURUTSHE). Their name derives from Mohurutshe, who according to some traditions was the first Kgosi among all BaKwena. Groups of BaHurutshe live primarily in South Africa and adjacent areas of southeastern Botswana. Those in Botswana came originally as refugees.

In 1853 the BaHurutshe booMokhubidu, now living at Mmankgodi in Kweneng District, migrated from the western Transvaal under the regent, Masega, acting for Thobega. Originally settled at **Dithubaruba**, in 1863 they moved to Mmankgodi with the BaLete. In 1874 the BaKwena Kgosi **Sechele I** intervened in booMokhubidu affairs by removing Masega, who had clutched the regency, and installing Thobega. Masega and a few followers then accompanied the BaLete to Ramotswa, where they expected to be free of Sechele. The location of Mmankgodi village shifted several times, having been situated at its present site since the 1930s.

The BaHurutshe booManyana, who live at Manyana in the Southern District, also originated in the western Transvaal, where by the **BaTswana-Boer War of 1852–1853** they were under the authority of the Boers. Their Kgosi, Mangope, was held hostage as a way of forcing the booManyana to join the Boers in their attack on the BaKwena. Some of the booManyana were with the Boers at the **Battle of Dimawe**. A booManyana group under Mangope's son Kontle defected at that time to the BaKwena, joining them at Dithubaruba. In 1858 Mangope brought the remainder of his people to the BaKwena and was settled by Sechele I at Dimawe. Upon Mangope's death in 1880, a succession dispute divided the booManyana; the largest faction under Kontle moved their Manyana village from the Dimawe hills to the present site, others settled in **Ramotswa,** and a few returned to the Transvaal (including the grandfather of Lucas Mangope, future president of the Bophuthatswana bantustan).

The drawing of the BaKwena-BaNgwaketse boundary between Mmankgodi and Manyana led to the 1881 dispute between the **BaNgwaketse** and the BaLete, culminating in the former's attack on Ramotswa.

From 1957 to 1958 another large migration took place from the Transvaal following a confrontation between the BaHurutshe there and the South African police. Some of these refugees settled in Peleng township, Lobatse.

I

INCORPORATION. This term refers to a long-standing threat of white governments in southern Africa to take control of Botswana and other black African territories. The threat has been present since the establishment of Boer republics north of the Vaal river in the 1840s and continued until the late 1980s. It was particularly rife during the early and mid-colonial period, when Britain periodically contemplated placing the Bechuanaland Protectorate under the control of the **British South Africa Company (BSACO)**, Southern Rhodesia, the Union of South Africa, and later the Central African Federation.

During the nineteenth century a number of BaTswana states preserved their autonomy from incorporation by the Transvaal Boers, the BSACO, and the Cape Colony through small-scale armed resistance, diplomacy, and some timely luck. They accepted British rule because of its remoteness and its potential usefulness as a barricade against white domination in the region. Thus BaTswana fought for and in other ways supported British troops in the 1899–1902 **South African War**. They also quickly perceived that the treaty of Vereeniging would lead not to British rule but white South African reconciliation. Before the Union was created in 1910, protest was mounted. In May 1908 when the four white-controlled colonies called for a National Convention to draw up a constitution for a self-governing South Africa, **Sebele I** of the BaKwena and Letsie of the BaSotho in Basutoland separately petitioned High Commissioner Lord Selborne requesting imperial safeguards for their people in the event of closer union. Selborne gave the appearance of responding favorably, but the black petitioners had in fact caused him merely to adjust the timing of his request to the Colonial Office that the High Commision Territories be incorporated into the future union. In December Selborne inserted into the draft South Africa Act a twenty-five-point schedule for incorporation. By then, however, Sebele's secretary **Peter Sidzumo** had launched a series of public and private appeals that helped to consolidate local opposition to the proposed union. The eagerness of South Africans to get their draft act through Parliament in London created its own resistance which allowed the growing voice of local opposition to reach London. DiKgosi **Bathoen I** and Sebele induced **J. Gerrans**, a Mafikeng trader, to act as the agent for the southern Protectorate diKgosi on his trip to London, and William Schreiner led the "Coloured and Native People's Delegation" which arrived in London to block or modify the South Africa bill before Parliament. The delegation failed to prevent enactment, but they managed to persuade *The Times* of London to print on its front page part of the transcript of the 7 January 1909 meeting, on the issue of the Union, between the southern diKgosi and acting Resident Commissioner Brian May and lodge the transcript in the official records. Within days of that meeting, petitions from all southern diKgosi followed (Kgosi **Khama III** remained aloof from the petition campaign and refused to associate with Gerrans). The decision on incorporation was delayed, and in 1910, in a move timed to coincide with the union, all the major diKgosi (this time including Khama III) forwarded another set of petitions favoring the status quo.

For the remainder of the colonial period, the specter of incorporation remained more or less constant in the Protectorate and an issue around which most BaTswana could be rallied. One factor was the presence of a small but vocal white farming community, which used the European Advisory Council and petitions to keep steady pressure on the Protectorate administration to negotiate closer ties with South Africa and Rhodesia. Fear of incorporation significantly informed the BaTswana approach to issues such as the administrative reforms of the 1930s, participation in the first and second world wars, cattle embargoes into South Africa, the fate of Namibia, internal mineral development, and nationalist politics.

Independence muffled but failed to silence the fear of incorporation. After Prime Minister H.F. Verwoerd's attempt in 1963 to entice the soon-to-be-independent High Commission Territories into the Republic of South Africa as "self-governing homelands," Botswana has rejected his and similar offers made from subsequent South African government officials. P.W. Botha's 1979 call for the creation of a southern African "constellation of states" was rebuked, as was his attempt in the 1980s to engage Botswana in an Nkomati-type accord, based as it is on white South Africa's self-image as a regional power. The coming of independence in Namibia and non-racial democracy in South Africa has finally ended the threat of political incorporation and improved prospects for greater regional economic cooperation. *See also* Administration; Battle of Dimawe; Councils; Herero; High Commission Territories; South Africa; South African War; Tshekedi Khama; World War II.

INDEPENDENCE. At midnight on 29 September 1966, the British flag was lowered and the blue, black, and white bars of the Republic of Botswana raised in the National Stadium at Gaborone and at similar ceremonies held across the country. Exactly eighty-one years prior to that day in London, without any BaTswana present, the British Crown had proclaimed a protectorate over the territory north of the Molopo River and south of the twenty-second parallel, thereby dividing this territory from **British Bechuanaland**. During the 1950s, September 30 was adopted as "Bechuanaland Protectorate Day," following a motion by **Bathoen II** in the African Advisory Council.

INDEPENDENCE PARTY (BIP). The Botswana Independence Party, the first political party to incorporate the term "Botswana" into its title—though this reference to the Bechuanaland Protectorate was already common in vernacular usage—

was formed in 1964 by **Motsamai Mpho**. In 1960 Mpho had helped to found the Bechuanaland **People's Party (BPP)**, from which he split in 1962. After two years attempting to gain recognition as the leader of the "true BPP," Mpho gave up and named his group the BIP. In the 1965 general election, the BIP won no seats, though Mpho was elected to the National Assembly in 1969. BIP support has been confined largely to the Northwest District. *See also* Elections; Motshidisi, Klaas.

INDEPENDENT CHURCHES. "Independent churches" is a broad term covering a wide variety of movements. Theologically they can be roughly divided into Apostolic, Millenial, Neo-Traditional, Pentacostal, and Spiritual churches. Various apostolic churches have emerged since the Apostolic Faith Mission entered the country in 1958. The millenial Jehovah's Witnesses (Watchtower) have been in Botswana since the 1950s, but they have few adherents. Among the more important neo-traditionalist churches is the Guta ra Mwari (City of God) movement, which was founded in Zimbabwe by prophetess Mai-Chaza and was spread in Francistown in 1946 by Tawozera Dube. Guta ra Mwari rejects Christianity as a white religion. In 1994 Guta had 5,000 members in Botswana. Spiritual churches make up the vast majority of independent churches, in terms of members, the largest being the **Spiritual Healing Church**, with 30,000 members. *See also* Mwali; Pentecostal Churches; Religion; Spiritual Healing Churches; Zion Christian Church.

INDIRECT RULE. Strictly speaking, Indirect Rule is a body of African colonial administrative policy developed in Northern Nigeria by **Frederick Lugard**, who through his writings (e.g., *Political Memoranda* and *The Dual Mandate* in British Tropical Africa) and example influenced a generation of colonial policymakers and administrators throughout the British Empire. Indirect Rule in each colonial territory was developed through what were called "Native Authorities" (such as emirs, chiefs, elders' councils), which were derived from traditional offices and customs and to which colonial officers attached a set of councils, tribunals, and treasuries for the performance of administrative and legal tasks. The Colonial Office favored the system because it utilized Africans to pay for and run the administration (thus sparing the British taxpayer), incorporated Africa into the British sphere without, so it claimed, destroying African culture (thus sparing the British conscience), and pointed Africa in the direction of self-government at the local level (thus sparing any thought that the empire must be held by force). As self-serving and paternalistic as Lugardian policy seems today, it then captured the imagination of the British left, who wanted Britain to protect Africans rather than run their lives or turn them over to white settlers.

Indirect Rule was a dead letter in Bechuanaland. The Protectorate was more than twenty years old before Lugard wrote his seminal *Instructions* and nearly forty before Lugard's theories became sacrosanct policy in the Colonial Office. By then, the British had all but forgotten the Protectorate, assuming that it and the other two **High Commission Territories** would ultimately be part of South Africa. In 1924 the Protectorate was removed one step further from Lugard's influence when it was transferred to the new Dominions Office. In the meantime, local administration remained where it had been since 1885—in the hands of diKgosi.

In the 1930s a form of administration disguised as Indirect Rule was unsuccessfully attempted in Bechuanaland. Following the 1933 Pim Report, which exposed the absence of social and economic development in the HCTs, Resident Commissioner **Charles Rey** introduced a set of Native Administration Proclamations, which he claimed were based on the policies of Lord Lugard and those of his principal disciple, Sir Donald Cameron. **Tshekedi Khama** and **Bathoen II** challenged Rey's proclamations, which bore close resemblance to native policy in the Union of South Africa and stood in marked contrast to Lugard and Cameron's. Tshekedi and Bathoen lost their fight with Rey in court, where in many ways the two diKgosi challenged the basis of British administration itself. They and other diKgosi succeeded in resisting the implementation of Rey's proclamations and in regaining much of their position. The proclamations of 1943, which followed Lugard and Cameron's lines more closely, were introduced with their approval. *See also* Administration; Arden-Clarke, Sir Charles; Khama III.

INITIATION. In SeTswana "bogwera" is used with reference to the initiation of young men, "bojale" with reference to young women. Only an individual who had been initiated could attain adulthood, hence making it the most important rite of passage in pre-colonial times. In the nineteenth century, initiation was the means by which persons between their early teens and mid-twenties were recruited into *mephato* (singular *mophato*), sometimes referred to as "age-regiments." *Mephato* were made responsible for the performance of military, police, and other social duties. For men initiation began with circumcision and was followed by intensive social and physical training that was carried out in secret away from the towns in deep bush, often during the coldest months. Training, which involved the learning of military tactics, hunting, and cattle herding, was extremely strenuous, sometimes resulting in death. On the other hand, a strong element of conservative social and political training was present in *bogwera*. Young men learned law and custom, with a strong emphasis on respecting social rank in all forms. Women's initiation was less physically demanding, but it also involved a strong element of conservative education. Initiation also forged lifelong individual friendships and imbued a sense of camaraderie among *mephato* members that cut across kinship ties and influenced social, political, and economic life in the community.

Around the turn of the century, circumcision schools were abolished by many diKgosi, often with approval of local missionaries and the colonial officials, who looked down on initiation. Types of modified initiation are still practiced by the BaLete, as well as the **Kgafela Kgatla**, whose Kgosi **Linchwe II** revived the institution in 1975. *See also* Regiment.

IPELEGENG ("Help Yourselves!"). A proto-nationalist group formed in the Bakgatla Reserve in 1937 to protest the suspension and banishment of Molefi, the BaKgatla Kgosi. Led by **Kgosi D. Lebotse**, a school teacher, and Rralefala Motsisi, onetime member of a black Johannesburg taxi owners' union, Ipelegeng was created to function outside the tribal structure and deal directly with the colonial administration. Motsisi and others wrote letters to the district commissioner, raised funds, and hired a Mafikeng lawyer to challenge the suspension order in court. It was banned within months of its formation. Its members, who included Molefi's mother, then established a chapter of the **Zion Christian Church**.

During **World War II**, "Ipelegeng II" emerged among the younger BaKgatla members of the AAPC, who initially raised money on Molefi's behalf.

Ipelegeng was also the name given to self-help drought relief programs in the later 1960s and 1970s. *See also* Molefi; Seingwaeng.

INTERNATIONAL RELATIONS. *See* External Relations.

ISANG PILANE (1886–1941). Regent of the **Kgafela Kgatla** (1920–1929) during the minority of his nephew **Molefi** and remembered for his unbounded energy and colossal memory. Isang was the second son of **Linchwe I** and the younger brother of **Kgafela**, who died in 1914. Between 1902 and 1906, Isang attended school in Cape Town at Zonnebloem College, where he passed his Standard VI examination. He became BaKgatla regent when his father was too old to continue as Kgosi and was forced out before his nephew was mature enough for the chieftaincy. As regent, Isang became a leading figure in the newly-formed Native Advisory Council and an advocate of modernization in the Reserve. He mobilized the BaKgatla in building the **Bakgatla National School**, imposed a strict code of social conduct on Reserve residents, led the Dutch Reformed Church council, and launched a number of schemes for the improvement of agriculture, stock breeding, water development, and specialized training of youth, girls included. Also, during Molefi's first reign, Isang served as a councilor, established the first borehole syndicates in the Protectorate, and, with Dr. Silas Molema, favored incorporation into the Union of South Africa. *See also* Archives; Regency; Water.

ISLAM. Muslims, who number 3,000 in Botswana, are almost exclusively of Asian origin, though Islam is a growing faith in the country. The earliest known Muslim was a trader named Buana, who settled in Mosopa in 1882 and was followed in 1884 by Buana Vahad, in Mosopa, then Molepolole. Other early settlers appear to have been Muhammad Ahmad and Sayad Osman, who established a trading store in Molepolole in 1891. Several years later Molepolole became the home of the Khan and Kablay families, many descendants of whom still live in Botswana. Between 1886 and 1967, Ramotswa was the country's center of Islamic activity, with the British Indian Mohammadan Society founded there in 1920 (it was then renamed the Bechuanaland [later Botswana] Muslim Association).

In 1967 the first mosque in the country was built in Lobatse, and in 1983 a second was erected in Gaborone, where the Botswana Muslim Association is headquartered. Mosques have been built since in Kanye, Francistown, Rasesa (near Pilane station), and Molepolole, which also has an Islamic school and center. *See also* Asians.

IVORY. In 1990 an estimated 67,000 elephants were located in Chobe and Ngamiland districts, representing roughly 10 percent of Africa's total population. They range over approximately 80,000 square kilometers, with the largest concentrations in Chobe, Linyati, Moremi Wildlife Reserve, Savuti, and the upper Ngwezumba. During the dry cold winter, they congregate in especially large numbers along the Chobe River on the northern Botswana border.

In the nineteenth century ivory, skins, and ostrich feathers from Botswana were traded for guns, wagons, and other articles from the Cape. Hunting of elephant was banned in 1983, and since 1989 the Botswana government has attempted to maintain its population in the 60,000 range through a culling scheme run by the Ministry of Tourism and Wildlife. In 1989 Botswana joined Zimbabwe, South Africa, Zambia, Malawi, and Namibia in an ivory-trading system (Southern African Centre for Ivory Marketing—SACIM) for supplying markets in Asia, as well as carvers in the immediate region. SACIM also cooperates in controlling elephant poaching and ivory smuggling. *See also* Economy; Traders; Viljoen, Jan.

J

JAMESON RAID (29 DECEMBER 1895–2 JANUARY 1896). The decisive event in averting Rhodesian white settler rule in Bechuanaland. In late 1895 Dr. Leander Starr Jameson, administrator of Rhodesia in the **British South Africa Company (BSACO)**, organized a small army at Pitsani Potlhogo in the Protectorate and used it to invade the Transvaal. Jameson's force was made up almost entirely of Bechuanaland's own Border Police, then being formed into the British South Africa Police during the transfer of the administration of the Protectorate from Britain to the BSACO. In the weeks before, the BSACO had received authority from the British, over the protests of many BaTswana diKgosi, to rule the entire Protectorate except for the undemarcated territories of BaNgwaketse, BaKwena, and BaNgwato.

Jameson's raid was intended to spark a rebellion among English-speaking residents of the South African Republic (SAR), in turn furthering Cecil Rhodes's dream of extending his political control to the Witwatersrand. It was orchestrated with coordination between Jameson and a group of Johannesburg plotters, who organized the Transvaal National Union and the Reform Committee. Both bodies were chaired by Charles Leonard, lawyer for the Secheleland Concessions Ltd., whose concession claims in the southern Protectorate had been used as a cover for communication between Leonard and Jameson. In the Protectorate, "Secheleland shareholders" was the code name for the Johannesburg plotters. Money was forwarded to them from the BSACO's "New Concessions Account," and the moment for the coup attempt was signaled with the telegraphed announcement of the "flotation" of new Secheleland shares.

The raid failed dismally. Jameson's arrest by SAR forces in the Transvaal led to a speedy eclipse of Rhodes's influence in southern Africa and a halt to the implementation of BSACO rule in the Protectorate. Britain restored its authority, apart from railroad concessions already made to the Company, and transferred Block land to the Company in 1905. *See also* Concessions; Three Kings in London.

JOINT ADVISORY COUNCIL. *See* Councils.

JOURNALISM. *See* Newspapers.

JOUSSE, PAUL (d. 1945). South African-born trader of French ancestry (born into a family of missionaries attached to the Paris Evangelical Missionary Society), Jousse became a manager for the Bechuanaland Trading Association (BTA) in Gammangwato during the reign of **Khama III.** When Khama bought out the concern of Garrett, Smith & Co. and began to outcompete the BTA, Jousse began agitating in the South African press against what he called Khama's "monopoly." In 1914 after he ran a series of articles under the pseudonym "Inquisitor," other local traders ostracized him, and Ba-Ngwato boycotted his stores. The high commissioner's investigation into the matter, however, caused Khama to incur a huge loss (he may have been the victim of a Rhodesian political/merchant conspiracy), and forced him out of trading. Jousse was himself removed to the Tuli Block, where he ran ranching and dairy operations until his death. *See also* Traders.

JUSTICE. Before the establishment of the Protectorate, justice in the Tswana states was administered by the diKgosi and ward headmen in the **kgotla.** Law was unwritten, and its source lay in custom and tradition. There was no distinction between civil and criminal laws. Under colonial rule, the **Order-in-Council of May 9, 1891** provided that "the High Commissioner may . . . provide for the administration of justice." The magistrate courts subsequently established, however, were intended for cases trying only non-Africans; the kgotlas of the diKgosi were to be left to function as before. In practice this dual system of justice—magistrate courts and Cape Colonial (Roman-Dutch) law for "Europeans," kgotlas and customary law for "Natives"—did not operate as envisaged. From the beginning magistrate courts had original jurisdiction over Africans in many instances, leaving customary, or kgotla, courts with all other cases involving Africans. Gradually customary courts and the justice they administered became regularized and the European and SeTswana legal systems were amalgamated. Since 1891 magistrate courts have remained paramount over customary courts.

The autonomy of the customary courts was weakened from the outset by the ban imposed on their dealing with cases of homicide. Customary law was also eroded by civil marriages, contracts, and other common law intrusions. In 1919 legislation was passed which provided for appeals against the decisions of diKgosi to a combined court of the Kgosi and the Magistrate. In 1927 all "witchcraft" trials were removed from customary courts. The Native Courts Proclamation of 1943 empowered magistrates to reverse the decisions of customary courts, strictly circumscribed their powers, and imposed upper limits for prison sentences and fines. In 1961 the African Courts Proclamation reaffirmed that the customary courts were to have no jurisdiction over non-Africans.

Since independence attempts have been made to integrate the two judicial systems. The Customary Law and Ascertainment Act of 1969 made it possible for all courts to apply either customary law or common law and enabled an individual to choose which type of court to hear his/her case. Confusion resulted. Thus in 1985 the Customary Court of Appeal was created to receive cases from customary courts, leaving the High Court to receive cases from magistrate courts and the Customary Court of Appeal.

K

KAA (BAKAA). A scattered people whose name is derived from *ba ka ya* ("they can go"). BaKaa share the totem *tlou* ("elephant"). They represent an offshoot of the Ba**Rolong** that settled in the Shoshong Hills sometime before or during the eighteenth century. In the late eighteenth century, they came under the Ba**Ngwato**. In 1849 the BaKaa fled to the Ba**Kwena**.

Then under the ailing Suwe, the BaKaa were led by his son Mosinyi, who kept the BaKaa together until his own death in 1892. The BaKaa then began to fragment. The *cause celebre* was a bogosi dispute between two of Mosinyi's sons. Segotsho had the backing of **Sebele I** of the BaKwena and other southern Protectorate diKgosi, while Selalabyannye, a minor, was put forward by his half-brother Tshwene and Tshwene's father-in-law **Khama III** of the BaNgwato. The BaKaa divided in November 1892, when Tshwene took his supporters and Selalabyannye to settle at Tlhagakgama (Bokaa) in the Kgatleng. Then, in 1894, Segotsho led his followers out of the Kweneng to found Kalamare, near Shoshong. In 1896, Tshwene broke from Selalabyannye and with his supporters occupied Shoshong, which Khama and the BaNgwato had abandoned in 1889. Other BaKaa wards are found in Sebina (Central District), Molepolole, Serowe, and leTswapong.

KALAHARI. *See* Kgalagadi.

KALANGA (BAKALANGA, also VAKALANGA). Often referred to in SeTswana as "Makalaka/BaKalaka," terms which are pejorative. BaKalanga are the people who live primarily in northeastern Botswana and adjacent western Zimbabwe and who speak IKalanga, a language closely related to ChiShona. The BaKalanga also share with ChiShona-speakers a common historical culture and have absorbed peoples of Tswana, Pedi, and Sotho origins. The BaKalanga constitute the largest non-SeTswana-speaking element in Botswana. Their traditional leaders are called *boShe* (singular *She*). Like the related Chi-Shona group name, VaKaranga, BaKalanga translates as "people of the Sun," in reference to the groups' mythical origin.

The modern BaKalanga are descended from the core element of the **Butwa** kingdom, which became divided into two major lines: the **BaLilima** and the **BaNyayi**. Under the Butwa monarchs known as Nichasike, the boShe of the Mengwe section of the BaKalanga served as regional governors in the area known as Bulila-gwa-Mengwe, which covers modern BuKalanga and the Northeast District as well as the Bulamangwe District in modern Zimbabwe.

Between 1825 and 1840, the Nichasike dynasty, already weakened by internal struggles and competition among the Mambo, Tumbale, and local boShe, fell victim to invasions from the southeast and west. In the late 1820s the Mambo and

Tumbale's forces united to defeat the invading BaNgwato under **Kgari I**. The kingdom collapsed, however, with invasion of the AmaNgoni of Zwangendaba. Around 1839 the last undisputed Mambo, Chilisamhulu Nichasike, committed suicide with many of his followers after being defeated by a breakaway AmaNgoni group led by the warrior queen, Nyamazuma. Soon thereafter, Nyamazuma was married by Mzilikazi of the Ama-**Ndebele**, merging their military forces. After 1840, some BaKalanga fled to the BaNgwato, including the BaKhurutshe who up to then had placed themselves under Mengwe, but most BaKalanga became subjects of the AmaNdebele, whose capital was built at guBulawayo (at modern Bulawayo).

The BaKalanga occupied an area known as the Tati, the control of which became the subject of dispute among the AmaNdebele, the BaNgwato, and European gold-seekers. After gold was discovered at Tati in 1867, the BaNgwato under **Macheng** and the AmaNdebele under Mzilikazi began a long-term dispute over their respective claim to the Bulilamengwe area. In 1880 Mzilikazi's son and successor Lobengula granted a mining concession to the Tati Company. Following the 1893 defeat of the AmaNdebele by Rhodes's **British South Africa Company (BSACO)**, the Bechuanaland Border Police, and BaNgwato regiments, the disputed territory was divided by the British. As a result, the BaKalanga in modern Zimbabwe came under the BSACO, those west of the Shashe river became BaNgwato subjects in an area known as BuKalanga (BuKalaka), and those in the Tati area (the present Northeast District) came under the rule of the Tati Company.

Tati Company rule was harsh. The Company alienated Kalanga land, imposed forced labor, and regulated the local economy to suit its own needs. Initially the company attempted to rule its BaKalanga subjects through the BaKhurutshe Kgosi Rauwe. After the BaKalanga appealed to the Protectorate resident commissioner in Mafikeng, the British established the Tati Native Reserve in the northern part of the Tati Concession for the BaKalanga. The land, however, was woefully inadequate, and many BaKalanga tried to solve their problems of land shortage by migrating into Zimbabwe or the Bangwato Reserve (Central District) or selling their labor on the Tati farms, in Francistown, and at the mines in Rhodesia, Namibia, and South Africa.

In Gammangwato (i.e., Central District), pressure on land also led to conflict. BaNgwato stockholders competed for pasture with BaKalanga agriculturalists. There was a modest boom in BuKalanga with local farmers selling their surpluses to the growing market of Francistown. In 1943 **Tshekedi Khama** attempted to end land disputes once and for all by imposing new boundaries between various BaKalanga peoples and their BaNgwato overlords. He also attempted to alter traditionally scattered BaKalanga settlement patterns by concentrating BaKalanga into Tswana-type villages. Many BaKalanga resisted, foremost among them being **John Madawo Nswazwi**.

After the 1930s, many BaKalanga regarded education as their principal means of advancement and established many self-help schools. The most notable of these was the Tati Training Institution, founded in 1932 by **K.T. Motsete**. The Institution was built by BaKalanga from the Tati Reserve and BaNgwato Reserve under the leadership of their boShe.

Two persistent tendencies merged among the BaKalanga during the colonial period: egalitarian nationalism, for which BaKalanga politicians have achieved prominence particularly in the **Democratic Party** and **Peoples' Party**, and ethnic separatism/traditionalism, which non-politicians have used to articulate BaKalanga resentment toward BaTswana predominance. *See also* Butwa; Lilima; Mwali; Nyayi; Talaote; Tati Concession; Villagization.

KANYE. Capital of the BaNgwaketse since 1853 and oldest of the major BaTswana capitals. Several nineteenth-century buildings, including the house of Bathoen I and the old LMS church, are still standing. In the 1860s Kanye prospered as a trade center for ivory, skins, and ostrich feathers, and in the 1870s it expanded greatly with the added settlement of Mmanaana Kgatla under **Mosielele Pilane**, who established the GaMafikana (Kgatleng) ward. In the twentieth century, Kanye was the first village in the Protectorate to introduce irrigation projects and public standpipes. A small asbestos mine at nearby Moshaneng, first opened in the 1920s, has been in continuous production since the 1950s. In 1991, Kanye had a population of 31,354, second only to **Molepolole** among the largest of Botswana's "rural settlements." *See also* Towns.

KEHERANJU, MONJUKU ("PHAKALANE") (1925–). Paramount leader of the OvaMbanderu section of the OvaHerero, based at Sehitwa. In the mid-1950s he used his position as headman to agitate for a move back to South West Africa and became a strong supporter of South West Africa National Union (SWANU). In 1959 he was deposed by BaTawana Regent **E. Pulane Moremi**, for interfering in the affairs of other OvaHerero wards. In 1960 while his case was being appealed, Keheranju left for Namibia, where the government recognized him as the OvaMbanderu paramount. He is still a resident of Epikuro District. *See also* Herero.

KEITSENG, NTWAESELE THATAYAONE ("FISH") (1919–). Keitseng was Botswana's leading member of the **African National Congress**. After he migrated to South Africa in 1940, he became a member of the African Mineworkers' Union then left the mines in 1947 and joined the ANC. He taught himself to read in a dispatch office and became a political organizer in Newclare Township. In 1956 he helped a large ANC group escape from police custody and gave himself up the day before the Treason Trial. A number of other BaTswana tried with him include **Motsamai Mpho**, Theo Musi, **Z.K. Matthews** and Joe Matthews. Keitseng was acquitted in 1959 and deported to Lobatse. He then became the ANC leader in Botswana until the 1980s, working mostly as a courier for fleeing exiles moving north. Keitseng was also involved in the formation of the **People's Party (BPP)** and its labor union, the Bechuanaland Trade Union Council. After the BPP split in 1962, he stayed in the **Independence Party** for a short time, before joining the **National Front** in 1965. He never stood for office, however, until 1990, when he was elected a councillor in Gaborone.

KGABO I (pre-1700). First Kgosi of the **BaKwena** of Botswana, renowned hunter and warrior. Sometime in the seventeenth century, during a drought, he left his brother, Mogopa of the BaKwena baga Mogopa, in the Transvaal region to settle in the hills around **Molepolole**. There Kgabo found and conquered two related groups of BaKgalagadi, the BaNakedi and the BaKgwatlheng. Kgabo's BaKwena then made the BaKgalagadi pay them tribute in karosses, which were traded over long distances. Kgabo's followers then included the BaNgwato and **BaNgwaketse,** who seceded in the eighteenth century.

KGABO, ENGLISHMAN M.K. ("LENYELESIMANE") (1925–1992). Founding member of the **Democratic Party (BDP)** and member of the Botswana cabinet from 1966 to 1989. Kgabo began his public career as a teacher, then as secretary to the BaKwena Tribal Administration. He emerged as a political leader in 1962 during the succession struggle between **Moruakgomo Sechele** and **Bonewamang Padi Sechele** (Kgabo supported the latter). Kgabo's organizational work for the BDP in the Kweneng established one of the party's strongest bases. Beginning in 1966 he was elected parliamentary member for Molepolole East six times until his retirement in 1989. For much of that time he also served as minister of Local Government and Lands. In retirement he chaired the 1991 Presidential Commission of Inquiry into "Land Problems in Mogoditshane and Other Peri-Urban Areas" and remained active in many community projects.

KGABOESELE, JOHN LEO (1910–1975). Headman of Peleng township, Lobatse, and nationalist politician. One of the early leaders of the **People's Party (BPP)** in the southern Protectorate and chair of the BPP Lobatse branch. He backed **Philip Matante** in the 1962 split, and in 1966 Kgaboesele was the only BPP candidate elected to the Lobatse Town Council. During the early 1960s he hosted a young Mozambican refugee, Samora Machel, who later became the first president of Mozambique (1974–1986).

KGAFELA (pre-1700). First Kgosi of the **Kgafela Kgatla**. According to some traditions, Kgafela or a successor by the same name was a female regent. Those unwilling to accept her authority broke away as the **Mmanaana Kgatla**.

KGAFELA KGATLA (BAKGATLA). The largest branch of the BaKgatla and the largest group of the eastern branch of SeTswana-speaking peoples living in Botswana. They were formed in the late seventeenth/early eighteenth century as an offshoot of the Mosetlha Kgatla in the western Transvaal, and by the early nineteenth century, under Pheto II (1795–1810), had absorbed numerous families and wards to become the dominant morafe north of Rustenburg. Following a civil war and other upheavals caused by the **mfecane**, they reconstituted themselves under **Pilane**, on the veld stretching northeast from the Pilansberg, the mountains named after him by the Rustenburg Boers. During the latter years of the reign of Pilane's son **Kgamanyane**, the BaKgatla suffered increasingly from Boer demands for land and labor. In 1870 Kgamanyane migrated with many of his people and entered the territory of the BaKwena of **Sechele I**, who allowed them to settle at **Mochudi**. The BaKgatla then challenged the BaKwena for outright control of this territory, especially the lands adjoining the Ngotwane and Madikwe rivers, and a protracted war resulted

(1875–1882). The BaKgatla won and have claimed ever since what was, until then, the western Kweneng.

The Kgatleng, as the Bakgatla Reserve/District is known locally, was used to resettle other Kgafela BaKgatla at the **river villages** of Sikwane, Malolwane, and Mathubudukwane, as well as in Morwa, but the Reserve was too small to absorb more than one-half the morafe. The BaKgatla in the Pilansberg lived on farms bought by **Linchwe I** and **Isang Pilane**, the most important of which are Saulspoort 269 (Moruleng) and Holfontein 593 (Mokgalwana). Since 1902 the Transvaal and Botswana sections of the BaKgatla have been under Kgamanyane's successors in Mochudi.

The Kgafela BaKgatla were instrumental in obstructing attempts by the **BSACO** to acquire land and concessions in the Protectorate and in contributing to the defeat of the Boers of the western Transvaal during the **South African War** (1899–1902). They are also the only morafe in the Protectorate/Botswana to have given the **Dutch Reformed Church** a mission monopoly. *See also* BaKgatla National School; Civil Wars; Mmusi; Molefi.

KGALAGADI (BAKGALAGADI). The term is used with reference to the people who either live in or near the Kgalagadi Desert in general or who speak dialects of SeKgalagadi, a Sotho-Tswana language related to but separate from SeTswana. "Kalahari" or more properly Kgalagadi, also is used to refer to the vast desert region of central and western Botswana. The major groups of SeKgalagadi-speakers, significant numbers of whom live in the Southern and Kweneng Districts as well as in the Central, Northwest, Ngamiland, Ghanzi, and Kgalagadi Districts, are BaKgwatheng, BaNgologa, BaBolaongwe, BaPhaleng, and BaShaga. Traditions allege that many BaKgalagadi were living under a BaKgwatheng paramountcy in the Dithejwane area (near present Molepolole), from whence they were driven west by encroaching BaTswana. Others were enslaved by the BaTswana as herders and domestic servants. Since that time, roughly around the beginning of the eighteenth century, the BaKgalagadi have been fragmented. In the nineteenth century BaKgalagadi hunters were important in the trans-Kgalagadi trade, and they were gradually subjugated by the BaTswana as the latter controlled the trade. As game was hunted out and cattle were moved deeper into the Kgalagadi, many BaKgalagadi found themselves herding for the BaKwena,

BaNgwaketse, and BaNgwato, who reduced many to servitude (*bolata*).

During the colonial period their condition scarcely improved. In the beginning the remoteness of the BaKgalagadi enabled them to avoid tax collectors and their BaTswana overlords to subordinate them in the usual way. In the 1930s, however, the colonial tax net enclosed male BaKgalagadi, many of whom became migrant laborers as a result. BaKgalagadi also came under increasing administrative control. In the BaNgwaketse and BaKwena reserves, unpopular chief's representatives were placed in charge of villages into which BaKgalagadi were forcibly settled. In the crown lands to the west of these districts, the government repeatedly attempted to create a BaKgalagadi paramountcy for administrative purposes, but a tangle of competing claims ended the effort in frustration. In the Ghanzi District, too, the 1930s brought hut tax and with it the introduction of a cash economy. Ultimately some BaKgalagadi were able to compete successfully with **Afrikaner** and **OvaHerero** cattle owners.

In the 1950s BaKgalagadi began to assert themselves through local development efforts, independent churches, and eventually party politics. *See also* Battle of Dutlwe; Bolata; Lost City of the Kalahari; Mosirwa Moapare; Puleng, Tumelo; Villagization.

KGAMANE (1828–1916[?]). Son of **Sekgoma I** of the BaNgwato and pretender to the BaNgwato throne. In 1859, he converted to Christianity together with his elder brother **Khama III** and was baptized the following year. In the 1870s he allied himself with his father against Khama but was forced out of Shoshong in 1875. After Kgamane flirted with the Boers as potential allies, Khama allowed him to return to Shoshong. In 1883 he attempted to take control of Shoshong while Khama was busy warding off AmaNdebele threats in the north. He was exiled to the Transvaal where he and **Kgari Macheng** remained thorns in their brother's side until the 1890s, when Kgamane was allowed to return to Gammangwato and was made governor of Shoshong. *See also* Rasebolai Kgamane.

KGAMANYANE. Son of Pilane and fifteenth Kgosi of the **Kgafela Kgatla**, who ruled from 1848 until his death in 1875. During the reigns of **Pilane** and Kgamanyane, the BaKgatla lived in the Transvaal under Boer rule. Kgamanyane was a wealthy ivory hunter and trader who accumulated many cattle. For years he got on well with the Boers, particularly Paul Kruger, who was Transvaal's commandant general before becoming its president. Kgamanyane assisted the Boers in their campaigns against the Pedi, Laka, and Sotho, helped them raid for cattle and slaves, and became very wealthy in the process. He married at least forty-four wives. From 1860 he lived on Paul Kruger's farm (Saulspoort), where at Kruger's encouragement he permitted Henry Gonin of the **Dutch Reformed Church** to establish a mission nearby at Welgeval in 1866. In 1869 resistance to Boer demands for BaKgatla labor led to rumors that Kgamanyane was plotting rebellion, whereupon he was rounded up. Kruger himself thrashed Kgamanyane publicly. In September 1870 Kgamanyane fled with many of his followers to the territory of the BaKwena of **Sechele I**, who allowed them to settle at Mochudi in 1872. Kgamanyane died in Mochudi in May 1875, and in August the BaKwena attacked the BaKgatla in order to drive them out of their territory. Bogatsu, Kgamanyane's brother, ruled as regent until the end of the year, when Kgamanyane's son **Linchwe I** was installed. *See also* Civil Wars.

KGAMPU KAMODI. A commoner who played a prominent role in BaNgwaketse affairs, particularly as the principal member of the BaNgwaketse Tribal Council during the regency of **Ntebogang** (1924–1928). Upon assuming power in 1928, **Bathoen II** abolished the Council and had Kgampu tried and exiled for witchcraft. He died sometime in the 1940s.

KGARAXUMAE. Elusive nineteenth-century Shua-Khoe leader whose resistance to the BaNgwato has taken on legendary status in oral tradition. He is credited with preserving his people's independence in the region around Nata for a generation. His legacy was subsequently taken up by such "social bandits" as **Twai Twai Molele**.

KGARI I ("PEBANE") (1775[?]–1826). Known for his strong personality, Kgari was Kgosi of the BaNgwato from 1817 until his death. Though only of the third *lapa* ("house"), Kgari named Sekgoma I his heir to bogosi. He is remembered as the "inventor" of the *kgamelo* system of *mafisa* among the BaNgwato and BaTawana. His rule coincided with the beginning of the effects of the **mfecane** in Botswana. He spent much of his reign leading northern BaTswana resistance against the **BaKololo**. A large faction of the then fragmented **BaKwena**

joined him, and he ransomed **Sechele I** from the BaKololo leader Sebetwane. A series of defeats, as well as drought, forced Kgari to attempt to recoup his losses by raiding the BaKalanga areas of northeastern Botswana and western Zimbabwe. After brief success raiding cattle among the BaKalanga, he was defeated and may have been killed near the Matopos hills. **Khama III** later used this campaign as justification for his claims of paramountcy over the BaKalanga.

KGARI, BAKWENA (1921–1977). Administrator for the Witwatersrand Native Labor Administration and for the Bechuanaland Protectorate government. Educated at **Tiger Kloof**, he was elected to parliament in 1965 for Serowe South. He served as minister of Home Affairs.

KGARI MACHENG ("LEPHUTSE") (d. 1913[?]). Pretender to the BaNgwato throne. He was the son of **Macheng**, who ruled from 1857–1859 and 1866–1872. Following Macheng's death in 1873, Kgari became the leader of his father's followers in exile in Gangwaketse. He returned to Gammangwato in 1898. *See also* Khama III; Ngwato.

KGARI SECHELE II (1904–1962). Kgosi of the BaKwena, 1931–1962. After the British deposed his elder brother **Sebele II**, the BaKwena appointed Kgari acting Kgosi. The British then officially declared Kgari Kgosi, though in doing so they violated SeTswana laws of succession and offended most of the BaKwena, who still considered Sebele II the rightful heir. Kgari depended on British support to enforce his authority, which was openly resisted until Sebele's death in exile in 1939. Thereafter Kgari was able to consolidate his power if not his legitimacy. During **World War II** he served as regimental sergeant-major in the AAPC. For the rest of his reign, Kgari governed in an authoritarian manner with British support. In 1952 Kgari represented the Protectorate at the Coronation of Queen Elizabeth II, though in the same year Kgari upset the British by insisting on accommodating a group of South African refugees within the Kwena Reserve.

During the 1950s Kgari turned down an invitation from **Bathoen II** and **Tshekedi Khama** to assume the ceremonial title of paramount chief or king of Bechuanaland within the context of a proposed Federated African Authority. In his later years, Kgari repeatedly maintained that BaKwena chieftainship would die with him. He opposed, but ultimately felt powerless to stop, the new democratic nationalist politics. In 1962 he chaired a meeting between **Seretse Khama** and the diKgosi of the southern Protectorate which failed to end mutual suspicions. *See also* Letlole Mosielele.

KGOSI. The plural form of Kgosi is diKgosi. Kgosi is a term often translated as "chief" or "king," but it has no suitable English equivalent. The office occupied by a Kgosi and the institutional prerogatives attached to the office are known as *bogosi*. The role of this title holder has also changed over time.

In the pre-colonial era any group of SeTswana-speakers, who looked on themselves as territorially independent (i.e., as a morafe), accepted the seniority of one lineage as well as the leadership of the male recognized as its senior descendant, on whom was bestowed the title Kgosi. By virtue of birth, the Kgosi retained for life this title and the authority of the office—he could be removed only through assassination or by being forced to flee. The Kgosi was also the supreme lawmaker, judge, military commander, prayer-giver, spiritual practitioner, and treaty-maker. His power was, however, restricted by the fact that his subjects had to be on the move more or less constantly. The ordinary requirements of farming, hunting, and herding led to considerable dispersal of families and individuals for much of the year, and the irregularity of rainfall and surface water often led to the breakup of settlements, scattering of populations, and violent competition within and among neighboring groups for scarce resources. Under such circumstances, it was impossible for a Kgosi to remain an absolute dictator for long, regardless of the will to become so. SeTswana history is full of failed attempts, and where diKgosi succeeded in building large, unitary states they tended to do so by serving the interests of a substantial part of the community rather than simply commanding obedience. As the SeTswana saying goes, *Kgosi ke Kgosi ka batho* ("the Kgosi is Kgosi by the grace of the people"). The morafe of the strongest Kgosi was in fact a fragile state that, given several years of strain, could decline rapidly (*See* Civil Wars).

The Kgosi acquired much better opportunities for gaining power and influence during the colonial period. For three generations after 1885, the government depended on diKgosi to administer much of the vast Protectorate. Until the 1950s, few white administrators were stationed inside the Protectorate. After boundaries were fixed and taxes introduced, Africans and even long-term European residents inside a "tribal reserve" had more or less to become obedient subjects of the Kgosi. The Kgosi was expected to control his people. A Kgosi could easily become an authoritarian, confident that the colonial government was in most cases prepared to back him.

The Kgosi's own subjects gave power to the "chief" as much as did the colonial government. They needed a Kgosi in office by whatever means necessary in order to manipulate the colonial system, minimize its ravages, and modernize the reserve because the government would not. Thus, the Kgosi became the focus of the hopes of the people as well as the colonial government, just as his favor and commitment became objects of their courtship. The Kgosi similarly enjoyed a corresponding freedom to spurn their affection, indulge their patience, and get his own way (or hers—for female rulers, all regents, *see* Gagoangwe, Ntebogang, and Moremi, P.). Many diKgosi greatly angered and/or disappointed the colonial government, and others had the same effect on their subjects. Yet only two diKgosi were removed permanently from office by the British—with great difficulty over loud public protest—and only one was assassinated (by a jealous brother).

Since independence, diKgosi have been demoted by the people and the central government. This trend is not connected with any radical loss of function. The modern Kgosi sits atop a "Tribal Authority," which remains part of local administration, the adjudication of disputes, allocation of land, communication of the concerns of the public and the government to one another, and the organization of community activities. He (no females have ruled since independence) is still treated with respect in public. The Kgosi is no longer in a position to exercise power, whether locally as an individual or nationally as part of a group. The so-called "House of Chiefs" meets in Gaborone in parallel with parliament, but its sessions are largely ceremonial; its members discuss common issues but exercise no veto over parliamentary legislation or its other proceedings. *See also* Bathoen I; Bathoen II; Kgari Sechele; Khama III; Letsholo; Molefi; Regency; Sebele II; Sechele II; Seepapitso I; Tshekedi Khama.

KGOSIDINTSI ("RADITSEBE") (1810[?]—1903). Half-brother to **Sechele I** After Sechele converted to Christianity, Kgosidintsi became the leader of the non-Christian section of the BaKwena and oversaw such important institutions as *bogwera* (**initiation**). At the time missionaries spoke of two factions within the morafe, but in fact the two brothers cooperated to ensure social harmony. Eventually Kgosidintsi advocated collaboration with the British as the surest way of preserving BaKwena autonomy. His influence was also crucial in the succession of **Sebele I**. *See also* Baruti Kgosidintsi, Sebele I.

KGOTLA. The SeTswana term for the basic socio-political unit within traditional Tswana society. The word (plural *dikgotla*; alternatively: *makgotla*; singular *lekgotla*) refers to the enclosures which serve as the loci for participatory decision-making and/or the public legitimization of decisions. DiKgotla exist and operate at all levels of Tswana society from the family cluster through larger lineage and ward groupings to the central kgotla of the morafe, which was presided over by the paramount Kgosi. The word is often used to identify the membership and location of a given kgotla ("I am of goraTsheko," etc.). (Le)kgotla may also refer to other collective organizations and institutions such as political parties (lekgotla la Domkrag, i.e. the **Democratic Party**), civic groups (lekgotla la chuto le tiro, Foundation of Education with Production), social societies, and the National Assembly (Lekgotla la Sechaba).

KGWEBE HILLS. A group of hills east of Lake Ngami, south of the tsetse fly belt, said to be named after a local BaSarwa chief. In the seventeenth and eighteenth centuries the hills' iron deposits were exploited, probably by Ba**Rolong** from the northern Cape and Ba**Kwena** from southern Botswana. The ore was apparently exhausted by the time the Ba**Tawana** settled there in 1795 and used the area's deep wells. Over the next century the hills were the site of decisive BaTawana victories over the BaNgwato in around 1810 and the BaKololo in 1854. In 1888 the area was ceded to concessionaires and became the base of **LMS** and BWCCO activities in the 1890s. Today Kgwebe is primarily a grazing area. *See also* Concessions.

KHAMA III (1835[?]–1923). Kgosi of the BaNgwato, 1872–1873 and 1875–1923. Leading supporter of British rule and widely known reformer. Born Khama Boikanyo Sekgoma, he was converted in 1859, along with his brother **Kgamane**, while in exile at Dithubaruba and baptized a Christian in 1860 by Heinrich Schulenberg of the Hermannsburg mission. In 1863 he successfully led the BaNgwato against the AmaNdebele.

His Christian beliefs led him increasingly into conflict with his father **Sekgoma I**, and his uncle, **Macheng**. In 1872, with BaKwena backing, Khama overthrew Macheng but failed to gain enough internal support to prevent Sekgoma from retaking the throne the following year. In 1875, Khama made his second bid for power, and this time he succeeded.

In the 1870s Khama foresaw the establishment of white hegemony and thereafter assiduously recruited British imperial support against the white settler threat. He was particularly adept at developing a political constituency in London through such figures as **John Mackenzie** to avert control from Cape Town. He also turned to the British in anticipation of their help in dealing with Boers wishing to enter his territory. In 1877, when the **Dorsland Trekkers** asked Khama's permission to cross Gammangwato, he asked the British to turn them back, which they refused to do. Nevertheless, seven years later, Khama enthusiastically welcomed the **Warren Expedition** and remained a loyal British subject thereafter. During the early colonial period, Khama frequently assisted, and volunteered to help, the British in establishing their authority in the Protectorate and in Central Africa. In return the British helped Khama to extend the boundaries of Gammangwato. By the time of the 1889 **Kopong Conference**, Khama was being shunned by other diKgosi, who called him the "white man's chief." In 1890 he assisted Rhodes's Pioneer Column in the early stages of **BSACO** conquest of Zimbabwe, and from 1892 to 1893 he offered to send his regiment against the diKgosi of southern Botswana who were then resisting the British administration. In 1893 BaNgwato regiments fought alongside the BBP in the war against Lobengula's army. After this campaign, Khama consolidated his hold on the BaKalanga communities of northern Botswana.

By 1894 Khama had come to realize the extent of the threat posed by the BSACO. At the same time internal opposition to Khama was mounting under the leadership of his brothers, Raditladi and Phetu Mphoeng. Khama joined **Bathoen I** and **Sebele I** in a visit to London to protest against the imminent handover of the Protectorate to BSACO control. The three diKgosi obtained limited guarantees of continued imperial protection, but only the failure of the **Jameson Raid** stopped the transfer.

Khama was greatly influenced by missionary teachings of Christian civilization. He attempted to abolish traditional institutions central to SeTswana culture: bogwera/bojale initiation schools), bogadi (bridewealth), rainmaking, polygamy, and the making and drinking of all forms of **alcohol**.

Khama's strained relationship with his son and heir **Sekgoma**

II seriously affected the morafe. Mainly because of Khama's autocratic methods, their conflict culminated in Sekgoma's exile (in 1898 to Lephephe, moving in 1907 to Nata with 2,000 followers); father and son were belatedly reconciled in 1920.

Following the demarcation of boundaries in 1899, Khama ruled over the largest reserve in the Protectorate. About a fifth of Khama's subjects were BaNgwato; the rest were BaKalanga, BaTswapong, and other subordinate groups. Khama ran his reserve by appointing district governors and creating a large administrative bureaucracy. In 1889 he moved the capital from Shoshong to Palapye and, in 1902, to Serowe, where it has been since. Khama was a shrewd and effective economist; in the nineteenth century he successfully introduced elements of private enterprise, privatized state cattle herds, and, in 1910, launched a trading company that became too profitable for the likes of big capital, the representatives of which had the British close it down in 1916.

In the twilight years of his reign Khama III grew disenchanted with British overrule, but he died a legendary figure in Great Britain and in international circles. Khama III was regarded as a model chief, and the reputation of "Khama the Great" has survived him by more than a half-century. *See also* Archives; Birwa; Civil Wars; Kalanga; Kgari Macheng; Kgamane; Initiation; Ratshosa Motswetle; Seleka; Three Kings in London; Zambia.

KHAMA, ELISABETA GOBITSAMANG (1846–1889). First wife of **Khama III** and mohumagadi ("queen") of the BaNgwato. She was named after Robert Moffat's daughter and became a Christian in April 1862, barely a month prior to her marriage to the youthful Khama. She was the mother of several daughters, one of whom, Bessie, married Khama's advisor, Ratshosa. Elisabeta's only son was **Sekgoma**, who later assumed bogosi. Undoubtedly, Elisabeta was the favorite among the four wives Khama married in his lifetime. She is popularly believed by BaTswana to have been the mother of Seretse, her grandson.

KHAMA, SEMANE SETLHOKO (1881–1937). The last of Khama's four wives, whom he married in 1900 after meeting her in church. Of BaLete descent, she was a devout Christian teacher. Semane bore **Tshekedi Khama** and his elder sister Bonyerile. She became unpopular in 1925 when **Sekgoma II** fell ill, and she and the Ratshosa family made efforts to have Sekgoma treated by a European doctor. When Sekgoma died, she and the Ratshosas were nearly lynched for murdering him through witchcraft. Nevertheless, during her last twelve years as mohumagadi, Semane attained great popularity. She promoted modern midwifery and medicine, perhaps because three of her children died young. Semane was active in the Women's Christian Temperance Union, earning the Union's banner for the highest number of recruits in 1933. In addition she promoted organized children's activities and was a long-time LMS deaconess. In 1936, she badgered Tshekedi into marrying Bagakgametse, her long-time match for him. This ill-fated union lasted but one year.

KHOE (also KXOE). The largest sub-grouping of languages within the **Khoisan** language family. About 80 percent of Botswana's Khoisan-speakers belong to such major Khoe groups as **Deti**, **/Gwi**, **Kxoe**, **Nama**, **Naro**, **Shua**, and **Tshu**. Outside of Botswana the Khoikhoi of the western Cape and original **Griqua** were also Khoe. Non-Khoe Khoisan speakers include the **Zhu** and **!Xo**. The word Khoe, along with such equivalents as Khoi, Kxoe, Kwa, and Qua, literally means "people." Those who use it to apply to themselves are often referred to by others as, inter alia, Ba**Sarwa**, **San**, or **Bushmen**.

KHOISAN. Along with Bantu, one of two language families indigenous to southern Africa. Khoisan is a linguistic term applied to the speakers of a wide range of languages (often grouped indiscriminately as "click" languages) spoken by the Khoikhoi (so-called "Hottentots") of antiquity, their **Nama** and Bastaard descendants, and by the so-called "bushmen" peoples of the dry regions of southern Angola, western and central Botswana, Namibia, and the northern Cape. In Botswana at least eleven major Khoisan languages, as well as a great diversity of dialects, are spoken by an estimated 60,000 people. Speakers of these languages are usually known to BaTswana as "BaSarwa." Khoisan-speakers for generations have practiced a variety of ways of life and have exhibited a range of physical characteristics. *See also* Bolata; Bushman; /Gwi; Hottentot; Khoe; Kxoe; Naro; San; Sarwa; Shua; Slave Trade; Tshu.

KHUKWE MOGODI (1829–1925). One of the first ordained MoTswana ministers of the **London Missionary Society (LMS)**. Mogodi was a MoHurutshe who fled Boer rule in the 1850s to live at Kuruman. He worked for Robert Moffat as a servant and was soon baptized and educated by his stern master. Later he attended the Mackenzie Bible School in Shoshong and was ordained.

In 1877 he accompanied James Hepburn on an unsuccessful attempt to establish a mission in Ngamiland. He then worked at Shoshong until 1883, when he was reassigned to Ngamiland, where he lived the rest of his life. He appears to have had indifferent success as a minister but did good work as royal amanuensis and as a hunter-trader. Except for the 1893–1896 period, he ran the LMS's religious and education programs in Ngamiland. By the late 1890s Mogodi had alienated many BaTawana by preaching against slavery, initiation, paganism, and casual sex. In 1905, after he argued with **Sekgoma Letshola-thebe**, the Kgosi asked the LMS to hold an inquiry into Mogodi's own slave-owning and trading activities. The LMS cashiered Mogodi, who moved with his family to the Boteti, where he lived out his years. *See also* Bolata; Maphakela Lekalake.

KHURUTSHE (BAKHURUTSHE). A branch of the BaHurutshe who came to be known as BaKhurutshe by their Ikalanga-speaking neighbors. By the end of the eighteenth century they were living in northeast Botswana. Around 1840 they were conquered by the AmaNdebele, but under the leadership of Sekoko in 1864 they fled to the BaNgwato at Shoshong. Sekoko's son Rauwe returned to the northeast in 1895 settling on what had been declared Tati Company lands. Rauwe supported a short-lived (1904–1908) independent BaKhurutshe Free Church, which was absorbed into the **Anglican** Church. In 1913 the morafe split. The largest group, led by Rauwe, moved into the Bamangwato Reserve and founded Tonota. BaKhurutshe Anglicans were persecuted off and on during the reign of **Tshekedi Khama**. The smaller group remained in the Tati, where they continued to suffer from lack of land. *See also* Ngwato; Ramokate, Pelaelo.

KOLOLO (BAKOLOLO). A group of BaFokeng bagaPatsa (classified as both southern BaTswana and as BaSotho), who invaded Botswana during the **mfecane** and settled briefly at **Dithubaruba** in the Kweneng District and in Ngamiland before moving north to Zambia. Their leader was Sebetwane (ruled 1820[?]–1851). He defeated most of the BaTswana groups that opposed him, causing the fragmentation of the pre-mfecane BaTswana states. He failed to defeat the Ba**Ngwaketse** under

Sebego I, who defeated his forces at Dithubaruba in 1826. The BaKololo made no attempt to establish control over wide areas, preferring instead to move in search of cattle to raid for the replenishing of their losses. Sebetwane is remembered as the greatest cattle thief in Botswana history. The BaKololo lost all their cattle inside Botswana on several occasions, at Dithubaruba, then in the Kgalagadi, and later in Ghanzi. In 1835 they took many BaTawana into captivity on their move toward southern Zambia. After settling along the Chobe river, Sebetwane's people attracted **David Livingstone**. Livingstone's faith in the SeTswana language as a medium for the whole of Central Africa was based on the false assumption that the BaKololo would expand. *See also* Battle of Dithubaruba.

KOMA, GAOBAMONG KENNETH SHOLO (1924–). Politician; founder and leader of the **National Front (BNF)**. Born in Mahalapye, Kenneth Koma first entered politics in the early 1950s during the BaNgwato Crisis, when he and many other young, educated men became vocal supporters of **Seretse Khama** against his uncle, **Tshekedi Khama**. During the 1950s and early 1960s, Koma spent most of his time in South Africa, Britain, Czechoslovakia, and the Soviet Union. While abroad he qualified as a lawyer, earned a doctorate in Moscow, became the secretary of the Union of African Students in Czechoslovakia, and married a Czech woman. He returned to the Protectorate in 1965 to witness the overwhelming victory of the **Democratic Party (BDP)**, about which he became disgruntled. Between April and October 1965 Koma held a series of meetings in Mochudi in which he attempted to forge a coalition of anti-BDP groups. Out of these meetings emerged the National Front.

A proponent of Scientific Socialism, Koma has since 1965 sought to unite a broad spectrum of BaTswana within the Front. In recent years he has pushed his party toward Social Democracy. He was elected for the first time to the National Assembly in 1984 as MP for Gaborone South and has remained in parliament ever since, serving all the while as the BNF leader.

KOPONG CONFERENCE (FEBRUARY 1889). The meeting between **Sidney Shippard**, the British deputy commissioner for the Protectorate, and the BaTswana diKgosi held at Kopong in February 1889, at which the southern Protectorate diKgosi joined together for the first time to protest British imperialism. The meeting was suggested by Sebele of the BaKwena the previous December after Shippard had hinted at the annexation of their territories "to the dominions of the Great Queen." Shippard sent with the invitations to the conference an agenda which included such issues as common defense against invasion; medicine and hospitals; hut tax; the opening of permanent waters; the telegraph; the railway; and the amicable settlement of all disputes between diKgosi. The agenda shocked the southern diKgosi who were not prepared for the proposed extent of British interference in their affairs. Shippard had in fact exceeded his authority. The meeting itself lasted long enough for **Bathoen I, Linchwe I,** and **Sebele I** to declare their opposition to the agenda, although **Khama III** was quite willing to cooperate. Shippard broke up the meeting with nothing achieved except the further alienation of the southern diKgosi from both himself and Khama III. Khama III later alleged that he had successfully opposed a scheme hatched by Sebele for the murder of Shippard. *See also* British South Africa Company; Grobler Affair; Orders-in-Council; Protectorate.

KOPPER, SIMON. *See* Nama-German War of 1904–1909.

!KUNG BUSHMEN. *See* Zhu.

KWELE, DANIEL (1928–1991). Politician of many stripes. He began his public service as a teacher and became the secretary of the North East District Council. He was the first president of the **National Front**, from which he later resigned following the entry of **Bathoen II**, joined the **Democratic Party (BDP)**, and became a vocal opponent of what he termed "feudalism." In 1979 he was elected to the National Assembly and was appointed assistant minister for Local Government and Lands, which he held until 1983. Kwele then resigned from the BDP and formed his own party, the Botswana Progressive Union (BPU), which failed to win a seat in the 1984 and 1989 elections. He was BPU president until his death.

KWENA (BAKWENA). Several BaKwena groups, who share the totem *kwena* (crocodile), live in southern Africa. In Botswana they are represented by the BaKwena-bagaKgabo (alternatively known as Baga-Sechele, or Baga-Molepolole), traditionally the senior morafe in Botswana. Their seniority has been attested in three respects. First, according to some traditions, all BaTswana had the crocodile as their totem. Second, the BaKwena claim to be the owners of the land that is now

Botswana, having conquered the BaKgalagadi and protected it in the nineteenth century from Boer incursions. (The date of BaKwena penetration into the Kgalagadi is unknown, but oral traditions suggest it was not later than 1700). Third, the Ba-Ngwato, BaNgwaketse, and BaTawana recognize their Ba-Kwena origin and defer to the BaKwena in matters relating to ritual seniority.

Modern BaKwena history begins with the reunification of the morafe by **Sechele I** (1829[?]–1892) following the disruptions of the **mfecane**. Under Sechele, the morafe greatly increased its numbers by absorbing refugees of both Tswana and non-Tswana origin. By placing these newcomers under the direct authority of the royal (BaKgosing) ward, Sechele was able to strengthen his bogosi and use it to capitalize on the growth in the trans-Kgalagadi trade. After 1850 the BaKwena became the most powerful and prosperous morafe in the region.

In the 1870s BaKwena power declined. The trans-Kgalagadi trade shifted northward, and new states such as the Ba**Ngwato** and **Kgafela Kgatla** asserted themselves. After 1875 they lost large portions of their southern and eastern territories and access to the Ngotwane and Madikwe rivers. Their herds remained comparatively small as a result. In the 1880s and 1890s the BaKwena lacked the resources to resist colonial rule, even though they and the other southern merafe were suspicious of British motives. In 1899 the BaKwena Reserve boundary was demarcated and the hut tax imposed. By then the ecological crises of the 1890s had decimated the population and driven many BaKwena into labor migration, a dependence which became central to the economy of the morafe in the twentieth century and remained so past Botswana's independence.

KXOE. Often referred to by outsiders as the "River Bushmen" or, in SeTswana, as "Banoka," the Kxoe are a branch of Khoe-speakers who have long survived by fishing and foraging in the swamps of the **Okavango Delta**. *See also* Khoe.

L

LABOR. *See* Employment; Migrant Labor; Trade Unions.

LAND TENURE. In pre-colonial times, the Kgosi and dikgosana were responsible for the allocation of land. The concepts of "private" and "public" land were not relevant, although wells and other improvements to the land were regarded as personal property. Families were allocated land for residential, farming, and grazing purposes. Once that land was allocated, it became inheritable by the family, though not transferable by them. And, because merafe tended to move their capitals every generation or so, no system of land ownership emerged.

In the colonial period land tenure assumed three forms: tribal, Crown, and freehold. Tribal land consisted of the "Native Reserves," most of which were demarcated in 1899. With the exception of the **Barolong Farms**, Africans were prohibited from owning land on an individual basis. The British recognized a "chief" in each reserve as the owner of all reserve land. Crown land was the area reserved by the British and made the property of the colonial state. Freehold land existed in areas owned by concession companies—in the Tati District, the Ghanzi Farms, and the Tuli, Gaberones, and Lobatse Blocks.

In 1968 the former reserves became Tribal Areas, and the use of land within was regulated by local Land Boards. Normally only individuals legally registered as members of the tribe may apply for land from their respective Land Boards. Since independence most of the Crown land has also been turned into Tribal Areas; what remained has been set aside for national parks and game reserves, or in a few cases made into freehold areas (e.g., the Molopo Farms). In 1976 the government initiated the Tribal Grazing Land Policy (TGLP) intended to promote "modern" ranching techniques, but the TGLP scheme failed miserably, leaving unclear the status of the land privatized under its auspices. More recently, the Botswana High Court has declared in the Matlo case (in which dubious testimony was admitted) that communal land in the Kweneng allocated before the establishment of Land Boards can be bought and sold without reference to land boards, but it is too early to tell whether communal land is being privatized as a result. The government has apparently ignored this ruling in removing "squatters" from Mogoditshane. In 1993 the Tribal Land (Amendment) Bill, which proposed making all land purchasable by any citizen, came before the National Assembly. It met stiff opposition from constituencies around Gaborone and Lobatse, where land pressures are greatest and where persons registered as members of the BaNgwaketse, BaKwena, BaTlokwa, and Kgafela Kgatla only are entitled to communal lands on the outskirts of these growing urban districts. *See also* Administration; Boundaries; British South Africa Company; Concessions; Economy; Reserves; Towns.

LAWYERS. In the late nineteenth century, BaTswana discovered the use of lawyers in protecting individual and group interests in their dealings with the British crown, the **BSACO**, the Protectorate, the South African governments, and each other. Because Cape law (i.e., Roman-Dutch) applied in the courts to which BaTswana had access, lawyers were hired for the purpose of challenging proclamations, protectorate rulings, the seizure of property, the disallowing of concessions, denial of group rights, and licensing of undesirable traders. Lawyers represented BaTswana charged in colonial courts with violations of noncustomary law, witnessed their purchase of land, helped prevent their arrest without legal process, corresponded on their behalf, and even loaned them money. Friendship and loyalty between lawyers and their BaTswana clients was not unusual. Douglas Buchanan, a Cape Town advocate, was Tshekedi Khama's confidant for nearly a quarter century. Others closer to the Protectorate, such as the Minchin & Kelly and Fraenkel firms in Mafikeng, de Kock in Rustenburg, Coulson in Zeerust, and Raphaely in Bulawayo, were well known to Africans in the Bechuanaland Protectorate. By 1910 royals embroiled in civil proceedings invariably resorted to lawyers.

Since independence, the legal profession has expanded greatly, particularly with the establishment of a law degree program at the University of Botswana. A self-regulating legal society has also been formed. *See also* Tshekedi Khama.

LEAPETSWE KHAMA (1939–1986). Eldest son of **Tshekedi Khama**. In 1960 Leapetswe abandoned his studies at Trinity College, Dublin to return home to take care of his late father's estate. He then became a Pilikwe headman and an early adherent of the **People's Party**. He served as Bangwato Tribal Authority, 1963–1973, succeeding **Rasebolai Kgamane**.

LEBOTSE, KGOSI D. Born in Mochudi; gadfly proto-nationalist, pioneer journalist. Son of a junior royal in the Ralebotsa ward and crony of **Molefi**, Lebotse helped found the **Ipelegeng** group, which was banned by the Protectorate government in 1937, and became a member of the **ZCC**, then a quasi-political religious sect. From 1947–1964 he edited the Argus-owned commercial weekly, *Naledi ya Batswana*. At independence, he joined the

Information and Broadcasting Department. *See also* Masire, Quett; Newspapers.

LEKALAKE MOITSHEKI (d. 1886). Prominent member of a famous family of traditional doctors, or dingaka. Lekalake was the son of Moitsheki Motsemme (RaLekalake), possibly of northern Transvaal origin, from a prominent clan of dingaka. Moitsheki trained among the BaTlhaping, then set up operations in the Kweneng after the **mfecane**, where **David Livingstone** interested him in Christianity and taught him basic literacy. Moitsheki worked as the missionary's cook to earn the cash to buy books. Nevertheless, he remained a traditionalist in his religion. Lekalake's father worked for various diKgosi, such as Moshweshwe, Gasebone, and **Kgamanyane**, but most notably for **Sechele I** and **Sekgoma I**, both of whom he taught. His family established their own village in the Kweneng, "founded on doctoring," but Sechele forced Moitsheki to relocate at **Dithubaruba** (ca. 1857). His son Lekalake then assumed prominence, and served Sechele as a ngaka. Lekalake then had a falling out with Sechele, moved to Shoshong, and involved himself in the intrigues of the period. Lekalake's sons and relatives became Christian converts, and his son **Maphakela Lekalake** became an ordained minister.

The Lekalake family illustrates how the fledgling **LMS** gained early converts and priests. A high percentage of this group were dingaka.

LENYELETSE MPETWANE SERETSE (1920–1983). Politician, vice president of Botswana, 1980–1983. Member of a prominent BaNgwato family and from his youth a close friend and political ally of his cousin, **Seretse Khama**. He had a gift for organization. When Seretse Khama was exiled to London, Lenyeletse led the group of young, educated BaNgwato who agitated for his return. He also supported such liberal causes as the end of prohibition in the reserve and the end of the **LMS** religious monopoly. He was interested in **trade unions** and organized the Serowe branch of the BPWU. He also organized sports and social clubs which often served as fora for political debate. Lenyeletse was a founding member of the **Democratic Party**. He served as BaNgwato tribal secretary in 1964, and in 1969 he entered the National Assembly, remaining in national office until his death. In 1974 he joined the cabinet, where he held portfolios in the ministries of Heath, Agriculture, and Local Government and Lands.

LESHOMA MASSACRE (15 FEBRUARY 1978). The worst single attack inside Botswana during the Zimbabwean Liberation War. On 15 February 1978, near the village of Leshoma in northeast Botswana, a **BDF** patrol was ambushed by Rhodesian security forces. Fifteen BDF soldiers and two BaTswana civilians were killed, and eight civilians were wounded in the attack. The ambush was apparently a premeditated attempt to intimidate the newly-formed BDF. In response to the massacre, the Botswana government took a harder line against the Rhodesians.

LETE (BALETE). The BaLete, who originated among the Transvaal AmaNdebele, have their capital at Ramotswa, Southeast District. According to oral traditions, they broke away from the Transvaal AmaNdebele (unrelated to Mzilikazi's AmaNdebele) under the leadership of Malete and settled among BaTswana groups in the western Transvaal. By the early nineteenth century the Ba-Malete (as they are sometimes called) had assimilated SeTswana language and culture. During the reign of Makgosi I (1820–1886), the BaLete came into conflict with the Boers and sought refuge with **Sechele I** of the BaKwena. In 1863 Makgosi left Sechele and established Mmankgodi, where from 1865 they were hosts to Lutheran missionaries. In 1875 they moved to Ramotswa in an area then claimed by the BaNgwaketse. During the **Civil Wars** they were allies of the **Kgafela Kgatla**. In 1881 the BaLete defeated and inflicted heavy casualties on a large BaNgwaketse force attacking Ramotswa. Ikaneng, Makgosi's son, was credited with leading the defense. Makgosi died in 1886, and Ikaneng succeeded (1886–1896), but for years his cousin Pule challenged his right to the throne. The British backed Ikaneng, and in 1891 Pule and his followers moved to the BaKwena and established the BaLete village of Gabane. Ikaneng was troubled by continued BaNgwaketse claims to Ramotswa and its environs and by the **BSACO**, to which in 1895 Ikaneng ceded his territory. The **Jameson Raid** led to the scrapping of the concession, and the British established a separate BaLete Reserve. The reserve was much too small and remained so, although the BaLete later bought adjacent farms and the BaNgwaketse transferred land to them in exchange for Crown land. The BaLete, many of whose early diKgosi did not convert to Christianity, are the only BaTswana group to have maintained bogwera and bojale throughout the colonial era and after independence. *See also* Initiation; Lutherans; Roman Catholics.

LETLOLE MOSIELELE (1911–1991). From 1940 until his death, Kgosi of the **Mmanaana Kgatla** at Thamaga. He succeeded his grandfather, **Gobuamang**, when his elder brother Diratsame refused bogosi. A strong ruler, Letlole often clashed with his overlord **Kgari Sechele**, most notably in the mid-1950s, when Letlole and other "headmen" in eastern Kweneng were sentenced to prison for failing to suppress **initiation**. Letlole appealed to the High Court, which overturned Kgari's judgment even though it had been backed by the British. Letlole was a member of the African Advisory Council, the JAC, and LEGCO. *See also* Councils.

LETSHOLATHEBE I (1830[?]–1874). Kgosi of the BaTawana,1847–1874. In 1835, when the BaTawana were attacked by the **BaKololo**, the young Letsholathebe escaped the fate of most BaTawana, who were either killed or captured, thanks to his nanny, who took him to live among the BaSubiya. Around 1839, he was discovered there by Mogalakwe, his uncle, and returned to his people, where he became Kgosi as a teenager. At the beginning of his reign he developed trading links with the BaKwena, leading to the first visit of **David Livingstone**, in 1849. During the 1850s as a consequence of a boom in the ivory trade, Letsholathebe imported guns and horses which he used to strengthen the BaTawana state. In 1854 his army repelled a BaKololo invasion. During his reign, the BaYei, BaKgalagadi, and BaSarwa inhabitants of Ngamiland were defeated militarily or threatened into subjugation. Some were sold into slavery. He had seven wives, and many of his children were influential into the 1930s. *See also* Slave Trade; Tawana I.

LETSHOLATHEBE II (1941–1981). Kgosi of the BaTawana, 1958–1981. Son of **Moremi II**, who died when Letsholathebe was six years old. Until he reached his majority, Letsholathebe's mother and Moremi's widow, **Elizabeth Pulane Moremi**, served as regent. Letsholathebe II was educated at Kroonstad, Orange Free State, where his boarding master was **Archibald Mogwe**, and in Southend, England, where he boarded with **Linchwe II**.

LETSHOLO. SeTswana term for a communal hunt involving all the adult males of the morafe and carried out on the orders of the **Kgosi**. After the hunt, but before they returned from the veld, the men held a meeting at which great matters of importance were discussed and decided upon. Because men were armed, contentious issues could lead to violence, although such instances were rare. Proceedings of the letsholo were supposed to be confidential, but during the colonial era they became a source of intelligence for the British. *See also* Motswasele II.

LILIMA (BALILIMA). One of two BaKalanga branches, considered to be the older. Apparently the BaLilima lived in Botswana during the Chibundule Dynasty (1450[?]–1680), when one of their chiefly lines provided the Chibundule Mambos. After the Chibundule were overthrown by the Changamire, many BaLilima moved west into the area northwest of modern-day Francistown. They are composed of numerous sub-groups and have assimilated many immigrants over the centuries. *See also* Butwa; Kalanga; Nyayi.

LIMPOPO RIVER. This famous river (the place, according to Rudyard Kipling's apocryphal "Just So" story, where the elephant got its trunk) forms part of Botswana's eastern border. The Botswana side of the Limpopo has never been the site of extensive settlement, due to **tsetse** and malaria. Such small groups as the Ba**Birwa** and Ba**Seleka** have lived in its vicinity. In the big game hunting era it was the site of much BaNgwato hunting. With the advent of colonial rule, the land was alienated and became the **Tuli Block.** White farmers in the area struggled to develop the area agriculturally, and poaching and cattle smuggling instead formed the basis of many livelihoods. As of yet the river, which is narrow and has a habit of drying up, has not been irrigated on the Botswana side. *See also* Boundaries, External; Land Tenure.

LINCHWE I (1859[?]–1924). Kgosi of the **Kgafela Kgatla,**1876–1920, born in Mmasebudule, western Transvaal, died in Mochudi. Son of **Kgamanyane** and his "Great Wife," Dikolo. During Linchwe's forty-four-year reign, the Kgafela Kgatla established themselves as one of the five major BaTswana groups in the Bechuanaland Protectorate. Between 1875 and 1882, they rebelled against the BaKwena of **Sechele I** and won control of the territory which the British demarcated as the BaKgatla Reserve in 1899. During the **South African War,** 1899–1902, BaKgatla regiments fought the Boers at the **Battle of Derdepoort** and in a number of other battles in the Transvaal. Until 1902 they controlled the territory north of Rustenburg on behalf of the British and captured a large number of cattle.

Between 1902 and 1920, Linchwe purchased fourteen farms around Saulspoort in the Transvaal where half of the BaKgatla were settled and ruled by Linchwe's brother, **Ramono Pilane**. Linchwe was baptized into the **Dutch Reformed Church (DRC)** in 1892 after divorcing two of his three wives. He abolished a number of traditions at variance with Christian practice, subsidized the mission, and saw to the building of the DRC church in Mochudi in 1904. He was predeceased by Kgafela Gisbren (d. 1917) and succeeded by **Isang Pilane**, who became regent in 1920 when Linchwe retired due to old age and ill health. *See also* Civil Wars; Maganelo; Molefi; Phiri, Thomas; River Villages.

LINCHWE II (1935–). Present Kgosi of the **Kgafela Kgatla** and only son of **Molefi** and his wife Motlhatse. Linchwe was installed in 1963, succeeding the Regent **Mmusi**, younger brother of his father, who had died in 1958. Educated at St. Joseph's College (Kgale), Emmarentia Geldenhuys School (Warmbaths, Transvaal), and Woodchester Park School (Gloucestershire, England). In 1966 he married Kathleen Nono Motsepe of the royal family of the Mmakau Kgatla in St. Mary's Cathedral, Johannesburg. From 1969 to 1972 Linchwe served as Botswana's Ambassador to the United States, and since independence he has been an active proponent of chieftaincy and traditional institutions. Linchwe has revived **initiation**, taken an active role in the tribal administration, vocally opposed attempts by the national government to reduce the authority of diKgosi, and has used the House of Chiefs as his principal forum to express views of a national character. He has also used his office for liberalizing purposes, such as opening the **kgotla** to women (1964). Though allied at times with opposition politicians, Linchwe II has remained outside any political party. Recently he has served as president of the Customary Court of Appeal and had his status as paramount of the Kgafela Kgatla of the Transvaal and Botswana confirmed by a South African court. *See also* Mitchison, Naomi; Mochudi.

LITERACY. Like most Africans elsewhere, BaTswana were illiterate until their languages were converted into written form by European missionaries keen on producing biblical texts in African languages. In the 1830s, following Robert Moffat's conversions, literacy increased as he and other **LMS** missionaries trained converts and their children to read and produced religious books and newspapers for them. Written composition in **SeTswana** began with translations of Christian texts by Moffat, who after producing a spelling book and catechism in 1826, published the Gospel of St. Luke four years later. Moffat's converts formed the core of BaTswana missionaries and the secretaries attached to BaTswana diKgosi. Another important agent of literacy was the Boer slave-owning class, who taught their *inboekelinge* (slaves, literally "apprentices") to read the Dutch Bible. In the 1860s and 1870s some ex-slaves settled on mission stations and became catechists and teachers.

By the 1870s BaTswana began organizing their own schools, and literacy spread. In 1876 the first single-volume SeTswana Bible appeared, and the Kuruman Press was founded. For the rest of the nineteenth century it produced grammars, religious texts, and newsletters in SeTlhaping, unfortunately a peripheral, southern dialect. Literacy became commonplace among the better-to-do BaTswana whose children attended regular classes following the surge in school-building that continued into the 1920s. The colonial government, however, neglected African education, leaving the matter entirely to African tribal administrations and to mission churches. Poverty, drought, and tax laws (driving many young people into migrant labor) discouraged education. Since independence, however, literacy has increased due to free primary and secondary schooling, as well as adult literacy programs run by the government. In 1990 the adult literacy rate in Botswana had reached 73.8 percent.

Oral SeTswana literature, much of which has been published, is rich in idiom, poetry, folktales, prayer texts, songs, and historical accounts. The extensive materials collected by **Isaac Schapera** reflect this abundant legacy. Modern SeTswana literature is a product of the twentieth century. D.P. Moloto, D.P.S. Monyaise, **Michael Seboni**, Sol Plaatje, Sam Mofoyane, and **Leetile Raditladi** are among its principal figures. The first SeTswana work of history, *Dico tsa Secwana* (1912), was compiled by the LMS missionary A.J. Wookey and has been since superseded by Schapera's edited volume, *Ditirafalo tsa Merafe ya Batswana* (1949). *See also* Education; London Missionary Society; Moffat, Robert; Newspapers; SeTswana; Slave Trade.

LITERATURE. *See* Literacy.

LIVINGSTONE, DAVID (1813–1873). Scottish missionary and explorer. He joined the **London Missionary Society** in 1838 and sailed to South Africa in 1840. In 1841 he stayed at **Molepolole**

with a faction of BaKwena under **Bubi**. In 1843 he joined Roger Edwards at his Mabotsa mission station among the **Mmanaana Kgatla** north of present Zeerust, western Transvaal. **Sechele I** of the BaKwena was at the time living at Tshonwane, east of present Ramotswa and under the protection of the Mmanaana Kgatla. In 1846 Livingstone became resident with the Ba-Kwena and shortly thereafter the BaKwena moved to Kolobeng, where Livingstone established the first mission church and school in what is now Botswana. Livingstone's initial and most important convert was Sechele, whom he taught how to read and write. By then Livingstone had already become unpopular among the Transvaal Boers, whom he criticized in the Cape and British press for enslaving African women and children under the guise of "apprenticeship." In 1849 Livingstone began the celebrated phase of his life, as an explorer, by trekking with a BaKwena trading party to Ngamiland. In 1852 he was at Kuruman when the Boers attacked the BaKwena and sacked Livingstone's mission station at Kolobeng. The Boers justified their attack by making a fairly strong case that Livingstone had been supplying guns to the BaKwena. Livingstone, who was a strong believer that slavery should be fought by whatever means necessary, indeed covertly assisted the Ba-Kwena in acquiring arms and ammunition. Soon after the Kolobeng attack Livingstone embarked on a career of exploration and never returned to work among the BaTswana. *See also* BaTswana-Boer War of 1852–1853; Slave Trade.

LOBATSE. A town in the southeastern corner of Botswana, headquarters of the Botswana Meat Commission and site of the High Court. In 1991 Lobatse and its suburbs constituted Botswana's fourth largest municipal district, with a population of 26,052.

The area around Lobatse had been settled by the BaNgwaketse by the late eighteenth century. In 1897 the town began to grow up around the railway station, which had been located at the railway's junction with the Zeerust-Kanye road. When whites started moving into the adjacent Lobatse Block after 1905, Lobatse became a service point for these farmers and, like **Francistown,** developed the racial earmarks of a white settlers' town. Africans were confined to Peleng location, excluded from the railway hotel, and denied access to schools and other services built for the European community. The Athlone Hospital, the first health facility erected in the Protectorate by the government, opened its doors in 1927, and whites had their own separate wing. In the 1960s the issue of racial discrimination gained the **People's Party** a popular following among Lobatse's African voters.

An **abattoir** was opened in 1934, but not until 1954 did it become a successful venture and spark real growth in the town's overall activity and population. During the 1920s Lobatse was designated as the future capital of the Protectorate, a development shelved for want of funds in the days of the Great Depression. *See also* Race Relations; Towns.

LONDON MISSIONARY SOCIETY (LMS). The most successful of the missionary churches in Botswana; until the late 1950s a majority of Christians among the BaNgwato, BaKwena, BaNgwaketse, and BaTawana belonged to the LMS. Though founded in 1795 as a non-denominational missionary society, the LMS mission effort depended primarily on Congregationalist ministers. From its base at Kudumane (Kuruman, in the northern Cape), the society began to seek converts among the BaTswana in 1817. Under **Robert Moffat**, the mission began to expand. Moffat's son-in-law **David Livingstone** was the first missionary to work in what is now Botswana. He lived among the BaKwena in 1841, from 1845 to 1851, and returned briefly in 1853. During the 1860s and 1870s, the LMS established missions among the BaNgwato (1862), the BaNgwaketse (1871), and the BaTawana (1877). In the nineteenth century the LMS introduced and spread literacy through its education and publishing facilities. The LMS's *Setswana Dictionary* (J. Tom Brown, compiler), originally published in 1875 and revised in 1895 and 1925, remained the standard orthography until 1993.

Missionaries gained their first converts from two distinct groups. In the northern Cape, they evangelized among refugees of the **mfecane**. Among the BaTswana to the north, however, the LMS succeeded in converting younger members of the elite, especially among dingaka (traditional doctors). By the turn of the century, most LMS preachers and teachers were BaTswana and drawn from the mfecane and dingaka converts.

LMS missionaries, in particular **John Mackenzie** and **W.C. Willoughby**, favored British imperialism in the region as a way of checking Boer and Cape colonialism. Mackenzie, a member of the **Warren Expedition**, was one of the most vocal supporters of British control north of the Molopo. Willoughby, as adviser to **Khama III**, organized the visit of Khama III, **Sebele I**, and **Bathoen I** to England in 1895 to protest against the handing over of their territories to the **British South Africa Company**.

Khama III was the Society's most famous convert; his energetic and apparently sincere attempts to Christianize the Ba-Ngwato were publicized worldwide. In 1923, at the end of Khama's reign, BaNgwato membership in the LMS reached 3,000.

LMS then declined as many BaTswana Christians became members in independent churches, but LMS missionaries provided the BaTswana with their first schools and western medical services. The LMS also built, in 1904, what became the first secondary school/college for BaTswana, **Tiger Kloof**, near Vryburg and, in 1962, Moeding College. During the 1930s the Society cooperated with the United Free Church of Scotland in building the Scottish Livingstone Hospital at Molepolole. Today known as the Botswana Synod of the UCCSA (United Congregational Church of Southern Africa), the LMS remains something of a force in the country. It currently has a membership of approximately 20,000 in fifty-nine congregations spread throughout the country, employs eight men and four women full-time ministers, and has twenty-three self-supporting ministers and twenty-three evangelists. *See also* Health; Khukwe Mogodi; Lekalake Moitsheki; Literacy; Merriweather, Alfred; Mogwe, Thatayone; Mothowagae Motlogelwa; Ratshosa, Simon; Religion; Three Kings in London.

LOST CITY OF THE KALAHARI. The most popular myth about the Kgalagadi Desert, of which there are many. The myth originated in *Through the Kalahari*, a book published in 1886 by G.A. Farini, also known as William Leonard Hunt. Hunt was an American showman-cum-charlatan who toured the Kgalagadi in 1885 to collect "bushmen" for his "missing links" exhibition which was to tour Europe and the United States. In his book and subsequent lecture tours, Hunt claimed to have found the ruins of a "great civilization." His "discovery" inspired several expeditions to find the "lost city."

LOWE'S CAVE. A cave in the eastern Kweneng, not far from Mochudi. One of several sites at which, according to tradition, both the BaTswana and the BaKgalagadi are alleged to have originated. Markings near the cave's entrance are claimed as the "footprints" of the ancients.

LOZI (MALOZI). A western Zambian state which had emerged by the eighteenth century. Between 1840 and 1864 it fell under the incoming BaKololo. The MaLozi maintained important trade and political connections with BaTswana to the south. King Lewanika (1878–1916) was an ally of **Khama III**, who was responsible for interesting the French Protestants of the Paris Evangelical Missionary Society in establishing a mission among the MaLozi. In 1885, following a coup which ousted Lewanika, **Moremi II** of the BaTawana sent a force to help reinstall Lewanika on the throne. For many years thereafter the BaTawana were given hunting rights in the MaLozi sphere. After 1890 the MaLozi became a protectorate of the **BSACO**, and their territory was known as Barotseland. The MaLozi then had a falling out with the BaTawana between 1898 and 1902, when Lewanika was pressured by the BSACO to make claims on part of BaTawana territory. By this time, small groups of MaLozi had begun to move away from BSACO control and settle in parts of the Bechuanaland Protectorate. In the 1950s and 1960s, some MaLozi attempted to have Barotseland included in the Bechuanaland Protectorate, or become an independent protectorate by itself, but their requests were rejected.

LUDORF, JOSEPH (d. 1872). Medical missionary who championed the unity and independence of BaTswana. In 1850 he was placed by the Wesleyan Missionary Society among the BaRolong at Lotlhakane. There he quickly won the trust of the young Kgosi **Montshiwa**. His outspoken support for the BaRolong during the **BaTswana-Boer War of 1852–1853** resulted in the destruction of his mission. He then moved with Montshiwa to Moshaneng, and from 1856 to 1857 lived at Thaba Nchu. A trained surgeon, his medical skills were in demand throughout Botswana. He also edited the first SeTswana paper, *Molekoli ua Bechwana* (BaTswana Visitor). In 1871 he played a leading role in upholding BaRolong land claims resulting in the Keate Award. Acting on Montshiwa's behalf, Ludorf then wrote to most of the independent diKgosi proposing that they form a united BaTswana state. To this end he drafted a constitution for the ''United Barolong, Batlhaping, and Bangwaketse Nation.'' The scheme won the additional support of the BaKwena but collapsed after Ludorf's death.

LUGARD, FREDERICK (1858–1945). This eminent British colonialist worked in Botswana between 1896 and 1897 as director of the British West Charterland Company (BWCC), which had acquired the Nicolls-Hicks Concession in Ngamiland. Hampered by **rinderpest**, Lugard's large and well-financed team prospected all over Ngamiland, but they failed to find gold and diamonds. In 1897 he left Botswana after accepting the position of governor-general of Nigeria, but he remained a BWCC board member until 1899. Lugard's brother E.J. Lugard was also a BWCC employee (1895–1899). Frederick Lugard's theoretical writings on colonial administration influenced Resident Commissioner **Charles F. Rey** in the 1930s but ultimately had little impact on the Bechuanaland Protectorate. *See also* Concessions.

LUTHERANS. The second oldest Christian denomination active in Botswana, the Lutheran church traces its local origins to 1857, when **Sechele I** accepted German (Hermannsburg) missionaries sent by the Transvaal Boers. The Lutherans took the place of the **LMS** mission, which had been abandoned by **David Livingstone** in 1851. Initially, the Lutherans made rapid progress with Sechele in evangelizing among the various merafe of eastern Botswana, and in the process they baptized such notables as **Khama III**. By 1866, however, the original missionaries had died, and Sechele once more welcomed back LMS missionaries. The Lutherans managed to stay active among the BaLete and some of their neighbors. Several communities in the western Kgalagadi, including Namibian refugee groups, have also historically been Lutheran.

Before 1966 three Lutheran mission societies were active in Botswana. The Hermannsburg Mission Society became the Botswana Circuit of the Lutheran Church. The Berlin Mission Society became the Cape Orange Circuit. The third was the Rhenish Missionary Society, which with the Berlin Mission was active in the Kgalagadi region. A fourth society, the Hanoverian Mission, which was active in South Africa from 1890, entered Botswana in 1969.

After Botswana's independence, a split occurred within the church at Ramotswa between those favoring a fully independent, local synod with a local ministry, known as the Evangelical Lutheran Church in Botswana (ELCB) and headed by Bishop Phillip Robinson, and those wishing to preserve existing links with the Evangelical Lutheran Church in Southern Africa (ELCSA), under Bishop Nthuping. After the Botswana High Court ruled that the church premises legally belonged to the ELCSA, the Botswana government encouraged reconciliation, but controversy flared in 1994 leading to a fracas in which people were injured and the local police had to restore order.

Thus, Botswana's Lutherans belong to one of three churches:

1. The ELCSA (1975), with 8,000 members, 32 parishes, and 20 pastors. It has grown largely out of the Hermannsburg Mission.

2. The ELCB (1978), with 16,305 members, 31 parishes, and 27 pastors. It incorporates Hermannsburg, Berlin, and Rhenish traditions.

3. The Lutheran Church of Southern Africa (LCSA), with 6,000 members and 10 parishes rooted in the Hanoverian Mission (1969).

M

MACHENG (1832[?]–1873). Kgosi of the BaNgwato, 1857–1859 and 1866–1872. Son of Regent Sedimo (1826[?]–1833) and his wife, the widow of **Kgari**. According to the custom of *seantlo*, Macheng was recognized as the senior brother of Kgama II (1833[?]–1835). When the childless Kgama died, Macheng and his mother were driven out of the morafe by his half-brother **Sekgoma I**. In 1842 Macheng was captured by the AmaNdebele, with whom he lived for fifteen years. In 1857 he was rescued by **Sechele I** of the BaKwena with the aid of **LMS** missionary **Robert Moffat**. In the same year Sechele installed Macheng as Kgosi of the BaNgwato. In 1859 Sechele deposed Macheng and restored Sekgoma I, but seven years later, Sekgoma abdicated in favor of Macheng. Once back in power, Macheng oversaw the rise of Shoshong as a trading center in competition with the BaKwena capital, Molepolole. Macheng also attempted, but failed, to extend BaNgwato influence northward and intervene in AmaNdebele affairs. In 1872 he was deposed for the last time by a BaKwena force led by Sechele's son and heir, **Sebele I**, and replaced by **Khama III**, his nephew.

MACINTOSH, PHINEHAS. *See* Flogging Incident.

MACKENZIE, JOHN (1835–1899). LMS missionary and colonial official. A Scotsman like **David Livingstone**, in whose footsteps he followed, Mackenzie reopened the LMS field abandoned by his predecessor in 1851 and established the first LMS mission among the BaNgwato in 1862. There he gained a strong devotion to the BaTswana and became an important influence on the Kgosi-to-be, **Khama III**. From the vantage of Shoshong,

Mackenzie also adopted a view of the region that later affected public opinion in Britain. He perceived major destructive effects brought about by the AmaNdebele (whose attack on Shoshong he witnessed in 1863) and the Transvaal Boers.

In 1868 Mackenzie published his popular book *Ten Years North of the Orange River*, in which he called for the British occupation of BaTswana territory for the protection of its inhabitants then threatened as well, so it seemed, by the Tati "gold rush." As head of the Moffat Institution at Kuruman in the 1870s, Mackenzie became sensitive to another growing threat, that of Cape colonial and Boer filibuster land-grabbing in the Griqualand west and the BaTlhaping/BaRolong territories. Mackenzie thereupon involved himself directly in events. He wrote and lectured extensively to reach a British audience and struggled to find a political role in southern Africa. In 1884 he gained appointment as deputy commissioner for Bechuanaland, but only months later he was dismissed by the High Commissioner Sir Hercules Robinson because of his opposition to the Cape Colony government.

Mackenzie fervently argued that all of Bechuanaland, as it was becoming known internationally, should be ruled from London, not Cape Town and that the white men who entered the area to settle should be selected English farmers, not local freebooters. In 1885 he converted General Charles Warren to his views and accompanied him on his expedition to establish the Protectorate. When they reached Shoshong, Khama III responded to Mackenzie's pleas by making his "magnificent offer" of land for English settlers and British sovereignty.

Warren's proposals for the full British administration of the new Protectorate were attacked by Robinson and shelved in London. Mackenzie returned to Britain to press for a more assertive British imperialism, but he failed to regain his former position of influence. *See also* London Missionary Society; Tati Concession; Warren Expedition.

MAFIKENG. Located in the northern Cape, this commercial town also served (1895–1966) as the administrative headquarters of the Bechuanaland Protectorate. Termed "Mafeking by British traders, who established their town in the years 1884–1885 next to the Tshidi BaRolong settlement by the same name. Mafikeng was an important commercial center in the region, connecting as it did principal wagon routes (and later, railway lines) between the Transvaal, Bechuanaland, and the Cape. In 1885 General Charles Warren established a military post nearby and made it the headquarters of the Bechuanaland Border Police, which patrolled British Bechuanaland as well as the Bechuanaland Protectorate. In 1895, when British Bechuanaland was annexed to the Cape, the British retained possession of a square mile sector on the edge of town, called the Imperial Reserve, which was used as the headquarters of the resident commissioner, Bechuanaland Protectorate, for the next seventy years. The railway arrived in 1896, before proceeding north to Bulawayo and east to Johannesburg. From 1899 to 1900, at the onset of the **South African War**, this important rail hub was besieged by the Boers.

During the colonial era, in addition to all administrative matters, Mafikeng was something of a headquarters for the territory's traders, lawyers, labor recruiters, and newsmongers. The first independent SeTswana newspaper, *Koranta ea Becuana*, was launched there, and the *Mafeking Mail and Protectorate Guardian* was a leading source of information and opinion. In 1965 on the eve of independence, the white residents of Mafikeng petitioned the South African government to allow the town to become part of the Republic of Botswana, but Pretoria refused. From 1980 until 1994 the white areas of Mafikeng formed part of the homeland of Bophuthatswana. *See also* Newspapers.

MAGANELO (1855[?]–1875). First-born son of **Kgamanyane**, Kgosi of the **Kgafela Kgatla** (1848–1875), and elder brother of **Linchwe I**, who succeeded Kgamanyane. In 1875, Maganelo was disallowed the succession on the grounds that his mother, Nkomeng, had been betrothed after Dikolo, the mother of Linchwe. Several months later Maganelo was killed in a battle with the **Mmanaana Kgatla** at Thamaga (then a cattle post), and opposition to Linchwe subsided. When Linchwe abdicated forty-five years later, in 1920, Maganelo's brother **Segale** revived the old claim and asserted that he himself or Maganelo's son, Ramorotong, should succeed. Ramorotong and **Isang Pilane** then clashed in the kgotla, and supporters of both met armed at a **letsholo** in the veld. Peace was restored when Segale backed down, and Ramorotong was then banished to Molepolole, where he died.

MAHARERO, SAMUEL (1846[?]–1923). Head of the Namibian Ova**Herero** and leader of their revolt against the Germans, 1904–1907. During the early phase of the German extermination campaign, Maharero led his people into Ngamiland. After

1905 his followers spread all over the Protectorate, and some joined Maharero during his sojourn in the western Transvaal (1907–1922). He settled at Mahalapye in 1922, where he was joined by many of his people. He died in Serowe. Maharero was succeeded by his son Frederick (1874–1953), who attracted additional OvaHerero to Mahalapye. *See also* Namibia.

MAKABA II (d. 1824). "Rramaomana." Kgosi of the BaNgwaketse, 1790–1824, and at the turn of the nineteenth century, the most feared Kgosi in the southern Kgalagadi. Makaba was a successful military leader who increased the size, power, and wealth of the morafe by means of cattle raiding. Under Makaba, the BaNgwaketse became preeminent in what is now the Southern District. BaKwena, BaRolong, BaTlhaping, and Mmanaana Kgatla were among the victims of his regiments, and the latter morafe temporarily became his subjects. In the early 1820s, when the effects of the mfecane were felt in the area, Makaba's sons and their BaKwena allies sabotaged his efforts to preserve BaNgwaketse unity. Makaba was killed in battle against the invading BaKololo, allegedly betrayed by his power-hungry son Sebego I, and his morafe was scattered. *See also* Gaseitsiwe; Segotshane; Tshosa.

MANUFACTURING. A comparatively minor component of the national economy, manufacturing accounted for 8% of the total Gross National Product at independence, peaked at 9% in 1982, and slipped to 5.7% in 1992, when roughly 22,000 Ba-Tswana, or 10% of the employable workforce, held jobs in the manufacturing sector. Lack of investment capital and affordable skilled labor, high utility and transport costs, a relatively small domestic market, and the openness of that market to South African goods through the Customs Union have been major obstacles to developing Botswana's manufacturing sector and are likely to remain so, now that South Africa's manufacturing sector is attracting investment after the dismantling of apartheid.

While apartheid South Africa suffered from sanctions, Botswana's government was able to stimulate mild growth in manufacturing through its Financial Assistance Policy (FAP)(1982+), a system of combining attractive terms for outside investment with subsidies for indigenous entrepreneurs. FAP failed, however, to reduce dependency on South African goods or capital, which flowed into the region at greater rates during the 1980s as a consequence of its isolation from international markets. Some successes have been apparent, nonetheless. The Selebi Phikwe Regional Development Project, for example, was touted as having created 5,000 jobs by 1995, most in textiles. *See also* Economy.

MAPHAKELA LEKALAKE (1853–1947). Son of **Lekalake Moitsheki**, he grew up at the cattle-post and did not undergo **initiation** until he was thirty. Soon after, in 1887, he was converted by a MoKwena preacher and baptized by A.J. Wookey of the **LMS**. In 1892, he went to Kuruman with Wookey and was entered in the Moffat Institution. After teaching in the Cape from 1896 to 1909, he attended Bible School at **Tiger Kloof**. Along with **Khukwe Mogodi**, he was the first African to be ordained as an LMS minister, in 1910. Until 1926, he preached at Kuruman, where he also served as boarding master at Moffat Institution, then worked for the rest of his career at stations inside the Bechuanaland Protectorate. He retired at an advanced age in 1941. Maphakela was one of the great LMS ministers and was the first Motswana to be profiled in *The Times* of London.

MARIJUANA. Known in Botswana as ''matekwane'' or more popularly by its Khoisan term, ''dagga.'' The drug of choice in Botswana after **alcohol** and a cash crop in such areas as the Kgatleng and BuKalanga. Dagga has for generations been a trade item and has been in particular demand among desert-dwellers. Colonial authorities made no attempt to suppress dagga production and consumption, and fines remain light. *See also* Griqua; Tobacco.

MARUPING, PETER (1935–). Born in Lobatse, Maruping was an early nationalist politician, entering the Bechuanaland Congress Party in 1961 before becoming secretary-treasurer of the **People's Party**, Matante wing. In 1964 he was jailed for alleging in a public meeting that the **Democratic Party** and the British were ''rigging'' the registration process for the forthcoming general election. He was defeated in the 1965 election by **Quett Masire**.

MASHWE, GEORGE. Mashwe, who was South African-born, played a significant role as a teacher and minister in the Kweneng, 1911–1916. Mashwe established the **Anglican** Church in Molepolole and was recruited by **Peter Sidzumo** to take part in a drive to reform BaKwena administration. In 1916 Mashwe and Peter Sidzumo's brother Richard were deported as undesirable aliens. *See also* Sechele II.

MASIRE, GLADYS OLEBILE MOLEFI (1933–). A MoRolong from the northern Cape, she attended **Tiger Kloof** in the years after her future husband had left. She became a friend of **Quett Masire**'s sister Gabalengwe and met her future husband on a visit to Kanye. They married in 1958. Mrs. Masire is the mother of the president's six children. She is prominent in charitable and philanthropic activities.

MASIRE, SIR QUETT KETUMILE JONI (1925–). Since 1980 the leader of the **Democratic Party (BDP)** and second president of Botswana, succeeding **Seretse Khama**. He was elected to his fourth term of office in 1994. Knighted in 1991, he is now called Sir Ketumile.

Masire was born in 1925 in Kanye to parents of common descent; he was the first child of an industrious shop assistant and cattle owner. Until he was thirteen, Masire was a herdboy, after which he attended school and showed remarkable aptitude, winning a government bursary to attend **Tiger Kloof** in 1944. In 1946, when both his parents died, he scrapped his plans to attend university, obtained teacher's qualifications, and assumed responsibility for his five siblings.

In 1950 Masire became headmaster of the new Kanye Junior Secondary School, where he taught until 1955. During these years he kept his interest in farming, his true love. Once he could afford to buy a tractor, he quit teaching. His modern methods of cultivation evoked howls from the conservative BaNgwaketse peasantry, but big yields brought him recognition in 1957 as the first African in the Protectorate to be awarded the Master Farmer Certificate.

Despite some run-ins with **Bathoen II**, his Kgosi, Masire was regularly placed on or elected to various committees in his district. When in 1958 he became the Botswana editor for the *Naledi ya Batswana* newspaper, his influence spread, and soon he was elected to the Ngwaketse Local Council, the African Council, and LEGCO.

In late 1961 he was tapped by Seretse Khama and others as potential southern organizer for the fledgling BDP. Masire then utilized his network of newspaper corespondents to set up a far-flung political organization. From the beginning the BDP was a partnership between Seretse, who provided leadership and charisma, and Masire, who provided the energy and organization needed for the sprawling party network. Masire also edited *Therisanyo*, the party paper.

From the beginning the BDP leadership had two factions. Based around Seretse were the patricians, who believed in the virtues of stability and rank. The other, favoring activist government and meritocracy, had Masire at its head.

In 1966, following independence, Masire became Botswana's first vice president and minister of Finance and Development Planning. By this time Masire had come to favor an all-out government effort to lift the country out of poverty, using the expertise of expatriate economists whom he cultivated. His program channeled foreign aid, loans, and mining revenues into the development of the educational, health, power, and transportation infrastructure and provided protection to nascent industries. Less successful efforts were made in promoting commercial farming and national self-subsistence in food.

During the 1960s Masire's plans were unpopular with the patrician wing and conservative bureaucrats, who pressured Seretse to unseat him. But Sir Seretse kept his faith in Masire, and the two formed an effective, long-term partnership. Masire's strengths complemented Seretse's weaknesses and vice versa. Quett's commitment to detail and hard work blended well with Seretse's ability to communiciate and keep the party popular. Masire was given great freedom by Seretse to pursue his vision of development.

Masire's lack of charisma dogged him somewhat, most notably in 1969 when he lost his seat to his old arch-rival Bathoen II, but Masire ran a hard race against hopeless odds, perhaps underestimated by Seretse himself. Seretse, then confident in Masire, kept him in parliament as a Specially Elected Member, and refused to demote him from the cabinet or the vice-presidency.

With Seretse's support and his election wins in 1974 and 1979 in GaNgwaketse, Masire's political stock continued to rise. His control over the budget and the successful development effort also gained him respect and increased his political clout. Masire succeeded to the Presidency in 1980 with overwhelming support in the party caucus and presided over the late Seretse's unfilled term until 1984, when he was elected in his own right. His devotion to hard work, along with his organizational and technocratic skills, were recognized as indispensable to the BDP. He was elected to his third term of office in 1994. *See also* Councils; Newspapers.

MASISI, EDISON SETLHOMO (1923–). Politician; born in Mosopa. Attended **Tiger Kloof** with **Quett Masire** and **M.P.K. Nwako** on a government bursary. From 1950 to 1964 he was a teacher in his home village. In 1964 he was recruited into full-time politics as a member of the **BDP** and as the party's local leader. Since 1965 he has represented Mosopa in the National Assembly and has held several cabinet posts. In 1989 he served as deputy speaker of the House, and was made assistant minister of Finance and Development Planning in 1992.

MATANTE, PHILIP PARCEL GOANWE (1921–1979). Co-founder of the **People's Party (BPP)**. Matante grew up in South Africa but claimed to be the son of Goanwe Matante of Serowe. During **World War II**, he served in the army with the rank of sergeant (1940–1945) in the AAPC, one of the few non-royals to hold top NCO rank. Not much is known of Matante's career prior to his settling in **Francistown** in 1957 as manager of a store, apart from the fact that he participated in **ANC** activities in the Johannesburg area. In 1959 he helped to launch the Tatitown Cultural Organization, which openly addressed political issues unlike its predecessor, the Francistown African Cultural Association (founded by **Leetile Raditladi**). Matante briefly showed interest in the **Federal Party** but found it too conservative and ineffectual. From February to October 1960 he struggled unsuccessfully to introduce his St. Philip's Apostolic Church into Gammangwato.

In December 1960 he joined with **K.T. Motsete** and **Motsamai Mpho** in founding the Bechuanaland People's Party. Matante blossomed as an orator; at BPP meetings, usually held in beer halls or football grounds, he fired his audience with almost religious enthusiasm by voicing their frustrations and grievances, which he blamed on the racist socioeconomic order in the Protectorate. In June 1962 tensions between Matante and Mpho irreparably split the party. The spark was Mpho's claim that Matante was responsible for financial irregularities and had attempted to have ANC refugee Maxwell Mlonyeni deported back to South Africa. Mpho was driven out and, by 1964, when Motsete was cashiered as well, Matante assumed sole control of the BPP.

In 1965 Matante's party captured three seats and became the opposition party in the National Assembly. As MP for Francistown, Matante led the opposition until his death in 1979. Following independence, Matante was the first MP to

call for the formation of a defense force. *See also* Botswana
Defence Force; Pan Africanist Congress.

MATHIBA MOREMI (1888[?]–1933). Kgosi of the BaTawana,1906–1932. Son of **Moremi II**, he became Kgosi with the
assistance of the British in place of **Sekgoma Letsholathebe**. A
weak and ineffectual ruler, in 1912 he moved the capital from
Tsau to **Maun**, but few of his subjects followed. As a result,
central authority in Ngamiland collapsed. In 1929, dismayed
by years of the paltry tax revenues received from Mathiba's
office, the British appointed two dikgosana to "assist" Mathiba. In 1932 they replaced him altogether with the brother of
Sekgoma Letsholathebe, **Monnamaburu Letsholathebe,** who
acted as regent. In the meantime, Mathiba, who had inherited
his father's chronic alcoholism and hangers-on, dissipated his
wealth. Mogalakwe Thabeng and other elders paid off his debts
in exchange for large grants of land. Mathiba died penniless.
See also Dithapo Meno; Motshabi Letsholathebe; Mphepheng.

MATHIBA OF BANGWATO (d. 1795[?]). Kgosi of the Ba-
Ngwato,1770[?]–1795, and founder of the BaNgwato state. During Mathiba's reign, the final separation between the BaNgwato
and Ba**Kwena** occurred. The BaNgwato moved north and eventually settled in the area of Shoshong. Before Mathiba's death,
the BaNgwato themselves divided. Kgama I, Mathiba's son,
drove out his father and eldest brother, Tawana, who took
refuge with the BaKwena. They subsequently settled in Ngamiland and established the Ba**Tawana** state. Mathiba fell out with
Tawana and tried to return to Kgama, who rejected him.
Mathiba, one tradition holds, moved to Lephephe, where he
committed suicide (another tradition locates his death in the
Kwebe Hills).

MATTHEWS, ZACHARIAH KEODIRELANG (1901–1968). Academic, politician, and diplomat. His grandfather left the Shoshong Hills area and settled among the BaRolong. "ZK" was
born in Kimberley and educated at Fort Hare, Yale, and the
London School of Economics. In 1942, after six years of
lecturing at Fort Hare, he became a member of the **ANC**
executive and in 1953 proposed the idea of drawing up a
"Freedom Charter," which was adopted. During the 1950s he
was a Treason Trialist and came to Botswana in 1961 after a
period of detention. In 1966 **Seretse Khama** appointed him
Botswana's first ambassador to the United States and the

United Nations. His brief tenure greatly enhanced Botswana's standing abroad. His son Joe became a prominent ANC activist and in 1961 was the first African to qualify as a lawyer in the then Bechuanaland Protectorate. In 1982, he jumped bail following indictment on embezzlement charges and in the 1990s moved to Natal, where he became an organizer for the Inkatha Freedom Party. *See also* Archives.

MAUN. Capital of the BaTawana since 1915. During its early history Maun was not a successful capital; the diKgosi complained that **tsetse** were keeping the people from them. In the 1930s and 1940s when tsetse were gradually eradicated from Maun, the village began to thrive. Since independence it has become a major tourist center as the gateway to the **Okavango Delta**. Since the 1980s, the heretofore sandy and inaccessible Maun has been connected by all-weather road to Francistown and assumed some of the earmarks of a modern town, with paved streets, electricity, television, newspapers, and the like. In 1991 its population stood at 26,769. *See also* Towns.

MAZEZURU. *See* Vapostori.

MBANDERU (OVAMBANDERU). Politically separate branch of OvaHerero. Beginning in the 1890s, many OvaMbanderu migrated into Botswana as refugees from German oppression, and they split into two separate groups, both mutually hostile. One is Nguvaqva ward, under the control of the paramountcy; the other is Kantu ward, under the leadership of a very wealthy commoner family. *See also* Keheranju, Monjuku.

MBUKUSHU (HAMBUKUSHU). For most of the nineteenth century they lived in the **Caprivi Strip** and southern Angola. In 1885 **Moremi II**, Kgosi of the **BaTawana**, established control over them when he returned with his army from BuLozi. A small minority were subject to **bolata**, but most were placed under control of BaTawana headmen. In the 1960s, several thousand additional HaMbukushu migrated into Ngamiland as refugees from the conflict in Angola. They were resettled between Gomare and Shakawe. *See also* Letsholathebe I; Lozi; Refugees; Slave Trade.

MERRIWEATHER, ALFRED MUSGRAVE (1918–). UCCSA missionary and medical doctor who has played a major role in the improvement of public health since 1944, primarily in the

Kweneng District. He pioneered serving remote rural areas through mobile health clinics. During the 1950s he contributed to the diagnosis of endemic (i.e., transmitted non-sexually) syphilis. With support from the World Health Organization (1955–1956) he organized a nationwide inoculation campaign using penicillin to eradicate this and other diseases. From 1961 to 1964 he was a member of LEGCO, becoming its speaker. He also served as the first speaker of the Botswana National Assembly, 1965–1968. Awarded the CBE in 1968, he became private physician to **Seretse Khama**, 1970–1980. Merriweather has authored several books on Botswana. He was also the founder president of the Botswana Medical Association (1965) and moderator (i.e., worldwide leader) of the United Free Church of Scotland, 1979–1980. *See also* Health.

METHODISTS. The Methodist Church in Southern Africa has approximately 5,500 members in Botswana in forty-five congregations. In the nineteenth century Wesleyan missionaries were particularly prominent among the Ba**Rolong**. Among the most notable of them was **Dr. Joseph Ludorf**. *See also* Religion.

MFECANE. An IsiXhosa/IsiZulu term ("the crushing"), also rendered in SeSotho as Difaqane, which refers to an extended period of tumult afflicting southern Africa in the early nineteenth century, marked by a "diaspora" of groups from Natal and the southern highveld into other regions as far north as the Zambezi and in some cases beyond. Mfecane/difaqane became commonly used in Botswana only after post-1966 school texts were introduced, and these terms have become controversial in recent years, because the origins of the tumult are being called into question. In the 1960s the mfecane was ascribed to the rise of Shaka of the AmaZulu, but recently other causes are being offered: drought, famine, and slave raiding by Dutch-speaking frontiersmen.

Whatever the term applied or its origin, the mfecane had its impact upon Botswana. During the first half of the nineteenth century, BaTswana were invaded by Ba**Kololo**, Ama**Ndebele**, and **Afrikaners**. BaKololo raided much of eastern and northern Botswana (1823, 1825–1840), while extensive raiding was carried out by AmaNdebele impis sent from their bases in the Transvaal (1832–1837) and western Zimbabwe (1838–1844). BaTswana cooperated with Afrikaners (Boers) in expelling the AmaNdebele from Mosega (1837) but came into conflict with the white settlers themselves in the 1840s, culminating in the

BaTswana-Boer War (1852–1853). Major consequences of the era include the fall of the kingdom of **Butwa** of the BaNyayi-BaKalanga, the reformation of states of BaKwena, BaNgwato, BaNgwaketse, and BaTawana, new military tactics, and the introduction of firearms.

According to oral traditions, early nineteenth-century Ba-Tswana on both sides of the modern Botswana-South African border shared a prophecy about the coming tumult. In Botswana, the prophecy is attributed to the BaKwena Kgosi **Motswasele II**; in South Africa, to the BaFokeng ruler Thethe. Before their deaths at the hands of political rivals, each is supposed to have said:

> If you kill me my people will not live together in peace. First will come the black ants who will scatter them [as portending, e.g., the BaKololo and AmaNdebele] Then will come the white [sometimes red and/or yellow] ants [Afrikaners] who will occupy the land and feed on the people.

See also Battle of Dimawe; Battle of Dithubaruba; Battle of Dutlwe; Battle of Matopos; Battles of Shoshong; Lozi; Military, Traditional; Sebego I.

MIGRANT LABOR. During the colonial era the major source of cash income for most households came from men and women who had migrated outside the Protectorate (mainly to South Africa but also to all other surrounding territories) to work in farms, factories, homes, and mines. Migrant labor dates back at least to the 1840s, when BaTswana began working on Boer farms, and it became significant to BaTswana economies after the discovery of diamonds in Kimberley in 1867. In 1878, African laborers in the diamond fields totaled more than 34,000, of whom BaTswana constituted nearly 1,900, or 5 percent. By the 1880s BaTswana made up one out of every five "new hands" hired at these mines. In the 1890s migrant labor became even more important with the rapid development of the gold fields combined with severe ecological crises and the introduction of the hut tax in 1899. Before **World War I** the Protectorate was well on its way to becoming a labor reserve for South Africa. By the 1930s only Ngamiland and the Kgalagadi were relatively free of dependence. After the depression, South African and Rhodesian recruiting agencies expanded their operations in the territory so dramatically that by 1943 one third of the adult male population was away (approximately 20 percent of these were in the African Auxiliary Pioneer Corps).

At independence, 25,000 BaTswana were working in the South African gold mines alone, and ten years later approximately 53,000 were working temporarily in different parts of South Africa. Since the late 1980s, the South African government has restricted migrancy, and fewer than 13,000 BaTswana worked there in 1993. *See also* Economy; Employment; Mining; Rinderpest; Trade Unions; World War II.

MILITARY, TRADITIONAL. By the late eighteenth century, the BaTswana of Botswana had developed sophisticated military cultures. Before the massive introduction of firearms the iron age armory of a MoTswana soldier consisted of several throwing spears (*marumo*), an assagai or short stabbing spear (*putlela*), a battle ax (*tshaka*), and a knife (*thipe*). Shields among such groups as BaKwena, BaNgwaketse, and BaNgwato were oval, three–four feet in length, and made of either ox or wild animal hide. Pockets in the shields were used for mounting spears and a hook for suspending the tshaka. BaNgwaketse preferred mostly white shields, while BaKwena opted for black. The bow and arrow, favored by **Khoisan** and Ova**Herero**, was known to BaTswana but generally used as a hunting, rather than military, weapon. Traditional battle dress consisted of a cape, preferably of leopard skin, and a frontal apron made from skins of other spotted or striped animals, necklaces containing personal charms and "war medicines," and bracelets and bangles usually made of copper wire and beads. Each community developed its own headdress, often incorporating ostrich feathers as well as *sebilo*, a substance made from iron oxide and fat. Traditional battle dress gradually gave way to European fashion during the nineteenth century. Headbands were increasingly used to identify opposing sides. The BaNgwato went the furthest in adopting European-style uniforms for dress parades during the time of **Khama III**.

Before the gun was introduced, the standard battle formation of BaTswana and Ba**Kalanga** was the "buffalo head," mistakenly thought to be an innovation of the Zulu Inkosi Dingiswayo (or his protégé, Shaka), in which the platoon was deployed in a center flanked by two "horns." During battle the horns attempted to outflank the enemy. This formation was also used in communal hunting. All adult male members of a BaTswana community were initiated as members of a particular age regiment. Guns, along with horses, became common in Botswana in the nineteenth century and played a vital part in victories over the BaKololo, Ama**Ndebele**, and **Afrikaners**. The

BaNyayi-BaKalanga had obtained some guns at an even earlier period through trade with the Portuguese. Some crude firearms of local manufacture were also developed. The BaKwena ruler **Sechele I** was a local pioneer in weapon technology. He began purchasing guns with percussion caps in the 1840s, acquired a cannon (now displayed at the Mafikeng Museum), and used breechloading rifles against the **Kgafela Kgatla** in 1876. As early as 1849 he ordered a volleygun, capable of firing its seven barrels simultaneously, as well as bullet molds. He also made use of trenches and stonewalls with gun pivots in his defenses. Such impressive advances in military technology failed, however, to make any BaTswana group a match for the might exercised in the region by the British military. *See also* BaTswana-Boer War of 1852–1853; Batswana-Boer War of 1881–1884; Battle of Derdepoort; Battle of Dimawe; Battle of Dithubaruba; Battle of Dutlwe; Battle of Matopos; Battle of Ngwapa; Battles of Shoshong; Initiation; Mfecane.

MINING. Botswana has rich deposits in diamonds, copper, lead, zinc, soda ash, and coal, but its wealth in this respect remained undiscovered until after independence from Great Britain was achieved in 1966. Because the Botswana government has been able to control the process of exploiting its mineral resources, it has been able to enjoy a sizable share of the income generated, unlike other mineral-rich African countries.

The first gold mining "rush" in southern Africa was to the Tati District in northeastern Botswana, when Europeans discovered gold there in 1867. Though the rush created **Francistown**, the Tati gold mines were only marginally profitable; apart from the 1930s they were worked throughout the colonial era and abandoned in 1964. In 1991, Monarch mine near Francistown was brought back into operation, with the expectation that it would generate approximately 100 pounds of gold per month until 2001. In addition to gold, asbestos and manganese were mined on a very small scale in the Bamalete and Bangwaketse reserves, but mining contributed nothing to the colonial Gross National Product. Cecil Rhodes and other mining magnates had great hopes for mining in Botswana, but none were realized until after independence.

In 1967 diamonds were found at Orapa, and the existence of major copper-nickel deposits was established at Selebi-Phikwe. Enormous coal deposits (seventeen billion tons) were discovered, and a modern coal mine was started at Palapye. Soda ash deposits at Sua Pan have been mined since 1991, when Soda

Ash Botswana (financed by the Botswana government and South African capital) opened its plant at Botswana's fourth mining town, Sowa (the others: Orapa, Selebi Phikwe, and Jwaneng). In full production, Sua Pan is designed to produce three million tons of soda ash and 650,000 tons of salt per annum and supply 60 percent of the South African market, and 100 percent of Zimbabwe's. Platinum and hydrocarbon in the Kgalagadi await development. In 1984 the total value of Botswana's mineral exports stood at $600 million and by 1992 had more than doubled to $1,283,246,400. *See also* British South Africa Company; Copper; Diamonds; Economy; Riley, Charles.

MITCHISON, NAOMI (1897–). Scottish author of many works of fiction who became interested in Botswana through her friendship with **Linchwe II**, when he attended school in England. She attended his installation in 1963 and thereafter wrote *Return to Fairy Hill* and numerous other works based on her visits to Mochudi and the **Kgafela Kgatla** and the southern African scene.

MMANAANA KGATLA (BAKGATLA BAGA MMANAANA). One of five branches of the BaKgatla, and the only one to reside exclusively within Botswana. Their diKgosi, who all trace descent from Kgosi Mosielele, are the traditional authorities of Mosopa, Thamaga, and the Gamafikana section of Kanye.

Mmanaana Kgatla history is a long quest for a territory of their own after their split from the **Kgafela Kgatla** before 1800. They lived in the western Transvaal until 1820, when they were defeated by **Makaba II** of the BaNgwaketse and brought under his rule. Following the overthrow of Makaba in 1824, the Mmanaana Kgatla regained their independence and, during the 1840s, were the dominant morafe in the western Transvaal. In the early 1850s, however, their power was broken by the Boers and they sought refuge with the BaKwena. In 1863 they settled at Mosopa in the territory of **Sechele I**.

In 1870 a bogosi dispute divided them. Mosielele broke away and settled with a minority group at Gamafikana. The larger faction followed **Pilane** to Kgobodukwe but in 1875 they returned to Mosopa. Thereafter they accepted the position of junior ally of the BaNgwaketse, the BaKwena having by then renounced their claim to Mosopa. Until 1930 Mmanaana Kgatla lived at peace in the land of their BaNgwaketse hosts.

Between 1930 and 1935 serious conflict developed between Kgosi **Gobuamang**, who had succeeded his nephews (sons of his brother Pilane), and the new and young Kgosi in Kanye, **Bathoen II**. In 1935 half the Mosopa population followed Gobuamang into exile at Thamaga, inside the Bakwena Reserve, while the remainder stayed in Mosopa under Kgabosetso, Gobuamang's son.

After Kgabosetso's death in 1945, the Mmanaana Kgatla paramount was his son, Kgosi Letlole, who ruled from Thamaga until his death in 1991, ending the paramountcy.

MMUSI (1915–). Second son of Kgafela and diffident brother of the bold **Molefi**, Kgosi of the **Kgafela Kgatla**. Mmusi was installed as acting chief (1936–1942) during Molefi's suspension and acted periodically during his brother's illnesses. He served in the AAPC from 1942 to 1945. From 1958 until 1963, between Molefi's death and the installation of **Linchwe II**, Mmusi served as regent and during Linchwe's ambassadorship to the United States, was once again acting chief. He was known best for ordering the inaugural meeting of the **Democratic Party** out of Mochudi (an action for which he has since recently apologized, saying he made a mistake). Mmusi retired as deputy chief in 1973, but resumed the regency when Linchwe II became president of the Customary Court of Appeal.

MOAGI, BEHRENS (d. 1947). Tribal secretary of the BaLete and long-time Native (African) Advisory Council member. He dominated BaLete affairs between 1936 and 1947. *See also* Councils.

MOCHUDI. Since 1872 the capital of the **Kgafela Kgatla**. Named after Motshodi, a BaKwena Kgosi of the early eighteenth century. His grave is located in present Mabodisa ward, the stones having been removed to cover graves of victims of the influenza epidemic of 1918. The modern Mochudi originated with the migration of a large section of the Kgafela Kgatla from the western Transvaal under Kgosi **Kgamanyane**. The original wards of Mochudi were built on the northern slopes of Phuthadikobo hill, and the town has since grown steadily outward. The kgotla and kgosi's kraal, as well as Linchwe II's house atop Phuthadikobo, were sited by Kgamanyane. The five major sections (dikgoro) of Mochudi are Kgosing, Morema, Mabodisa, Tshukudu, and Manamakgothe. Each of these are subdivided into wards, or dikgotla, the total in Mochudi being forty-eight. The town is distinguished by its many well-decorated walls and rondavels in the original section, stone-walled homesteads atop Manamakgoteng, the DRC church (1904) and sprawling ex-mission establishment, the huge rondavel of **Isang Pilane** near the main kgotla, and the Phuthadikobo Museum atop Phuthadikobo hill (reached by foot behind the main kgotla). In recent years, Mochudi's outlying areas, particularly between the old town and the railway, have been developed to accommodate the growing number of employees who commute to the nearby capital, Gaborone. In 1991, Mochudi's population stood at 25,542. *See also* Bakgatla National School; Dutch Reformed Church; Linchwe I; Linchwe II; Molefi; Towns.

MODIMO. Setswana for single, supreme being; God. The word in its singular form predates the introduction of Christianity. Such a concept accounts for the existence in Botswana of non-Christian church movements, such as the Elects Apostolic Movement. *See also* Independent Churches; Religion.

MOETI SAMOTSOKO (1895[?]–1963). As headman of the Maun BaYei during the regency of Elizabeth Moremi, Moeti sought British recognition as "chief" of the BaYei of Ngamiland. In 1961 he led a campaign of civil disobedience against Pulane's BaTawana tribal administration. His political career commenced in 1948 with the BaYei agitation, and he was later voted in as BaYei headman. He was a bitter opponent of the regent, who in 1949 took away some of his land. Moeti, less than a forceful politician, served as a figurehead for younger types coming up. In his private life, Moeti led a rags to riches existence, without effort. As a young man he married his cousin, who provided a substantial dowry. In addition, she earned him big animal herds through her agricultural and trading activities. In 1957 Moeti divorced his wife after forty-two years, having used her money to build himself a large, well-furnished house in Maun. *See also* Moremi, Elizabeth; Mpho, Motsamai.

MOFFAT, ROBERT (1795–1883). Scottish missionary who founded the first **LMS** mission among BaTswana, at Kudumane (Kuruman) in 1820, as well as the LMS Institute at Kuruman for the training of catechists and missionaries. Probably more than anyone Moffat was responsible for the codification of the SeTswana language and the spread of literacy among BaTswana. In 1830 he acquired a printing press from which he produced the first volume in SeTswana: the Gospel according to St. Luke. By 1857 he had translated and published the Bible in its entirety. Moffat's daughter Mary married **David Livingstone** in 1843.

Moffat, whose missionary career commenced in the time of the **mfecane**, became identified with assisting the BaTswana against a range of threats. He was an important figure in the 1823 defense of Dithakong; together with his son-in-law he was involved in helping the BaTswana to arm themselves in defense of the Transvaal Boers, prior to the 1852–1853 war. He also assisted **Macheng** in returning to the BaNgwato (1857–1858). *See also* Literacy.

MOGAE, FESTUS GONTEBANYE (1939–). Vice president of Botswana since 1992, a leading figure in the planning of Botswana's post-independence economic development. A product of Moeng College, he took a BA (Honours) in Economics at Oxford and an MA in Development Economics at Sussex. In 1969 Mogae joined the Ministry of Development Planning, under **Quett Masire**, and rose to permanent secretary in 1975. After secondment to the International Monetary Fund as its executive director, he became the permanent secretary to President Quett Masire in 1982. In 1989 he was specially elected to the National Assembly and appointed assistant minister of the Ministry of Finance and Development Planning. In 1994 he won the Palapye seat, signaling a shift in his ambitions from senior bureaucrat to leading politician. Mogae has established himself as a strong advocate of governmental fiscal responsibility and a free market economy.

MOGALAKWE TAWANA (b. 1795[?]). Regent of the BaTawana, 1840[?]–1847, and uncle of his protégé **Letsholathebe I**. Around 1835 he and other BaTawana were taken to Zambia as captives by the BaKololo. He led an escape of the BaTawana (ca. 1839) and found his nephew on his return to the Okavango. Mogalakwe rebuilt the BaTawana state through a combination of recruiting subjects and raiding cattle from the BaYei and **Deti Khoe**. He is said to have established the kgamelo system of patronage that outlasted his rule by more than a century. His descendants played a long, prominent role in BaTawana politics as "traditional defenders of the chieftainship." In reward for their loyalty, Mogalakwe's descendants were given control of the Hainveldt region as a private grazing sanctuary.

MOGWE, ARCHIBALD (1921–). Long-time politician, member of the **Democratic Party**, and government minister. Mogwe is a MoNgwaketse from an old family of **LMS** converts and priests who grew up in Molepolole. Like his father and grandfather, "Archie" was educated at **Tiger Kloof**, where he was a star pupil. In 1944 he became a teacher and spent a decade in the Free State as boarding master of Modderpoort School. He then joined the Bechuanaland Protectorate civil service. In the 1960s he was one of two BaTswana promoted to senior (super-scale) civil service positions. In the 1970s he entered politics and won reelection in GaNgwaketse until 1994, when he lost his seat. For years he served as minister of Mineral and Water Affairs and as minister of External Affairs, where he distinguished himself. During the 1970s Mogwe became a forthright advocate of universal standards of human rights for all of Africa.

MOGWE, THATAYONE (1863–1923). Influential teacher and minister of the **LMS**. Born in GaNgwaketse, he attended school as a teenager in Kuruman under the tutelage of Roger Price and J.T. Brown. From 1893 to 1901 he was the head teacher at the Kanye school and was then made the LMS minister in Mathseng. During this time he served as tutor to **Seepapitso I** in preparation for the Kgosi's schooling at Lovedale. In 1915 Mogwe was ordained at **Tiger Kloof** and was posted to head the Kanye LMS mission. Until his death he was politically, as well as religiously, influential in GaNgwaketse. His grandson **Archibald Mogwe** became an MP and member of the cabinet.

MOKGOSI I (1810[?]–1886). Kgosi of the BaLete,1830[?]–1886, and primarily responsible for rebuilding his morafe following the **mfecane**. In these years, which were spent in the western Transvaal, the BaLete replenished their herds by obtaining cattle in exchange for working as ironsmiths for the merafe around them. Mokgosi chafed under Boer rule and left for the Kweneng in 1852. He remained there until 1863, when Sechele I demanded tribute, and moved with his followers to Mmankgodi, where he remained until 1875, when he resettled at **Ramotswa**. *See also* Lutherans.

MOKGOSI III (1920–1968). Kgosi of the BaLete, 1945–1966. He was an active member of the African Advisory Council, JAC, and LEGCO. Mokgosi had a reputation for independent and progressive views. He supported **Seretse Khama** during the early 1950s and proposed **Oratile Ratshosa** as regent. He was tolerant of political party activity in his reserve.

MOLEFI (1909–1958). Kgosi of the **Kgafela Kgatla, 1929–1936** and 1945–1958. Born as the first son of Kgafela Linchwe and **Seingwaeng,** Molefi succeeded his uncle, **Isang Pilane,** who had acted as regent since the retirement of Molefi's grandfather **Linchwe I.** Molefi was an outspoken and popular figure whose reign was nevertheless marred by personal problems and conflict with his uncles and Protectorate officials. Molefi and Isang quarreled over the Linchwe estate, resulting in a major inquiry in 1935. The following year, after a series of incidents ending with his allowing the Machama regiment to create a two-day disturbance in Mochudi, Molefi was suspended from office by Resident Commissioner **Charles Rey** and replaced with his younger brother, **Mmusi.** In 1937 Molefi was banned from the Bakgatla Reserve. Until 1945, popular agitation for Molefi's return was led by the Bakgatla Free Church under **Thomas Phiri,** a proto-nationalist movement known as **Ipelegeng,** and the **Zion Christian Church (ZCC),** made up of ex-Free Church and Ipelegeng members including his mother, Seingwaeng. Molefi regained the confidence of the colonial government by serving in **World War II** as a sergeant-major of the AAPC and was reinstalled in September 1945. The second half of his reign, however, was equally troubled.

A person of great extremes, Molefi was known both for his fair judgments in kgotla as well as his harshness in dealing with opponents. He banned the ZCC in 1947, even though it had worked for his reinstatement, and banished its unrecanting members, including Seingwaeng and his uncle Bakgatla Pilane, who had looked after his own children during his exile. Molefi squandered his inheritance and the revenues from his office on luxuries and entertainment, but often he spent it on his friends, who came from all segments of society. In 1958, his health had greatly deteriorated through alcoholism and tuberculosis, and Molefi overturned his car at Phapane, dying almost immediately. He was succeeded by Mmusi, who acted as regent until Molefi's son **Linchwe II** was installed in 1963.

MOLELE, TWAI TWAI. A social bandit from Nata, of **Shua** descent, who made a name for himself in the early twentieth century by resisting BaNgwato rule and breaking colonial hunting laws. In the 1890s Molele and his family, along with the rest of Nata's population, were enslaved by BaNgwato regiments. In 1898 the family apparently murdered several Zambian migrant workers passing through the area, but nothing was proved. Molele was constantly harassed by Khama's overseer Oitsile, who killed his pregnant daughter. Oitsile barely escaped a lynching, but soon after the Molele family deserted the cattle in their charge. For the next sixteen years they lived a life of banditry on Crown land, "poaching" wildlife and stealing BaNgwato cattle. They then obtained mafisa cattle from **Tshekedi Khama**. In 1944 the family and some other Shua, out of fear of having their "poaching" activities reported, killed two British airmen who crash-landed in the desert. Due to a lack of evidence the courts could not prove murder, and the Moleles escaped punishment for a crime they now admit to freely. The British administration banished the family to Shashane in 1946. *See also* Sarwa.

MOLEMA, MODIRI SILAS (1892–1965). Medical doctor, author, and political activist. A Tshidi MoRolong kgosana born in Mafikeng, he studied medicine at Glasgow University, graduating in 1919. In 1920 he published *The Bantu: Past and Present* which, together with his later biographies of diKgosi Moroka and **Montshiwa**, pioneered black southern African historiography.

Molema was best known as an African spokesman. Influenced by the writings of W.E.B. DuBois and the Pan African Movement, Molema became active in both South African and Protectorate politics, joined the **African National Congress**, and was a member of the Native (African) Advisory Council (NAC), the Joint Advisory Council, and the African Council. During the 1920s he advocated the election of NAC representatives, a reform adopted by the Tshidi BaRolong. He worked closely with BaTswana diKgosi, in particular **Tshekedi Khama** and **Bathoen II,** in opposing the British administrative reforms of the 1930s. He attempted unsuccessfully to mediate between the opposing factions in the BaNgwato crisis of the 1950s. Molema was also a leading advocate of LEGCO, though he failed to be elected in 1961. *See also* Councils; Rolong.

MOLEMA, SILA THELESHO (1852–1929). MoRolong royal and early nationalist politician. In 1878 he organized the first day school among the BaRolong boo Ratshidi. From 1888 he served as tribal secretary to Kgosi Montshiwa and his successors. He commanded the BaRolong regiments during the siege of Mafikeng. In 1901 he purchased the *Bechuanaland Gazette or*

Koranta ea Becoana, which under his direction existed for a number of years as the first black-owned SeTswana newspaper. In 1909 he represented "Bechuanaland" at the South African Native Convention where he was instrumental in getting the body to support the continued existence of the Bechuanaland Protectorate as well as Lesotho and Swaziland outside the nascent Union of South Africa. During the 1920s he served on the Native (African) Advisory Council and in 1927 played a behind-the-scenes organizational role in the petition and subsequent mission to the **high commissioner** by **Tshekedi Khama, Sebele II,** and **Ntebogang**. He was the father of **Dr. M.S. Molema** and served as a mentor for such figures as journalist, activist, and author Sol Plaatje and **Peter Sidzumo**. *See also* Newspapers.

MOLEPOLOLE. Capital of Kweneng since 1863 and "gateway to the Kgalagadi." The historic center of the village is the hill, Ntsweng. In the 1860s and 1870s Molepolole prospered as the nexus of the trans-Kgalagadi trade in ivory, ostrich feathers, and karosses. In 1901 **Sebele I** moved his kgotla off the hill into the valley below, known as Borakalalo. In 1915, his son **Sechele II** moved the royal kgotla back up to Ntsweng. A powerful faction of dikgosana refused to accompany him, however, and the village remained geographically divided. In 1933 when the British tried to unite the two villages by locating the kgotla of **Kgari Sechele** at a site between, both segments refused to budge. In 1937 the British forced the Borakalalo and Ntsweng segments to move next to Kgari Sechele and in the process destroyed most of the historic buildings at Ntsweng. In 1990 Molepolole was the largest rural town in Botswana, with a population of 36,930. Botswana's first diamond-cutting factory, operated by Lazar Kaplan Company, is located there [the second, Debswana, is located in **Serowe**]. *See also* Towns.

MONNAMABURU LETSHOLATHEBE (1875[?]–1947). Political leader in Ngamiland. Monnamaburu was a strong supporter of his brother **Sekgoma Letsholathebe,** whom he accompanied into exile. From 1917 to 1923 he was head of the BaSekgoma faction in Chobe, following the death of David Letsholathebe. In 1924 he returned to Maun and in 1932 was appointed regent in place of **Mathiba Moremi**. In turn, the British replaced him as regent with Dibolaeng. After 1934 he served as the headman of Tsau. *See also* Motshabi Letsholathebe.

MONTSHIWA (1812[?]–1896). Kgosi of the Tshidi BaRolong, 1849–1896, the period when they were divided by Boer and British imperialism. In 1853, after the Tshidi BaRolong fought the Boers at Mosite, Montshiwa fled with his people to Moshaneng, northwest of Kanye. He returned to the Molopo area in 1877. Montshiwa is credited with mediating between the Kgafela Kgatla and the BaKwena in 1881, helping to gain a truce in the **Civil Wars**, which disturbed all of southern Botswana, and gathering support for a united front against Boer filibusters and Cape settler land-grabbing. In 1884 he accepted John Mackenzie's offer of British protection, which led to the **Warren Expedition**. The resulting proclamation, making British Bechuanaland a British colony and Bechuanaland a protectorate, led ultimately to the permanent division of the Tshidi BaRolong, who straddled the two Bechuanalands. In 1895 British Bechuanaland was annexed to the Cape Colony over the protests of Montshiwa. The Tshidi BaRolong south of the Molopo became the subjects of the Cape Colony and, after 1910, South Africa. Only Montshiwa's people north of the Molopo, in the **BaRolong Farms** he created in the year of annexation, escaped this fate. *See also* Besele Wessels; Mackenzie, John; Mafikeng; Rolong; Three Kings in London.

MOREMI II (1855[?]–1891). Kgosi of the BaTawana, 1876–1891. On ascending the throne he contacted various missionary bodies, inviting them to establish a presence in Ngamiland. By then the BaNgwato church of the **LMS** had already claimed Ngamiland as their mission field. James Hepburn, LMS missionary at Shoshong, moved quickly with the encouragement of **Khama III** to preempt potential rivals. He converted Moremi in 1877. In subsequent years, the LMS church in Ngamiland grew slowly as a branch of the BaNgwato church. In 1882 and again in 1884 Moremi's regiments fended off AmaNdebele incursions. Under Moremi, the BaTawana expanded their control over the entire Ngamiland region.

MOREMI III (1915–1946). Moremi Mathiba ("Mawelawela") was Kgosi of the BaTawana, 1937–1946. Groomed by the British as a young man, he was sent by Resident Commissioner **Charles Rey** to receive military training at the Gaberones Police Camp and then to **Tiger Kloof** for three years. His independent streak surfaced early. On school holidays he worked with **Tshekedi Khama** to delay Rey's cherished 1934 Proclamations, though later as chief he was forced to implement them. And at Tiger

Kloof he seduced the school nurse, who became his wife. Ultimately, Moremi was disliked by the British as much as he became popular among his own people. He was known as a fearless hunter and an opponent of autonomy for the OvaHerero. During **World War II** his popularity declined. In 1941 he began recruiting for Ngamiland's volunteer forces and had to contend with widespread desertion and apathy. In his final years, Moremi neglected his duties and alienated the British as well as the majority of the BaTawana. *See also* Moremi, Elizabeth.

MOREMI, ELIZABETH PULANE neé SEECO (1912–1994). Wife of **Moremi III**, regent of the BaTawana, 1947–1964, and member of the British Empire. She was born in the Orange Free State of BaRolong parents, gained an education, and met her husband while working as a nurse at his school, **Tiger Kloof**. They married in 1937 and had three children, including **Letsholathebe II**, her eventual successor. When Moremi III was suspended by the British in 1945 for misbehavior, Pulane was appointed tribal treasurer, and her good work prompted the government to recommend her as regent in 1946 when her husband died in a car crash.

Pulane's regency, though troubled, was energetic. One of her first acts was to retain the services of her late husband's MoNgwato secretary **Leetile Raditladi,** whom Moremi had hired just prior to his death. Raditladi's reforms brought accounting and administration to the BaTawana for the first time. As a result, older but powerful reactionaries bore him resentment, and their suspicions intensified as Raditladi and the regent became romantically involved. The conservatives, who used as their representative **Moshuga Moremi** mobilized against what they called the "two foreigners." In 1952 Pulane fired Raditladi, after the revamping of the administration was complete, and then suffered a steady reduction of her powers by her opponents. Nevertheless, Pulane proved to be an able administrator and, with British support, she maintained her authority. She stood down from the regency in 1964 in favor of her son Letsholathebe II and lived out her working years as matron of Francistown Teacher Training College. *See also* Moeti Samotsoko; Regency.

MOROKA, WALTER MOKGOSI. Kgosi (1955–1960) of Moroka's BaRolong of northeastern Botswana and the last Kgosi to be dethroned in the colonial period. The occasion of his installation was anything but propitious. In 1955 the British removed his father, as they feared he would fail to prevent the local influence of Ephraim "The Prophet" Moyo, a Zimbabwean millenialist. Walter himself had been convicted of robbing the Tati Company in 1951 and as Kgosi set up a cattle-running scheme to steal Rhodesian animals. He was caught and deposed by his own morafe.

MORUAKGOMO SECHELE (1932–1979). Eldest son of **Sebele II** and pretender to the BaKwena throne. His mother was Susan, of coloured origin, who in 1928 became Sebele's second wife according to SeTswana law (i.e., *bogadi*). Moruakgomo was born in Ghanzi during the period of his father's forced exile. Following the death of **Kgari Sechele** in 1962, Moruakgomo's uncles and the majority of the BaKwena promoted his succession. Moruakgomo's cousin, and son of a civil marriage, **Bonewamang**, was supported by a minority. After holding an inquiry, the British rejected the claims of both parties and made **Neale Sechele** the new Kgosi.

MOSHUGA MOREMI (1889–1972). Leading member of the BaTawana royal family. The senior uncle of **Moremi III**, he was passed over as regent in favor of his nephew's wife Elizabeth Pulane in 1946. He led the opposition against Pulane and fought to preserve feudal privilege. *See also* Moremi, Elizabeth.

MOSINYI, GOARENG SEGOTSO (1915–). Politician, member of the BaKaa royal family. Product of **Tiger Kloof** and Lovedale, Mosinyi was the son of a Kalamare headman and married into the Kgamane family. From 1943 to 1948 Mosinyi served as BaNgwato tribal treasurer. He supported **Seretse Khama** during the 1948–1949 crisis and in 1950 accompanied him into exile at Lobatse. After 1956 Mosinyi became a member of the BaNgwato tribal council, the African Council, and LEGCO. In 1962 he became a founding member of the **Democratic Party**. From 1965 to 1989 he was the MP for Shoshong, then he retired. He served in the cabinet. *See also* Kaa.

MOSIRWA MOAPARE (1890[?]–1944). Kgosi of the BaNgologa of Hukuntsi, 1931–1944. Resident Commissioner **Charles Rey** met Mosirwa in 1931 and subsequently tried to make him "paramount chief" of the BaKgalagadi in order to implement his schemes for the reform of native administration. The non-BaNgologa BaKgalagadi opposed his "paramountcy," but

Mosirwa's authority over the BaNgologa, who had until then been scattered, was recognized. The British also regarded his son and successor, Moapare, as the only reliable BaKgalagadi headman.

MOTHOWAGAE MOTLOGELWA (d. 1944). MoNgwaketse **London Missionary Society** evangelist and founder of the King Edward Bangwaketse Free Church. Mothowagae was among the early evangelists of the LMS. He worked first as an LMS teacher from 1874 to 1880. Educated at Kuruman Bible School, he became a full-time preacher in 1884. In 1893 he took charge of the Ngwaketse "free school," which charged nothing and competed with its sister LMS "fee school." In 1901 he refused to accept an assignment to preach in distant Lehututu. Hoping to puncture his pride, the LMS gave him an "ordination exam" in Latin. In 1902 he broke from the LMS to found his own church, which initially gained support from his fellow evangelists and many dikgosana. In addition to a large following in Kanye, he was also popular in Mosopa, where his supporters, including Kgosi **Gobuamang**, built him a church. Mothowagae's appeal was based on personal charisma, respect for traditional customs, and promises of educational reform. Kgosi **Bathoen I** tried to suppress the sect, because he suspected it might be part of a plot to usurp him and install Kwenaetsile, his own brother. In 1911, after Bathoen's death, Kgosi **Seepapitso I** carried out his father's banishment order and sent Mothowagae into exile at Lekgolobotlo. His followers, who were not allowed to join him, trickled back to the LMS after his death.

MOTSETE, KGALEMAN TUMEDISHO (1899–1974). Co-founder and first president of the **People's Party (BPP)** and author of Botswana's national anthem "Fatshe la Rona." Born in Serowe, Motsete was the first MoTswana to obtain an LMS bursary for higher education. He spent most of the 1920s in London, where he earned bachelor's degrees in Theology and Music and qualified as a music teacher. He also taught introductory SeTswana to Resident Commissioner-Designate **Charles Rey.** After returning to Bechuanaland in 1929, Motsete set out to be a schoolteacher in Serowe, but he clashed with **Tshekedi Khama.** From then he became one of Tshekedi's most vocal critics. In 1932, with the support of local BaKalanga leaders (*boShe*), he established the Tati Training Institution, the first secondary school in the Protectorate. Financial difficulties forced its closure in 1941. He then left the Protectorate to teach in South Africa and Nyasaland. In 1944 he co-founded the Nyasaland African Congress, the party which led Malawi to independence in 1964. Motsete returned to Bechuanaland after the war, and during the 1950s he acted as tribal Education secretary in Gammangwato, where he also became involved in the pro-**Seretse Khama** agitation. After the stagnation of the **Federal Party**, in which he was briefly active, Motsete co-founded the People's Party in December 1960. During and after the BPP split in June 1962 he supported **Matante**. During this period he became an informer for the South African Police regarding the activities of the **ANC** in the Protectorate, thereby undermining **Motsamai Mpho**. In 1963, after Motsete and Matante had a falling out over tactics, Motsete's political influence declined. He stood as the only BPP (Motsete) candidate in the 1965 general election, in Lobatse, and lost his deposit. Though he participated in the discussions which led to the formation of the **National Front** after 1965, Motsete retired from active politics to his home in Mahalapye.

MOTSHABI LETSHOLATHEBE (1870[?]–1934). ''MmaKgabo,'' elder sister of **Sekgoma Letsholathebe** and niece of **Khama III**. In 1923 she became leader of the remaining BaSekgoma in Chobe, who left the area following her death as she had no heirs. Her property was inherited by her brother's usurper, **Mathiba Moremi**. *See also* Monnamaburu Letsholathebe.

MOTSHIDISI, KLAAS KEBOTSE (1932–). Politician and labor leader. ''KK'' emerged as a labor leader while working in a Palapye garage for Tommy Shaw. He was a member of the BaNgwato tribal council in the late 1950s and became a founding member of the **People's Party (BPP)** for which he served as secretary in 1961. Following the 1962 party split, Motshidisi became secretary-general of the BPP (Mpho). In the early 1960s he was also involved in trade union activities, becoming general secretary of the short-lived Bechuanaland Trade Union Congress. After independence, he joined the civil service and subsequently was appointed Commissioner of Labour, where he earned a reputation for hard work, fairness, and devotion to duty. He retired in the early 1990s and reentered politics, in 1994 standing for election to the National Assembly as the **National Front (BNF)** candidate for Palapye. He lost. He nevertheless remains an important BNF figure. *See also* Mpho, Motsamai; Trade Unions.

MOTSWASELE II (1785[?]–1821). Kgosi of the BaKwena, 1807[?]–1821. He was assassinated in a **letsholo** by his political enemies, who considered him a despot. Oral tradition relates that before he was killed, Motswasele prophesied the coming of the **mfecane** as a form of vengeance on the **BaKwena**. *See also* Sechele I.

MPHEPHENG (1820[?]–1910). Mother of Makaba and **Moremi II**, Kgosi of the BaTawana. Of BaNgwato descent, "Mmama-kaba" was captured by the AmaNdebele as a young, unmarried mother and was taken to Zimbabwe. Several years later she escaped with her sister and child, trekking across the Kgalagadi to Ngamiland. She then was married by a MoTawana, but soon caught the eye of one of his age-mates, **Letsholathebe I**, and became his first love. Over time, she came to be considered his wife and bore him two sons, Makaba (who died young), and Moremi. When Letsholathebe's first wife died childless, she became the senior wife and Moremi, the heir. From 1860 to 1863 she was the guardian of the orphaned Helmore children, with whom she corresponded until her death. As *mohumagadi* she opposed **Sekgoma Letsholathebe** and lived long enough to see her grandson **Mathiba Moremi** oust him.

MPHO, MOTSAMAI KEYETSWE (1921–). Co-founder of the **People's Party (BPP)** and long-term political figure in Ngami-land. Mpho was born into an industrious and free BaYei family of Maun and was sent to **Tiger Kloof** by his schoolmaster uncle. There he became religious and in 1948 was sent to South Africa, where he worked in the Crown Mine as a welfare officer with his former boarding master until 1953. He then obtained part-time employment with a religious organization and devoted his spare hours to organizing for the ANC in the West Rand. He served as secretary of the ANC branch in Roodepoort and three years later was arrested for treason, along with 155 others. After a year in jail, he was released. He was later rearrested and, following four months in detention, deported in 1960 to the Protectorate.

Though absent in South Africa for twelve years, Mpho had maintained his involvement in Protectorate politics. He was a spokesperson for the rights of BaYei and a regular contributor to *Naledi ya Batswana*. Immediately on his return, Mpho assumed the position of secretary-general of the BPP. After the party split in 1962, he founded the **Independence Party (BIP)**, which failed to gain a seat in the general election of 1965. Mpho was elected to the National Assembly in 1969 and again in 1974, but he lost his seat in 1979 and has failed to regain it in the three elections held subsequently. Today Mpho is the leader of the Independence Freedom Party, which united the BIP with the Freedom Party, led by Leach Tlhomelang. *See also* Newspapers.

MPHOENG, PHETHU (1880[?]–1951). Grandson of **Sekgoma I** of the BaNgwato and chief's representative in Mmadinare, 1904–1951. Educated at Lovedale, in 1903 he divorced Leina Rauwe and married Milly, the daughter of **Khama III**. His father had been exiled by Khama, but Phethu gained the latter's loyalty and introduced a fervent pro-Khama and LMS administration in Mmadinare. He fell out with **Sekgoma II** after the Ratshosa family circulated stories that he was a despot, and Phethu was expelled in 1924. When **Tshekedi Khama** assumed the regency in 1926, Phethu led the opposition against Tshekedi's enemies, the Ratshosa brothers, and subsequently he and his brother, Oteng, became Tshekedi's right-hand men. Like Tshekedi, he strongly opposed **Seretse Khama**'s marriage in 1949. A teetotaler, upright Christian, and hard worker, Phethu was a successful cattle and store owner, and he found time as well to indulge in cattle-running through his association with the Brink family. In his old age Phethu went blind. *See also* Ratshosa, Motswetle; Ratshosa, Simon.

MUSEUMS. Calls for a Botswana-based museum were sounded as early as the 1930s, but the first museum, the National Museum and Art Gallery in Gaborone, was not built until 1968. In 1976 the National Museum became a department in the Ministry of Home Affairs. Since independence, non-governmental attempts to develop local museums have had mixed results. In the early 1960s a museum was operated for a few years in Kanye under the patronage of **Bathoen II**, who then became active in establishing the National Museum. In 1976 Sandy Grant opened the Phuthadikobo Museum in the converted building once used as the **Bakgatla National School**. It now serves also as a craft and education center. The Botswana Museums Association joins regional and non-governmental museum organizations, such as in Serowe (Khama III Memorial Museum 1985), in Molepolole (Kgosi Sechele I Museum 1992), in Francistown (Supa Ngwao Museum 1993), and in Maun (1994). Since 1987 calls to establish a unified museums service have had no result to date. Small cultural museums are run at D'kar (BaSawra/Khoe), Etsha (HaMbukushu), and an archaeological site museum in the Tsodilo Hills was scheduled for opening in 1995.

MWALI. The Mwali religion (Ikalanga; "Mwari" in other Chi-Shona dialects), originated as the state religion of the **Butwa** kingdom and was later adopted by the occupying Ama**Ndebele.** Like other institutionalized religions, Mwali consists of many congregations which overlap ethnic and territorial boundaries. Believers of Mwali stretch from the Central and Northeast Districts of Botswana across central and southern Zimbabwe, and into parts of Mozambique and South Africa. The central oracle is situated in Njelele in the Matopos hills. Mwali is a "high God cult," in which small congregations of believers communicate their problems through messengers and priests, who in turn relay messages back to their congregations from the regional oracles, or shrines, of Mwali. Individuals and groups may also travel personally to the oracle in order to pray, make sacrificial gifts, and consult with priests. The priests who maintain the various oracles are male/female descendants of oracle founders. In Botswana, there are three oracles. The principal members of Mwali are Ba**Kalanga,** though congregations are found among the Ba**Khurutshe** of Tonota, and the BaTswapong in the Tswapong hills. Several neo-traditional churches, such as the Guta ra Mwari, are offspring of Mwali. *See also* Independent Churches; Religion.

N

NAMA (NAMA-KHOE). A people of Cape and Namibian origin and who speak Nama, a form of **Khoe,** sometimes referred to as Namaqua and another term applied to the group. They are referred to pejoratively as "Hottentots" or, in SeTswana, as "MaKgothu" (literally people of copper, which alludes to their one-time metallurgical skills). Unlike other Khoe groups, the Nama acquired a significant number of guns during the nineteenth century, leading to their temporary hegemony of southern and central **Namibia** during the mid-nineteenth century, when they for a while dominated many OvaHerero. Members of several of their branches entered the Protectorate during the **Nama-German War of 1904–1909,** and the Anglo-German boundary cut across their hunting areas. *See also* Herero.

NAMA-GERMAN WAR OF 1904–1909. In 1904 the **Nama** of southern **Namibia** and adjacent areas of Botswana rose in revolt against the Germans. In January 1905 they were defeated at the Battle of Swartfontein and their most important chief, Hendrick Witbooi, died soon after. For the next three years, the Nama adopted hit-and-run tactics under such guerrilla leaders as Jacob Marenga, Abraham Morris, and Simon Kopper, who outmaneuvered the Germans in the desert and relied on *tsamma* melons for water. The Nama ignored the 1890 border drawn by the British and Germans across the Nama's western Kgalagadi homeland, and the Bechuanaland Protectorate Police (BPP), South African Cape police, and German Schutztruppen cooperated to arrest the rebels (after the war a number of BPP officers were awarded German medals).

In September 1907 an Anglo-German force killed Marenga and others inside British Bechuanaland. Kopper remained at large, repeatedly ambushing the Germans in the summer of 1907–1908. In hopes of forcing Kopper into a showdown, the Germans dispatched additional troops to Botswana's southwestern border. After Kopper's men wiped out a six-man German patrol just inside Namibia on 3 March 1908, the Germans notified the British **high commissioner** of their ordering a German force of 520, mounted on camels, to cross the border in pursuit. On March 15, the Nama spotted the force near their principal camp at "Seatsub" pan located inside what is now Gemsbok National Park. Kopper, thinking it a small patrol rather than the main invasion force, moved out of the camp with a number of his men, weakening the camp's defenses. The Germans attacked the camp at dawn on the 16th, making effective use of their four machine guns. The Nama returned fire from behind their barricades and trenches, killing the German commander, Friedrick von Erckert. The defenders withstood a bayonet charge but, after two-and-a-half hours of fighting, retreated fearing encirclement. The Germans reported eleven of their troops dead and nineteen wounded and counted fifty-eight Nama corpses, including a woman. The Battle of Seatsub was the last major engagement of the war. The elusive Kopper frustrated the Germans, who entered into secret negotiations with the British. In 1909 Kopper and the British signed a treaty, Kopper agreeing to settle peacefully with his followers at Lokgwabe. The Nama were granted additional land rights in the then Kgalagadi Crown lands as well as some "compensation" from the Germans in return for their promise to refrain from recrossing the border.

NAMANE, GAMELEMO VICTORIA (1905–). Pioneer female teacher and nurse. A MoNgwaketse adopted into the royal family, Victoria witnessed the assassination of **Seepapitso I** and was raised by the regent, **Gagoangwe**. She was educated in Kanye and became a qualified teacher in the early 1920s. She then left teaching and became one of the first BaTswana nurses, training and working at the Kanye hospital from 1925 to 1935. She returned to teaching, however, because it offered more opportunities to people of her ability. For many years she taught at Tlokweng, where she retired. In her old age she has become a supporter of the women's movement.

NAMIBIA. Botswana's neighbor to the west and north. In 1884 it was occupied by the Germans as South-West Africa, taken by South African forces in 1915, and in 1922 it became the League of Nations mandate of South Africa, under the control of which, in spite of the revocation of the mandate in 1966, it remained until Namibian independence in 1990. Between 1965 and independence, the South West Africa People's Organisation (SWAPO) waged from Angola a guerrilla-style liberation war against the South African Army along the northern border with its military wing, PLAN (People's Liberation Army of Namibia). Until independence SWAPO was recognized by the United Nations as the legitimate representative of the Namibian people, and in the two elections held since independence it has won large majorities in the national parliament. SWAPO's first and only president Samuel Nujoma has been Namibia's first and only elected president.

Over the generations, colonial events inside Namibia reverberated in Botswana. The brutal phase of German occupation drove many Namibians into exile in the Bechuanaland Protectorate, and after the South African takeover, BaTswana opposed its incorporation into the Union and Republic of South Africa. In 1946 diKgosi led by **Tshekedi Khama** played an important role in blocking South African attempts to gain approval in the new United Nations for such a step. In the two decades or so prior to independence, many Namibian political refugees began their journey into active exile by crossing into Botswana, and the war between SWAPO and South Africa unsettled northwestern Botswana along the border from Ghanzi to Kazungula.

Namibia's geographical position has also forced the Botswana government, as the colonial rulers before them, to contemplate a rail or road link connecting Walvis Bay, in independent Namibia's possession since 1994, to eastern Botswana through the Kgalagadi Desert. As of 1995 the "Trans-Kalahari Road," long a dream, was in the process of becoming a reality, with all-weather roads connecting most of the distance between Jwaneng and Gobabis via Kang. *See also* Caprivi Strip; Herero; Maharero, Samuel; Nama; Rey, Charles; World War I.

NARO (NARO-KHOE). Botswana's largest Khoe-speaking group, based in the **Ghanzi** area. Misrepresented as Nharo, the Naro call themselves Ncoa-Khoe ("red people"). The Naro remained independent into the 1850s and appear to have had a centralized form of leadership. Under **Dukuri**, they hunted, foraged, raided cattle, and were involved in trade with peoples of the **Okavango Delta** and northern Cape. In 1854 they stole cattle from the BaTawana, then under attack from the BaKololo. They held out against BaTawana retaliatory raids for several years before their leaders were killed by the BaTawana, who had lured them with the ruse of peace negotiations. From then until 1895 they lived under BaTawana headmen **Hendrik Van Zyl**, of Boer descent, being especially notorious. In 1880 the Naro killed him.

In 1895 the Naro had their land alienated by the British administration which hoped to placate the **BSACO** by giving the area in question to Boer settlers. The administration arranged for a Namibian "expert," known as "Sjambok" Hahn, to declare the area "uninhabited," alleging that only "nomadic" Naro were living there. In this manner, Naro land rights were ignored, and in 1898 Boer settlers arrived to occupy what became known as the Ghanzi Farms.

Since 1898 the Naro have lost even more land to commercial farming in the area and have been reduced to being poorly-paid farm workers plagued by alcoholism, family breakdown, violence, and a lack of education.

In recent years they have taken a prominent role with other BaSarwa communities in the Ghanzi area in asserting their land and political rights, among others. Grassroots organizations and non-governmental organizations have consolidated into the Kuru Development Trust, based at D'Kar, where a small "Bush People" cultural and art center is located. *See also* Khoe.

NATA. The region northeast of the **Boteti River** bordering on the Makgadikgadi pans. The region's **Shua**-Khoe remained independent until 1890, and for much of the nineteenth century they lived under chief **Kgaraxumae.** His subjects apparently lost their cattle to BaNgwato raids. In the early 1890s the **BaNgwato** colonized the area in order to graze cattle there. In the process they conquered and enslaved the region's inhabitants in a systematic and brutal fashion. Their control only increased between 1907 and 1920 when **Sekgoma,** son of **Khama III,** lived in exile in Nata. Cattle owners in Serowe appointed overseers to look after their slaves and animals, which they visited irregularly. Nata women were raped on a regular basis by BaNgwato men. **Tshekedi Khama** continued to exploit the region, but when commercial ranches opened in Nata in the 1950s, **bolata** came to an end due to mass desertions. Nata obtained better administration and services in the 1940s, when conditions there were exposed following the murder of two British airmen. Today, Nata remains poor, and the cattle posts of the Khama family and other BaNgwato are still located there. *See also* Molele, Twai Twai.

NATIONAL FRONT (BNF). The Botswana National Front was founded in 1965 under the leadership of **Kenneth Koma.** The BNF regards itself as an alliance of a broad spectrum of interests and groups, though it began as a coalition of parties defeated in the 1965 election and several alienated diKgosi. In southern Botswana, most of the **People's Party** members joined the BNF. Among traditional authorities, the Front made a major breakthrough in 1969, when **Bathoen II** abdicated his bogosi and joined the party as president. In the 1969 general election, the BNF won three of the four seats in the Southern District, which has remained a BNF stronghold. Since then the BNF has also gained strength in the urban areas, particularly in Gaborone, where in the 1984 election it captured the capital's two seats. It has increased its share of the vote in each national election, despite internal disorganization and financial problems, to become Botswana's second party rivaling the dominance of the **Democratic Party.** The BNF had its best showing in 1994, when it captured thirteen of the thirty-nine seats in the National Assembly and more than 37 percent of the popular vote. *See also* Dingake, Michael; Elections; Motshidisi, Klaas.

NDEBELE (AMANDEBELE). A militarily-powerful people led by Nkosi Mzilikazi, of the Khumalo clan. During the **mfecane** of the early nineteenth century, Mzilikazi fled Natal with his followers to escape the authority of Shaka of the AmaZulu. On their long trek north, Mzilikazi's group absorbed large numbers of captives and refugees from SeSotho- and SeTswana-speaking peoples. The AmaNdebele core dwindled with time, and only the SiNdebele language and culture, together with Mzilikazi's organization, held his mobile state together. Around the period 1823–1837, before settling ultimately in western Zimbabwe, Mzilikazi established his capital in the western Transvaal at eGabani near Mosega, south of present-day Lobatse, from which his armies raided among the southern BaTswana. From 1838 to 1839 they moved through eastern Botswana. From Zimbabwe they attacked the BaNgwato and BaKwena in 1843, were defeated by the BaNgwato at Shoshong in 1863, and raided the BaTawana in 1882 and 1884. Mzilikazi's son and successor, Lobengula (ruled 1870–1894), competed with the BaNgwato for control of northeastern Botswana. The dispute was finally resolved in 1893 when **Khama III** joined the **BSACO** and the Bechuanaland Border **Police** in attacking and destroying the AmaNdebele army. Lobengula died soon thereafter. *See also* Battle of Dutlwe; Battles of Shoshong; Grobler Affair; Kalanga; Macheng.

NEALE SECHELE (1917–1985). Kgosi of the BaKwena, 1963–1970. Neale was the son of **Baruti Kgosidintsi** and *mohumagadi* Phetogo, divorced senior wife of **Sechele II,** and he grew up claiming membership in the royal family. He was educated at Tati Training Institution and **Tiger Kloof.** In 1963 Neale Sechele was recognized by the British as Kgari Sechele's successor in a controversial judgment. In 1970 he was deposed on account of his general incompetence. *See also* Bonewamang P. Sechele; Kgari Sechele; Moruakgomo Sechele; Sebele II.

NEWSPAPERS. During the early nineteenth century coverage of events in Botswana appeared in many South African papers, notably *The Friend* (Bloemfontein), *The Graham's Town Journal*, the *Natal Mercury*, the *Colesburg Advertiser*, *Zuid-Afrikan*, and the *Transvaal Argus*, among others. Later, Botswana news was printed in the important northern Cape newspapers, e.g., *The Bechuanaland News & Vryburg, Mafeking and Malmani, Protectorate Chronicle* (1883–1901); *Vryburg Advocate and Bechuanaland Gazette* (1886–1887); *Mafeking Mail and Protectorate Guardian* (1899–1900, 1903–1921, 1960–); *Northern News* (Vryburg); and *Diamond Fields Advertiser* (Kimberley). Throughout the twentieth century the English press in

South Africa has played an important role in informing Ba-
Tswana. By the 1930s the Johannesburg newspapers enjoyed a
wide readership in the Protectorate, especially *The Star*, *Rand
Daily Mail*, the *Sunday Times*, and *Bantu World*.

The earliest SeTswana newsletters were printed by missionaries in the mid-nineteenth century. These included *Molekoli
ua Bechwana* (1856–1857), published in Thaba Nchu at the
Wesleyan mission by **Joseph Ludorf**; *Mokaeri oa Becuana le
Muleri oa Makuku* (1857–1859), published by William Ashton,
of the **LMS**, Kuruman; and *Mahoko a Becwana* (1883–1898),
also Kuruman, LMS. By the 1880s, some BaTswana were also
reading SeSotho newspapers and, during the early twentieth
century, issues from the English/IsiXhosa press of the eastern
Cape. The first independent (i.e., non-mission) SeTswana
newspaper was *Koranta ea Becoana* (1901–1908), edited by
Sol Plaatje and **Peter Sidzumo** and published in Mafikeng by
Silas Molema. *Tsala tsa Batho* (1910–1916), also edited by
Plaatje, was published in Kimberley. In the western Transvaal,
the Lutheran mission at Bethanie published *Masupa-Tsela*
from 1913.

SeTswana articles, some dealing with Protectorate affairs,
appeared in such newspapers as *Abantu-Batho* (the SANNC/
ANC organ from 1912–1930) and the multi-lingual newspapers
of the **Communist Party of South Africa**: *The South African
Worker* and *Inkululeko*. In the late-1920s, **the Dutch Reformed
Church** in Mochudi began producing a SeTswana newsletter,
Lesedinyana la Sechaba, which lasted into the 1930s, by
which time the government had begun to produce its quarterly
educational journal *Labone la Sechaba* (1936–1940), which
was then followed by the SeTswana/English *Bechuanaland
Protectorate Government Newsletter* (1939–1946). In 1936 the
government agreed to submit SeTswana articles to *Umteteli
wa Bantu*, a newspaper sponsored by the Bantu Press and the
Chamber of Mines. These articles were also forwarded to the
Bantu World, published by the Bantu Press in Johannesburg.
Articles on Botswana also appeared in *The African World*, *The
African Voice*, and in the Communist Party of South Africa
organ, *Usembenzi & Inkululeko*. During **World War II** the
Bantu Press published a newspaper for BaTswana and Ma-
Swati members of the AAPC: *Indlovu/Tlou* (1940–1944). This
newspaper's success led to the cooperation of the Protectorate
government and the Bantu Press in a more ambitious venture
that catered to BaTswana in the Protectorate and South Africa.
The result was the English-SeTswana newspaper, *Naledi ya*

Batswana, which ran from 1944 to 1955 and from 1957 to 1964. In 1962 the government brought out its first monthly English-SeTswana journal, *Kutlwano*. The colonial newsletter *The Bechuanaland Newsletter* (1961–1964) grew into the *Bechuanaland Daily News Bulletin* (1964–1966), which eventually became the republican-government-run *Botswana Daily News/Dikgang tsa Gampieno* (1966–).

Other SeTswana publications include the *Tiger Kloof Magazine* (1916–1956); *Therisanyo* (1964–), published by the **Democratic Party**; *Digkang tsa Mochudi* (1968–1969), published by the Mochudi Community Centre; *Masa-Dawn* (1964), published by the **People's Party**; *Phua-Phaa* (1969–), published by the **National Front**; and *Lesedi* (1962–), published at Moeng College.

Independent, privately-run newspapers did not appear in Botswana until the 1980s and then only as weeklies. The four major independent newspapers are based in Gaborone. The *Botswana Guardian* (an outgrowth of the *Mafeking Mail and Bechuanaland [Botswana] Guardian*), appears each Friday, and its sister paper, *The Midweek Sun*, on Wednesday, the former with a circulation of approximately 20,000. *Mmegi wa Dikgang/The Reporter*, appears on Friday, with a circulation of 15–20,000. The smaller *Gazette* appears on Wednesday. Small newspapers circulate in other towns, such as the Francistown *Voice* and Maun's *Okavango Observer*, but they and the many domestic magazines tend to come and go. Still, the journalist's profession has established itself tentatively in the country, as evidenced by the recent formation of the Botswana Journalist Association (BOJA), which has membership in the International Federation of Journalists. BOJA was also active in establishing the Media Institute of Southern Africa (MISA— headquarters in Windhoek) in 1992, a federation of journalists outside South Africa, but certain soon to include democratic South Africa. MISA's secretary-general is Methaetsile Leepile, former editor of Botswana's *Mmegi wa Dikgang*. Conversely, pre-democratic South Africa's Defence Force set up newspapers and persons posing as journalists in Botswana as part of its total strategy. One of these, *Newslink*, based in Gaborone, operated as recently as the early 1990s with a total budget of 3.5 million Rand. *See also* Lebotse, Kgosi; Literacy; Masire, Quett; Raditladi, Leetile.

NGWAKETSE (BANGWAKETSE). One of the largest and most important merafe, the BaNgwaketse derived their name from

Ngwaketse, an early Mokwena kgosana from whom the di-Kgosi of BaNgwaketse trace their descent. For that reason, the totem of the BaNgwaketse is the same as that of the BaKwena, the *kwena* (crocodile). By the reign of **Makaba II**, the BaNgwaketse had become independent of the BaKwena (bagaKgabo) and prosperous from cattle-raiding. During the **mfecane** the group fragmented into rival factions, which were not reunited until the reign of **Gaseitsiwe**. In 1853 they settled at **Kanye** and during the 1860s grew wealthy primarily through trade in ostrich feathers. After 1870 they established their northern border with the BaKwena, with whom they allied in the **Civil Wars**. In 1881 they were defeated by the BaLete at Ramotswa and subsequently were threatened by Boer expansionism. They accepted the protection of the British in 1885 but in the next decade under **Bathoen I** joined other BaTswana in trying to limit British authority. During Bathoen's reign, Christianity consolidated its presence. Ecological crises and the introduction of the hut tax in the late 1890s led to dependence on **migrant labor**, which increased among the BaNgwaketse until after independence.

Under the long and stable rule of **Bathoen II**, the BaNgwaketse preserved their bogosi when this institution faced serious crises in many other parts of the Protectorate. *See also* Gagoangwe; Mmanaana Kgatla; Mothowagae Motlogelwa; National Front; Ntebogang Ratshosa; Sebego I; Seepapitso II; Seepapitso IV; Segotshane; Senthufe; Tshosa Makaba; Tshosa Sebego.

NGWATO (BANGWATO, BAMANGWATO). A BaKwena offshoot which under Kgosi **Mathiba** (1777[?]–1795[?]) became independent. Their name derives from Ngwato, who according to tradition was the son of a BaKwena Kgosi. Ngwato is said to have fled from his brother and evaded a search party with the aid of a *phuti* (duiker), thus accounting for the use of *phuti* as the royal totem among the BaNgwato and their descendants, the BaTawana.

Under **Sekgoma I**, the BaNgwato expanded greatly in territorial size, asserting their paramountcy over what is now the Central and Northeastern Districts of Botswana. In 1848 Sekgoma pushed the BaKaa out of the Shoshong hills and then began incorporating the BaTswapong, BaTalaote, and other neighboring peoples. The BaNgwato competed with the BaKwena for control of the profitable trade routes to Ngamiland and central Africa, prompting BaKwena intervention in Ba-

Ngwato affairs between 1857 and 1872. After **Khama III** became their Kgosi, the BaNgwato established themselves as the stronger morafe. Khama III cooperated with the British and the **BSACO** in the early 1890s as a means of incorporating the territories occupied by the Ba**Kalanga** and Ba**Birwa,** over which the BaNgwato and AmaNdebele had long disputed. When reserve boundaries were demarcated in 1899, the Bamangwato Reserve was the largest; approximately one-third of the Protectorate's population thereby became Khama's subjects. From his headquarters in Palapye and, after 1904, Serowe, Khama created a system of provincial governors to control this "empire," in which the BaNgwato "proper" constituted no more than a fifth of the total reserve population (Bamangwato).

In the twentieth century Khama and his son, **Tshekedi Khama,** attempted to stem the tide of BaNgwato dependence on **migrant labor,** but this task proved hopeless. By the 1930s Gammangwato had become another of the Protectorate's labor reserves, though an elite of large cattle holders continued to dominate local affairs. The major challenge to the status quo within the reserve came from its numerically largest group, the BaKalanga. During the 1950s a new order emerged in Serowe as a result of the bogosi crisis of 1949–1956, between Tshekedi and his nephew, **Seretse Khama.** The bogosi itself was seriously weakened, and elements of democracy began to develop in local government structures. *See also* Kgamane; Kgari Macheng; Macheng; Ratshosa, Simon; Sekgoma II.

NIKODEMUS, KAHEMEMUA (d. 1945). Leader of the Mbanderu OvaHerero from 1896, when his uncle, also named Nikodemus, was executed by the Germans, until his death. In the 1890s Nikodemus and most Mbanderu fled the Germans in Namibia, crossed into the Protectorate, and settled in Ngamiland. There he came into conflict with the Ba**Tawana** Kgosi **Mathiba Moremi,** and in 1916 he petitioned the British against what he alleged was BaTawana oppression of his people. Concerned that Nikodemus would openly defy Mathiba, the British resettled his people on the Chobe River. Grazing was inadequate, so in 1922 Nikodemus moved with about half of his followers to settle along the **Boteti,** where they remain today. In the 1920s Nikodemus continued to worry the British as a local champion of Marcus Garvey's **Universal Negro Improvement Association,** which called for the redemption of Africa from white rule. *See also* Keheranju, Monjuku.

NSWAZWI III, JOHN MADAWO (1875–1960). Leader of prolonged BaKalanga resistance to BaNgwato overrule. Nswazwi became leader *She* (pronounced "shay") of the BaKalanga-bakaNswazwi in 1912. Both Nswazwi and his father before him were able to collaborate peacefully with **Khama III.** The "troubles" with the BaNgwato began much later, during the rule of **Tshekedi Khama.** Conflict erupted as part of increased land competition between BaNgwato cattle holders and BaKalanga farmers, as well as tightening administrative control from Serowe, but it took the form of a personal confrontation between Nswazwi and Tshekedi.

In 1926, when Nswazwi's people abandoned a communal labor project, Tshekedi fined Nswazwi for insubordination. In 1929 Nswazwi clashed with Tshekedi over a levy to finance Tshekedi's trip to London and then forwarded a petition to the **resident commissioner.** In it he protested the levy as well as Tshekedi's failure to render Nswazwi a percentage of the hut tax, to bring about development among the BaKalanga, particularly in education, and the destruction of BaKalanga cattle posts by Ba**Sarwa** herders of the BaNgwato. When Resident Commissioner Roland Daniel simply referred the matter back to Tshekedi, Nswazwi and five other BaKalanga were hauled off to Serowe and confined for two years. Nswazwi's people responded by refusing to acknowledge the authority of Tshekedi's new chief representative to Bukalanga, **Rasebolai Kgamane.** The regional press and a member of the European Advisory Council took up their cause. In 1931 another petition arrived in Mafikeng demanding Nswazwi's return, full independence from the BaNgwato, and recognition of the Ikalanga language. The British held an inquiry in 1932 and gained a compromise: Nswazwi's release for the dropping of demands for independence. Relations nevertheless remained strained.

In 1943 Tshekedi revived tensions to the breaking point when he imprisoned Nswazwi once again for "insubordination." After his release in 1945, Nswazwi returned to his village against the orders of Tshekedi and the British. The BaKalanga then drove away the men ordered to remove him from the village, thus challenging the will of the government. The British and Tshekedi sent in a regiment and policemen, both heavily armed, and gained backup support from Southern Rhodesian troops and a few of their planes, which overflew the village. Nswazwi and 122 others were rounded up and taken to Serowe. For two years, the BaKalanga protested by refusing to pay their hut tax through the BaNgwato collectors. They also employed lawyers to prepare an appeal to the Privy Council in London. Then, in 1947, the British gave Tshekedi permission to subdue the protest. In late September 2,000 BaNgwato, in regiments under Oteng Mphoeng, moved on Nswazwi's village, with seventy-nine police standing by as "observers." The result was a weeks-long campaign of terror in the general area, from which 1,600 BaKalanga refugees fled into Southern Rhodesia. The houses of refugees were destroyed, their property seized and sold. In 1948 John Nswazwi was allowed to join his people in exile in Southern Rhodesia, where he remained until his death. *See also* Pedi; Villagization; World War I; World War II.

NTEBOGANG RATSHOSA (1882–1979). Female regent of the BaNgwaketse, 1924–1928, during the minority of **Bathoen II.** Ntebogang was the sister of Kgosi **Seepapitso II** and second wife of the MoNgwato royal Ratshosa Motswetle, by whom she bore three children. After his death in 1917, she returned to GaNgwaketse, where she assumed importance following the assassination of Seepapitso. She was appointed regent by her dying mother **Gagoangwe** whereupon she brought stability to a morafe that had experienced seven years of drift under three regents. Six councilors were appointed to assist her; she ruled, however, in partnership with only one—**Kgampu Kamodi**, who was also a member of the **Seventh Day Adventist Church.** Ntebogang continued many of the development projects initiated by her late brother. She expanded Kanye's water supply and established a bull camp as a step toward the introduction of scientific breeding in the reserve. Under her patronage, the SDA set up in Kanye and outlying villages a medical mission that became a model for the Protectorate. In 1927 she joined **Tshekedi Khama** and **Sebele II** in protesting colonial inroads into the power of diKgosi. As a direct consequence, the British backed petitioners demanding Bathoen II's recall from school and placed him on the throne. *See also* Kanye; Moremi, Elizabeth; Regency; Tshosa Sebego.

NURSING. The nursing profession was introduced to Botswana by Dominican sisters who arrived in 1890 with the Rhodesian "pioneer column." Throughout the colonial period nursing was confined to women working in the Protectorate's few hospitals. Many women missionaries served as nurses. The first attempt to train local nurses was organized in 1925 by Dr.

Arthur Kretchmer of the **Seventh Day Adventist Church (SDA)** at the SDA Kanye Hospital. Similar efforts were made at the Molepolole Midwifery Clinic in 1926 (superseded by the Scottish-Livingstone Hospital after 1931), Athlone Hospital (1930+); Sekgoma Memorial Hospital (1931+), Maun Midwifery Centre (1936+), Maun Hospital (1937+), and Sefhare Hospital (1938+).

Initially BaTswana women nurses were offered only apprentice training, rather than certificate courses, and functioned more as laborers than medical professionals. In 1934 a curriculum of Nursing for **High Commission Territories** was developed, but by 1944 not a single person had graduated in the Protectorate. Botswana's first registered nurse was Grace Kgari, who completed her training in South Africa in 1948. Following the adoption of a new curriculum in 1947, the Teichlers, a medical family, promoted nursing education at Derdepoort in the 1950s and in Mochudi after 1960. Between 1958 and 1969 nursing development was promoted by the High Commission Territories Nursing Council. Eventually, some Botswana hospitals became accredited nursing schools prior to independence, and by 1970 the country had 250 registered nurses.

After 1966 the profession expanded with the national medical service operated by government. Unionization and the implementation of American-style education led to a great independence for nurses within the national health system. Today, most of the country's 2,807 nurses are members of the Botswana Nursing Council, which oversees nurses' training.

Nurses are trained for registration at the National Health Institute, which has taught with a new curriculum since 1970. It is located on the grounds of the Princess Marina Hospital, Gaborone. Since 1980 degree-level nursing has been provided at the University of Botswana, Gaborone. *See also* Health; Namane, Gamelemo.

NWAKO, MOUTLAKGOLA PALGRAVE KEDIRETSWE (1922–). Central district civil servant and politician. Nwako is the son of a MoNgwato headman of Palapye and was educated at Khama Memorial School and **Tiger Kloof,** where he was an associate of **Quett Masire.** After he joined the Bamangwato tribal council in 1961 he became known as an upstart "radical." Nwako was a founding member of the **Democratic Party,** its first assistant treasurer, and its most active campaigner in LeTswapong. From 1961 to 1964 he was elected to the African Council, and from 1965 to 1994 he was MP for Tswapong

North. From 1977 to 1989 he held the portfolio as minister of Commerce and Industry, and since 1989 he has been speaker of the National Assembly.

NYAYI (BANYAYI). Of the two branches of the Ba**Kalanga** in Botswana, the BaNyayi are the larger. Their totem is *moyo* ("heart"), and they are properly known as Moyo-Varozwi. They are thought to have been of VaShona (Vakaranga) origin and to have entered eastern Botswana in the seventeenth century from the central Zimbabwean plateau. Under one of their chiefs, Nichasike (Portuguese, Changamire), they overthrew the Chibundule Dynasty of the Butwa kingdom in ca. 1680.

The name BaNyayi, literally "spies," was a pejorative used by the Ba**Lilima**, the royal family of the Chibundule, to refer to these Moyo-Varozwi as outsiders. Under the Nichasike Mambos, a BaNyayi royal was appointed as the monarch's "teeth," overseeing the once-powerful BaLilima. The descendants of this appointee became known as the Mengwe (from meno, "teeth"), while the region of governance itself has been known since as Bulilima-gwa-Mengwe. Of the BaNyayi subgroups, the Mengwe are paramount, while other groups include the Talaote, Nambia, and Tshangate.

O

OKAVANGO DELTA. One of the world's largest inland deltas, containing over 3,000 square miles of surface water, the Okavango is situated in a basin in northwestern Botswana into which drains the Okavango River. The river itself originates on the Benguela Plateau in Angola. Since the late nineteenth century, many schemes for the exploitation of the delta's water have been advanced to benefit the territory and the region as a whole. In 1920, E.H.L. Schwarz suggested that the climate of the subcontinent could be improved by channeling the Okavango into a series of lakes; the consequent increase in evaporation would greatly increase the region's rainfall. To date the idea of rechanneling the waters of the Okavango—for making lakes, irrigating agricultural schemes, supplying eastern Botswana across a Kgalagadi pipeline, or similar plans—have come to nothing. In 1986 the government announced a comprehensive technical and feasibility study of water transfer from the Okavango-Chobe region, but political problems associated with the international status of the two rivers in Angola and Namibia became obstacles. Greater still were local and international conservation pressures applied to resist almost any use of the Okavango-Chobe system.

ORATILE RATSHOSA neé KHAMA (1890–1965). Daughter and eldest child of **Sekgoma II**, Kgosi of the BaNgwato (1923–1925); wife of **Simon Ratshosa**. In 1926 she and her husband's family came into conflict with the new regent, **Tshekedi Khama** and were sent into exile, during which she was aided by the **Haskins** family. She and other female descendants of **Khama III** fought to alter the system of impartible inheritance through the eldest son, basing their effort on the kgotla edicts of Khama. Their agitation was stymied by the BaNgwato gerontocracy and by Tshekedi's personal hatred. Moreover, the government refused to sanction Khama's edicts, claiming that the edicts did not fall within "traditional customs." During Tshekedi's regency, Oratile refused to return to Serowe from exile. In the early 1950s some BaNgwato who backed **Seretse Khama** put her forward as an alternative to the regency of **Rasebolai Kgamane**. Oratile never returned to Serowe, though her son Galebolwe eventually settled there.

ORDERS-IN-COUNCIL. An Order-in-Council was a command or instruction given with the authority of the British sovereign and by advice of the Privy Council. In practice it was simply an administrative decree of the British cabinet. Many of the decrees governing the creation, administration, and dissolution of the Bechuanaland Protectorate were "Orders-in-Council." *See also* Administration, Orders-in-Council, 1890 and 1891; Proclamation.

ORDERS-IN-COUNCIL, 1890 AND 1891. These two decrees of the British crown established the legal and territorial authority of the **high commissioner** of the Bechuanaland protectorate. Under the Foreign Jurisdiction Act, the Order-in-Council of 1885 declared the Protectorate to exist south of the twenty-second parallel but remained silent on the character and content of British authority.

The Order-in-Council of 1890 authorized the high commissioner to make laws on behalf of the Queen and extended her authority north of the twenty-second parallel to include what is now northern Botswana.

The Order-in-Council of 1891, which followed acceptance of

the **Bramestone Memorandum**, gave legislative powers to the high commissioner for "the administration of justice, the raising of revenue, and generally for peace, order and good government of all persons within the limits of this order including the prohibition and Punishment of acts tending to disturb the Public peace." The same order made the high commissioner's authority subject to the secretary of state for the Colonies in London.

The powers of the high commissioner under the 1891 Order are the powers of the modern Botswana Government as defined in the 1966 Constitution. *See also* Foreign Jurisdiction Act; Justice; Proclamation.

P

PAN AFRICANIST CONGRESS (PAC). Formed in South Africa in 1958 by a group of "Africanists" who seceded from the Transvaal wing of the **African National Congress (ANC)**, the PAC espoused black nationalism and mass consciousness, in contrast to the ANC Freedom Charter, and prescribed in its manifesto "an Africanistic Socialistic democratic social order." Its success at arousing large crowds in boycotts and defiance campaigns led to its being banned in 1960, the imprisonment of its leader, Robert Sobukwe, and the exiling of many others, including the charismatic Potlake Leballo. The PAC-in-exile and its military arm, "Poqo" (IsiXhosa, literally, "standing alone") proved ineffective, and they suffered from protracted internal feuding, poor organization, and misalliances.

In Botswana, the PAC influence was important, but momentary. The leader of the **People's Party (BPP)**, **Philip Matante**, was close to PAC leaders; his approach to politics reflects PAC thinking and methods, and BPP achievements paralleled those of the PAC. Francistown, Matante's political base, was where PAC exile Matthew Nkoana established an office in 1962 for the forwarding of recruits to Angola and elsewhere for guerrilla training. But in 1963 a series of incidents ended the usefulness of the town as a PAC base, and its "White House," which housed refugees, was bombed, a plane used for airlifting them north destroyed, and several refugees kidnapped.

After Botswana's independence, PAC refugees were welcome to live inside the country but not to use it as a base of operations. The PAC had many sympathizers among South African exiles who in the 1960s and after made Botswana their permanent home. David Sibeko, the PAC leader assassinated in Dar es Salaam in 1979, is buried in the Gaborone cemetery. *See also* Refugees.

PARASTATALS. Many corporations are wholly-owned by the Botswana government. The most important are

Parastatal	Estab-lished	Role
National Development Bank (NDB)	1963	Commercial, industrial loans
Botswana Meat Commis-sion (BMC)*	1965	Wholesale and export of beef products
Water Utilities Corpora-tion (WUC)*	1970	Dam/borehole construction, water utilities
Botswana Power Corpora-tion (BPC)*	1970	Power plants, electric utili-ties
Botswana Development Corporation (BDC)	1970	Business loans, expertise
Botswana Housing Corpo-ration (BHC)	1971	Public housing units
Botswana Livestock De-velopment Corporation (BLDC)	1972	Cattle-holding farms
Botswana Agricultural Marketing Board (BAMB)*	1974	Wholesale local grain, grain products
Bank of Botswana (BOB)*	1975	Monetary policy
Botswana Railways (BR)*	1986	Railway management

*monopolies

Apart from the BOB, parastatals have suffered in general from mismanagement, waste, and corruption. In 1992 a public scandal involved the Botswana Housing Corporation general manager and the assistant minister of Local Government and Lands, the ministry overseeing the BHC, regarding a major kickback arrangement with a South African-based construction company. BHC losses at the time were estimated to have run into tens of millions of dollars. The government admitted publicly that "a growing number of [our parastatal organis-ations] appear to be afflicted by inefficiency, mismanagement and corruption."

PARKS/GAME RESERVES. In Botswana, a game reserve is an area set aside for the protection of game; a national park is an area in which human settlement is prohibited. Botswana has nine parks and reserves, which make up 17 percent of its land surface. The first game reserve was the Gemsbok Reserve (after independence, Gemsbok National Park) in the southwest. It was created in the late 1930s as an extension of the South African Gemsbok National Game Park and was administered by South African game wardens (i.e., the Le Riches family). About five hundred people were removed from their settlements along the Nosop River and resettled at Bokspits as a result of a South African request that the park/reserve be depopulated.

Resident Commissioner **Charles Rey** lobbied for the creation of a large game reserve/park in the Chobe District; his dream was only realized in 1960 with the creation of Chobe Wildlife Reserve, which was gazetted as a national park in 1968.

In 1961 the Central Kalahari Game Reserve was set up as a result of growing international concern about the fate of the "Bushmen." The reserve was to become a hunting area exclusively for these people, although the area was by no means exclusively inhabited by them. The decision not to declare the area a "bushman reserve" was made for various reasons: the costs of administration, opposition of Ghanzi farmers, and the perception that the future de-proclamation of a game reserve would be less controversial than of a "bushman reserve." Since the early 1960s international concern has shifted away from the fate of the "bushmen" to the fate of the game. In the 1980s the possibility of the complete depopulation of the reserve in order to protect the game was raised.

Parks

Chobe National Park
Gemsbok National Park
Nxai Pan National Park

Reserves

Central Kalahari Game Reserve
Khutse Game Reserve
Mabuasehube Game Reserve
Maikaelelo Game Reserve
Makgadikgadi Pan Game Reserve
Moremi Game Reserve

See also Bushmen; Sarwa.

PEDI (BAPEDI). Sotho-Tswana peoples in northern Transvaal, southern Zimbabwe, and eastern Botswana. Their language,

SePedi, is northern Sotho, and amounts to a label applied to the dialects common to the entire region. The BaPedi totem is *khupe* ("hare"). A number of BaTswana and BaKalanga groups claim BaPedi origin, and some still use the language. BaPedi moved into the Botswana area in the mid-eighteenth century, when they were offered land by the Nichasike of the Ba**Kalanga**. In the Tati District, the BakaNswazwi Kalanga so trace their descent, as do the BakaSelolwane Kalanga. The languages Se**Birwa** and SeTswapong are often classified, like SePedi, as northern Sotho.

PENTECOSTAL CHURCHES. The Church of God in Christ (1,300 members), founded in 1935, was the first successful Pentecostal church, though its founders, William Sebolau in Molepolole and Dickson Muthume in Kanye, had to survive heavy-handed persecution at the hands of diKgosi such as **Kgari Sechele.** During **World War II,** Sebolau evangelized actively as a member of the AAPC.

Pentecostal churches were usually introduced by returning migrant laborers and were regarded as subversive of local political monopolies of the **LMS** or **DRC.** DiKgosi, backed by the British, often fined, jailed, and/or exiled those who refused to abandon such churches. Pentecostal leaders, such as **P.G. Matante,** subsequently emerged as prominent nationalist critics of "chiefly autocracy." As elsewhere, the Pentecostal movement in Botswana has proved to be highly schismatic. Among the major offshoots are the Free Church of Botswana, with a membership of 2,700. *See also* Independent Churches; Puleng, Tumelo; Religion; Zion Christian Church.

PEOPLE'S PARTY (BPP). The Bechuanaland (later Botswana) People's Party was formed in December 1960 by **K.T. Motsete, Motsamai Mpho,** and **P.G. Matante** in order to protest the racially-based structure of the Legislative Council (LEGCO). Although many of its members were experienced in South African protest politics, the party drew much of its inspiration and nearly all of its financial support from nationalists north of the Zambezi. The BPP, which attacked racism and social deprivation, quickly became popular in townships along the rail line. In their attempts to gather support in the rural areas, however, they abandoned their initial anti-diKgosi posture.

In 1962 the party's progress was interrupted by the formation of a well-organized rival, the **Democratic Party**, and by a major split (the first of three such splits) in the BPP itself. The split erupted following a dispute between Matante and Mpho. Matante was accused of misappropriating party funds and attempting to get ANC refugees deported; Mpho, of wanting to relocate party headquarters to his own advantage. Tensions reached a climax on June 19, 1963, when Matante and Mpho brawled publicly in Lobatse over the keys to a party Land-rover. Soon, the party split into three groups: BPP (Matante); BPP (Mpho) [Mpho going on eventually to found the **Independence Party**]; and in 1964, Matante expelled Motsete, who formed BPP (Motsete). These divisions and a continuing failure to mount an effective campaign in the rural areas led to a disastrous defeat in the 1965 general election: the party won only three seats—in the Northeast District and Mochudi. Since 1965 the BPP has further declined, to the extent that its support is confined almost solely to the Northeast. In 1965 the BPP captured 14.2 percent of the total votes cast; in the most recent election of 1994, it garnered a mere 4 percent. The BPP has not been represented in the National Assembly since 1989. *See also* African National Congress; Councils; Pan Africanist Congress.

PHIRI, THOMAS (1860[?]–1941). Phiri was an early evangelist, the first African ordained as minister of the **Dutch Reformed Church,** and, in his later years, an independent church leader. Born in Saulspoort, western Transvaal, Thomas was the son of Franz (Moroke) Phiri of the Bakgatla baga Mosetlha, converted by Henry Gonin, DRC missionary among the Saulspoort Ba-Kgatla. Like many early DRC converts, Franz at one time had probably been a slave of the Transvaal Boers. Thomas Phiri attended Morija Training Institution in Lesotho and worked as a teacher/evangelist in Saulspoort and Kimberley. In 1892 he moved to Botswana at the request of **Linchwe I,** whom over the years he served as interpreter, secretary, and teacher. Based in Malolwane and later in Sikwane, he was ordained in 1907 after attending Wellington Institute in the Cape. Throughout his life, Phiri rankled under DRC control. He came into conflict with many missionaries, as well as with his first pupil, the regent **Isang Pilane,** and was suspended several times by the church for misbehavior. He flirted with Ethiopianism in 1918 and in 1937 formed the breakaway BaKgatla Free Church, which attracted those protesting the suspension of **Molefi** and most of the DRC congregation in the "**river villages.**" After Phiri's death, the Free Church was gradually displaced by the DRC.

PHUTHADIKOBO MUSEUM. *See* Bakgatla National School.

PILANE (1790[?]–1848). Kgosi of the **Kgafela Kgatla,** 1824–1848, and progenitor of the Pilane line, from which BaKgatla diKgosi have been elected ever since. Eldest son of Pheto II's second wife and his successor by virtue of the fact that the sons of Pheto's first wife had been murdered by Motlotle, who tried to usurp the throne while regent (1821–1824). Pilane succeeded after Motlotle was himself assassinated, but the BaKgatla, then situated north of Rustenburg, were also troubled by invasions from the **BaKololo** and AmaNdebele. Pilane survived numerous attempts on his life and spent most of his adulthood in exile. After Mzilikazi was driven north by the Boers in 1837, Pilane returned and reunited the BaKgatla, using his widespread trading and political contacts to build up their cattle herds. Pilane and his people lived near the farm of Andries Potgieter, early Boer leader, and Pilane was in contact with ivory traders north of the Limpopo River. Pilane's son **Kgamanyane** became very wealthy under Boer rule before migrating with many of his followers into Botswana and settling at Mochudi.

PILANE, AMOS KGAMANYANE (1888–1984). Teacher, councilor, historian. Born in Mochudi, son of Mogale Kgamanyane, Amos Pilane taught for years in local DRC schools. He was the leading member of the three-man Council of Regency (1942–1945) that acted in the place of Acting Chief **Mmusi,** who entered the AAPC, and before the reinstallation of **Molefi,** with whom he was privately allied. He was a councilor under Molefi and **Linchwe II,** member of the African Advisory Council, and noted source of **Kgafela Kgatla** historical traditions.

PILANE, MOSIELELE/PHEKO (1843–1889). Kgosi of the **Mmanaana Kgatla,** 1870–1889. During the **Civil Wars,** Pilane managed to preserve his people's autonomy. After a period at Kgabodukwe, where he was an ally of the BaKwena, he returned to Mosopa in 1875 and reached an agreement with **Gaseitsiwe** which allowed the Mmanaana Kgatla to live as an autonomous group in GaNgwaketse. *See also* Gagoangwe; Ngwaketse.

POLICE. *Local police.* According to traditional SeTswana law, offenders are held accountable for their acts by various bodies and courts, depending on the context, though a case may be appealed to or directly reach the **Kgosi,** who renders the final judgment and sentence if need be. No standing police force existed in pre-colonial times, though age regiments (*mephato*) were sometimes used for law enforcement. Messengers were sent to arrest those attempting to sidestep justice, and men recognized as *maotlana* ("punishers") were delegated the task of carrying out floggings in the **kgotla.**

During the colonial era, regiments were used by some di-Kgosi to arrest and/or punish insubordinate groups, whereas Tribal Police gradually displaced maotlana and dealt with individuals on behalf of diKgosi and the courts.

State police. The first colonial police force was the Bechuanaland Border Police (BBP), formed in 1885. The BBP exercised authority in the Protectorate as well as in **British Bechuanaland**, where most of its officers and troopers were stationed until 1888. The responsibilities of the BBP operating north of the Molopo River were ill-defined, with police work overlapping administrative duties and involvement in boundary and border issues. The BBP also became a de facto arm of the **British South Africa Company (BSACO)** and participated in the 1893 war against the AmaNdebele and was dissolved so that its members could take part in the ill-fated **Jameson Raid.** In 1896 it was replaced by the Bechuanaland Mounted Police, a section of the Rhodesian-based BSACO police.

In 1903 the Bechuanaland Protectorate Police Force (BPPF) was formed as the Protectorate's first unit operating under the supreme command of the **resident commissioner,** in this case **Ralph Williams,** who was responsible for its formation (thereafter all resident commissioners held the rank of lieutenant-colonel, BPPF). The BPPF was largely an African force made up of mainly BaSotho recruits, numbering no more than 200 at any time. Not until 1948 were BaTswana encouraged to join. The BPPF's major preoccupation was hut tax collection, but it also patrolled veterinary cordons, dealt with customs and immigration, and provided communication and transport services for the administration.

In the years leading toward independence, a Police Mobile Unit (PMU) was established to deal with mounting political tension and to increase intelligence gathering. In 1966 the BPPF was changed to the Botswana Police Force. In 1977 the PMU formed the core of the new **Botswana Defence Force (BDF),** which was used to police Botswana's borders. The BDF's first commander was Mompati Merafhe, past PMU commander. The Botswana Police Force, like the Defence Force, is administered from the Office of the President of

Botswana. The police are responsible for the enforcement of the national laws, the gathering of national intelligence, the regulation of traffic and communications, and the investigation of criminal misdeeds. To date, the police have not been used to serve the objectives of one political group or another, and Botswana has been devoid of political prisoners. The prison system operates independently of the police and is housed in the Ministry of Labour and Home Affairs.

POPULATION. *See* Census.

PRESBYTERIANS. The Presbyterian African Evangelical Church has 1,500 members in ten parishes. It was introduced in 1949 to Botswana (at Tonota) by Rev. J. Molawa, where he met opposition from the **London Missionary Society** and the BaNgwato diKgosi. The Presbyterians were not registered officially until 1973. *See also* Religion.

PROCLAMATION. In the British constitutional system, a proclamation was a formal order issued by the sovereign or his/her representative *without* the assent of parliament. Between 1891 and 1959, the proclamation was the principal legislative device for administering the Bechuanaland Protectorate. In effect, it was a high commissioner's decree approved by the secretary of state for the Colonies (after 1931 the dominions secretary) and "proclaimed" (i.e., published in the government's *Gazette*) throughout the Protectorate. *See also* Administration; Foreign Jurisdiction Act; Justice; Orders-in-Council.

PROTECTORATE. A term not to be confused with protection, unless it is used as a euphemism for colonial territory. In the British colonial system, a protectorate was a territory under the Crown which was regarded as not being strictly British territory or part of its dominions (i.e., used for white settlement, such as Canada and South Africa). In theory, a protectorate was created through a "treaty with" (i.e., by "invitation from") indigenous authorities. In the case of the Bechuanaland Protectorate, it was established in the wake of the **Warren Expedition,** whereby the British army alleged it had gained the consent of diKgosi in southern Botswana for the establishment of British authority over the territory north of the Molopo River. British authority over such territory was made official by the **Foreign Jurisdiction Act of 1890.**

The advantage of the "protectorate" concept was that the

British Crown could claim in parliament that most of the administration of such a territory, and by extension its expense, remained the responsibility of indigenous authorities, whereas the territory belonged to the British "sphere," thereby disallowing claims of rival European powers. After the **South African War,** Britain intended to allow Bechuanaland to be incorporated into the Union of South Africa.

Protectorate status provided no protection as such to Bechuanaland's African inhabitants, who were taxed, subjected systematically to racially-based exclusions, deprived of much of their arable land, and reduced to dependency on labor migration. The extent of their protection derived from the fact that Great Britain and the Union of South Africa regarded Bechuanaland as unsuitable for mining or ranching. *See also* Bramestone Memorandum; Incorporation.

PULENG, TUMELO. MoKgalagadi religious and political leader. After **World War II** he founded the Church of Christ and gained a large following among the BaKgalagadi of the western Kweneng. The BaKwena Kgosi **Kgari Sechele** tried to suppress his church and for many years kept him prisoner at Molepolole. In 1970 Puleng was elected headman of Letlhakeng, the first MoKgalagadi to hold this post after decades of BaKwena overrule. *See also* Kwena.

R

RACE RELATIONS. The history of race relations in Botswana is long, complex, and multi-faceted. In the early nineteenth century, a modest number of Europeans and "mixed race" persons began to enter the area. They came as hunters, traders, craftsmen, missionaries, criminal fugitives, wagon-based cattle keepers, or as a combination of any of these. Some elected to become subjects of diKgosi and integrate themselves, partly or wholly, into SeTswana society; others lived in the town in their own section, under a Kgosi's protection. In political and economic matters, the diKgosi maintained preeminence over these outsiders until the colonial era.

Protectorate laws removed whites, people of mixed ancestry, and Asians from local African authority, although many non-Africans living in reserves chose to respect local norms and the Kgosi's authority. Racial alienation developed as diKgosi lost control over traders and as non-African residents took advantage of their privileges in the colonial structure by obtaining special schools and hospital wards, as well as their own representatives on the various **Councils.** Some whites openly called for **incorporation,** which was opposed by the overwhelming majority of Africans. Outside the reserves in the settler-dominated towns and farming blocks, as well as in the Rhodesian owned and operated railway cars and stations, an entrenched and rigid racial caste system reflected the pattern found in settler societies in other parts of eastern and southern Africa.

In the Protectorate, however, tendencies toward integration were more persistent than elsewhere. The cattle industry in particular gave rise to patterns of economic interdependence across racial lines. On the eve of independence, such links worked to counter separatism within the white community. Also, the comparatively small number of non-Africans posed less of a threat to African "paramountcy" in the Protectorate than in other places. In the political campaign leading up to independence, the **People's Party** made race relations a major issue, but the large majority of African voters supported the **Democratic Party,** which advocated non-racialism. Since independence a tolerant racial climate has existed in spite of a significant, economically privileged expatriate urban population. *See also* Asians; Boyne, Henry; Buys, Coenraad; Chand, Abdul Rahim; Coloureds; England, Russell; Flogging Incident; Francistown; Ghanzi Farms; Haskins, James; Head, Bessie; Hirschfeldt, Max; Hume, David; Jousse, Paul; Livingstone, David; Lobatse; London Missionary Society; Lugard, Frederick; Mackenzie, John; Merriweather, Alfred; Mitchison, Naomi; Moffat, Robert; Moruakgomo Sechele; Retief, Deborah; Reyneke, Johan; Riley, Charles; Rowland, Richard; Steinberg, Benjamin; Tuli Block; van Rensburg, Patrick; van Zyl, Hendrik; Willoughby, William.

RADIO. Radio communications, which originated as a network among police posts, was established in 1934. The Bechuanaland Protectorate established the territory's first radio service in 1936 with receivers at Maun, Kanye, Serowe, Palapye, Tsabong, Ghanzi, Gaberones, Mafeking, and Molepolole. A short wave transmission, its main function was providing information to administrators throughout the territory. The first SeTswana broadcast was in November 1936, when diKgosi **Tshekedi Khama** and **Bathoen II** broadcast messages to their people from Mafeking, regarding their court case challenging the reforms of **Charles Rey**. Regular broadcasting began in early 1937 with the opening of station ZNB-Mafeking, which broadcast nine hours a week, Monday through Friday and Sunday evening. The Witwatersrand Native Labour Association set up its own separate network in the late 1930s at Francistown, Mohembo, and Kazangula. During **World War II,** limited spare parts caused a decline in the system, including its propaganda efforts and colorful SeTswana war stories, narrated by Levi Moumakwa, the territory's first announcer in SeTswana. For some years an argument arose as to whether Protectorate radio fell under the jurisdiction of the postmaster-general of South Africa. In the 1950s little SeTswana programming was transmitted, apart from that aimed at schools and farmers. By 1962, forty-three stations operated on the Protectorate network, but broadcasting was still limited, mainly confined to the Education department. South African pressure and later Botswana government policy prevented development of independent radio, despite the submission of applications as early as the 1950s. In 1962 the British Broadcasting Corporation (BBC) helped to expand broadcasting facilities inside the Protectorate and established a base in the new capital, Gaborone, in February 1965. At independence, the BBC operation became Radio Botswana. In 1968 a report by John Synson ("Report: Information Functions of Government") set out the development of radio as an arm of government development policy. Efforts by broadcast officers, such as Brian Egner (1968–1969) and Potlako Molefe (1969–1977), tried to raise the radio's status, but government was unwilling to allow them or radio broadcasting any autonomy. Radio has remained just another government department under the civil service regulations. A second, semi-commercial government station (RB2) was introduced in Gaborone in 1990.

RADITLADI, LEETILE DISANG (1910–1971). Founder of the territory's first political party—the **Federal Party**—and pioneering SeTswana playwright, poet, and journalist. Born in Serowe, the great-grandnephew of **Khama III** and grandson on his mother's side of **Ratshosa Motswetle**, he attended **Simon Ratshosa**'s primary school, **Tiger Kloof**, Lovedale, and Fort Hare College. A member of a prominent BaNgwato family, in 1937 he was exiled following allegations that he had impregnated the wife of **Tshekedi Khama** and conspired with her to bewitch Tshekedi's mother. Thereafter he became an unbending critic of "chiefly autocracy."

In 1938 Leetile joined the civil service as a clerk and inter-preter, and in 1944 his cousin, **Moremi III,** Kgosi of the BaTawana, had him transferred to Ngamiland and requested his services in the tribal administration. Within months, Mo-remi died accidentally, but his widow-cum-regent, **Elizabeth Moremi** retained him in office. With her support, though much to the chagrin of the cattle-based elite, Leetile supported BaYei autonomy in 1948 while regularizing BaTawana administration generally. His romantic involvement with the regent strength-ened the convictions of his local opponents that Leetile was power-hungry. In 1953, when they threatened to kill him, Leetile left Ngamiland for good.

He moved to Francistown, operated the Mimosa Cafe (which belonged to the Ratshosa family), and worked for the local office of the Witwatersrand Native Labor Association (WEN-ELA). He became involved, too, in politics, first as a founder of the Bamangwato National Congress (BNC) as a pressure group for **Seretse Khama.** There he associated with other up-and-coming political figures: **K.T. Motsete, Lenyeletse Seretse, M.P.K. Nwako,** and **Kenneth Koma.** British opposition to this effort kept him in Francistown. In 1954 he revived the Bechua-naland Protectorate African Workers' Union and in the same year founded the Francistown African Cultural Organisation. The latter served as a forum for educated township dwellers. Following the return of Seretse Khama, Leetile moved back to Serowe in 1957 and attempted to revive the BNC. In 1959, when the British announced the imminent formation of LEGCO, Leetile formed the Bechuanaland Protectorate Fed-eral Party (BPFP), which was also known as the Liberal Party. The BPFP manifesto declared its opposition to the domination of local and Protectorate politics by diKgosi. In particular, the BPFP had in mind Leetile's old rival, Tshekedi.

BPFP growth was stunted at an early age when Leetile accepted the position of subordinate african authority in Maha-lapye. the party was finally eclipsed in the early 1960s by the rise of the **People's Party** and the **Democratic Party.** During his latter years, Leetile was pushed aside by the new generation of politicians, many of whom had begun their careers in organiza-tions he had formed.

Leetile was a prolific author and journalist. He regularly contributed articles to *Naledi ya Batswana* under the nom de plume "Observer." He is still recognized as one of the giants of SeTswana literature. His works include *Sefalana sa Menate* (a collection of poetry), the historical dramas *Sekgoma* and

Motswasele II, and the novel *Ditshontsho tso Lorato*. Social justice and royal despotism are themes central to nearly all of his writings. *See also* Newspapers.

RAILWAYS. Botswana's principal lifeline to the outside world is the railway running along its eastern border. With a total length of 642 km, the railway exits into Zimbabwe at Bakaranga (near Ramokgwebana) in the north and into South Africa at Ramatlabama in the south. The original line was built in 1897 by the **BSACO**, after **Bathoen I**, **Khama III**, and **Sebele I** granted to the Crown a strip of land in the eastern portion of their respective territories. These land strips were then transferred to the BSACO and became the Tuli, Gaberones, and Lobatse Blocks. The railway ended the wagon trade and contributed significantly to the deforestation of eastern Botswana. It also placed considerable strain on the Imperial budget: prior to 1909, the government paid the BSACO £20,000 per annum for the use of the railways, the second largest item of expenditure after the police. Only in 1950 with the introduction of an annual railway tax of £140,000 did the government begin to acquire significant revenues from the railway.

Rhodesian control of the railway was gradually challenged. In 1963 the Southern Rhodesian government attempted to use the railway to transfer a political prisoner to South Africa. The train was stopped at Mahalapye, and the prisoner was taken off by British officials, thereby establishing local sovereignty over the Rhodesian-owned line. Independent Botswana prohibited separate cars and other facilities for whites and blacks on the railway. In 1974 **Seretse Khama** announced his government's intention to nationalize the railway and, after 1980 negotiations with newly-independent Zimbabwe produced an agreement, Botswana assumed control of the operation of all rail traffic inside its borders in 1987.

The railway is operated by the parastatal Botswana Railways, with its headquarters in Mahalapye since 1994. Roughly 85 percent of its revenues are derived from freight. In 1992, Botswana Railways conveyed 430,000 passengers and 2.4 million tons of freight. Branch lines operate between Palapye and Morupule (16 km), serving the hydroelectric plant, and between Francistown and Sua Pan (175 km), connecting the new soda ash mine. Work on a branch line from Palapye to Selebi Phikwe commenced in 1994.

RAMOKATE, PELAELO (1899–1959). Kgosi of the Tati section of the BaKhurutshe, 1943–1959. Descended from the old royal line, Ramokate attended **Tiger Kloof**, worked as a tax collector, and served as de facto Kgosi for years prior to his installation.

RAMONO PILANE (1860[?]–1917). Younger brother to **Linchwe I**, early DRC convert, first MoKgatla royal to receive formal education (at Morija, 1888–1890), teacher, military leader, and appointed Kgosi of the Kgafela Kgatla of the Transvaal (Saulspoort), 1903–1917. Ramono, also known as "Mokolometsa," is the father of Tidimane Pilane, Kgosi at Saulspoort since 1949. *See also* Battle of Derdepoort; Dutch Reformed Church; Kgafela Kgatla; Segale.

RAMOTSWA. Present administrative headquarters of the Southeast District and, since 1875, the capital town of the BaLete.

In 1881 it was the scene of a major battle between the BaLete and the BaNgwaketse, who claimed the territory and wished to impose suzerainty over the BaLete. In the battle, which took place at Magopane hill on the west side of the village, the BaLete heavily defeated the BaNgwaketse regiments, who left more than eighty dead in the field. Muzzle-loaders were used by both adversaries.

Since its founding, Ramotswa has also been the principal mission station of the **Lutherans**, whose Hermannsburg missionaries followed the BaLete from the Kweneng, where they had begun their conversions. In addition to a church, the Lutherans at Ramotswa have established a thriving medical mission at the BaLete Lutheran Hospital. In 1980 the Ramotswa congregation divided over its continued membership in the South African church, a split which reverberated among Lutherans throughout Botswana and raised difficult legal problems that Botswana's courts have had to resolve.

Ramotswa is the site of the Bolux flour mill, a joint venture involving the Botswana Development Corporation and multinational financial/technical investment, for the processing of flour as a substitute for imports from South Africa and as an export to central African markets. Built in 1985, it processes 200 tons of wheat daily. Still, the town's residents are heavily dependent on jobs in Gaborone, making modern Ramotswa a dormitory community. *See also* British South Africa Company; Civil Wars; Mokgosi I; Roman Catholics.

RASEBOLAI GOREWANG "GEORGE" KGAMANE (1907–1973). African Authority of the BaNgwato, 1953–1964. Grandson of **Kgamane**, Rasebolai was appointed chief's representative in BuKalanga, 1930–1941. From 1941 to 1946 he was a regimental sergeant-major in the AAPC, the highest ranking MoNgwato. In 1949 he followed **Tshekedi Khama** into exile. The British appointed Rasebolai African authority over the BaNgwato in 1953 in spite of the fact that the morafe had rejected him as Kgosi on three separate occasions. His appointment was regarded as a victory for Tshekedi. After Tshekedi and **Seretse Khama** reconciled in 1956, Rasebolai enjoyed broad popular acceptance. He was made an Officer, Order of the British Empire in 1960.

RATSHOSA MOTSWETLE (d. 1917). MoNgwato of the royal family who in the 1880s became advisor to **Khama III** and overseer of his cattle. He married Khama's eldest daughter Besi, by whom he had ten children, including Johnnie, **Simon**, and Obeditse. He was well-educated and understood European methods of administration and was opposed to the religious and educational monopoly exercised by the **LMS** in Gammangwato. In 1895 he accompanied Khama to Cape Town. He was a critical influence when Khama decided to expel **Sekgoma II**, Raditladi, and **Mphoeng,** and in 1897 assumed the position of tribal secretary, previously held by Sekgoma. While Sekgoma was in exile, Ratshosa pressed Besi's claim as heir to the throne. His ambitions subsided after Besi's death in 1902. He then married **Ntebogang,** future regent of the BaNgwaketse, by whom he had three children.

After **Tshekedi Khama** was born to Khama's fourth wife, Ratshosa threw his support behind the exiled Sekgoma. Ratshosa's strategy paid off for his family, because Sekgoma reconciled with Khama in 1916 and became heir once again. Upon Ratshosa's death in 1917, his son Johnnie took over his father's position as advisor to the Kgosi. When Khama died in 1923, Ratshosa's sons, Johnnie and Simon, controlled Sekgoma, but Sekgoma's death two years later reduced their influence and placed the Ratshosas at loggerheads with the young regent, Tshekedi.

RATSHOSA, SIMON (1883–1939). Son of **Ratshosa Motswetle** and Besi Khama, leading critic of **Tshekedi Khama,** and advocate of a greater role for the educated elite in Protectorate affairs. From a family opposed to LMS hegemony, he was educated at Lovedale and Zonnebloem and, in 1902, was turned down by the LMS as a teacher. His father and **Khama III** therefore had him appointed principal of the Serowe Public School, which had been established in 1904 by the Ratshosa anti-LMS faction to cater to small numbers of children of the elite. Until 1922 he controlled BaNgwato education, but Simon was expelled from the LMS on grounds of "immorality," which prompted his grandfather, Khama III, to fire him from the principalship.

Simon's wife was **Oratile Khama Ratshosa**, only daughter of **Sekgoma II**, successor to Khama in 1923. They had a son, Galebolwe. Simon and his brother Johnnie had considerable influence over Sekgoma, but the Kgosi himself died in 1925, ushering in an era of conflict between the Ratshosas and Khama's son by his fourth wife, Tshekedi. After Sekgoma's death, the Ratshosa brothers tried to use as their power base a council which had been appointed to advise Gorewang, the caretaker regent. Soon thereafter, however, Tshekedi became regent, abolished the council, and fired Johnnie as tribal secretary. In April 1926, after ignoring requests to report for regimental duties, the three Ratshosa brothers (including Obeditse), were ordered by Tshekedi to be publicly flogged for failing to respect his authority. Johnnie received his lashes, but Simon and Obeditse broke away, seized their guns, and returned to the kgotla. They fired at Tshekedi, wounding him only slightly. Simon spent the next four years in jail, then lived in Francistown for the remainder of his life.

From exile, he wrote several manuscripts and numerous letters which attacked the autocratic power of diKgosi and claimed that slavery was rife in the Protectorate. He called for the British to limit such abuses by appointing "tribal councils" of leading educated "progressive" BaTswana. His writings were read only by colonial officials and white liberals, though his charges of slavery reached the public and led to an inquiry in 1932 and 1933. *See also* Bolata; Raditladi, Leetile.

REFUGEES. A land historically unattractive to white settlers or mining companies, Botswana has had magnetic properties for Africans facing persecution in neighboring territories. In the 1850s and 1860s, the BaNgwaketse and BaKwena welcomed a number of African groups moving away from the oppressive rule of the Boers. Among them were BaLete, BaTlokwa, Kgafela Kgatla and Mmanaana Kgatla, and BaHurutshe. The first influx of refugees during the Protectorate era was that of the Mbanderu OvaHerero escaping the Germans in South West Africa in the 1890s. In 1904–1905, in the midst of brutal German oppression, at least 2,000 other OvaHerero followed. They were granted sanctuary by the BaTawana and settled mainly in Ngamiland. Until **Namibia** gained its independence in 1990, the OvaHerero of Botswana periodically made requests to return to their homeland, but they were refused permission to do so. Since 1990, only a small fraction have returned.

In 1958 up to 500 Ba**Hurutshe** fled from the area around Zeerust in **South Africa** across the border into the Protectorate following the violent suppression of protests against the introduction of pass books for women. Many lived for several years in Peleng township outside **Lobatse,** but most returned eventually to South Africa.

After the Sharpeville shootings and the suppression of the **ANC** and the **PAC** in the early 1960s, a steady flow of refugees from South Africa began. These included returning residents, such as **Philip Matante** and **Motsamai Mpho,** who became important political figures, as well as nationalist leaders from other territories such as Samora Machel and Oliver Tambo. Given the Protectorate's close proximity to South Africa and the cooperation of police across colonial borders, a few hundred refugees at most remained in the Protectorate at any one time, its function being a transit point to the north, especially after Zambian independence in 1963, rather than a permanent haven for refugees.

During the years 1967–1969 more than 4,000 Ha**Mbukushu** entered Botswana at Mohembo, fleeing the Portuguese campaign against guerrillas in southern Angola. Most were successfully settled in northern Ngamiland.

The war for the liberation of **Zimbabwe**, which reached its peak in the late 1970s, created the largest influx of refugees into Botswana. By 1979 more than 30,000 were settled in three refugee camps. After the end of the war in 1980, most of these refugees returned to Zimbabwe. Dukwe camp, on the Nata-Kazungula road, was kept in existence mainly to cope with refugees from the hard-pressed Matabeleland region of Zimbabwe, where troops of the newly-independent government crushed political opposition. In 1988 Dukwe camp accommodated about 4,000 refugees, most having come from Matabeleland but many others from South Africa and Namibia. Only a handful of refugees still remain in Dukwe.

Since Botswana's independence in 1966, government policy toward refugees has been open-door, qualified only by a ban on the territory being used as a springboard for violent attacks on its neighbors. After the South African raids on alleged ANC targets in Botswana in 1985 and 1986, the government and the public became less sympathetic toward refugees, particularly those claiming economic hardships. Still, in the past generation, thousands of Africans have made Botswana their home. When South Africa held its first democratic elections in 1994, those eligible to vote in Botswana numbered approximately 35,000.

REGENCY. Since pre-colonial times, the appointment of a regent (*motswaraledi*, SeTswana) between the reigns of recognized diKgosi has often been necessary, though risky for the legal heir, when made to an ambitious person. A regent is usually the most senior adult uncle of the future **Kgosi** (usually a minor), but a grandmother, senior aunt, mother, or brother may be installed. Constitutionally, the regent enjoys the same authority as a Kgosi, but the regent's powers are diminished by virtue of his or her lack of legitimacy with respect to succession. A regent has no eligibility to bogosi, barring the death of all descendants of diKgosi senior to his own line. A few pre-colonial regents attempted executing all who stood between them and bogosi, but none achieved complete success. During the colonial era, ambitious regents attempted to secure their rule through force of personality, place the legitimate heir in difficulty with the colonial administration, or both. *See also* Gagoangwe; Pilane; Moremi, Elizabeth; Ntebogang Ratshosa; Sebego I; Sekgoma Letsholathebe; Tshekedi Khama; Tshosa Sebego.

REGIMENT. Pre-colonial SeTswana societies were organized horizontally into parallel male and female age-regiments, into which were recruited persons of roughly the same age. Members within a given regiment were still expected to observe a strict personal code of discipline and demonstrate loyalty to one another. Regiments were formed through **initiation,** *bogwera* for young men, *bojale* for young women. In the twentieth century, initiation was abolished in most merafe, but regiments are still formed.

The purpose of regiments has changed over time. In precolonial Botswana, female regiments were used for tending the Kgosi's fields. Male regiments were commonly used for cattle-raiding, military defense, and carrying out decisions reached in public assembly. Political disputes were often conducted in a manner that pitted members of one or a group of regiments (supporting one or another royal candidate) against the claims of others.

In colonial times, both female and male regiments became the Kgosi's main source of public labor and construction.

RELIGION. Historically, Botswana has been an area of extremely varied religious institutionalization. Indigenous religious beliefs vary widely among the BaTswana, Ba**Kalanga**, and **Khoisan** groups, for whom the published literature is extensive. As well, Botswana has felt the impress of Christian missionary activity since the mid-nineteenth century and, since the beginning of the twentieth, increasingly strong independent church development.

Although Christian church membership accounts for only about 30 percent of the citizenry (the majority gravitating to Pentecostal and other independent evangelical sects) Botswana's important social rituals, such as those connected with marriage and death, are pervaded by Christian church symbols, dress, and practices. The ecumenical movement is also the better financed, better organized, and far more influential. Since 1966 the major churches have cooperated in running social programs under the banner of the Botswana Christian Council (BCC), which has been joined by a variety of Christian organizations. Headed in 1994 by Rev. Joseph Matsheng, the BCC had its Headquarters in a new office building in Gaborone. BCC committees include high-ranking members of the government, and the Council is affiliated with the All Africa Conference of Churches.

As of 1994, membership in world religious groups in Botswana was estimated as follows:

Religion	*Total Members (est.)*
Christian	392,035

(Largest Groups)

Roman Catholic	47,000
Lutheran—three churches	30,300
Spiritual Healing Church	30,000
London Missionary Society	20,000
Zion Christian Church	18,000
Bahai	5,000
Islam	3,000
Hindu	2,000

See also African Methodist Episcopal Church: Baptists; Buddhists; Dutch Reformed Church; Independent Churches; Methodists; Modimo; Mwali; Pentecostal Churches; Presbyterians; Seventh Day Adventist Church; Vapostori; Zambia.

REOKWAENG, EYES (1916–1989). Politician. As headman of a section of Letlhakeng during the 1940s, he resisted BaKwena attempts to consolidate that village under a chief's representative. In 1964 he was recruited by **Quett Masire** to organize the **Democratic Party** in western Kweneng. He represented the constituency of Kweneng West in the National Assembly, 1965–1984.

RESERVES. Proclamation 9 of 1899 established five reserves: Bangwaketse, Bakwena, Bakhatla, Bamangwato, and Batawana. Three others were created later: Bamalete (1909), Tati (1911), and Batlokwa (1933). Inside a reserve, the sale of land was not permitted, as it was held to be the property of the "tribe" under the authority of their "chief" or "tribal authority." *See also* Administration; Boundaries; Kgafela Kgatla; Kgosi; Kwena; Lete; Ngwaketse; Ngwato; Proclamation; Tati Concession; Tawana; Tlokwa.

RESIDENT COMMISSIONER. The principal administrative officer responsible for the Protectorate was known from 1885 to 1891 as deputy commissioner, from 1891 to 1964 as resident commissioner, and from 1964 to independence as Queen's commissioner. Except for the 1885–1895 period, when he was based at Vryburg, the commissioner's offices were located in the Imperial Reserve, **Mafikeng**, until February 1965, when they were shifted to Gaborone.

Deputy Commissioner for the Protectorate (and Administrator of British Bechuanaland)

1885–1891   **Sidney Godolphin Alexander Shippard**

Resident Commissioner, Bechuanaland Protectorate

1891–1895   Sidney Godolphin Alexander Shippard
1895–1897   Frances James Newton
1897–1901   **Hamilton John Goold-Adams**
1901–1906   **Ralph Champney Williams**
1907–1916   Francis William Panzera
1916–1917   Dr. Edward Charles Frederick Garraway
1917–1923   James Comyn Macgregor
1923–1927   **Jules Ellenberger**

1928–1930	Roland Mortimer Daniel
1930–1937	**Charles Fernand Rey**
1937–1942	**Charles Noble Arden-Clarke**
1942–1946	Aubrey Denzil Forsyth Thompson
1946–1950	**Anthony Sillery**
1950–1953	Edward Betham Beetham
1953–1955	William Forbes MacKenzie
1955–1959	Martin Osterfield Wray
1959–1964	**Robert Peter Fawcus**

The Queen's Commissioner for the Bechuanaland Protectorate

1964–1965	Robert Peter Fawcus
1965–1966	Hugh Selby Norman-Walker

See also Administration; High Commissioner.

RETIEF, DEBORAH ("BORRIE"). Longest-serving member of the **DRC** mission in **Mochudi**, 1887–1929. Born in Paarl. The present hospital in Mochudi was named in her honor.

REY, CHARLES FERNAND (1877–1968). Resident commissioner, 1930–1937, and pugnacious reformer. After serving in Abyssinia (Ethiopia), Rey was appointed by Dominions Secretary Leopold Amery to reorganize and improve the Protectorate's economy and administration. His efforts to reform the administration with the Native Proclamations of 1934 were largely thwarted, mainly due to the resistance of **Tshekedi Khama** and other diKgosi, but also because his superiors and subordinates in the colonial structure failed to back him. At one time or another Rey was at loggerheads it seemed, with every member of the Protectorate administration, European and African. Nevertheless, his plans for economic development were far ahead of their time. They included building a railway to Walvis Bay, using Okavango waters for irrigation, creating secondary industries around cattle, and introducing large-scale mining, especially in **copper**. Rey did manage to open a small **abattoir** at **Lobatse** and begin a beef export industry; build dams and sink boreholes in cooperation with the merafe; establish tribal treasuries to finance local development projects; and found **radio** and air services. However, the British government remained marginally committed to the development of the Protectorate, because at the time **incorporation** of the Protectorate into South Africa was considered as inevitable, and Rey retired a frustrated and disillusioned man.

See also Cattle; Namibia; Okavango Delta; Resident Commissioner; Water.

REYNEKE, JOHAN. Popular **DRC** missionary in **Mochudi**, 1923–1934, a time of internal political turmoil among the **Kgatla Kgafela**. His gentle manner, willingness to compromise, and hard work helped restore the fortunes of the mission, which had declined since the outbreak of the **South African War of 1899–1902**. During his time, a nurse and doctor were added to the mission staff, the Protectorate's first vernacular mission paper appeared (*Lesedi la Sechaba*, also known as "Lesedinyana"), and the Reverend navigated his circuit on an Overland motorcycle.

RHODES, CECIL. *See* British Bechuanaland; British South Africa Company.

RHODESIA. *See* Zambia; Zimbabwe.

RILEY, CHARLES (1860–1941). Riley ("Magagane") was a trader and proprietor in the early Protectorate. A "coloured" whose descendants were white, Riley arrived in Botswana in 1882 and traded in southern Bechuanaland, where he became well known and trusted by the diKgosi. He was instrumental in the negotiation of several key concessions involving **Bathoen I, Sebele I,** and **Linchwe I.**

Riley used his connections and quick understanding of the trading laws to open up liquor stores and hotels. By 1900 he was based in Ngamiland, where he set up a trading store and became a close friend of BaTawana Kgosi **Sekgoma Letshola-thebe.** When Sekgoma was deposed in 1906, he gave Riley his power of attorney, with which Riley pressed Sekgoma's legal claims for several years, eventually reaching the High Court in London. When the case failed, Riley had a falling out with Sekgoma over expenses. Eventually Riley was compensated by the British. Riley settled in Ngamiland, making the new capital of **Maun** his home. His son Harry built the hotel that still bears his name. *See also* Coloureds.

RINDERPEST. A livestock epizootic which originated in the Horn of Africa and swept south, passing through the Protectorate in 1896 along the rail line with mortality rates averaging roughly 90 percent of the country's **cattle**. Some small areas escaped harm, but the nation as a whole was devastated. Its appearance compounded an ecological malaise that caused more suffering than has been experienced at any other time in Botswana's recorded history. Disease and drought accompanied rinderpest, and drought, famine, locusts, and disease followed in its wake. In some areas, human mortality exceeded 20 percent.

In the long term, rinderpest may have made the distribution of cattle more egalitarian. In the early twentieth century, migrant laborers began returning from South Africa, having purchased cattle with their earnings and competing with the old aristocracy that had been hard-hit by the epizootic. *See also* Okavango Delta; Tawana; Tsetse; Zambia.

RIVER VILLAGES. The three villages of Sikwane, Malolwane, and Mathubudukwane are situated on the Madikwe River on the border between Botswana and South Africa. They were founded between 1882 and 1884 by leading **Kgafela Kgatla** from the Saulspoort area of western Transvaal and were sited by Kgosi **Linchwe I** as part of his plan to preserve BaKgatla access to the Madikwe River and protect the Derdepoort drift, a vital road link between **Mochudi** and Saulspoort. These villages supported a flourishing **DRC** mission community. Sikwane was the base used by regiments of the Kgafela Kgatla, under **Ramono**, to attack Boer emplacements in Derdepoort during the **South African War of 1899–1902.** *See also* Battle of Derdepoort.

ROADS. Botswana has approximately 2,200 miles of bituminized national roads, almost all of which have been built since independence, nearly half of which were constructed between 1988 and 1992. Botswana's all-weather road system links Gaborone to all of Botswana's major towns and mining centers, and connects Botswana to South Africa, Namibia, Zambia, and Zimbabwe. The trans-Kgalagadi road to Gobabis via Jwaneng and Kang, the most ambitious of Botswana's road development projects, was nearing completion in 1995. *See also* Air Transportation; Railways.

ROCK ART. This well-known art form has been associated with so-called "Bushmen" throughout southern Africa in the precolonial era. Botswana appears not to have had as many painters as its neighbors, probably because few rock outcroppings are found here. Nor do those extant follow the mystic style depicting trance-dancing, as is common in South African paintings. The most famous, and numerous, paintings are the animal representations at Tsodilo hills in Ngamiland. Similar work can be found in the Tati, Savuti, and some southern hill areas, notably Manyana-Dimawe. A set of abstract rock engravings also exists in the Ghanzi area.

ROLONG (BAROLONG). A large section of BaTswana with groups scattered throughout Botswana and South Africa. Ba-Rolong are found in the extreme south, northeast, and west of Botswana and in the northern Cape Province and the Orange Free State of South Africa. Perhaps the best known BaRolong in Botswana are members of the Tshidi BaRolong who live on either side of the Molopo river, which divides Botswana from South Africa. As early as the eighteenth century and until the **mfecane**, the Tshidi BaRolong and other BaRolong probably controlled the trade of the western Kgalagadi, and they retained control of the Lehututu-Hukuntsi pans until 1885. They used this area, known as "Matsheng," as a place of refuge, trading, hunting, and tribute collecting. During the second half of the nineteenth century the Tshidi BaRolong were ruled by Kgosi **Montshiwa**, with whom diKgosi in southern Bechuanaland cooperated to stem the tide of Boer and British expansion. In 1885 Tshidi BaRolong territory was divided when the area south of the Molopo was proclaimed **British Bechuanaland** and, in 1895, annexed to the Cape Colony. In the latter year, separate Tshidi BaRolong reserves were created on both sides of the border, that to the north becoming known as **Barolong Farms**.

Among the other BaRolong of Botswana, the community of northeastern Botswana dates to 1897, when a group of Seleka BaRolong (not to be confused with the Ba**Seleka**) originating from Thaba Nchu in the Orange Free State, moved from the Transvaal under the leadership of Samuel Moroka to the Tati area, where they established a village known by their leader's name. In the nineteenth century other groups of BaRolong settled in many of the villages of Kgalagadi, including **Ghanzi**.

ROMAN CATHOLICS. The largest world religious group in Botswana in terms of members (47,000). Catholic missionaries began work in 1886 in Mafikeng. Bishop Meysing of Kimberley bought Kgale farm from the Lonergans, a Catholic family, giving rise to the St. Joseph's Mission (opened 1928 under Fr. Rittmuller). In 1929, St. Theresa Mission was established in

Lobatse by Fr. Ortman. The Catholic mission was staffed by German priests (the Oblates of Mary Immaculate) and Dominican and Franciscan sisters. A primary school and clinic were built at St. Joseph's, and in 1935 the first foothold was gained in a reserve when the BaLete gave permission to Fr. Kress to start a mission at **Ramotswa**. Kgale school began to teach Junior Certificate level in 1945 and by 1954 was teaching to matriculation standard. In 1952 the Catholic missionary effort in Botswana became the responsibility of the largely Irish Passionist Order and quickly overcame one of its principal obstacles to progress—British and BaTswana prejudice against the German priests.

The 1950s and 1960s were a period of extraordinary growth in the Catholic church in Botswana as the opposition of the diKgosi gradually disappeared: missions were established at Francistown, Morwa, Mahalapye, Serowe, Palapye, and Mochudi. The Catholics were particularly active in the fields of education and medicine. The first MoTswana priest to be ordained was Fr. Joseph Motsumi in 1958. In 1966 the Diocese of Botswana was created and Monsignor Urban Murphy became its first Bishop (succeeded by the Right Rev. Boniface Tshosa Setlalekgosi). In 1987, the Catholic population of the country was estimated to be 40,000 (compared to 1,500 in 1950). Testimony to their advance was the Pope's visit in 1988. *See also* Religion.

ROWLAND, RICHARD MONTSHIWA (1879–1945). Early trader and confidant of BaNgwaketse diKgosi. From Mafikeng, Rowland was of mixed ("coloured") descent but could pass for white. He moved to **Kanye** in 1912 as a trader. Alongside his many trading ventures, he acquired a mining concession and ran the Moshaneng asbestos mine until his death. Kgosi **Seepapitso II** used Rowland to reorganize local commerce and to increase local cattle prices. Rowland was also crucial to Seepapitso's road and dam-building schemes. Always close to local diKgosi, he became an advisor and aide to **Bathoen II**, and also hired Johnny Masire (father of future president, **Quett Masire**) as his store manager. During the 1930s depression he raised much charity for poor relief. Rowland was very popular among the BaNgwaketse, and upon his death they demanded his burial locally. He was a Member, Order of the British Empire. *See also* Mining.

S

SAMUEL MAHARERO. *See* Maharero, Samuel.

SAN. A **Khoe** term, usually pejorative and rejected by Khoe-speakers in Botswana and Namibia, that is used to refer to people of low social status and/or foragers. In recent decades it has been embraced by many non-Khoe-speakers, and by academics in particular, as a generic reference to replace the uncomplimentary **Bushmen**. It is often combined with Khoi to refer to the speakers of the so-called "click languages." *See also* Khoisan.

SARWA (BASARWA). SeKgalagadi, later SeTswana, term for Khoisan-speakers of the Kgalagadi. "Masarwa" is the pejorative. Many of these people were enslaved by the BaKgalagadi prior to the eighteenth century, just as the BaKgalagadi and BaSarwa were enslaved by incoming BaTswana groups in the eighteenth and nineteenth centuries. In Botswana, the issue of BaSarwa civic rights is still controversial. As recently as 1994, a report by Alice Mogwe to the Botswana Christian Council contained allegations that police in remote areas were subjecting BaSarwa detainees to physical and sexual abuse. Police have also been accused by BaSarwa in the Ghanzi area of ignoring their complaints regarding abuse of their children by area residents. *See also* Bolata; Bushmen; /Gwi; Khoe; Khoisan; San; Shua; Slave Trade; Tshu; Zhu.

SAUNDO, CHOMBO (d. 1977). A MoYei from Shorobe who established himself as the leading Ba**Yei** politician in the 1950s and 1960s, using **Moeti Samotsoko** as his front man. Convicted for his part in the 1961 BaYei civil disobedience campaign, he acted as "chief" of the BaYei separatists after the death of Samotsoko in 1963 and became an active member of the **Independence Party** in the mid-1960s. In his private life, Saundo was a large cattle owner, notorious in Ngamiland as a cattle thief, and was alleged to have participated in ritual murders.

SCHAPERA, ISAAC (1905–). Noted scholar in southern African studies and honored for his prolific writing on the peoples of Botswana. Born in the Cape Province, South Africa, of East European Jewish descent, he began his research in 1929 in the Bechuanaland Protectorate and returned often over the next two decades. His published work includes *The Handbook of*

Tswana Law and Custom, Married Life in an African Tribe, Migrant Labour and Tribal Life, Praise Poems of Tswana Chiefs, Rainmaking Rites of the Tswana Tribes, and *Tribal Innovators,* all of which have become classics. Schapera's work on BaTswana societies represents, according to Meyer Fortes, "the most complete and comprehensive body of knowledge relating to the history, the social and political life and the contemporary situation of any single group of African peoples as yet assembled." Altogether he has published more than fifteen books, edited seven others, and produced more than 100 articles, texts, and reports related to the peoples of Botswana. Schapera is the retired professor of Social Anthropology, London School of Economics, and resides in London.

SEBEGO I (1800[?]–1844). Regent of the main faction of the BaNgwaketse, 1825–1844, during the crucial period known as the **mfecane.** Allegedly he betrayed his father **Makaba II,** and he then became regent for Gaseitsiwe, son of Tshosa Makaba II. Sebego was an effective military leader, and in 1826 his regiments drove out the Ba**Kololo** from southern Botswana. In the 1830s, his army defeated the Ama**Ndebele** at Dutlwe, but he fled into the Kgalagadi to avoid retribution. He moved to Ghanzi, which he conquered in 1834. Sebego then attempted to murder Gaseitsiwe and his brother by poisoning them. Gaseitsiwe's younger brother succumbed, but the heir fled with his mother and gained refuge among the BaRolong of **Segotshane,** whereupon support for Sebego began to crumble. Malaria and lack of water for his cattle soon forced him south, and he settled in Lehututu until 1835. There he ruled through terror, even once burning alive an entire village of Ba**Kgala-gadi.** Such acts earned him the sobriquet, "hard-hearted crocodile" (*kwena,* or crocodile, was the BaNgwaketse's totem, which among BaTswana is commonly used as a proper title of their Kgosi, or regent). In 1842 Sebego returned to GaNgwaketse, where he was attacked by his enemies. He died in 1844 of natural causes on a trip to the northern Cape with his followers. He was survived by his son **Senthufe,** who led the most important faction among the BaNgwaketse until 1853 and possibly later. *See also* Battle of Dithubaruba; Battle of Dutlwe.

SEBELE I (1838[?]–1911). Kgosi of the BaKwena, 1892–1911, son of and successor to **Sechele I.** His reign was marked by internal discord, ecological crises, and strained relations with the Protectorate administration. During the 1850s he was educated at the LMS school at Kudumane (Kuruman) and became literate in SeTswana and Dutch but never mastered English. In the 1870s he emerged as a military leader. In 1872 his forces helped to install **Khama III** at Shoshong, but in 1875 he gained notoriety for cowardice in the battle between the BaKwena and **Kgafela Kgatla** at Mochudi during the **Civil Wars**.

In 1885 he opposed the British declaration of the Protectorate and throughout his reign tried to limit British interference in BaKwena affairs. Upon succession his position was precarious: he had already become embroiled with the British, who in 1892–1893 forced him to back down by threatening to destroy Molepolole as an example to BaTswana in general. His authority was also challenged by his elder half-brother Kgari, who by 1895 was recognized as Kgosi by nearly half of the morafe. That year, Sebele's visit to London with Khama and **Bathoen I** helped to bolster his standing with the British and BaKwena, and after Kgari died in 1896 the British allowed Sebele to reassert his authority throughout Kweneng and send Kgari's sons and die-hards into exile.

Between 1896 and 1899, **rinderpest**, drought, and disease destroyed stock and decimated the BaKwena. For much of this period Sebele abdicated his responsibilities by retreating to his cattle post and rejecting British offers of food for his people. During the **South African War of 1899–1902**, Sebele was nearly removed by officials who had been convinced by missionaries and Sebele's enemy **Baruti Kgosidintsi** that Sebele was anti-British. Undeterred, Sebele continued criticizing Protectorate rule for such actions as collecting hut tax and demarcating boundaries at BaKwena expense. Sebele's most important contribution was leading the 1908–1909 campaign against **incorporation** of the Protectorate into the proposed Union of South Africa. *See also* Boundaries; British South Africa Company; Concessions; Kaa; Kopong Conference; Lete; Mmanaana Kgatla; Sechele I; Sidzumo, Peter; Three Kings in London; Tlokwa; Warren Expedition; Williams, Ralph.

SEBELE II, KELEBANTSE A SECHELE (1892–1939). Controversial Kgosi of the BaKwena, 1918–1931; exiled to Ghanzi by the British. After a year's schooling at **Tiger Kloof**, Sebele ran away to the Witwatersrand, where he worked as a mines clerk, 1912–1916. In 1917–1918 he served in the Bechuanaland Protectorate unit of the **South African Native Labour Contingent** in France. Upon his return he succeeded his father **Sechele II**

and quickly came into conflict with a faction of dikgosana who criticized his private life and his advocacy of such traditional practices as bogwera (**initiation**). During the 1920s this faction, even though supported by Protectorate officials, failed to remove Sebele, because he had strong support within the morafe, particularly among commoners. In 1927 Sebele began cooperating with **Tshekedi Khama** and other diKgosi in resisting British efforts to reduce their powers. After **Charles Rey** became **resident commissioner** in 1930, Sebele's removal was thought essential before Rey's Native Administration reforms could be introduced. In 1931 Rey seized on complaints received from **Molepolole** about bogwera to portray Sebele as a threat to the public peace. He was then lured to **Mafikeng**, arrested, and deported by rail to Ghanzi via **Namibia**. The majority of the BaKwena rejected the legitimacy of Sebele's deposition and the succession of **Kgari Sechele**, hand-picked by the British. When Sebele II died in 1939, the BaKwena had his body returned to Molepolole and buried it as befitting their Kgosi. *See also* Councils; Moruakgomo Sechele; World War I.

SEBESO, G.G. (1908–1992). MoTswapong teacher and politician. Past headmaster at Shoshong school and soldier veteran of **World War II**, Sebeso became sub-African authority in Palapye in 1953 and held the same office in Mahalapye in 1964. In 1965 he stood for the **Democratic Party** in Tswapong South, which he won and held until his retirement in 1989.

SEBONI, MARTINUS. Tax collector, councilor, and co-regent of the BaKwena (1941–1945). He played an important role in both the affairs of his morafe and the Protectorate as a whole. He helped **Tshekedi Khama**, **Bathoen** II, and the British draft the 1943 Proclamations and was active in the African Advisory Council. His last major public action was to sponsor his nephew **Bonewamang**, who claimed bogosi in 1962.

SEBONI, MICHAEL (1912–1975). Son of **Martinus Seboni**; leading author and academic. He held a Ph.D. from the University of South Africa (1958) and was for many years a lecturer at Fort Hare College, where he headed the Department of Bantu Languages. He is best known for his contributions to SeTswana literature, including the novel *Rammone wa Kgalagadi* and the biographies *Kgosi Isang Pilane*, *Kgosi Sebele II*, and *Dr. Modiri Silas Molema*. Through such works as *Maboko Maloba le Maabane* and *Diane le Maele a Setswana*, he tried to preserve elements in the SeTswana language and to promote its growth by grammars, translations, and other works. His nephew Barolong Seboni, at the University of Botswana, is a poet, writer, and social commentator. *See also* Matthews, Zachariah.

SECHELE I (1810[?]–1892). "RraMokonopi." Kgosi of the Ba-**Kwena**, 1829[?]–1892, and champion of BaTswana autonomy. Following the murder of his father **Motswasele II** in 1821, the morafe fragmented and Sechele went into exile. Around 1833 he assumed leadership of a group of BaKwena then based at Lephephe and began the long process of reunification which was finally completed in 1845 with the death of his rival **Bubi**. By then **David Livingstone** had converted him to Christianity. As of the late 1840s Sechele had gained control of the booming trans-Kgalagadi trade in ivory and, later, in ostrich feathers.

After 1850 many BaTswana, sometimes whole merafe, fled the Boers in the western Transvaal and took refuge with Sechele. The most numerous of these were the **Mmanaana Kgatla** of Mosielele. In 1852 at the **Battle of Dimawe**, Sechele's army repelled a large Boer commando sent to arrest Mosielele. In 1853 Sechele traveled to Cape Town and petitioned Queen Victoria to disallow the Sand River Convention (1852) and permit him to buy guns to defend himself against the Boers. His request was ignored, but guns, and even a cannon, were later smuggled into the Kweneng. The BaKwena and their allies also moved to **Dithubaruba** Hill, where stone fortifications were built, deterring a second Boer attack. In 1853 Sechele and the Boers reached a truce, and Kwena-Boer relations, which were normalized with the arrival of Hermannsburg missionaries (1857–1858), lasted for thirty years. In 1860 Sechele visited Pretoria as the guest of President Marthinus Pretorius. In 1868, when Boer farmers in the Marico district talked of occupying BaHurutshe land, Sechele threatened war against the South African Republic (SAR), and the SAR convinced the farmers to back down. Sechele accepted the Hermannsburgers (**Lutherans**) sent from the Transvaal, because the **LMS** had not returned after Dimawe. Under Sechele's patronage, the Hermannsburg missionaries branched out to the **BaNgwato, BaLete, BaHurutshe**, and Mmanaana Kgatla. The BaKwena also profited from the Kgalagadi-Transvaal trade, one result of which was the introduction of metal plows.

Sechele was at the height of his power in 1872, dominating political and economic affairs in what became Botswana. For years he repeatedly involved himself in BaNgwato affairs, a process which ended in the consolidation of power of the Christian faction, led by **Khama III**. After 1875 his control was challenged by the **Kgafela Kgatla**, who wrested the western portion of BaKwena territory, and by the BaNgwato, who broke the BaKwena monopoly of the trans-Kgalagadi trade. When they declared the Bechuanaland Protectorate in 1885, the British regarded Sechele and Khama as the two principal diKgosi. Sechele opposed the **Warren Expedition** and spent the last years of his reign resisting British inroads into his authority. *See also* Afrikaners; Baruti Kgosidintsi; Civil Wars; Kgamanyane; Linchwe I; Macheng; Mfecane; Moffat, Robert; Ndebele; Sekgoma I; Traders.

SECHELE II KEALEBOGA SEBELE (1860[?]–1918). Kgosi of the BaKwena, 1911–1918. His short reign was troubled by political conflict. Like his father **Sebele I**, his authority was challenged by a group of digkosana led by **Baruti Kgosidintsi**. In 1912 when Sechele sanctioned the establishment of the **Anglican** Church, **LMS** missionaries supported the dikgosana in a campaign to discredit him before the British.

The resulting conflict split **Molepolole** into the Ntsweng and Borakalalo factions and occasioned the first BaKwena tribal council. The council, which was controlled by Sechele's sibling rivals Kebohula and Moiteelasilo soon lapsed as Sechele asserted his authority by promoting junior headmen into powerful positions and reviving bogwera. After his death, however, political quarreling continued, disturbing the reign of his heir **Sebele II**. *See also* Initiation; Mashwe, George; Sidzumo, Peter.

SEEPAPITSO II, BATHOEN GASEITSIWE (1884–1916). Kgosi of the BaNgwaketse, 1910–1916, his reign terminated by his being assassinated. On his accession, Seepapitso was the most educated Kgosi in the Protectorate. During his short reign he was an energetic ruler who tried to modernize the politics and economy of his morafe. He built up a strong bureaucracy around his secretary Peter Kgasa. He was also the first Kgosi to begin the recording of **kgotla** and other public proceedings. Among his development projects were the Makgodumo dam and the sinking of boreholes, which allowed Kanye to become the first village with standpipes. The British admired his efficiency and trusted his loyalty (during **World War I**, his regiments intercepted and captured a pro-German Boer force under General Pienaar at Segwagwa on 1 January 1915), but his independent spirit often made them uncomfortable.

He was assassinated in the kgotla by his younger brother Moeapitso, who was subsequently hanged at the insistence of their mother **Gagoangwe**. Moeapitso's motive has never been clearly established, but the dikgosana, fearing that Seepapitso's reforms might threaten their wealth and privilege, may have incited him. *See also* Bathoen I; Bathoen II; Kanye; Mothowagae Motlogelwa; Ntebogang Ratshosa; Tshosa Sebego.

SEEPAPITSO IV (1934–). Kgosi of the BaNgwaketse,1969–. Perhaps the most outspoken of contemporary diKgosi, Seepapitso's independent frame of mind was apparent early. In 1965 he founded the short-lived Botswana National Union, a political party superseded by the **National Front (BNF)** in the same year. Seepapitso himself stayed out of the BNF and assumed bogosi in 1969 after his father **Bathoen II** abdicated the position and entered politics as president of that very party. Seepapitso was elected chairman of the House of Chiefs the following year. Over the years he has been a staunch defender of customary law and local land rights. In 1994 the national government suspended him as Kgosi, a move vigorously protested by his people. It was a major campaign issue in GaNgwaketse in the 1994 national elections.

SEGALE (1860[?]–1926). The "Fighting Chief." Segale was the older half-brother of **Linchwe I**, an early **DRC** convert and mission teacher in **Mochudi**, and along with Linchwe's brother **Ramono** a leader of the Makoba regiment, which played a key role in the **Battle of Derdepoort** and in the BaKgatla campaign in the western Transvaal during the **South African War of 1899–1902**. For sometime after the war Linchwe appointed Segale Kgosi of the Protectorate Kgatla and Ramono Kgosi of the Saulpoort Kgatla, designating himself as Paramount. The war made Segale anti-Boer and pro-Protectorate. He became a staunch opponent of DRC missionaries and established his own school in Mochudi with his own money. In letters to *Koranta ea Becoana*, he attacked the British Transvaal government for continuing Boer laws. Segale led BaKgatla opposition to **incorporation** from 1908 to 1910 and served as an important councilor under Linchwe I and **Isang Pilane**. *See also* Kgafela Kgatla; Kgamanyane.

SEGOKGO, MOTLATSI KESEABETWE (1928–1977). Politician, born in Tlokweng. In 1964 Segokgo resigned as head teacher at Batlokwa National School to enter full-time politics in the **Democratic Party**. He was elected to the National Assembly in 1965 and served in the cabinet as minister of Finance (1965–1969); Commerce, Industry and Water Affairs (1969–1974); and Mineral Resources and Water Affairs (1974–1977).

SEGOLODI, MOANAPHUTI RAMPODU (1894–1949). Extravagant but troubled MoNgwato royal and sometime civil servant. He was born in Ngamiland as the son of Rampodu, an exiled MoNgwato royal who became the first secretary to the BaTawana and headman over the HaMbukushu. Moanaphuti, who schooled in Maun, acquired his father's position in 1914. In 1927, after years of flamboyant living underwritten by considerable personal indebtedness and by embezzlement of public funds, Moanaphuti was exiled. He was thrown out of Kanye in 1928 but accepted by **Tshekedi Khama** of the BaNgwato, when he had become persona non grata elsewhere. Soon he fell out with Tshekedi and became part of the anti-Tshekedi agitation launched by the Ratshosa brothers, who by then had become his in-laws. Gifted at intrigue and fond of packing two six-shooters in public, Moanaphuti succeeded in alienating others as well. In 1929, the year he was found guilty of killing Tshekedi's cattle, he raised the banner of protest against Tshekedi the tyrant, evaded regimental work, and placed the touring pair, **Ballinger & Barnes**, in contact with the Protectorate's leading malcontents. When Tshekedi had him hauled into the kgotla to hear complaints against him, Moanaphuti was pummeled by an angry mob assembled for the occasion, and then summarily flogged. Fueled for another round of agitation, Moanaphuti organized (with other disgruntled BaNgwato) an anti-Tshekedi petition against flogging and regimental work that succeeded in getting the British to reduce the Kgosi's powers regarding these practices. **Charles Rey**, determined on reducing the power of Tshekedi and other diKgosi, nevertheless found ample grounds to have Moanaphuti thrown out of Gammangwato in 1931. Fortunately he was able to return to Ngamiland and obtain work in the tribal administration and, eventually, the Protectorate government. *See also* Ratshosa, Simon.

SEGOTSHANE (d. 1885). Regent of a BaNgwaketse faction, 1825–1852. In 1823 he joined his elder brother **Tshosa Makaba**, in an unsuccessful attempt to overthrow their father, **Makaba II.** He then took refuge among the BaRolong. Following Makaba's death in 1825 he gathered together the BaNgwaketse opposed to the followers of the regent **Sebego** (including until 1832 **Gaseitsiwe**, heir to the throne). In 1842 he defeated Sebego, and in 1852 he led the BaNgwaketse into battle with the forces of **Sechele I** against the Boers in 1852, after which Gaseitsiwe succeeded, probably in 1853. *See also* BaTswana-Boer War of 1852–1853.

SEINGWAENG (1883–1967). Wife of Kgafela, mother of **Molefi** and **Mmusi,** and leader of conservative protest during the 1930s and 1940s in the Bakgatla Reserve. The daughter of a blacksmith, she was born in Mmathubudukkwane and educated by **Thomas Phiri.** As a founder member of **Ipelegeng** and the Mochudi chapter of the **Zion Christian Church (ZCC),** she helped oppose the official removal and banishment of Molefi from bogosi (1936–1945). Before and after Molefi's reinstatement, the ZCC also became vocal against modern social ills and westernization. In 1947 Seingwaeng and other hard-core members were banished by Molefi from the reserve. She lived the balance of her life in the **Tuli Block** on the ZCC-owned farm Lentswe-le-moriti. A large, strong woman, she was known for her courtesy and open-handedness.

SEKGOMA I ("MMAPHIRI")(1810[?]–1883). Sekgoma was the son of **Kgari I** by a junior wife and on three occasions occupied the office of Kgosi of the BaNgwato: 1835[?]–1857, 1859–1866, and 1872–1875. During his interrupted reigns, the BaNgwato emerged as a regional power. He executed AmaNdebele envoys demanding tribute in 1844 and subsequently defeated a punitive expedition. In 1848 his regiments drove the BaKaa out of Shoshong, which Sekgoma then made his capital. During his first reign he expanded the morafe, incorporating the BaTswapong and groups of BaBirwa and BaKgalagadi. In 1857 **Sechele I** of the BaKwena, fearful of Sekgoma's growing power, deposed him and installed Sekgoma's half-brother **Macheng.** When Macheng proved to be a potential ally of Mzilikazi of the AmaNdebele, Sechele returned Sekgoma to power. Restoration was accompanied by the extension of Hermannsburg (**Lutherans**) missionary activity from Molepolole to Shoshong with the support of Sekgoma's two sons **Khama III** and **Kgamane.** In 1863 the last AmaNdebele raiding party was defeated outside Shoshong by regiments under Khama. From 1865 to 1866 conflict between Christian and traditional factions forced Sekgoma to abdicate in favor of Macheng. In 1872 Sechele deposed Macheng and installed Khama, who was unable to prevent his father from regaining the throne. Tensions marked the next three years, as BaNgwato divided between those loyal to Sekgoma and Kgamane and those in the Christian faction led by Khama. In 1875 Khama seized control, and Sekgoma fled to Molepolole. He was allowed to return to Shoshong before his death in 1883. *See also* Battles of Shoshong.

SEKGOMA II ("Leraraetsa")(1869[?]–1925). Kgosi of the BaNgwato,1923–1925, and father of **Seretse Khama**, first president of Botswana. The prime of Sekgoma's adult life (1889–1916) was spent outside the capital as a result of his estrangement from his father **Khama III**. As crown prince, Sekgoma wanted some say in morafe affairs, but Khama, who had usurped his own father, regarded him as a challenger. Around 1895 Khama punished him and his followers by confiscating some of their cattle. When Sekgoma spoke against Khama in the **kgotla**, Khama silenced him thenceforth. Finally, in 1898 Khama alleged that Sekgoma was disloyal and exiled him to Lephephe. The next year the **resident commissioner** held an inquiry to determine ownership of kgamelo cattle held by Sekgoma and his followers and declared Khama the owner. The question arose again in 1907, when Sekgoma moved to **Nata**; only then did Khama abolish the kgamelo system. When Khama fell ill in 1916, father and son reconciled and Sekgoma was restored as heir.

Sekgoma's brief reign was troubled by competition and conflict between the Ratshosa and Mphoeng factions. In 1925 he made excessive demands on his people to hold a great pageant to welcome the Prince of Wales, but to Sekgoma's great disappointment the Prince made only a fleeting visit to Serowe. *See also* Gasetshwarwe; Mphoeng, Phethu; Oratile Ratshosa; Ratshosa Motswetle; Tshekedi Khama.

SEKGOMA LETSHOLATHEBE (1874[?]–1914). Kgosi of the BaTawana, 1891–1906. An ambitious regent who made himself Kgosi, Sekgoma used administrative reforms to undercut his political enemies and raise allies among commoners. He grew up in the shadow of his elder brother **Moremi II**, who shunned him. Sekgoma was raised on a distant cattle post where he underwent **initiation** with local Ba**Sarwa**. In 1889 he assumed power in a coup when Moremi was absent. In the following months he lost two battles to Moremi, but he returned to assume the regency in 1891 upon the death of his brother. Moremi's son **Mathiba** was then a minor. As regent, Sekgoma soon claimed the right of succession over the claims of Mathiba's supporters. He solidified his position by incorporating commoners and subject peoples into the royal (kgosing) ward and resorting to torture, patronage, marriage alliances, and forgery to silence or discredit his opponents.

In 1906 an anti-Sekgoma coalition of dikgosana, traders, missionaries (Sekgoma did not convert to Christianity), and **Khama III** persuaded the British administration to depose Sekgoma and install Mathiba. While Sekgoma was in Kimberley receiving medical treatment, a pro-Mathiba coup was launched in Tsau, then the BaTawana capital, and Sekgoma was detained while returning, first by Khama and then by the British. After staging an inquiry-cum-election, Resident Commissioner **Ralph Williams** declared Mathiba the rightful Kgosi. Sekgoma was held in Gaberones, but with the help of **Charles Riley** and others, he managed to challenge the legality of the inquiry and his detention without trial by taking the **high commissioner** to court. In 1909 his case reached the Court of Appeals in London, which refused to make a ruling on the grounds that under the **Foreign Jurisdiction Act of 1890** the high commissioner's power in the Protectorate was absolute. In 1911 Sekgoma went free and the following year settled in Chobe, where he was joined by a majority of Ngamiland's population. *See also* Motshabi Letsholathebe.

SELEKA (BASELEKA). A people long resident in the upper Limpopo valley (on both sides of the modern Botswana-South African border). Like the BaLete, the BaSeleka were originally "Transvaal Ndebele" who assimilated the Sotho-Tswana language of their neighbors. Earliest oral traditions support their claim that they had adopted the *phuthi* (duiker) as their totem prior to the mid-eighteenth-century arrival of the BaNgwato in their area. Around 1828, the BaSeleka joined forces with the BaNgwato in an unsuccessful invasion of the BaNyayi-BaKalanga ("Rozwi") kingdom. Thereafter their Kgosi Kobe established himself at Ngwapa (old Seleka), the defenses of which protected them against Sebetwane's BaKololo and Mzilikazi's AmaNdebele. They were later effective, too, against the state-building efforts of **Sekgoma I** of the BaNgwato. By the time of the 1885 declaration of the Protectorate, the BaSeleka had maintained their independence and had provided refuge to some noted exiled BaTswana, such as the twice-deposed **Macheng** and the rival-brother of **Khama III, Kgamane.** In 1876, following a visit by a British labor recruiter, BaSeleka began to migrate seasonally to Kimberley to work in the diamond mines and return with guns purchased with their earnings. The BaSeleka arsenal was sufficient in May 1887 to require a 4,000-man BaNgwato force, backed by a detachment of Bechuanaland Border Police, to dislodge them. They were expelled to the Transvaal. In 1895 much of the BaSeleka lands inside the Protectorate were ceded by Khama III to the **British South Africa Company** as part of the **Tuli Block.** Two years later a BaSeleka faction, under Baitswe, junior son of Kobe, was allowed to resettle in the Bamangwato Reserve on condition that its members accept Khama's overrule. Descendants of the Baitswe group live today in the village of "Seleka." *See also* Kalanga.

SENANG DITSELA (1818[?]–1945). Perhaps the longest-living MoTswana on record, this MoKaa Methuselah lived an eventful life. As a boy growing up during the **mfecane**, he accompanied the losing BaNgwato war party to the Matopos in 1826. When the AmaNdebele raided the BaKaa (ca. 1835), he was captured and then trained for the military, entering Mzilikazi's Chindebadala regiment, and fought against the Boers, BaNgwaketse, and BaNgwato. After spending his middle age in Ndebele territory, he "retired" to BoKaa in the mid-1880s. In 1911 he married a twenty-nine-year old. By the 1930s his longevity began to attract attention worldwide. Senang was interviewed by South African Broadcasting Corporation, National Broadcasting Corporation, and the British Broadcasting Corporation radio services and was the subject of numerous newspaper articles.

SENTHUFE (d. 1885). Son of **Sebego I**, after whose death in 1844 he became the leader of the BaNgwaketse remnants of his father's followers. He played an important role in the **BaTswana-Boer War of 1852–1853.** His men fought at Dimawe and subsequently repulsed a Boer attack on Kanye. By 1853 he was living uneasily with **Gaseitsiwe** at **Kanye.** In 1857 Gaseitsiwe defeated Senthufe, who fled to **Sechele I** of the BaKwena. In 1859 he was allowed to return to Kanye.

SENTSHO LEGONG. A MoHurutshe millenarian prophet, a self-proclaimed "Jesus Christ," who led an early anti-mission/

anti-European movement in the southern Protectorate. His influence reached a climax in 1908, when Sentsho's group briefly seized control of Mmankgodi village and burned down the local **LMS** church. Sentsho was arrested by **Sebele I** and handed over to the British, who placed him in a lunatic asylum. Sentsho had a reputation as a talented rainmaker, and his name is still associated with good rainfall. *See also* Hurutshe.

SERETSE KHAMA, SIR (1921–1980). First President of the Republic of Botswana, 1966–1980. Son and heir of **Sekgoma II** of the BaNgwato, he was four years old when his father died. During his minority, Seretse's uncle **Tshekedi Khama** ruled as regent. In 1948 while studying law in London, he married Ruth Williams (later Lady Khama), a white Englishwoman. The same year he returned to Serowe and faced his uncle, who vehemently opposed the marriage. Tshekedi asked Seretse to choose between his people and his wife, but in June 1949 Seretse turned the tables at a momentous kgotla meeting where he asked the BaNgwato to choose between Tshekedi and Seretse. Only seventeen headmen and fewer than forty commoners backed Tshekedi; an estimated 8,000 stood and thundered applause for Seretse.

At first the Dominions Office was willing to recognize Seretse, but their own racial prejudices played an important role in events leading to a banishment decision. The Dominions Office first set up a judicial inquiry in order to find reasons not to install him. The findings (the Harrigan Report) were then closeted because they revealed that the only obstacles to Seretse's recognition were white Southern Rhodesian objections (official and unofficial) to his mixed marriage. Records now available show that Dominions Office officials were more racially agitated than was apartheid South Africa's president, D.F. Malan, who personally was somewhat indifferent. The unofficial protest of the pro-British Union Party, then out of power, may have influenced Britain more than the Malan government's communications. In 1950 Seretse was invited to London for talks and offered a post in the Jamaican civil service. Seretse refused, and the British banned him from returning to the Protectorate and suspended forever his right to assume bogosi.

Although banishment turned Seretse and Ruth into international celebrities, the British remained adamant and Seretse stayed in exile in London (1950–1956). Seretse used this time to establish ties with other African nationalists. Meanwhile,

BaNgwato still held Seretse to be their Kgosi. In June 1953 they rioted in the kgotla, and three BaSotho policemen were stoned to death.

In 1956 Seretse was allowed to return to the Protectorate. He and Tshekedi soon reconciled and renounced their own and their children's claims to bogosi. Seretse then took an active part in BaNgwato and Protectorate affairs, and after Tsheke-di's death in 1959 he became the leading MoTswana in the territory. In September 1961 Seretse responded to much urging and declared his intention in the Serowe kgotla to form a political party, which led to the Democratic Party **(BDP)**. Seretse and his right-hand man **Quett Masire** recruited local notables and created a strong network of support throughout the Protectorate. In 1963 when offered the bogosi by the BaNgwato, he refused. In 1965 his party won an overwhelming mandate to lead Botswana to independence.

Under Seretse's presidency, Botswana went from one of the world's poorest and most beleaguered countries to a model of human rights and economic development. Largely through his influence, Botswana resisted policies that would alienate its neighbors, overstretch its own resources, or use force against opponents inside the country. Though in 1966 Botswana was almost entirely surrounded by white-dominated governments, Seretse became a noted critic of their racially-based laws and sympathizer of Black liberation, while declaring Botswana's territory out of bounds to the liberation struggle itself. A believer in realpolitik, he offset Botswana's military weakness by making it a showcase for African non-racialism, modera-tion, and democratic rule.

SEROWE. Capital of the BaNgwato since 1902 and one of the largest traditional settlements in Botswana. In 1991 its popula-tion stood at 30,264. The previous capitals of Shoshong (1848) and Palapye (1889) had been abandoned mainly because of wood, grass, and water depletion, although in the latter case proximity to the railways and its attendant social "evils" were factors. *See also* Towns.

SETSWANA. The national language of Botswana and one of two official languages, the other being English (at present, English is the only language used in the National Assembly and the Government *Gazette*, though the use of SeTswana is under review).

SeTswana is a major branch of the Sotho-Tswana language

cluster, which is part of the southern Bantu family. SeTswana is thus closely related to SeSotho, SePedi (i.e., northern Sotho), SeKgalagadi, and SiLozi. SeTswana comprises many dialects, such as SeKgatla, SeTlhaping, and SeNgwato. Se-Tswana is the first language of approximately six million people in southern Africa, nearly five million of whom live in South Africa. Setswana is widely used in radio, television, and the music industry.

SeTswana was codified as a language in the 1840s, when French missionaries in Lesotho determined that "Sesotho" was a language separate from SeTswana. The **LMS** published the first SeTswana grammars and spellings, based largely on SeTlhaping. In modern Botswana, SeTlhaping has been abandoned as the basis of the national language.

SeTswana is spoken in southern Botswana slightly differently in tone and vocabulary than it is in the north. *See also* Literacy; London Missionary Society.

SEVENTH DAY ADVENTIST CHURCH (SDA). The SDA, which currently has an estimated 11,000 members, was introduced by American medical missionaries. In 1922, after receiving permission from the British to set up a mission at **Kanye** on condition that it provide medical services, Dr. Arthur Kretchmer began medical work at Kanye and in 1923 was given permission to do missionary work. The SDA became active in other villages in the Bangwaketse reserve. Since then the SDA has played a major role in developing medical care in the Southern District, and in 1937 it opened a hospital in Maun. *See also* Ntebogang Ratshosa; Nursing.

SHAMAKUNI. A Tonga-speaking family of middle-Zambezi people present in the vicinity of the Chobe River since at least the eighteenth century. Sometimes referred to as BaSubiya, a group to which they have since belonged. In the 1830s, they were incorporated into the Ba**Kololo** state, which in 1864 was succeeded by the BaLozi state. In 1876, after a succession dispute, a portion of them broke off and settled along the Chobe. They were never completely subordinated by the BaTa-**wana,** although an attempt to dominate them was made by the exiled **Sekgoma Letsholathebe** and his successors, who lived in the Chobe area (1912–1923).

SHIPPARD, SIDNEY GODOLPHIN ALEXANDER (1838–1902). First deputy commissioner of the Bechuanaland Protectorate (he was recommissioned in 1891 as **resident commissioner**). At the time he was also the administrator of British Bechuanaland. Shippard, who is noteworthy for his promotion of the interests of Cecil Rhodes, his friend since Oxford days, was regarded with great suspicion by the early southern diKgosi. They dubbed him *morena maaka* ("lord of lies"). Shippard's 1886 land settlement robbed the BaRolong and BaTlhaping of 92 percent of their land. In 1888 he traveled to Bulawayo, where he played a central role in securing the Rudd Concession, which paved the way for the takeover of Zimbabwe by Rhodes's **British South Africa Company (BSACO)**. Thereafter Shippard worked to assure that the Protectorate served BSACO's interests, and his relations with the southern diKgosi became increasingly acrimonious. In 1892 and again in 1894 he pushed for British military action against the BaKwena. On leaving office in 1895, Shippard joined the BSACO's board of directors. *See also* Grobler Affair; Kopong Conference.

SHOMOLOKAE SEBOLAI (1843[?]–1918). Born in Kuruman, Shomolokae was an early **LMS** missionary, appointed to Ngamiland in 1883. He worked in the **Okavango Delta,** among the BaYei, having to recover from many bouts with malaria. He was the first to reduce SeYei to writing, translating parts of the Bible into that language. His biography *Apostle of the Marshes*, written by J.T. Brown, appeared in 1925. Opposed to BaTawana suppression of the BaYei, Shomolokae was among the first of Botswana's abolitionists. *See also* Bolata.

SHUA. A major **Khoe** group inhabiting the region between **Nata** and Leshoma. During the twentieth century, most Shua communities were placed, usually forcibly, under the rule of the BaNgwato. *See also* Bolata; Kgaraxumae; Molele, Twai Twai.

SIDZUMO, PETER J.J. Born in South Africa. As BaKwena tribal secretary, 1908–1913, he organized BaTswana opposition to **incorporation** into the Union. After many frustrating years as an interpreter and journalist in the northern Cape, he was recruited by **Sebele I** to work for him in Molepolole. Sidzumo's educational background and his many contacts helped the BaKwena and other BaTswana to participate in black politics in **South Africa**. Sidzumo co-authored (with Sebele) a series of petitions and newspaper articles protesting white government policies in general and incorporation in particular. He coordinated these efforts with other tribal administrations. During his brief tenure with the BaKwena, Sidzumo also tried to inaugurate the BaKwena National School as a secular English-medium school with an emphasis on technical training, lines which then were considered radical. In 1913 he was pushed out of the Protectorate by British officials who were disturbed by his activities and influence. Peter was succeeded as tribal secretary by his brother, Richard, who also served during this period as secretary-general of the Bechuanaland and Griqualand Provincial Congress of the South African Native National Congress, precursor to the ANC. In 1916 the British banished Richard and the Anglican leader **George Mashwe**. *See also* Anglicans; Newspapers; Sechele II.

SILLERY, ANTHONY (1903–1976). Colonial administrator and founder of the colonial school of Botswana historiography. He was **resident commissioner** from 1946 to 1950, and dealt with the fall-out from the banishment of **Seretse Khama**. Not confident he was up to the task, the Dominions Office replaced him. His works include *The Bechuanaland Protectorate* (1952); *Sechele: The Story of an African Chief* (1954); *Founding a Protectorate* (1965); *John Mackenzie of Bechuanaland: A Study of Humanitarian Imperialism* (1971); and *Botswana: A Short Political History* (1974).

SLAVE TRADE. Like other parts of Africa, Botswana was affected by slave trading, though not to the same extent. It appears increasingly likely that in the Ngamiland area the **BaYei** and **BaSarwa** in particular were sold into the Atlantic Trade between 1775 and 1820. After 1840 Angolan slavers operated in the Caprivi area, and until approximately 1910 many **Khoe** and HaMbukushu in northern Ngamiland were kidnapped and sold. They were destined to work on plantations in Angola and São Tome. At about the same time, slave trading began in southern Botswana. Between 1790 and 1820 **Griqua** and other Khoi raiders seized southern BaTswana (especially women and children) on the Cape frontier, and some BaTswana sold children to these groups. Slave raiding and slave trading increased with the arrival of **Afrikaners** in the Transvaal. Aided by **Kgafela Kgatla** and other Transvaal African groups, the Boers raided people bordering Afrikaner settlements and captured several thousand African women and children, who were used as domestic servants, laborers, artisans, hunters, and herders. In southern Botswana, slave trading with the Boers seems not to have occurred, but the BaTawana of Ngamiland exported slaves to the Transvaal, via such Boer traders as **Jan Viljoen**, these being children of malata who failed to pay sufficient tribute. This trade ended around 1877. *See also* Bolata; Caprivi Strip.

SLAVERY. *See* Bolata.

SOUTH AFRICA. South Africa has been over many generations an integral part of the Botswana experience, as is reflected in many entries in this *Dictionary*.

Before the Union of South Africa was established in 1910, BaTswana were preoccupied with defending themselves against a range of white adversaries. Quite apart from the Transvaal Boers, against whom BaTswana had learned to defend themselves, the major threats were posed by nameless company agents, mining prospectors, concessionaires, and uniformed policemen. All of the aforementioned spoke English, and most of them—along with many of the officials of the Bechuanaland Protectorate—were particularly responsive to the needs of the big men whose wealth and power were built on gold and diamonds, and whose vision for the region required the extension of British political control. BaTswana opposed the proclamation of the Bechuanaland Protectorate while recognizing their powerlessness to prevent it. When the South African War broke out in 1899, few BaTswana fought in the defense of Britain. Of those who did, the BaNgwato repelled an invasion of their own territory, and the Tshidi BaRolong defended themselves in the siege of **Mafikeng**. The only BaTswana who attacked Britain's opponents were the **Kgafela Kgatla**, who carried on their own "private war" with the Rustenburg Boers in the western Transvaal.

The Union created a single, all-powerful political force in the region which threatened to embrace Bechuanaland. The South African government demonstrated through its laws and law enforcement the inferior position accorded to all Africans and their predisposition to coerce black labor for the benefit of the white community. During the Union period, BaTswana at home fought **incorporation** into South Africa while in increasing numbers they worked in South Africa in order to survive, much less advance, economically.

South Africa was the only land of opportunity for the people of the Protectorate, poor or wealthy. BaTswana brought home, in addition to a little cash, the symbols of black South African culture. Most who grew up during that period acquired at least part of their informal education in South Africa, and most leaders of independent Botswana went to school there.

After the National Party took power in 1948 and launched policies based on apartheid, BaTswana had to contend with a South African government that perceived African nationalism as a direct threat. Though Botswana made no direct or veiled threats in its dealings with South Africa, or allowed others to use Botswana for such purposes, it was the victim of numerous cross-border attacks, bombings, sabotage, and other punitive acts directed from Pretoria. As recently as March 1988, South African Defence Force commandos entered Gaborone, Botswana's capital, at night, murdered three BaTswana women and a South African refugee man, and incinerated their house. Botswana persisted, nevertheless, in openly condemning the South African government and its policies, helped to create the Front Line States and the **Southern Africa Development Coordination Conference (SADCC)**, favored sanctions, and established a prosperous, democratic, non-racial society that stood in contrast to apartheid South Africa.

Since the 1994 democratic elections in South Africa, Botswana-South Africa relations have entered a new phase. Time will tell whether, in economic terms, South Africa's revival in a post-sanctions era will strengthen or undermine Botswana's previous advances in commerce and small manufacturing that, in certain respects, were underwritten by sanctions. Also, Botswana's costly investment in its military has gained a momentum of its own, making it difficult to scale back without repercussions. South Africa's historical economic strength in the region may grow, rather than diminish, and create at least a temporary vacuum of investment, skills, and development that could sap the resources of surrounding countries. Certainly, the flow of people and goods between Botswana and South Africa has already accelerated. Border crossings, which used to consume hours in some cases because of police searches on the South African side, have become minor formalities on the South African side and perversely difficult on the other. Numbers of skilled and professional BaTswana find themselves in demand, particularly in the Witwatersrand. Botswana's external relations in the region, which have been developed in concert with countries north of the Limpopo, have also undergone change. SADCC, which was formed partly as a means of reducing dependency on apartheid South Africa, has been abandoned and replaced with the **Southern African Development Community (SADC)**, of which South Africa is a member. International support for regional integration has so far proved to be substantial. *See also* BaTswana-Boer War of 1852–1853; British South Africa Company; Customs Union; Diamonds; External Relations; Migrant Labor; Mining; Refugees; South African Native Labour Contingent; South African War (1899–1902); Tiger Kloof.

SOUTH AFRICAN NATIVE LABOUR CONTINGENT (SANLC). The SANLC was a black unit of the Union of South Africa's Defence Force that saw active service in France (1916–1918) during **World War I**. The contingent included the Bechuanaland Protectorate Company, consisting of 555 BaTswana under the command of Lt. Louis Glover, who subsequently became a prominent advocate of multi-racial politics in the Protectorate. BaTswana NCOs included future Kgosi **Sebele II**. White racial fears led to the confining of the SANLC in closed compounds when off duty. Protests against these conditions, as well as reservations voiced by white South Africans about the force, resulted in the early demobilization of the contingent. After the war, many BaTswana veterans refused to accept their SANLC service medals.

SOUTH AFRICAN WAR (1899–1902). Sometimes referred to as the (Second) Anglo-Boer War, the South African War was a major turning point in Botswana history because it led to white reconciliation and the creation of the Union.

Between October 1899 and May 1900, Bechuanaland was also an important war theater. Transvaal Boer commandos besieged **Mafikeng**, attacked Seleka Kop in an abortive attempt to capture Palapye and move north, and then established laagers along the Bechuanaland border to prevent Rhodesian forces from relieving Mafikeng. In November they attacked **Lobatse** and Gaberones camp, blew up the bridge at Sepitse (near Khale hill), and gathered reinforcements at Derdepoort, opposite Sikwane. On November 25, **Kgafela Kgatla** regiments overran the Derdepoort laager and forced a Boer retreat, thus freeing the Rhodesians to move south along the rail line. Through the assistance of the Tshidi Ba**Rolong**, in the form of reconnaissance, sorties, and communications, the British held Mafikeng until May, when the Rhodesians broke through Boer lines after advancing from **Kanye**. Thereafter BaTswana contributed to the war with wagons, draught oxen, cattle, food, drivers, scouts, laborers, and military intelligence. Perhaps the greatest impact was made by Kgafela Kgatla regiments acting as a surrogate force in the western Transvaal after the war entered its guerrilla phase. Until the end of the war, the BaKgatla controlled the area north of Rustenburg to the Limpopo River, engaged several Boer commandos in battle, and divested Boer farms of their cattle.

The Treaty of Vereeniging, which was signed by the Boers and British, contained the suggestion that the Bechuanaland Protectorate, along with the other **High Commission Territories**, might be in the future absorbed by the Transvaal government. This proviso, in slightly altered form, was included in the 1909 Act of Union. *See also* Battle of Derdepoort; Incorporation.

SOUTHERN AFRICAN DEVELOPMENT COMMUNITY (SADC). On 17 August 1992, the heads of state and governments of the **Southern African Development Coordination Conference (SADCC)** met in Windhoek to sign a treaty creating SADC to replace SADCC. South Africa officially joined SADC at a meeting in Gaborone in 1994. SADC, with its headquarters in Gaborone, functions through the structures and institutions that were created by SADCC.

The change from SADCC to SADC reflected a stronger commitment to regional cooperation. The aim of SADC is to strengthen the work initiated by SADCC. Some of its objectives are 1) to achieve development and economic growth, reduce poverty, and improve the quality of life of the peoples of southern Africa, 2) to develop common political values, systems, and institutions, 3) to promote and defend peace and security, 4) to promote development through collective self-reliance and interdependence, 5) to promote productive employment and the use of the resources of the region, 6) to protect the environment, and 7) to promote links among the people of the region. It remains to be seen whether SADC will achieve its objectives, but early signs are encouraging. For example, SADC peace intiatives in Lesotho and Mozambique in 1994 were successful.

SOUTHERN AFRICAN DEVELOPMENT COORDINATION CONFERENCE (SADCC). Following a meeting of the Front Line States in Arusha in July 1979 on development coordination, the first SADCC conference was held at Luanda in April 1980 among the FLS heads of state and the heads of the other independent southern African states, including soon-to-be-independent Zimbabwe. The nine conference members were Angola, Botswana, Lesotho, Malawi, Mozambique, Swaziland, Tanzania, Zambia, and Zimbabwe. Namibia became a member after gaining independence in 1990. **Seretse Khama** is often cited as the architect of SADCC. After its initial appeal for support at Maputo in September 1980, SADCC was financed largely by donor agencies, with emphasis on regional cooperation in transport and communications, food security, and energy. Botswana's special responsibilities were crop research in semi-arid tropics and animal disease control. The SADCC secretariat was located in Gaborone.

Progress under SADCC in integrating the region's economic development was what one observer called "modest," noting that the combined GNP of the members constituted but a third of South Africa's and was not likely to grow significantly without its much stronger neighbor. A South African-led regional integration process, which began with the emergence of mining in the Witwatersrand in the late nineteenth century, and which was resisted by SADCC as a means of reducing its dependence on apartheid South Africa, appears to have been accepted with the disbanding of SADDC in 1992 and the formation of the **Southern African Development Community**. *See also* Economy; External Economic Relations; External Relations.

SPIRITUAL HEALING CHURCH. The largest independent Church in Botswana, with 30,000 members in 1994. Founded in 1950 at Matsiloje near Francistown by the prophet Mokaleng Motswasele, who had been influenced years earlier by the local Pentacostal evangelist Harry Morolong and by the prophetess Christina Nku, founder of the St. Johns Apostolic Faith Mission. In 1948 Mokaleng was given permission by George Moroka, Kgosi of the Ba**Rolong** of the Northeast District to start his own church, which he initially named the Apostolic United Faith Coloured Church. The church's name changed several times until 1973, when the present name was adopted. The Spiritual Healing Church's better-known offshoots are the St. Faith Holy Church (5,000 members) and the Revelation Blessed Peace Church (3,000). *See also* Independent Churches; Pentecostal Churches; Religion; Spiritual Healing Churches.

SPIRITUAL HEALING CHURCHES. In addition to the large **Spiritual Healing Church**, many Christian churches in Botswana may be categorized as spiritual healing churches. Their origins are commonly associated with persecution at the hands of local authorities, and sometimes women figured prominently in their establishment. Christ the Word of God Church was introduced by Nanani Nkomo of Mpoka village in 1944, following Nanani's persecution by She Havanga. Gideon Sibanda, persecuted in Maitengwe, established the Followers of Jesus Christ. In 1949 the Faith Gospel After Church of Christ was introduced in Tswapong by Robert Modikwa. Mrs. Kebueng Modutwa and Miss K. Photonono founded the Foundation Truth Sanctuary in 1956 following their persecution in Ga-Ngwaketse. They and their followers were expelled to Motlobo. Erastus Medupe introduced the Galatia Church in Zion into Serowe in 1956, whereupon he was sent into exile at Paje and then arrested. Samson Kebeng, who established the General Apostolic Church in the 1960s in Kanye, suffered persecution as a result. Other notable churches include the General Foundation Apostolic Church, founded in Jerusalem, Tswapong, by Letsomane in 1949, and the Gospel Church of God—Johane Church of God, established by John Masowe after his arrival in Botswana in 1943. Masowe's group were also known as the **Vapostori**, or Mazezuru. *See also* Independent Churches; Religion.

SPORTS. In pre-colonial days, stick-fighting, calf-racing, and morabaraba (African-style checkers) were popular pastimes. As early as the 1870s organized sports were introduced to Botswana by cricket-playing miners in the **Tati Concession**. Up to the 1930s, white settlers were avid fans of football (soccer), tennis, cricket, and rifle shooting. By the 1930s football, tennis, and cricket were popular sports among black South Africans and began to spread to the Bechuanaland Protectorate. In 1949 the Southern Protectorate Soccer League, Northern Protectorate League, Mafeking Football Association and Western Transvaal League merged to form the Bechuanaland Union African Soccer League, which was affiliated with other South African leagues. Bechuanaland Union club teams competed for the "Moraka-Baloyi Cup." These clubs were promoted by di-Kgosi, migrant laborers, the scouting movement, and the schools. During the 1940s, mixed-race tennis competitions were patronized by **Bathoen II**. Netball and track-and-field (athletics) were also appearing at this time. Fast-pitch softball, brought back to the Protectorate by returning veterans of **World War II**, was organized by the police in the 1950s and eventually became, under the tutelage of U.S. Peace Corps volunteers, independent Botswana's most popular sport after football until the late 1980s.

Sports are organized through the National Sports Council in the Ministry of Home Affairs but are dependent almost totally on support from gate-takings and the private sector. Fully professional sports do not exist in the country, and national teams representing Botswana in international competitions in southern Africa receive bus transportation only from the government. The new national stadium, which was built in 1985 and 1986 at a cost of $18 million to reach international standards in football and athletics, was made possible through a national fund-raising effort payable against a government loan.

Botswana's various sporting "codes" (associations) maintain individual memberships in international sporting bodies and compete regularly in the Commonwealth Games in track and field, bowling, and boxing. Botswana was represented in the Olympics for the first time in 1984, the same year they sent a men's softball team to the International Softball Federation World Championships. Botswana was a signatory of the 1976 Gleneagles Agreement, which banned sporting contacts with South Africa, but sporting relations between South Africa and Botswana have resumed since 1994.

STEINBERG, BENJAMIN (1920[?]–1975). Born in Lobatse, Steinberg was a Serowe trader and cattle dealer with Protectorate-wide business interests. He was a member of the European Advisory Council before becoming a founding member and first treasurer of the **Democratic Party** in 1961–1962. In 1965 he became the first elected white MP, representing Botletle constituency. *See also* Councils.

STOCK MARKET. *See* Economy, Post-Colonial.

SUA PAN. *See* Mining.

SUBIYA (BASUBIYA). A small group located in the Chobe area, of varying origins, properly known as Bekuhane. *See also* Shamakuni.

T

TALAOTE (BATALAOTE). A group of Kalanga-BaNyayi. Between 1840 and 1863 they paid tribute to both the AmaNdebele and BaNgwato and therefore occupied an area disputed by the two. In 1863 they aided the BaNgwato against the AmaNdebele, who inflicted vicious reprisals on the BaTalaote. Many BaTalaote were captured, while others scattered. Some resettled in Shoshong. After the AmaNdebele were crushed in 1893, the BaTalaote head, Simelamela, went to Zimbabwe to bring back the old captives. **Khama III** allowed them and the other BaTalaote to settle under Simelamela at Mmadinare. *See also* Kalanga; Nyayi; Sekgoma I.

TATI CONCESSION. In 1880, following the 1867–1870 gold rush, Lobengula granted a concession to some businessmen who then organized the Northern Light Company (1880–1888), which became the Tati Concession and Mining Exploration Company, Ltd. (1888–1895), then Tati Concessions Ltd. (1895–1914), and eventually the Tati Company Ltd. (1914–1954), which was then bought out and reorganized under the same name (1954–). By 1911 the British recognized Tati Concessions as having complete ownership over the "Tati District" (the modern Northeast District). When mining proved to be unprofitable, the company turned to exploiting the land and its resources such as firewood. All forms of commerce were monopolized by the Company, and farms were sold exclusively to Europeans. Labor costs remained low because of the extreme land pressure inside the Tati Native Reserve, which constituted less than 20 percent of the Tati District area. Tati Company control in the Northeast District ended only in 1969, although the Tati Company Ltd. is still in existence. Additionally, two mining concessions were also made in the Tati District: the Premier Tati Monarch Reef Company Ltd. (1895–1918) and the Tati Blue Syndicate Ltd. (1893–1914). *See also* Concessions; Francistown; Kalanga; Khurutshe.

TAUTONA. Literally "the big lion" in SeTswana, this term has long been used as a title of address for supreme political leaders. During the early nineteenth century, it was commonly used to refer to the AmaNdebele Nkosi Mzilikazi. During the colonial era it referred to the **high commissioner**. Since 1966 it has been reserved for the president of the Republic of Botswana.

TAWANA (BATAWANA). The BaTawana originated as an offshoot of the BaNgwato following a bogosi dispute (ca. 1795–1800). Under **Tawana**, their first Kgosi, they settled in the Kgwebe hills of what is now Ngamiland. Moremi I (1820[?]–1828) succeeded his father Tawana after a war between the two. He moved the morafe to Toteng on the shores of Lake Ngami. Between 1835 and 1840 the BaKololo established supremacy over them, and many BaTawana were taken to Zambia as hostages. Rebuilding the fragmented BaTawana state began under the regent Mogalakwe (1840[?]–1847[?]), who initiated a process of incorporating the BaYei, HaMbukushu, BaKgala-gadi, and BaSarwa of Ngamiland, a process completed under Letsholathebe I. Varying patterns of subordination between the BaTawana and these subject groups emerged, including clientship and bolata, a form of slavery. In the second half of the nineteenth century, trade in ivory strengthened the BaTawana state and enabled Moremi II to arm his regiments and establish a cavalry. In 1883 they repulsed the AmaNdebele and in 1885 sent an expeditionary force to BuLozi (western Zambia) to assist Lewanika.

British rule came relatively late, but it devastated bogosi. Without consulting Sekgoma Letsholathebe, or making any treaty, the British established a permanent presence in 1894. In 1906 in the wake of a triangular power struggle among Kgosi, dikgosana, and commoners, the British helped the dikgosana gain ascendancy in the morafe by deposing Sekgoma and installing Mathiba Moremi. Bogosi never recovered.

The rinderpest of 1896–1897 reduced cattle numbers but contracted the tsetse fly belt, and cattle multiplied steadily thereafter. In the 1920s the BaTawana were probably the largest stock holders in the Protectorate—several leading di-Kgosana had herds of 5,000 or more. By the 1930s, however, tsetse returned to its former domain and exacerbated conflicts by shrinking fly-free grazing areas. In the same decade, the people of Ngamiland became increasingly dependent on labor migration as the Witwatersrand Native Labour Agency (WEN-ELA) established roads and airlinks around the Okavango Delta. After World War II, the BaYei and OvaHerero began to challenge BaTawana supremacy. See also Moremi III; Moremi, Elizabeth; Moshuga Moremi; Traders.

TAWANA I (d. 1820). "Mpuru." Kgosi of the BaTawana, 1800[?]–1820 and founder of the BaTawana state. The BaTawana were known as the BaMpuru until the 1840s. The eldest son of Mathiba, Kgosi of the BaNgwato, he was designated by his father as heir. Tawana's succession was disputed by his brother Kgama, who claimed that Tawana's mother, who was a Mo-Kwena, was junior to Kgama's mother. In the ensuing civil war, Kgama defeated Tawana and Mathiba, who then took refuge with the BaKwena at Lephephe. They later trekked northwest to the Kgwebe hills in an area over which the BaKwena claimed authority. In 1810 the forces of Kgama attacked the BaTawana settlement but were routed; thereafter two independent BaNgwato states emerged. In 1820, Tawana died in battle fighting his son Moremi I, who had attempted to seize bogosi. *See also* Kgama I.

TAXATION. Plans to introduce taxes date from 1888, but their introduction was delayed until 1899, by which time colonial fears of revolt had subsided. The original "hut tax" of 10/- became a poll tax of 20/- in 1907 and in 1919 was supplemented by a 3/- "native tax," which was channeled to a "Native Fund" primarily for education and other social and agricultural services decided on by the Native (later African) Advisory Council, constituted in 1920 for that purpose. In 1939, the poll tax and supplementary tax were paid in a lump sum of 25/-, the amount raised periodically thereafter until 1965. In 1949, however, a graduated, or graded, income tax was introduced ("one of the few experiments," commented Lord Hailey in 1957, "in the graduation of a personal tax payable by Africans."). The purpose of the graded tax was to provide revenue for tribal treasuries, which since their formation in 1938 had been dependent on a percentage of the collection of poll taxes, which were drawn into the government revenues. Provisions for income tax, payable by non-Africans after 1922, were applied to all persons in 1964 and underwent considerable revision in 1973. Government revenues from income tax are comparatively small, depending as they do on a small percentage of the total population. In 1983 they constituted a record 14% of central government revenues, a proportion that fell below 10% in 1985 and has remained there since. In contrast, mining revenues have remained above 75% since the 1970s. Other forms of government tax revenues have been maintained at modest levels, such as commercial profits taxes, which have a ceiling of 35% with a flat tax rate of 15% on dividends. *See also* Economy.

TELECOMMUNICATIONS. Botswana maintains a modern telephone and telecommunications system operated by the government parastatal, Botswana Telecommunications Corporation (BTC). Its nearly 40,000 telephones are connected internationally through its satellite station at Khale hill, south of Gaborone. BTC provides telex, telegraph, facsimile, and radio communications services to all parts of the country. The national telephone directory, issued annually, is available by writing Directory, Botswana Telecommunications Corporation, P.O. Box 700, Gaborone.

THEMA, BENJAMIN C. (1912–). Educationist and politician. Born in Ranaka, Bangwaketse Reserve. A product of **Tiger Kloof** and Healdtown, in 1936 Thema became the SeTswana teacher at Tiger Kloof. He was the first president of the Bechuanaland Student Association, formed in 1939. In 1946 he founded the Tshidi Barolong Secondary School in **Mafikeng** and served as its principal until 1955. During his tenure, Thema obtained a masters degree in Education (1948). He then became headmaster of Moeng College until 1964, when he resigned and entered the **Democratic Party**. By then his achievements in education had made him a national figure. In 1962 he was made a member of the British Empire. In the 1965 election he won the Lobatse seat to the National Assembly. From 1966 until 1974, when he retired from politics, Thema served as minister of Education (until 1969 known as Education, Health and Labor).

THREE KINGS IN LONDON (1895). The visit of diKgosi **Bathoen I**, **Khama III**, and **Sebele I** to England was an event that has assumed mythical proportions in popular historiography. It is often used, mistakenly, to credit these three leaders for having "invited" the British to rule Bechuanaland in order to prevent South Africans (especially the Boers) from taking over the country. Such was not the case. The facts are as follows.

   In 1895 following an idea that originated as Khama's visit to the **LMS** in England for the 1795–1895 centenary celebrations, the three diKgosi chose to visit London and protest the imminent transfer of the Bechuanaland Protectorate to the **British South Africa Company (BSACO)** and British Bechuanaland to the Cape Colony. They did so because in June 1895 the Cape parliament legislated for the annexation of British Bechuanaland, and by then the plans of BSACO President Cecil Rhodes to take over Bechuanaland had become clear. In July Bathoen, Khama, Sebele, and **Linchwe I** sent petitions to the British requesting imperial, rather than BSACO, rule. Bathoen, Khama, and Sebele then decided on a journey to England for the purpose of making a personal appeal to the Queen (the Tshidi Ba**Rolong** had petitioned against Cape annexation and their acting Kgosi, **Besele Wessels**, attempted to travel with

Bathoen et al., but he was stopped at Cape Town by the British). **W.C. Willoughby**, LMS missionary and confidant of Khama III, organized the visit and acted as interpreter. They arrived in England in September.

The visit was a great, popular success. The LMS had prepared the ground through the recent publication of J.D. Hepburn's *Twenty Years in Khama's Country*, which had turned Khama into a Christian hero. Edwin Lloyd's *Three Great African Chiefs* appeared before the end of their visit. Prior to their meetings with the Queen and the Colonial Secretary Joseph Chamberlain, the diKgosi addressed large assemblies up and down Great Britain and swung public opinion behind their cause. In the meantime, Rhodes was moving quickly to establish BSACO rule over the entire Protectorate.

The three diKgosi achieved little. Chamberlain upheld his decision to hand over the entire Protectorate to the BSACO. Chamberlain did give certain guarantees to Bathoen, Khama, and Sebele concerning their respective lands, but he made it clear that their yet-to-be demarcated "reserves" were to be completely surrounded by BSACO-controlled territory. The 1895 agreement they signed with Chamberlain also surrendered a strip of land in the eastern Protectorate for the railway (built 1897), which led to the creation of the Tuli, Gaberones, and Lobatse Blocks. The diKgosi agreed to submit to taxation as well. In return, they gained only the reassurance that within their respective territories they could continue to rule their people "much as at present." They returned home in December and were received as heroes, but they had failed to alter events.

The **Jameson Raid**, which occurred on the heels of their arrival back in the Protectorate, lost the BSACO its opportunity to rule Bechuanaland. Only when news of the raid reached Chamberlain did he decide to postpone indefinitely the BSACO takeover of the Protectorate. *See also* Orders-in-Council, 1890 and 1891.

TIGER KLOOF. School of Botswana's leaders. Founded in Vryburg, northern Cape, in 1904 by **W.C. Willoughby** of the **London Missionary Society**, this primary, industrial, secondary, and bible school for boys was originally intended for Gammangwato, but LMS plans were opposed by **Khama III** and **Ratshosa Motswetle**, who feared an LMS hegemony in Bamangwato Reserve. As such, Tiger Kloof became a boarding school for wealthy blacks and "**coloureds**" from across southern Africa. Most of Botswana's LMS priests were trained there. After 1919 girls were admitted. By the 1920s it had established itself as the school of the BaTswana elite. Such diKgosi as **Bathoen II**, **Moremi III**, and **Neale Sechele** went there. In the 1930s and 1940s Tiger Kloof trained students who would lead Botswana to independence and beyond. Botswana's first two presidents, **Seretse Khama** and **Quett Masire**, attended, as did future cabinet ministers **Gaositswe Chiepe**, **Moutlakgola Nwako**, **Edison Masisi**, and Washington Meswele, and many other leading political, educational, and civic figures. In 1955 the school lost its South African government subsidy, due to new National Party apartheid regulations, and folded. *See also* Archives.

TIRELO SECHABA (TS). A national service scheme launched in 1980 for the purpose of temporarily employing secondary school graduates in developmental and education projects prior to their admission to university and other tertiary institutions. Tirelo Sechaba was a response both to primary teacher shortages and to the public wish to require young scholars to compensate the country in some way for the free tertiary education they were about to receive and gain some maturity in the process. Begun as a voluntary program, it became compulsory in 1985 because of the lack of interest shown, but TS failed to acquire a clear purpose or provide meaningful projects for its enrollees, who were consigned to a one-year commitment with a subsistence allowance. It was discontinued in 1996.

TLOKWA (BATLOKWA). The BaTlokwa of Botswana are related to other BaTlokwa in South Africa and Lesotho. The name Tlokwa derives from the site, "Tlokwe," located near Potchefstroom in the Transvaal. The BaTlokwa who eventually settled in Botswana had established their identity by the reign of Bogatsu (d. 1817[?]). While in the Transvaal the BaTlokwa came increasingly into conflict with the Boers and, around 1852 they took refuge with **Sechele I**. The BaTlokwa were led by Matlapeng (1835[?]–1880), Bogatsu's grandson, who fled after shooting a Boer (the man had tried to rape his wife). In 1872 Matlapeng moved his people to Tshwene-Tshwene, where during the **Civil Wars** they allied themselves with the **Kgafela Kgatla** against the Sechele's BaKwena. In 1887 Kgosi **Gaborone**, settled his people in Tlokweng, at a site known as Moshaweng with the permission of **Sebele I**, whose senior authority Gaborone accepted. A part of Sebele's territory, which included the area occupied by the modern capital city of Gaborone, was detached in 1895 to form what in 1905 became the Gaberones Block, and from 1905 to 1932 the BaTlokwa paid rent to the **British South Africa Company (BSACO).** In 1932 the British acquired the land from the BSACO and created the Batlokwa Reserve.

The BaTlokwa and Ba**Lete** are the only BaTswana groups to have maintained **initiation** for men and women throughout the colonial period. Their reserve has always been too small to serve the agricultural and veterinary needs of the morafe, although several small farms adjacent to the Reserve were purchased through a tribal levy.

The original BaTlokwa town, Tlokweng, has been swallowed by the urban sprawl emanating from the nearby capital of Gaborone, and Tlokweng has become a de facto part of Botswana's largest city. The suburb of Tlokweng, classified by the government as a "rural settlement," with a population of 12,501 in 1991, has manufacturing, service, and residential areas, though BaTlokwa still have access to arable and grazing land.

TOBACCO. An indigenous variety known as *motsoko* has been used in Botswana for generations. In pre-colonial times, tobacco was a luxury, although especially indulged in by women and children. Often smoked or taken as snuff, its use came under fire from missionaries, who appear to have been responsible for reducing tobacco consumption among women, few of whom today smoke or take snuff. Cigarette smoking, however, is common among men.

TOURISM. Botswana's wildlife and other natural wonders have attracted tourists for decades, but its "tourist industry" was born in the 1970s when improved communications and infrastructure made the game parks and other wildlife areas of the **Okavango Delta** and Chobe/Kasane area more accessible. Government, fearful of mass tourism and its supposedly deleterious effects, has until recently favored a "high-cost, low volume" approach. In contrast to Swaziland and Lesotho, for example, it has eschewed entertainment centers with which to attract tourists from South Africa. Yet it has been less apprehensive about exposing its abundant wildlife to the outside world, as indicated by having its Department of Wildlife in the Ministry of Commerce and Industry, and the tourism trend of the 1980s and 1990s has been one of rapid expansion.

New foreign investors have found tourism more profitable than any other sector in Botswana. Hotel capacity grew by 65% in the 1979–1983 period, and by 1984, sixty-four tour companies were operating in the country, as opposed to only twenty-eight in 1981. As of 1992, the nation had seventy-six hotels and safari camps, with a capacity of 3,058 beds. Still, Botswana's potential for tourism is far from being realized. The vast majority (83%) of Botswana visitors come from its immediate neighbors, South Africa, Namibia, and Zimbabwe, and a full 35.6% of all visitors spend but one day inside the country. Only 104,438, or 300 persons per day, entered the country in 1992 for holiday purposes (11% of all arrivals). The 1993 Tourism Act hopes to stimulate more activity.

Expanding Botswana's tourism requires considerable investment as well as land use policy changes that pose risks to the government and private sectors. The government has suffered approximately $1 million loss of annual tourism revenues because outside tour operators avoided registering in Botswana while sending in parties that paid none of the normal fees for hunting and sightseeing. Since 1992 a tourist industry licensing board and a national advisory council have been functioning, but the lightly-funded Tourism Development Unit in the Ministry of Commerce and Industry has not been upgraded to departmental status. For Botswana to tap more heavily the international, as opposed to regional, market, the country will have to invest heavily in promotion and accept losses at least in the short term. In 1993, for example, an international recession cost Botswana's hotel and tour operators an estimated $250,000.

TOUTSWE. A state that existed in modern-day Central District around 850–1300 A.D. Known only through extensive archaeological remains, Toutswe was a state based around enormous cattle herds comparable to those of independent Botswana. Toutswe had a capital and several regional centers. Wealth appears to have been built primarily around trade of such commodities as gold, ivory, metal, meat, and flint. Toutswe appears to have been undermined by the rise of Great Zimbabwe and an apparent decline in cattle herds after 1300. Recent work suggested that the region continued to be heavily populated after that time, in contrast to earlier theories of desertification caused by overgrazing. Toutswe has a pottery style similar to that of Zimbabwe, but its settlements are similar to modern BaTswana large villages. *See also* Archaeology and Prehistory.

TOWNS. In addition to Gaborone, which was proclaimed a city in 1986, Botswana has six other designated "urban districts," which are situated on alienated communal land and are governed by a town (city) council, the members of which elect one of their own as mayor. Councils are responsible inter alia for the zoning and servicing of urban land, regulating public transport, licensing of petty traders, and the disposal of waste (control of utilities, such as water, telephones, and electricity, is exercised by parastatal corporations subject to the national government). They are responsible to the Minister of Local Government and Lands and defray a portion of their expenses through the collection of local tax.

During the colonial period, large settlements in the Reserves were known as "towns," but today, Molepolole, Kanye, and other densely-populated sites in district communal areas are designated as "rural settlements." Urban districts are defined as having 5,000 or more people and less than 25 percent of their population engaged in agriculture or made up of persons virtually solely employed (as in Sowa). Based on the 1991 census, the following populations were present in Botswana's largest Urban Districts and Rural Settlements.

Urban Districts

1.	**Gaborone** (city)	133,463
2.	**Francistown**	65,244
3.	Selebi Phikwe*	39,772
4.	**Molepolole**	36,930
5.	**Lobatse**	26,052
6.	Jwaneng*	11,188
7.	Orapa*	8,827
8.	Sowa*	2,228

Rural Settlements

1.	**Kanye**	31,354
2.	**Serowe**	30,264
3.	Mahalapye	28,078
4.	**Maun**	26,759
5.	**Mochudi**	25,542
6.	**Ramotswa**	18,683
7.	Palapye	17,362
8.	Mogoditshane	14,246

9. Thamaga	13,026
10. Tlokweng	12,501
11. Mosopa	11,444
12. Tonota	11,129
13. Tutume	10,070
14. Letlhakane	8,583
15. Bobonong	7,708
16. Gabane	5,975
17. Shoshong	5,592
18. Ghanzi	5,550
19. Kasane	4,336

*See Mining

See also Villagization.

TRADE. *See* Economy; Traders.

TRADE UNIONS. Trade unionism has not been a success in Botswana, mainly because of the small industrial workforce and the hostile attitude of government (the main blot on Botswana's reputation for democracy and human rights). Trade unions began to make their presence felt only after the formation of mass political parties in the early 1960s. Two trade unions had been organized prior to this date—the Francistown African Employees' Union in 1948 and the Bechuanaland Protectorate Workers' Union (BPWU) in 1959—but their memberships had been small, and their leaders, corrupt and/or inefficient. The **People's Party (BPP)** brought these two unions together in the Bechuanaland Trades Union Congress (BTUC) in 1962. Under BTUC President **Klaas Motshidisi**, trade unionism adopted a more radical stance. Several effective strike actions were organized, but BTUC influence declined after the defeat of the BPP in the 1965 elections. Also in 1965 the **Democratic Party (BDP)** formed the Bechuanaland Federation of Labor (BFL) to counter the efforts of the BTUC, but by 1969 the BFL had disappeared. The BDP was in fact deeply suspicious of the trade union movement and its potential for economic and political disruption.

The Trade Union Act of 1969 effectively destroyed this potential. The Act made legal strike action virtually impossible, imposed regulations which made the formation of new trade unions very difficult (at least thirty members and at least 25 percent of the work force), and, by specifying that there had to be separate trade unions for each trade or profession, prevented the establishment of "general" unions—often the most effective and powerful type of trade union. Significantly, in 1971 when a Botswana Employers Federation was formed, no restrictions on membership or freedom of operation were imposed.

At the same time, government brought in an American trade union "expert," Paul Rasmussen from the African American Labor Center, to set up a trade union education center and teach trade unionists the doctrine of non-participation in politics. In 1972 the government-sponsored Botswana Federation of Trade Unions was established and made responsible for negotiating agreements on labor policy, but it was little more than a puppet of the state. The government's response to the only serious mass industrial action taken by workers in the history of the Republic, the Selebi Phikwe miners' strike of 1974, was to send in the paramilitary Police Mobile Unit, allow the Company to dismiss all the workers and rehire only those who would "cooperate," and convict and sentence thirty-four workers to jail. In 1978 the eleven trade unions registered in the country had fewer than 6,000 members, over half of whom were in the public sector. By the early 1980s less than 20 percent of eligible workers were members of a trade union and the trend of this proportion has since been downward.

The Botswana Mine Workers Union has had some success in bargaining with Debswana, the major mining company in the country. The Botswana government has dealt harshly, however, with workers in categories, particularly unskilled, that extend more broadly within the economy. In 1991, for example, when the Manual Workers Union (which included many government employees) struck for higher monthly salaries, the government fired 10,000 government workers and then incorporated its industrial-class employees into the civil service, which legally bars strike actions.

Of the 173 conventions adopted by the International Labour Organization since 1919, the government of Botswana has ratified but two: those concerning a weekly day of rest and accident compensation.

TRADERS. Since the mid-nineteenth century, traders have been an important part of the rural economy, centered as it has been on the respective town capitals and connected to outlying villages. Until the 1890s Bechuanaland was part of an active regional trade in **ivory** and other game products, and many European traders entered the area as a result. Some stayed on as shopkeepers and made **Kanye, Molepolole,** or one of the other major towns their permanent home. Often they operated on the basis of **concessions** awarded by diKgosi in return for an annual sum. Asian traders began to enter Bechuanaland before the **South African War of 1899–1902** and afterward became established primarily in the southeast.

Until the 1920s traders benefitted from government restrictions, established local oligopolies, fixed prices, and bribed diKgosi. They also established the deeply-resented "good-for" system of exchange in the same reserves, which obligated Africans selling their stock and grain to accept paper slips as payment and to redeem them only in purchase of goods from the trader's store. Selling and buying values were determined by the trader, often to his advantage. By the 1920s traders using good-fors had become the target of petitions, and protests against traders were commonplace in Native (later African) Advisory Council minutes.

Gradually, traders were forced to recognize local authority. In legal terms, they were licensed by the Protectorate government, but in practice a license was usually issued only with the consent of the **Kgosi** affected. Moreover, the Kgosi's power of local law-making and law enforcement, as well as determining stand-rents, placed traders under his de facto control. Until after **World War II** in many reserves and alienated European blocks, diKgosi had a major say on such issues as shop hours, grain/stock transactions, weights and measures, liquor sales, and credit. Traders had to maintain working relationships with diKgosi. The latter needed the former as well, who often was the sole source of industrially-manufactured goods and available cash and credit within the reserve. But the trader, who as a rule enjoyed local protection only by limiting profits, depended on diKgosi to restrict competition. As a result, traders often became localized individuals who confined their trading activities to the reserve. Trading syndicates were unknown, South African commercial houses were boxed out of the Protectorate, and internal commercial centers were absent. The only trading networks consisted of family-owned stores, such as those run by the Haskins family in the Bamangwato Reserve (Central District). Volumes of trade remained small, costs relatively high, and trading income was supplemented through labor recruitment, government contracting, mechanical repair, and grain storage.

African traders were few before independence, lacking not only capital but the social and political niche enjoyed by second, and sometimes third, generation resident European and Asian traders. The preferred method of capital investment in the Reserve, where land was public property, was in **cattle**. The risks of cattle ownership, great as they were in a land of drought and lungsickness, were far lower than they were for a fledgling entrepreneur, who would have to raise considerable sums to acquire goods from a distant supplier, transport them at great cost, rent a shop (which could not be used as collateral), and sell to a cash-poor public accustomed to dealing in credit.

The dearth of indigenous traders and the absence of an entrepreneurial tradition has placed independent Botswana in a vulnerable position. The rapidly-growing commercial sector in all urban areas has been dominated by outside, principally Witwatersrand-based, entrepreneurs and syndicated companies. *See also* Asians; Boyne, Henry; Chand, Abdul Rahim; Councils; Economy; Fleming, George; Gerrans, J.; Haskins, James; Hirschfeldt, Max; Hume, David; Jousse, Paul; Race Relations; Riley, Charles; Rowland, Richard; Van Zyl, Hendrik.

TRIBE. This term used with reference to various people is becoming regarded as a pejorative, as it has become in the rest of Africa. Officially "tribe" is used as a synonym for the SeTswana term *morafe* (plural, *merafe*), and refers to such groups as BaNgwato, BaKwena, BaNgwaketse, etc., which are made up of groups, or wards, of diverse origin whose members historically respected the authority of a single **Kgosi** or were forced to do so. During the colonial period, a member of a tribe was the legal inhabitant of a Reserve and corresponded to a "citizen" of the formerly independent state. In contrast to other parts of Africa, where tribe often has a very vague or recent meaning, in Botswana it originates in the pre-colonial period and has acquired since the establishment of the Protectorate a legal definition. In 1968 a person was for the first time entitled to become a member of a tribe by recognizing the jurisdiction of the Kgosi/kgotla official known as the "tribal authority." On the other hand, "tribesman" as a legal definition has been eliminated recently with regard to land.

For persons who categorize themselves as BaTswana, "tribalism" connotes membership in one of the officially-recognized tribes. On the other hand, those non-BaTswana who in the past have strived to gain official recognition as groups on a par with, and distinct from BaTswana, such as BaKalanga,

BaKgalagadi, BaYei, etc., have invested in their "tribalism" a much stronger ethnic content. *See also* Kgotla; Land Tenure; Reserves; Sarwa.

TSETSE. The tsetse fly is an insect which can transmit sleeping sickness (trypanosomiasis rhodesiense) to humans, and nagana (trypanosomiasis vivax; t. congolense; and t. brucei) to animals. Both diseases can be fatal (especially the latter). The earliest known reference to the disease in Botswana was made by Andrew Smith in the 1830s when passing along the **Limpopo River**. K.J. Andersson and **David Livingstone** noted its presence in their travels through Ngamiland in the 1850s. The **Okavango Delta** and the Chobe River systems have proved to be almost ideal environments for the tsetse fly, having both ground cover for breeding and a large game population which acts as a "reservoir" for the blood parasite the fly transmits. The massive epizootic of **rinderpest** greatly reduced the extent of the fly by destroying the cattle and game "hosts," but by the early 1930s the fly had returned to the area previously covered. The methods of tsetse fly control (mainly tree clearing and game shoots) employed by both the BaTswana and the British, including a Tsetse Fly Control Unit formed in 1943, proved ineffective before 1961 tests of residual insecticide then began in Ngamiland, and in 1967 large-scale application of Dieldrin (and later DDT) began to be used as a new method to control and eradicate the fly. Dieldrin and DDT were replaced after 1974 by Endosulfin, a safer and less harmful insecticide. In 1979 the Botswana government approved a plan to eradicate the tsetse fly permanently from Ngamiland. The plan has not yet been implemented, however, due at least in part to fears expressed by conservationists that the eradication of the fly would lead to the replacement of game by cattle.

TSHEKEDI KHAMA (1905–1959). Regent of the BaNgwato, 1925–1950. From his assumption of power on behalf of his young nephew **Seretse Khama**, and until his death thirty-four years later, Tshekedi was the most influential figure in the Bechuanaland Protectorate.

His reign began violently. In 1926, after Tshekedi abolished a briefly-constituted tribal council dominated by the Ratshosa brothers and dismissed Johnnie Ratshosa as tribal secretary, **Simon Ratshosa** and Obeditse Ratshosa tried to assassinate Tshekedi in the Serowe kgotla. The British imprisoned the Ratshosas and also punished them by burning their houses and personal belongings, in accordance with traditional law. The brothers then took Tshekedi to colonial court and won compensation for the destruction of their property. Tshekedi, who felt this judgment undermined his authority, appealed the case in London after imposing a levy on the BaNgwato to fund his trip. The Privy Council upheld Tshekedi but suggested that guidelines needed to be established in the Protectorate for the exercise of "native law and custom." The ultimate result was the Native Proclamations of 1934, drafted by Resident Commissioner **Charles Rey**.

Tshekedi and Rey naturally drew into conflict. Since 1927 Tshekedi had worked closely with other diKgosi and led them in resisting colonial efforts to diminish their authority. When Rey arrived in 1930 with the task of drafting and implementing reforms, Tshekedi became the mastermind of the opposition to Rey's Native Proclamations, and the battle over the proclamations often took the form of a personal confrontation between the regent and the resident commissioner. In 1933, when Tshekedi sentenced a white youth in Serowe to be flogged, Rey seized on the incident as a pretext to suspend him from power and exile him to Francistown. But official opinion in Britain and South Africa overwhelmingly favored Tshekedi and forced Rey to recall him. By then working in tandem with **Bathoen II** through court actions, Tshekedi failed to have the 1934 proclamations revoked, but his tenacity outlasted that of the government. The proclamations were never fully implemented, Rey was replaced in 1937, and the new resident commissioner, **Charles Arden-Clarke**, accommodated Tshekedi by making extensive modifications in the 1943 proclamations.

Tshekedi also garnered British support for his pretensions as an absolute monarch in Gammangwato. Tshekedi, who doubted the loyalty of many members of the BaNgwato elite, had them exiled or imprisoned. His targets included Johnnie Ratshosa; **Oratile Ratshosa**, Seretse's half-sister; Baboni and Bonyerile, daughters of **Khama III**; his own wife, Bakgagametse; Disang, Lebang, and Leetile Raditladi; **Moanaphuti Segolodi**, who had charged Tshekedi with tyranny; and **Gasetshwarwe**, son of **Sekgoma II**, who served seven years hard labor. Tshekedi also caused much resentment by making extensive use of regimental labor and public levies. The British supported Tshekedi's autocratic rule over his subject communities. Determined to uphold the religious monopoly of the **LMS** within the reserve, Tshekedi detained pro-Anglican BaKhurutshe leaders in Serowe. In the 1920s and 1930s the

British and Tshekedi together swept under the carpet the BaSarwa slavery issue which had been spotlighted by Simon Ratshosa. Tshekedi's most persistent and troublesome opponents, however, were the BaKalanga, who found in John Nswazwi their champion. The regent's harsh treatment of the BaKalanga is perhaps the most censurable aspect of his reign.

After World War II, Tshekedi stood as the most articulate opponent of incorporation and took part in the international fight against South Africa's attempts to annex Namibia. His ambitions to become a leading African statesman, however, were compromised by his refusal in 1949 to relinquish the regency in favor of his nephew Seretse after the latter's marriage to a white Englishwoman. Tshekedi gained little support in Gammangwato for his stand; after the BaNgwato declared Seretse to be their Kgosi, Tshekedi led forty-two of his headmen into self-imposed exile in the Kweneng. In 1950 the British decided to banish both Seretse and Tshekedi from the reserve, but after lobbying in London, Tshekedi obtained permission to settle with his followers (the "Bo-Rametsana") in Pilikwe in 1952.

During the mid-1950s Tshekedi continued to play an important role in Protectorate affairs. He joined others in calling for the creation of LEGCO. In 1956 Tshekedi met and reconciled with Seretse in London and supported the return of his nephew, who was allowed back into the Protectorate that year. The two then worked together on the BaNgwato tribal council. In 1959 Tshekedi made his final contribution by negotiating the mineral agreement which led to the establishment of the copper mine in Selebi Phikwe and began modern mining development in Botswana. *See also* Anglicans; Ballinger-Barnes Tour; Bolata; Flogging Incident; Kgari Sechele; Khurutshe; Mining; Motsete, Kgaleman; Proclamation; Raditladi, Leetile; Regency; Villagization.

TSHEKO TSHEKO (1923–1969). Politician, born in Ngamiland. Tsheko, who was educated at Maun Tribal School and **Tiger Kloof**, became a teacher in Francistown in 1943. From 1945 until 1964 he worked in the BaTawana tribal administration then resigned to enter politics as the **Democratic Party** leader in Ngamiland. He was a member of the National Assembly and served in the cabinet as minister of Agriculture, 1965–1969. *See also* Moremi, Elizabeth.

TSHOSA MAKABA (d. 1823). Senior son of Makaba, Kgosi of the BaNgwaketse. In 1823 he was killed in an unsuccessful rebellion against his father. His son, **Gaseitsiwe**, assumed the throne in 1846. *See also* Makaba II.

TSHOSA SEBEGO. Regent of the BaNgwaketse, 1919–1924. Appointed after the deaths of regents Kgosimotse (d. 1918) and Malope (d. 1919), Tshosa was stripped of power in 1923 by **Gagoangwe** and formally replaced by her daughter **Ntebogang Ratshosa** in 1924. Allegations that Tshosa's irresponsibility had led to financial improprieties involving the tribal secretary, Peter Kgasa, precipitated his removal.

TSHU. A collective name for a number of **Khoe** communities in eastern Botswana. The Tshu language or dialect cluster is now limited to a few hundred speakers.

TSODILO HILLS. Northwestern Ngamiland hill formation, site of hundreds of rock paintings, and focus of recent archaeological research. As early as 400 A.D., Tsodilo was an important center of regional trade. *See also* Rock Art.

TSOEBEBE, ARCHELAUS MOLELEKI (1904–1986). Educator, civil servant, union organizer, politician. MoSotho by origin and born in Matatiele, Lesotho, he attended Lovedale and Fort Hare College. Between 1932 and 1938 he served as principal of the **Bakgatla National School** in **Mochudi**. There in 1937 he founded the Bechuanaland Protectorate African Teachers' Association and served as its first general secretary (1937–1939). He subsequently joined the civil service and in 1949 founded the Bechuanaland Civil Servants' Association, of which he was president until 1959. He was elected to the Bamangwato tribal council in 1960 and between 1961 and 1964 he was a member of LEGCO. Having been a member of the **People's Party**, but disappointed by the party's refusal to recruit rural, or "tribal," support, Tsoebebe helped to found the **Democratic Party** and became its first vice president. From 1965 to 1969 he represented Bobonong in the National Assembly and served as minister of Works and Communications.

TSWANA (BATSWANA). *See* Birwa, Hurutshe, Kaa, Kgafela Kgatla, Khurutshe, Kwena, Lete, Mmanaana Kgatla, Ngwaketse, Ngwato, Rolong, Talaote, Tawana, Tlokwa, Tribe.

TULI BLOCK. A freehold farm area along the **Limpopo River** in eastern Botswana. In 1895 **Khama III** of the BaNgwato granted the block to the British who made it available to the **British South Africa Company (BSACO)**. Tuli, which was a border strip in **tsetse** country, gave BSACO troops in Rhodesia legal access to Gaberones and Pitsani, from which the **Jameson Raid** was launched. Khama III had surrendered the strip for the building of the railway. In 1910 Africans living in the BSACO-controlled Tuli Block (as it was known after 1905) were told that they could remain only as tenants. In 1920 the BSACO began selling the land to white farmers, a process which led to the removal of most Africans living in the block. One group of Ba**Birwa**, the followers of Malema, resisted their removal. In the 1960s a minority of the white farmers in the block tried to form the Tuli Block Democratic Party for promoting racial separatism and the **incorporation** of the Protectorate into South Africa. *See also* Race Relations; Three Kings in London.

U

UNIONS. *See* Trade Unions.

UNIVERSAL NEGRO IMPROVEMENT ASSOCIATION (UNIA). Founded in the United States by Jamaican-born Marcus Garvey, the UNIA's call for "Africa for the Africans" spread to southern Africa after **World War I**. The UNIA attracted dock workers and war veterans, and Garvey's ideas were transmitted through African newspapers, particularly those of the African National Congress (**ANC**) and the Industrial and Commercial Workers Union (**ICU**). In the 1920s the UNIA gained followers among the Ova**Herero** and Ba**Tawana** of Ngamiland and the western Kgalagadi, largely through the efforts of Samuel Shepperd, a OvaHerero UNIA organizer. Shepperd addressed numerous meetings at which the red, black, and green colors of the UNIA were displayed. The Garveyist movement was also associated with Bishop Alexander's African Orthodox Church, which the British barred from entering the Bechuanaland Protectorate. *See also* Nikodemus, Kahememua; Religion.

UNIVERSITY. *See* Education.

V

VAN RENSBURG, PATRICK (1931–). Educationist, development theorist, author, and founder of the **Brigades** movement. Born of Afrikaner descent in Durban, van Rensburg arrived in Botswana in 1961 and founded Swaneng Hill School in **Serowe** in the following year and, subsequently, Madiba and Shashe River schools at Mahalapye and Tonota, respectively. At these schools and in the Serowe Brigades movement, which he also initiated, van Rensburg introduced ideas that combined education with agricultural and artisan production as a stimulus to local, community development. Since then van Rensburg has propagated his ideas by writing extensively, traveling widely, and establishing organizational vehicles, the most important of which is the worldwide "Foundation for Education with Production," with headquarters in Gaborone.

VAN ZYL, HENDRIK (1828–1880). Hunter-trader and first Boer settler in the Ghanzi area, where he arrived in 1869. For a decade, van Zyl used Ghanzi as his base for hunting for and trading in **ivory**, and his cruelty and greed gained him notoriety throughout the Kgalagadi. He claimed personal authority over, and tried to collect tribute from, the people of Ghanzi and southern Ngamiland until the Ba**Tawana** under **Moremi II** drove him out of the area. He fled to **Namibia**, where he was killed. *See also* Dorsland Trek; Ghanzi Farms; Naro; Race Relations; Traders.

VAPOSTORI ("Apostles"). Also known in Botswana as the Mazezuru, the Vapostori, as they refer to themselves, are members of the Apostolic Sabbath Church of God (ASCG). The ASCG was founded in 1932 in Southern Rhodesia by Johane Masowe (d. 1973). In 1951 a group of 200 Vapostori led by Ebrahim Moyo settled in the Northeast District of the Protectorate at Moroka village. By 1955 most had moved to **Francistown**. After 1957 tensions within the community led to new settlements being founded at Shashe, **Serowe**, and **Lobatse**, and later **Gaborone** and Selebi Phikwe. The Vapostori manufacture and sell goods such as baskets, tinware, and carpentry products, as they are not allowed to work for others. Their theocratic leadership and separatist views have kept them aloof from the rest of the population. *See also* Religion.

VILJOEN, JAN W. (1812–1893). After 1851, Viljoen was field-cornet of Marico District in the Transvaal and led a life closely linked with BaTswana. Politically, Viljoen was a dove regarding the BaTswana and opposed to the Boer attack on Dimawe in 1852. Afterwards he helped ease tensions and for the next quarter of a century served often as the Transvaal representative to the BaTswana merafe as well as to the AmaNdebele.

Viljoen's diplomacy may have had something to do with the fact that he made his living in Botswana, where he went on annual journeys to engage in hunting, especially for **ivory**. He killed hundreds of elephants in northern Botswana and western Zimbabwe. Viljoen was also involved in slave trading. The duties of a field-cornet included providing labor to Boers in his district, and Viljoen met Marico's needs in this respect by importing at least several hundred *malata* from the BaNgwato and the BaTawana. He was observed in 1869 departing Ngamiland with a large number of children in chains. Viljoen's slave train is depicted in a color sketch reproduced in *The Northern Goldfield Diaries of Andrew Baines*. *See also* BaTswana-Boer War of 1852–1853; Bolata; Slave Trade.

VILLAGIZATION. From the 1930s to the 1950s the Protectorate attempted, in conjunction with the diKgosi, to compel people who traditionally lived in scattered homesteads to relocate in villages. Their purpose was to increase administrative efficiency, but the government often legitimized these efforts as an enforcement of SeTswana norms, which favored large villages. The policy was carried out mainly against non-Tswana and most concertedly in Ngamiland among the BaYei, in the Bamangwato Reserve among the BaKalanga and the BaBirwa, and in the western areas of the Kweneng and Bangwaketse reserves among the BaKgalagadi. Villagization caused general resentment and sometimes resistance, because it undercut local economic patterns while increasing the rate of tax collection and **migrant labor**. The policy was never completely successful and in some areas was a complete failure. *See also* Kgosi; Nswazwi, John; Taxation.

W

WANKIE CAMPAIGN (1966–1968). A turning point for Botswana in the liberation wars in Zimbabwe and South Africa. In the Wankie campaign, guerrilla fighters of the Zimbabwe African People's Union (ZAPU) and the **African National Congress (ANC)** failed to establish northern Botswana as a safe haven. At the time elements within the two liberation movements conceived of newly-independent Botswana as a potential "Cambodia" for their "Ho Chi Minh Trail to South Africa."

After an initial incident, August–September 1966, Botswana reaffirmed the former British policy of welcoming political **refugees** from the two white-minority-ruled countries, while forbidding them to use Botswana territory to launch attacks. A second, larger, infiltration occurred in August 1967, during which time a thirty-four-man ANC unit under the command of Chris Hani surrendered to Botswana's paramilitary Police Mobile Unit (forerunner of the **Botswana Defence Force**). After heated debate in cabinet, it was decided to charge the captured combatants with illegal possession of "weapons of war." In 1969 the ANC and ZAPU, having failed to infiltrate western Zimbabwe, called off their Wankie campaign, whereupon Botswana repatriated their imprisoned cadres to **Zambia**.

WARREN EXPEDITION (1885). The first manifestation of British rule in the Bechuanaland Protectorate was Sir Charles Warren's expeditionary force, which passed through **Kanye, Molepolole, Mochudi**, and Shoshong in April and May 1885. The Warren Expedition was the outcome of the 27 January 1885 **Order-in-Council** in which Britain unilaterally declared its Protectorate over the territories of South Africa north of the Cape Colony, south of the twenty-second parallel, west of the South African Republic (SAR), and east of the twentieth meridian of east longitude. This area included all of modern Botswana south of Selebi Phikwe. A **protectorate** was proclaimed in order to prevent the joining together of the SAR and German South West Africa, to retain Britain's access to central Africa, and to secure law and order in areas adjacent to the diamond mines of the Cape Colony.

Warren and a small force rode north of the Molopo River with orders to inform **Khama III** of the BaNgwato and **Sechele I** of the BaKwena regarding the proclamation of the Protectorate. He was accompanied by the ex-missionary **John Mackenzie**, who along with Warren also used the expedition to gain BaTswana support for settling English farmers in the territory. Their envisaged English-Tswana alliance would then be used to obstruct expansion by the Transvaal Boers and Cape British. Warren and Mackenzie met Khama and Sechele, as well as **Gaseitsiwe** of the BaNgwaketse and **Linchwe I** of the **Kgafela Kgatla**. Only Khama accepted the proclamation without reservation. To Warren and Mackenzie's pleasure, he also made his "magnificent offer" of land for English settlement in the north and northwest as well as along his border with the SAR.

Warren exceeded his instructions by formally accepting this

offer and negotiating agreements with Khama, Gaseitsiwe, and Sechele. The latter two also made land offers after Khama had done so, though theirs and Khama's were for areas disputed by other rulers. Khama gave to the British the right to make laws and govern in his territory with respect to both blacks and whites (in effect ceding his sovereignty), whereas Sechele agreed that Britain could make laws for white people only.

In June 1885 the Colonial Office set aside these agreements and rejected Warren's recommendations for English settlement, but the agreements were later used to justify the **Order-in-Council of 1891**, which established the legal foundation for British rule in the territory. *See also* BaTswana-Boer War of 1881–1884; Boundaries, External; British Bechuanaland.

WATER. Apart from the **Okavango Delta**, surface water is very scarce in Botswana, but subterranean supplies are relatively plentiful. The history of water development has been, therefore, one of drilling for wells, or what are called "boreholes." In the nineteenth century, the use of ground water was limited to shallow surface pits, usually in dry river beds or depressions where the water table was within a few yards of the surface. With the introduction of gasoline and diesel drilling rigs in the 1920s, boreholes could be drilled to the depths of a hundred yards or more. Boreholes made possible the settlement and grazing of huge expanses of previously under-utilized grassland, including much of the Kgalagadi Desert. Some diKgosi, such as **Isang Pilane**, realized the potential of borehole development in the 1920s, but the government did not react until the 1930s, when Resident Commissioner **Charles Rey** secured grants from London for sinking wells along the cattle trek-routes across the Kgalagadi. By then indigenous use of the new technology had already begun to accelerate. Isang's organization of borehole syndicates in the Bakgatla Reserve was being replicated by large cattle owners in many parts of the Protectorate. As a result, many syndicate owners also gained control of grazing land around the boreholes by default, making it effectively their private property. Nearly 400 private boreholes were drilled in the decade after World War II, compared with 220 drilled by government. At independence, over 5,000 boreholes had been sunk in Botswana. By 1985, this figure had doubled, and over 80 percent of the people had come to depend on boreholes for their water.

Boreholes have helped to extend the land available for grazing, thereby increasing the national herd, but their proliferation and improper management have threatened the national range with overgrazing and long-term deterioration.

The growing urban populations in the country have created another demand for water resources, which in the largest urban centers boreholes cannot meet. Since **Seepapitso II** initiated dam building to help supply **Kanye**, dams have been constructed in many locations, but the periodic scarcity of water brought on by drought has rendered some of them unreliable. In the 1980s, following a period of drought, the government raised the level of the Gaborone Dam more than 100 feet in order to increase storage capacity, and together with another recently-constructed dam at Bokaa, the Gaborone Dam has been able to withstand the effects of recent dry years. In 1990 Botswana and South Africa began joint surveys for the purpose of locating dams on the **Limpopo River.** Other studies are being undertaken on the Shashe and Motloutse rivers. Another late 1980s undertaking, the Okavango Integrated Water Development Project, was intended to deliver water from the Okavango Delta to Orapa town and diamond mine, which have depended on underground water, but environmental groups noting its potential harm to the Delta environment have succeeded in halting its progress.

In the years ahead, Botswana is likely to face a crisis of major proportions. The Ministry of Mineral Resources and Water affairs has estimated that by the year 2020, Botswana will, at the present rate of consumption by stock and humans, have used up all water resources presently known. *See also* Cattle; Drought.

WHITE SLAVES OF MOLEPOLOLE. In the precolonial era, a number of Boer smiths and wagoners settled among the Ba-**Kwena**. In 1925 their descendants' existence was discovered by the South African press, which carried reports distorting the character of the loyalty of the whites to their **Kgosi** and community. These "white slavery" stories were also published in Britain. *See also* Molepolole; Race Relations.

WILLIAMS, (SIR) RALPH CHAMPNEY (1848–1927). Resident Commissioner, 1901–1906. Williams's contact with the Protectorate began in 1885 with the **Warren Expedition**, in which he served as intelligence officer. As an early proponent of Cape expansion and an ally of Cecil Rhodes, he soon fell out with Warren, whose scheme for annexation and English settlement he helped defeat with his pamphlet, "The British Lion in Bechuanaland."

Ironically, Williams became the first **resident commissioner** to regard the Protectorate administration as being independent of others in the region. In the crucial, post-South African War period, he guarded the Protectorate from the inroads of the Cape and Transvaal administrations, established the policy of rule through diKgosi, created the Bechuanaland Protectorate Police, and reformed the administration of the territory.

One of his last and most controversial acts was to depose **Sekgoma Letsholathebe** of the BaTawana. Williams later became governor of Newfoundland, 1909–1913. To the BaTswana Williams was known as "Ramaologa." *See also* British South Africa Company; Police.

WILLOUGHBY, WILLIAM CHARLES (1857–1938). Missionary, educationist, scholar. Willoughby was an **LMS** missionary to **Khama III**, and he acted as his advisor, particularly from 1893 to 1896, and even as his secretary (1893–1894). In 1895 he accompanied Khama, **Sebele I**, and **Bathoen I** on their visit to London and acted as their interpreter in negotiating with the British government. From 1904 to 1914 he was the first principal of **Tiger Kloof**, which became the main center of higher education for BaTswana. After retiring from mission work in 1917 he devoted his time to scholarly pursuits and published several noted early works in "Bantu Studies," in particular his book *Soul of the Bantu* (1928). His papers, which are a valuable source on the history and culture of pre-colonial and early colonial Botswana, are housed at Selly Oak Colleges, Birmingham, England. *See also* Education; Three Kings in London.

WOMEN. Since the pre-colonial era, women have performed vital economic and social roles, and some women in royal families have exercised political influence, but with few exceptions all women have occupied an inferior position in society and especially so with respect to legal rights. In rural areas, where since the early twentieth century most resident adults have been female, women were responsible for all cultivation, only plowing being the responsibility of men. During the growing season women lived with their children away from the town at the lands, where they raised a variety of grains, melons, beans, and pulses. Males not in town or involved as **migrant laborers** normally remained with family stock at cattle posts located farther still from the main settlements. In the months preceding harvest, women foraged for wild roots and berries to feed themselves and their children. Their extensive knowledge of these wild food resources, as well as their raising of crops and food preparation, enabled BaTswana to survive over the generations. Only women of wealthy families, who had access to agricultural and herding labor, were likely to live in town free from such duties.

As men's legal dependents, women had no choice of residence or any rights to property. Until marriage a daughter lived under the authority of her father or guardian (usually an uncle), thereafter under the husband's or, in the instance of his death, his brother. Divorce ended with the return of the woman to her previous residence (usually not with her children, who remained with the father's family). Cattle and land ownership was reserved for the males of her governing lineage, though her eldest male child was entitled to receive his father's full inheritance (unless she was a junior wife, in which case her children might not receive anything). Men were known to pass wealth and knowledge to their daughters as a way of depriving sons they disliked, but they did so seldomly, secretly, and at risk to family relations. Only *malata* servants were regarded as possessions of wealthy BaTswana females. Women were excluded from the care of cattle, attendance at **kgotla**, and, apart from the royal family, in holding any office of authority. They held, in effect, the status of children, i.e., minors.

The spread of the cash economy, which now pervades Botswana, has greatly altered female economic and social roles but failed to elevate significantly their legal position. In rural towns the long-term absence of males in search of wage employment has lowered marriage rates and increased female responsibilities for their own support and that of their children. Whereas in the colonial period men were impelled by tax laws to seek work abroad; young single women left their towns in order to establish themselves independently. In the rural towns of modern Botswana may be found elderly women who spent their working years in South Africa and returned to their original homes to retire with their life savings. Like those who remained behind, they tend to be single and heads of households of their children, though by virtue of working abroad they have the capital to build their own houses and support themselves independently. In the urban centers of Botswana, which have grown rapidly since independence, large numbers of single mothers head households supported through their own wages and salaries.

Long term pressure on women to be self-supporting has occurred alongside their involvement in **education**, **nursing**, and religious organizations. Historically, females have made up the majority of students attending primary and secondary schools in the country, though their proportion diminishes past puberty (roughly 60 percent of the girls who drop out of school do so on account of pregnancy). Consequently, literacy between men and women is virtually equal (roughly 73 percent for men, 69 percent for women), and women may be seen occupying positions in all private and public sectors in the country. Botswana's long-serving Minister of Foreign Affairs, and presently Minister of Education, **Gaositswe Chiepe**, is now one of four women members of the National Assembly and one of two sitting in the cabinet. Margaret Nasha, former director of Information and Broadcasting and deputy secretary of Foreign Affairs, has been appointed as a specially-elected member and assistant minister of Local Government, Lands and Housing. The other MPs are Joy Phumaphi neé Mannathoko, an ex-university radical, and Mrs. Kokorwe, representing Thamaga. All are members of the **Democratic Party (BDP)**. Women voters and activists have played decisive roles in the BDP and the **National Front**, but they hold at best second-ranking positions in these two major parties.

The Botswana Constitution bars discrimination on account of gender, but women lack essential protection in many respects. Child support, a burning issue, has been left to district and customary courts to resolve, with few fathers compelled to meet their obligations. Married women lose legal control of property, such as a common checking account, which are recorded in the name of their husbands. According to the Citizenship Act of 1982, citizenship for the children of married women is likewise determined by their husbands. Until recently, such children were not entitled to Botswana citizenship by birth unless their fathers were BaTswana citizens. Otherwise they were foreigners, like their fathers. In 1991, however, a woman MoTswana attorney, Unity Dow, challenged the Act as discriminatory and won her case before Botswana's High Court in **Lobatse**.

This victory, and others that lay in the future, result from concerted efforts on the part of female organizations in the country. Among the most active and outspoken is *Emang Basadi* ("Stand Up, Women!"), formed in 1986 by leading professionals such as university law professor Athaliah Molokomme, and journalist/politician Clara Olsen. Emang Basadi is devoted to enhancing the social, economic, and political position of women and has directed its energies especially toward the removal of discriminatory laws. Other active women's organizations include the Botswana Council of Women (1965), the Young Women's Christian Association (1962), Christian Women's Fellowship (1975), Women on Development (1981), and several business and professional women's clubs. *See also* Alcohol; Bolata; Family; Gagoangwe; Head, Bessie; Initiation; Khama, Elizabeta; Khama, Semane; Labor Migration; Masire, Gladys; Mphepheng; Moremi, Elizabeth; Motshabi Letsholathebe; Namane, Gamelemo; Ntebogang Ratshosa; Oratile Ratshosa; Population; Religion; Retief, Deborah; Seingwaeng; Zion Christian Church.

WORLD WAR I. World War I involved Botswana, in the region and in Europe. In late 1914, Protectorate police and their auxiliaries assisted the Rhodesians in occupying the **Caprivi Strip**. At Segwagwa in the southern Protectorate, on 1 January 1915 BaNgwaketse regiments dispatched by Kgosi **Seepapitso II** intercepted and captured a pro-German rebel force under General Ben Pienaar, then proceeding to link up with German forces in South West Africa.

During the war, 555 BaTswana enlisted in Protectorate units of the **South African Native Labour Contingent (SANLC)** and served in France. They were made up of 203 BaNgwaketse, 127 **Kgafela Kgatla**, 74 BaKwena, 49 BaLete, 32 BaTlokwa, and 70 from the Tati Native Reserve. The Kgafela Kgatla also supplied 312 men and the BaLete 93 to assist in the occupation of German South West Africa. Disturbances within the SANLC led to its recall before the war ended. **Khama III** refused to send any men to the front, although the BaNgwato along with the BaTawana, BaNgwaketse, and Kgafela Kgatla contributed a total of £2,000 toward the war effort. A small, but as yet undetermined, number of BaTswana also served in the East Africa Campaign. *See also* Namibia.

WORLD WAR II. A period of suffering and dislocation in the Protectorate. Between 1941 and 1944, 10,027 BaTswana enlisted in the African Auxiliary Pioneer Corps (AAPC) of the British Army. The AAPC, which consisted of twenty-four companies, served in the central/eastern Mediterranean theaters in the AA Batteries, Smoke, Bridgebuilding, Salvage, and Labour Contigents. An unknown, though certainly much smaller, number enlisted in South African units. About 20 percent of the adult male population saw active service, the highest proportion of any colony or dominion in Africa. Among Protectorate European officials, 42 percent were released for military service. Recruitment of BaTswana was the responsibility of the diKgosi. Recruitment was spread across the entire territory, and much of it was coercive. DiKgosi were keen to recruit large numbers to demonstrate loyalty to the Crown and forestall **incorporation** into South Africa. At the conclusion of the war a total of 847 BaTswana had been killed, wounded, or disabled.

In the wartime Protectorate, the British introduced a "war lands" policy to reduce food imports. Grain and labor quotas were set to induce production on communal lands (*masotla*), but chronic labor shortages and drought crippled all arable farming in the territory. AAPC allowances and migrant labor remittances provided needed cash and saved the Protectorate from famine, but dependence on **migrant labor** intensified during the war and increased thereafter. When the soldiers returned from the front, their impact on local and national politics was blunted by their need to support themselves and their families by becoming migrant laborers. The war had a significant impact on the nation's future leaders, especially the generation in school during the war. The general public also became interested in news about the Protectorate, the southern African region, and the rest of the world (including word of BaTswana companies at the front) as communicated for the first time through SeTswana **radio**, local newspaper reporting, and film shows.

Following the war, three BaTswana companies totaling 1,000 men formed part of the High Commission Territory Corps (HCTC), a volunteer force. Between 1946 and 1949 the HCTC was reduced in size due to South African pressure but served ably in the Middle East, most notably in Palestine. BaTswana distinguished themselves as guards and police against the backdrop of rising violence between Jewish settlers and Arabs in the closing phase of the British Mandate. Among other awards, members of these companies received a George V medal and four British Empire Medals. *See also* High Commission Territories; Newspapers.

X

!XO. A language group spoken throughout southwestern Botswana along with related dialects /Xam, /Nuhki, and //Xegwi.

!Xo-speakers have in the past been identified with "**Bushmen**," "**San**," or BaSarwa. *See also* Khoe.

Y

YEI (BAYEI). The BaYei, whose ancestors migrated from southern Zambia no later than the eighteenth century, constitute the largest group in Ngamiland. They lived originally in scattered homesteads, not in villages like BaTswana, and had no traditional institution equivalent to bogosi. When the BaTawana settled in Ngamiland in the nineteenth century, the BaYei were unable to resist these less numerous, but militarily more powerful, state-builders. The BaTawana evolved the system of botlhanka, or **bolata**, which subordinated the BaYei and deprived them of such rights as owning or inheriting property, defending themselves in **kgotla**, and even exercising authority over their own children. Many BaYei were partially assimilated as "Makuba," a pejorative term the BaTawana often applied to the BaYei generally. Though originally fishing people and agriculturists, many BaYei became stock holders. In the 1930s they were also encouraged to settle in SeTswana-type villages along the edge of the **Okavango Delta,** and increasing numbers became involved in **migrant labor**.

After **World War II**, an outspoken BaYei minority advocated separatism as a way of elevating their status. In 1948 they petitioned the British for rights to their own dikgotla, the use of land without having to pay rent or labor, and the inheritance of property. The BaYei were granted their own dikgotla, but the BaTawana claimed that botlhanka had ceased to exist and so rejected the other demands. The separatists continued to agitate for reform, including the establishment of a BaYei reserve with their own "chief." When local government reforms were implemented in the late 1960s many of the grievances of the separatists were resolved. *See also* Independence Party; Moeti Samotsoko; Moremi, Elizabeth; Mpho, Motsamai; Raditladi, Leetile; Saundo, Chombo; Shomolakae Sebolai; Tribe; Villagization.

Z

ZAMBIA (before 1964, Northern Rhodesia). The Republic of Zambia and the Republic of Botswana, though sharing a very small common border, have important historical connections. **Archaeology** indicates the existence of trade between the regions of western Zambia and Botswana over many centuries. During the nineteenth century the Lozi state in western Zambia was allied with the Ba**Tawana** and Ba**Ngwato** against the Ama-**Ndebele**. Many early European traders and missionaries entered Zambia from Botswana; the Paris Evangelical Mission in BuLozi, for example, was established with the encouragement of **Khama III**. After the 1896–1897 **rinderpest** devastated cattle herds in the Bechuanaland Protectorate, **cattle** from Northern Rhodesia played a role in the regeneration of stock. During the interwar period the copper mines of Northern Rhodesia also became a market for Bechuanaland's beef, which had been denied access to South Africa by the weight restrictions. From Botswana's independence in 1966 to that of Zimbabwe's in 1980, Zambia was Botswana's only majority-ruled neighbor, and its only road and air link to the north. In 1968 President Kenneth Kaunda became the first head of state to visit Botswana, and Botswana and Zambia developed a special relationship as "front-line" states. The two countries exchange High Commissions, and Botswana's high commissioner in Lusaka is responsible for Botswana's affairs in central and eastern Africa. *See also* Cattle; External Relations; Kololo; Refugees; Southern African Development Coordination Conference.

ZHU (!XHU). A language group concentrated in northwest Botswana and eastern **Namibia**. Today Zhu-speakers number some 6,000, two-thirds of whom live in Botswana. Perhaps the world's most famous anthropological "specimens," the Zhu (whom past anthropologists have mystified as "!Kung Bushmen"), have been studied more than any ethnic group in Africa. In the 1950s they were popularized by the Marshall family as "Harmless People," who lived in a "remote" area. They were said to have a lifestyle based entirely on hunting and gathering unchanged since the Stone Age. In the 1960s a large number of professional anthropologists descended on the Zhu to study seemingly every aspect of their existence. Results of their studies claimed that the Zhu lived in "primitive affluence" in a society with few personal possessions and tensions. Zhu popularity reached its peak in the early 1980s with the appearance of the Hollywood blockbuster *The Gods Must Be Crazy*, featuring a Zhu character as star. Although the ideas of the Marshalls and others live on in the popular imagination, modern scholarship has rejected them. Abundant archaeological, anthropological, and historical research has demonstrated that all people in the area occupied by the Zhu have been involved for at least a millennium in complex forms of food production, including stock raising, that they have interacted at all levels over considerable distance, and that they have been connected to long-distance trade and the exchange of ideas. *See also* Archaeology and Prehistory; Bushmen; Khoe; San.

ZIMBABWE (Southern Rhodesia, 1894–1965; Rhodesia, 1965– 1980). The histories of Zimbabwe and Botswana have been interconnected for centuries. Circa 1200 –1800 A.D. a series of states emerged within Zimbabwe which controlled large areas of northern Botswana. Moreover, recent archaeological excavations of cattle sites in the tsetse-free areas of Botswana suggest that the foundation of the Great Zimbabwean civilization was built in part on cattle surpluses accumulated in Botswana. In the nineteenth century, Botswana was Zimbabwe's "avenue of conquerors." Before establishing themselves in western Zimbabwe, the AmaNdebele of Mzilikazi fought their way north through parts of Botswana and absorbed BaTswana and BaKalanga into their society. The "pioneer column," which passed north through eastern Botswana, was launched from Mafikeng by Cecil Rhodes and his British South Africa Company (BSACO) for the purpose of establishing a toehold in Rhodesia, and the subsequent BSACO defeat of the AmaNdebele was made possible by the Bechuanaland Border Police and the armed regiments sent by the BaNgwato. The failure of the Jameson Raid prevented Rhodes's next step of taking over the administration of the Bechuanaland Protectorate.

Many people share historic ties across the two borders. To the north, Ikalanga-speaking peoples lived on either side, and along Botswana's eastern-most border such people as the BaBirwa have many relatives in southwestern Zimbabwe. For generations, the northern Limpopo watershed draining northeastern and eastern Botswana and western Zimbabwe has been an area of considerable social interaction.

Following Rhodesia's "Unilateral Declaration of Independence," the Zimbabwean liberation war was launched in 1966 and necessarily involved Botswana, which had just gained its own independence. Guerrilla fighters passing through Botswana from Zambia led Botswana to establish its good-neighbor policy, i.e., that it would not allow its territory to be used as a base for attacks on its neighbors, while at the same time giving a standing welcome to all political refugees. Botswana refused to establish official relations with Rhodesia, though the border posts remained open and the trains continued to run. Violations of Botswana's territory by Rhodesian security forces was a major factor in the formation of the **Botswana Defence Force** in 1976.

Since 1980 and Zimbabwe's admission to the Front Line States and the Southern African Development Coordination Conference, Botswana has developed close political and economic ties with Zimbabwe. The flow of people and goods, particularly in Botswana's direction, has steadily increased. In 1992 Zimbabweans constituted more than 25 percent of all visitors to Botswana. Many enter the country (especially by train to Francistown and Gaborone) for the purchasing of commodities for reselling in Zimbabwe. *See also* Archaeology and Prehistory; Cattle; External Relations; Grobler Affair; Lilima; Nyayi; Railways; Refugees; Wankie Campaign; Vapostori.

ZION CHRISTIAN CHURCH (ZCC). The ZCC, among the largest Christian churches in Botswana, originated in the northern Transvaal among the Ba**Pedi**, who since the nineteenth century had developed a strong, independent Christian church tradition. The Church of Zion was founded in 1924 by Engenus Barnabas Lekganyane near Pietersburg at a site now known as Morija. In 1937 the ZCC entered the Bechuanaland Protectorate in the Bakgatla Reserve as a device to restore **Molefi** to bogosi, but it spread as a response to growing concern among the common people, particularly women, about the deterioration of family and social life. In the 1940s and 1950s, the ZCC was suppressed by diKgosi, who regarded it as a vehicle of political protest and a source of village disturbance. A number of ZCC leaders and their followers were driven into exile or forced to leave the church itself. Since independence, when constitutional rights to religious freedom have been more rigorously protected, the ZCC has rooted itself in most towns and villages of the Republic. In 1947, following the death of founder Engenus Lekganyane, the ZCC divided into two independent churches, each headed by one of Engenus's sons, Edward and Joseph. The Zion Christian Church (Edward Lekganyane), with approximately 18,000 members, is now headed by Bishop Barnabus (son of Edward) Lekganyane and uses the silver star as its emblem. The St. Engenas Zion Christian Church (Joseph Lekganyane), uses the silver dove and recognizes Joseph Lekganyane as their bishop. They too, have approximately 18,000 members. *See also* Pentecostal Churches; Religion; Seingwaeng; Women.

Bibliography

This bibliography is selective, giving attention to noteworthy published books and articles (and a few dissertations), as well as to publications inside Botswana that are relatively unknown outside. Most Botswana publications may be obtained through the Botswana Book Centre, Box 91, Gaborone (FAX: 215–568). Government publications are available through the relative ministry, and some may be obtained from the Government Printer, Private Bag 0060, Gaborone.

Those works that are noted with an asterisk [*] are recommended for inclusion in any basic library collection on Botswana.

The bibliography's organization follows the outline below.

I. Bibliographies

II. General Works and Collections
   A. Collections, Interdisciplinary Studies
   B. Descriptions, Guides, and Maps
   C. Government Statistics and Surveys

III. Specialized, Disciplinary Studies
   A. Culture and Society
      1. Anthropology, Ethnology, and Sociology
         a. Bushman, or BaSarwa, Studies
         b. Other Studies
      2. Art, Music, and Crafts
      3. Communications, Press, and Publications
      4. Dictionaries, Language, and Linguistics
      5. Literature and Folklore
      6. Demography, Migration, Populations, Settlement, Urbanization
      7. Education
      8. Women
      9. Religion
   B. Economics
      1. General
      2. Agriculture

I. BIBLIOGRAPHIES

Botswana is still underserved in terms of bibliographic research, though the situation has improved in the last decade. Even so, there are still a large number of books and articles on many topics that have never appeared in any bibliography. An assiduous search is therefore necessary for turning up these titles. Research should begin with the starred titles.

Archibald, J. E., comp. *The Works of Isaac Schapera: A Selective Bibliography*. Johannesburg: Department of Bibliography, Librarianship and Typography, University of Witwatersrand, 1969.
Balima, M. G., comp. *Botswana, Lesotho, and Swaziland: A Guide to Official Publications, 1868–1968*. Washington, D.C.: Library of Congress General Reference and Bibliography Division Reference Department, 1971.

Botswana Government. *National Bibliography of Botswana*. Gaborone: National Library Service, 1969.

Botswana Society. *Index of Botswana Notes and Records, Volumes 1–24* [1969–1992]. Gaborone: Botswana Society, 1993/1994.

Eicher, S. F. *Rural Development in Botswana: A Select Bibliography, 1966–1980*. Washington, D.C.: African Bibliographic Center, 1981.

Gardner, S., and P. E. Scott. *Bessie Head: A Bibliography*. Grahamstown: National English Literary Museum, 1986.

Giffuni, C. "Bessie Head: A Bibliography." *Current Bibliography on African Affairs* 19, no. 3 (1986/87): 203–211.

Grant, S. "Index to Botswana Society Publications." *Mmegi/The Reporter* 8, no. 29 (1991): 17.

*Hitchcock, R., and Q. N. Parsons. *An Index to the Publications of the Botswana Society 1969–1989*. Gaborone: The Botswana Society, 1991.

Jones, K. L., comp. "A Select Bibliography of Botswana Material for 1983." *Botswana Notes and Records*, 17 (1985): 183–186.

———. "A Select Bibliography of Material Published About Botswana During 1982." *Botswana Notes and Records*, 16 (1984): 147–149.

Kerven, C. K., and P. Simmons. "Bibliography on the Society, Culture and Political Economy of Post-Independence Botswana." *National Migration Study*. In Botswana Government. Gaborone: Government Printers, 1981.

Kgathi, D. L., and Q. N. Parsons comp. *The Brigades Movement: An Annotated Bibliography*. Gaborone: National Institute of Research, 1981.

Lekaukau, T. M. *A Guide to the Public Archives of Botswana: Volume I 1885–1965*. Gaborone: Botswana National Archives, 1984.

Lestrade, G. P. "Bibliography of Tswana Language and Literature." In C. M. Doke, "A Preliminary Investigation of the State of the Native Languages of South Africa." *Bantu Studies* 7 (1933): 77–85.

MacKenzie, C. *Bessie Head: A Bibliography*. Grahamstown: National English Literary Museum, 1992.

Middleton, C. *Bechuanaland: A Bibliography*. Cape Town: University of Cape Town School of Librarianship, 1965.

Mohome, P., and J. B. Webster. *A Bibliography on Bechuanaland*. Syracuse, N.Y.: Syracuse University Program of Eastern African Studies, 1966.

* Morton, B. *Pre-colonial Botswana: An Annotated Bibliography and Guide to the Sources*. Gaborone: The Botswana Society, 1994.

* Morton, B., and Q. N. Parsons. *Colonial Botswana: An Annotated Bibliography, 1885–1935*. Gaborone: The Botswana Society, forthcoming.

Parsons, Q. N. *A Consolidated Checklist of Theses and Dissertations on Botswana*. Gaborone: National Institute of Research, 1982.

———. *The High Commission Territories, 1909–1964*. Kwaluseni: Swaziland Libraries Publications. No. 3, University of Botswana, Lesotho and Swaziland, 1976.

Schapera, I. and A. Kuper. "Select Bibliography" and "Select Supplementary Bibliography." In *The Tswana*, I. Schapera. London: International African Institute, 1976 edition. Reprint, 1979: 77–89.

Shillington, K., comp. *Essays on the History of Botswana: A Bibliography of History Research Essays Presented in Part Fulfillment of the B.A. Degree of the University of Botswana, 1976–1984*. Gaborone: University of Botswana Department of History, 1984.

Stevens, P. *Bibliography of Bechuanaland*. Cape Town: University of Cape Town School of Librarianship, 1947.

*van Varmelo, N. *A Bibliography of Journal Articles Relating to South African Anthropology to 1950*. Johannesburg: University of Witwatersrand Press, 1976.

Veenendaal, E. M. *Botswana's Environment: A Second Annotated Bibliography*. Gaborone: National Institute of Development Research and Documentation, University of Botswana, 1989.

Weimer, B. *A Bibliography on Education in Botswana and Related Fields*. Gaborone: National Institute of Research, 1976.

Youngman, F. *Adult Education in Botswana, 1960–1980: An Annotated Bibliography*. Gaborone: National Institute of Research, 1981.

II. GENERAL WORKS AND COLLECTIONS

A. Collections, Interdisciplinary Studies

* Barrett, T. M., Colclough, and D. Crowley, ed., *Proceedings of the Conference on Sustained Production from Semi–Arid Areas, Gaborone, 11–15 October, 1970. Botswana Notes and Records* Special Issue, No. 1 (1971).

Botlhole, Molebelli I. C. K. *Directory of On-Going and Completed Research on Botswana, 1984–1987*. Gaborone: National Institute of Development Research and Documentation, University of Botswana, 1991.

* Cooke, J., and A. Campbell, ed. *Proceedings of the Seminar on Botswana's Environment*. Gaborone: Botswana Society, 1985.

* Crowder, M., ed. *Education for Development: Proceedings of a Symposium Held by the Botswana Society at the National Museum and Art Gallery, Gaborone, 15–19 August, 1983*. Gaborone: Botswana Society/Macmillan Botswana, 1984.

Harvey, C., ed. *Papers on the Economy of Botswana*. London: Heinemann, 1981.

* Hinchey, M. T., ed. *Proceedings of the Symposium on Drought in Botswana*. Gaborone: Botswana Society, 1979.

* Hitchcock, R. K., N. Parsons, and J. Taylor, ed. *Research in Botswana. Proceedings of the Research for Development Symposium*. Gaborone: The Botswana Society, 1988.

* Hitchcock, R. R. and M. R. Smith, ed. *Settlement in Botswana: The Historical Development of a Human Landscape*. Marshalltown: Botswana Society/Heinemann Educational Books, 1982.

Jeske, J., ed. *Proceedings of the Seminar on Botswana's External Trade in the Light of the Lome Convention*. Gaborone: National Institute of Research, 1978.

Kerven, C., ed. *Migration in Botswana: Patterns, Causes and Consequences. National Migration Study Final Report*. 3 vols. Gaborone: Central Statistics Office, 1982.

—————. *Workshop on Migration Research, National Migration Study*. Gaborone: Central Statistics Office, 1979.

* Morton, R. F., and J. Ramsay, ed. *Birth of Botswana: The History of the Bechuanaland Protectorate, 1910–1966*. Gaborone: Longman Botswana, 1988.

Nteta, D., and Hermans, J., ed. *Sustainable Rural Development: Proceedings of a Workshop Held by the Botswana Society in Gaborone, Botswana, 13–15 April 1992*. Gaborone: The Botswana Society, 1992.

Oomen, M. A., F. K. Inganji, L. D. Ngcongco, ed. *Botswana's Economomy Since Independence*. New Delhi: Tate McGraw-Hill, 1983.

Photenhauer, L., ed. *Tourism in Botswana: Proceedings of a Symposium Held in Gaborone, Botswana, 15–19 October 1990*. Gaborone: The Botswana Society, 1991.

Picard, L. A., ed. *Politics and Rural Development in Southern Africa: The Evolution of Modern Botswana*. London: Rex Collings, 1985.

* *Proceedings of the Symposium on the Okavango Delta and its Future Utilization*. Gaborone: Botswana Society, 1976.

Stedman, S. J., ed. *Botswana: The Political Economy of Democratic Development*. Boulder: Lynne Reinner, 1993.

Werbner, R. P., ed. *Land Reform in the Making: Tradition, Public Policy and Ideology in Botswana*. London: Rex Collings, 1982.

Wylie, E., ed. *Minutes of Remote Area Development Workshop*. Gaborone: Ministry of Local Government and Lands, 1978.

B. Descriptions, Guides, and Maps

Botswana Government. *Botswana in Pictures 1986*. Gaborone: Government Printer, 1986.

Botswana Government. *Guide to the Villages of Botswana*. Gaborone: Government Printer, 1973.

Botswana Government. Department of Surveys and Lands, List of Maps (Write Map Office, Department of Surveys and Lands, Ministry of Local Government and Lands, Private Bag 006, Gaborone).

Campbell, A. C. *The Guide to Botswana*. 3rd ed. Gaborone: Winchester Press, 1980.

—————. *Sites of Historical and Natural Interest in and around Gaborone*. Gaborone: National Museum, 1978.

Laure, J. *Botswana*. Chicago: Childrens Press, 1993.

Main, M. *Kalahari: Life's Variety in Dune and Delta*. Johannesburg: Southern Book Publishers, 1987.

Main, M., J. Fowkes, and S. Fowkes. *Visitors' Guide to Botswana: How to Get There, What to See, Where to Stay*. Johannesburg: Southern Book Publishers, 1987.

Parsons, Q. N., ed., *The Botswana Society Social Studies Atlas*. Gaborone: The Botswana Society, 1988.
Phuthadikobo Museum. *Guide to Mochudi*. Mochudi: Phuthadikobo Museum, n.d.
United States Government. *Background Notes, Botswana*. Washington, D.C.: Department of State, Bureau of Public Affairs, Office of Public Communication, 1993.
Winchester–Gould, G. A. *The Guide to Botswana*. Gaborone/Johannesburg: Winchester Press, 1968.

C. Government Statistics and Surveys (For Government Reports, contact the relevant Ministry)

Agricultural Statistics Unit (Private Bag 003, Gaborone)
    Agricultural Surveys, 1967–
    Agricultural Statistics, 1980, 1990
    Farm Management Survey, 1981
    Livestock and Crop Surveys, 1978–
Central Statistics Office (Private Bag 0024, Gaborone)
    Census Report, 1971, 1981, 1991
    Employment Surveys, 1974–
    External Trade Statistics, 1983/84 +
    Household Expenditure Survey, 1968–1970
    Labor Force Survey, 1984–1985
    Migration in Botswana: Patterns, Causes and Consequences. Final Report, National Migration Study. Vols. 2, 3, 1982
    National Accounts of Botswana, 1978–1979
    Rural Income Distribution Survey, 1974–1975
    Statistical Abstracts, 1966–
    Statistical Bulletin, 1975–

III. SPECIALIZED, DISCIPLINARY STUDIES

In addition to the work of Isaac Schapera, whose published works are essential reading for anyone studying Botswana in the non–scientific areas, recommended studies in the categories below are indicated by an *.

A. Culture and Society

1. Anthropology, Ethnology, and Sociology

a. Bushman, or BaSarwa, Studies

Biesele, M. et al. "Hunters, Clients and Squatters: The Contemporary Socioeconomic Status of Botswana Basarwa." *African Study Monographs* 9, no. 3 (1989): 109–151.

Bleek, D. F. *The Naron: A Bushmen Tribe of the Central Kalahari.* Cambridge: Cambridge University Press, 1928.

Cashdan, E. A. *Subsistence, Mobility, and Territorial Organization Among the G//anakwe of the Northeastern Central Kalahari Game Reserve, Botswana.* Gaborone: Ministry of Local Government and Lands Report, 1977.

Cashdan, E. A. and Chasko, W. Jr. *People of the Middle and Upper Nata River Area: Origins, Population, Economics, and Health.* Gaborone: Ministry of Local Government and Lands Report, 1977.

Caye, V. M., and S. R. Koitsiwe. *Report on a Survey of Basarwa in Western Kgatleng District.* Gaborone: Ministry of Local Government and Lands Report, 1976.

Chasko, W. J. et al. "Sero–Genetic Studies on the 'Masarwa' of Northeastern Botswana." *Botswana Notes and Records* 11(1979): 15–23.

Childers, G. W. *Report on the Survey/Investigation of the Ghanzi Farm Basarwa Situation.* Gaborone: Government Printer, 1976.

Clements, V. C. "The Masarwas, or Bushmen of the Kalahari." *African Monthly* 5 (1908): 29–33.

Denbow, J. *See under* History, archaeology.

Dornan, S. S. *Pygmies and Bushmen of the Kalahari.* London: Seeley Service, 1925.

Ebert, J. I. et al. *Report and Recommendations for Land Allocations and Basarwa Development in the Sandveld Region of the Central District, Botswana.* Gaborone: Ministry of Local Government and Lands/District Council Serowe Report, 1976.

Gordon, R. J. *The Bushman Myth: The Making of a Namibian Underclass.* Boulder, Colo.: Westview Press, 1992.

———. "The !Kung in the Kalahari Exchange: An Ethno–Historical Perspective." In *Past and Present in Hunter–Gatherer Studies.* Edited by C. Schrire, 195–224. New York: Academic Press, 1984.

Guenther, M. G. *Farm Bushmen: Socio–Cultural Change and Incorporation of the San of the Ghanzi District, Republic of Botswana.* Gaborone: Ministry of Local Government and Lands Report, 1974.

———. *The Farm Bushmen of the Ghanzi District, Botswana.* Stuttgart: Honschul-Verlag, 1979.

Harpending, H. and L. Wandsnider. "Population Structures of Ghanzi and Ngamiland !Kung." In *Current Developments in Anthropological Genetics.* Vol. 2, *Ecology and Population Structure.* Edited by M. H. Crawford and J. H. Mielke, 29–50. New York: Plenum Press, 1982.

Heinz, H. J. "The Nexus Complex among the !Xo Bushmen of Botswana." *Anthropos* 74 (1979): 465–480.

Hitchcock, R. K. "Foragers on the Move: San Survival Strategies in Botswana Parks and Reserves." *Cultural Survival Quarterly* 9 (1985): 31–36.

———. The Ethnoarchaeology of Sedentism: Mobility Strategies and Site Structure among Foraging and Food producing Populations in the Eastern Kalahari Desert, Botswana." Ph.D. diss., University of New Mexico, 1982.

* ———. *Kalahari Cattle Posts: A Regional Study of Hunter-Gatherers, Pastoralists, and Agriculturists in the Western Sandveld Region.* Gaborone: Government Printer, 1978.

Hitchcock, R. K., J. I. Ebert and M. C. Ebert. *Preliminary Anthropological, Archaeological, and Ecological Investigations in the Central District of Botswana, September–December 1975.* Gaborone: Ministry of Local Government and Lands, 1975.

Howell, N. *Demography of the Dobe !Kung San.* New York: Academic Press, 1979.

Jenkins, T. et al. "Sero–Genetic Studies on the G/wi and G//ana of Botswana." *Human Heredity* 25 (1975): 318–328.

League of Nations. *Report on the Masarwa in the Bamangwato Reserve, Bechuanaland Protectorate.* Prepared by J. W. Joyce, VI. B. Slavery. 1938. C 112M. 98. 1938 VI, Annex 6, 57–76.

* Lee, R. B. *The !Kung San: Men, Women, and Work in a Foraging Society.* Cambridge: Cambridge University Press, 1979.

* Lee, R. B. and I. DeVore, ed. *Kalahari Hunter–Gatherers: Studies of the !Kung San and Their Neighbors.* Cambridge: Harvard University Press, 1976.

London Missionary Society. *The Masarwa (Bushmen): Report of an Inquiry by the South Africa District Committee.* Alice, South Africa: Lovedale Press, 1935.

Marshall, L. *The !Kung of Nyae Nyae.* Cambridge: Harvard University Press, 1976.

Parsons, Q. N. "Frantz of Klikko, the Wild Dancing Bushman: A Case Study in Khoisan Stereotyping." *Botswana Notes and Records* 20 (1988): 71–76.

Passarge, S. *Die Buschmänner der Kalahari.* Berlin: Dieter Reimer, 1907.

Rudner, I. "A Note on the Beliefs of Modern Bushmen Concerning Tsodilo Hills." *Southwest African Scientific Society Newsletter* 3/4 (June/July 1974).

Russell, M. "Slaves or Workers? Relations between Bushmen, Tswana, and Boers in the Kalahari," *Journal of Southern African Studies* 2, 2 (1976): 178–197.

Sanders, A. J. G. M. "The Bushmen of Botswana—From Desert Dwellers to World Citizens." *Africa Insight* 19, no. 3 (1989): 174–182.

———. "The Bushmen of Botswana—From Desert Dwellers to World Citizens." *Law and Anthropology* 4 (1989): 107–122.

Schapera, I. *The Khoisan Peoples of South Africa: Bushmen and Hottentots.* London: Routledge and Kegan Paul, 1930.

Schrire, C. "An Inquiry into the Evolutionary Status and Apparent Identity of San Hunter–Gatherers." *Human Ecology* 8, no. 1 (1980): 9–31.

Silberbauer, G. *Bushman Survey Report.* Gaborones: Bechuanaland Government, 1965.

———. *Hunter and Habitat in the Central Kalahari.* Cambridge: Cambridge University Press, 1981.

Silberbauer, G., and A. Kuper, "Kgalagari Masters and Bushman Serfs: Some Observations." *African Studies* 25, no. 4 (1966): 171–179.

Steyn, H. P. "Aspects of the Economic Life of Some Nharo Bushman Groups." *Annals of the South African Musuem* 56, no. 6 (1971): 275–322.

Tagart, E. S. B. "Report on the Conditions Existing among the Masarwa in the Bamangwato Reserve of the Bechuanaland Protectorate." *Official Gazette of the High Commissioner for South Africa*, 122, no. 1662 (May 12, 1933).

Tanaka, J. *The San, Hunter–Gatherers of the Kalahari: A Study in Ecological Anthropology*. Translated by D. W. Hughes. Tokyo: University of Tokyo Press, 1980.

Thomas, E. M. *The Harmless People*. New York: A. Knopf, 1958.

Tobias, P. V. "Bushman Hunter–Gatherers: A Study in Human Ecology." In *Ecological Studies in Southern Africa*. Edited by D. G. S. Davis, 67–68. Den Haag: Uitgevenig Dr. W. Junk, 1964.

———. "On the Increasing Stature of the Bushmen." *Anthropos* 57 (1962): 801–810.

van der Walt, L. A. et al. "Endocrine Studies on the San (Bushmen) of Botswana." *South African Medical Journal* 52 (1977): 23–32.

Vierich, H. I. D. *Interim Report on Basarwa and Related Poor Ba–Kgalagadi in Kweneng District*. Gaborone: Ministry of Local Government and Lands Report, 1977.

———. "The Kua of Southeastern Kalahari: A Study in the Socio–Ecology of Dependency." Ph.D. diss., University of Toronto, 1981.

Weissner, P. "Risk, Reciprocity, and Social Influences on !Kung San Economics." In *Politics and History in Band Societies*. Edited by E. Leacock and R. Lee, 61–84. Cambridge: Cambridge University Press, 1982.

Wilmsen, E. N. "The Real Bushman is the Male One: Labour and Power in the Creation of Basarwa Ethnicity." *Botswana Notes and Records* 22 (1990): 21–36.

———. "Seasonal Effects of Dietary Intake on Kalahari San." *Federation of American Societies for Experimental Biology Proceedings* 37 (1978): 65–72.

* ———. *Summary Report on Research on Basarwa in Western Ngamiland*. Gaborone: Ministry of Local Government and Lands Report, 1976.

Wily, E. "A Strategy of Self-Determination for the Kalahari San (The Botswana Government's Programme of Action in the Ghanzi Farms)." *Development and Change* 13 (1982): 291–308.

Woolard, J. "The Active Chemical Components of the Basarwa Arrow-Poison." *Botswana Notes and Records* 18 (1986): 139–141.

Yellen, J. E. and H. Harpending. "Hunter–Gatherer Populations and Archaeological Inference." *World Archaeology* 4 (1972): 244–253.

b. Other Studies

Allen, S. A. "Maps of Traditional Tribal Sub–Divisions among the Balete of Ramotswa." *Botswana Notes and Records* 12 (1980): 119–135.

* Alverson, H. *Mind in the Heart of Darkness: Value and Self-Identity among the Tswana of Southern Africa.* New Haven: Yale University Press, 1978.

Alverson, M. *Under African Sun.* Chicago: University of Chicago Press, 1987.

Ashton, E. H. "Notes on the Political and Judicial Organization of the Tawana." *Bantu Studies* 11 (1937): 67–83.

Breutz, P. -L. *The Tribes of the Mafeking District.* Pretoria: Department of Native Affairs, 1956.

———. *The Tribes of the Marico District.* Pretoria: Department of Native Affairs, 1953.

———. *The Tribes of Rustenburg and Pilansberg Districts.* Pretoria: Department of Native Affairs, 1953.

Brown, C. "Kgatleng Burial Societies." *Botswana Notes and Records* 14 (1982): 80–83.

Campbell, A. C. "Bangwaketse Marriage and Dissolution of Marriage." *Comparative and International Law Journal of Southern Africa* 1 (1970): 212–214.

Comaroff, J. *Body of Power, Spirit of Resistance.* Chicago: University of Chicago Press, 1985.

———. "Chiefship in a South African Homeland: A Case Study of the Tshidi Chiefdom of Bophuthatswana." *Journal of Southern African Studies* 1 (1974): 36–51.

———. "Competition for Office and Political Process among the Barolong Boo Ratshidi of South African, Botswana Borderland." Ph.D. diss. University of London, 1974.

———. "Rules and Rulers: Political Processes in a Tswana Chiefdom." *Man,* n.s., 13 (1978): 1–20.

———. *The Structure of Agricultural Transformation in Barolong.* Gaborone: Government Printer, 1977.

Fortman, L. "Seasonal Dimensions of Rural Social Organization." *Journal of Development Studies* 21 (April 1985): 377–389.

Gibson, G. D. "Double Descent and its Correlates among the Herero of Ngamiland." *American Anthropologist* 58 (1956): 109–139.

———. "Herero Marriage." *Rhodes–Livingstone Journal* 24 (1958): 1–37.

Grant, S. "The Revival of Bogwera in the Kgatleng—Tswana Culture or Rampant Tribalism? A Description of the 1982 Bogwera." *Botswana Notes and Records* 16 (1984): 7–17.

Gulbrandsen, O. *Privilege and Responsibility: On Transformations of Hierarchical Relations in a Tswana Society.* University of Bergen, Department of Social Anthropology, 1987.

* Head, Bessie. *Serowe: Village of the Rain Wind.* London: Heinemann, 1981.

Jennings, A. E. *Bogadi: A Study of the Marriage Laws and Customs of the Bechuana Tribes of South Africa.* Tiger Kloof: London Missionary Society, 1933.

Kerven, C. "Underdevelopment, Migration and Class Formation in the N.E. District of Botswana." Ph.D. diss. University of Toronto, 1977.

Kjaer-Olsen, P. *Sociology of Rural Enterprises.* Gaborone: Economic Consultancies (Pty) Limited, 1980.

Koofiman, K. F. M. *Social and Economic Change in a Tswana Village.* Leiden: Afrika-Studiecentrum, 1978.

* Kuper, A. *Kalahari Village Politics: An African Democracy.* Cambridge: Cambridge University Press, 1970.

———. "Preferential Marriage and Polygyny among the Tswana," In *Studies in African Social Anthropology: Essays Presented to Isaac Schapera.* Edited by M. Fortes and S. Patterson. London: Academic Press, 1975.

———. "The Social Structure of the Sotho-Speaking Peoples of Southern Africa." *Africa* 45, nos. 1 & 2 (1975): 67–81, 139–149.

Larson, T. J. "The Bayeyi of Ngamiland." *Botswana Notes and Records* 21 (1989): 23–42.

———. *The BaYeyi of Ngamiland.* Gaborone: The Botswana Society, 1994.

———. "Death Beliefs and Burial Customs of the Hambukushu of Ngamiland." *Botswana Notes and Records* 17 (1985): 33–36.

———. "The Hambukushu of Okavangoland." Ph.D., diss., University of Port Elizabeth, 1966.

———. "Kinship Terminology of the Hambukushu of Ngamiland." *Botswana Notes and Records* 9 (1977): 85–89.

———. "The Political Structure of the Ngamiland Mbukushu under the Rule of the Tawana." *Anthropos* 60 (1965): 164–176.

Matthews, Z. K. "Marriage Customs among the Barolong." *Africa* 13 (1940): 1–24.

Morton, B. "Larson's Book Lacks Full Information on Bayeyi." *Mmegi/The Reporter* 10, no. 10 (1993): 17.

Odell, M. J. *Sociological Research and Rural Development Policy.* Gaborone: Rural Sociology Unit Report 19, 1980.

Passarge, S. "Das Okawangosumpfland und seine Bewohner." *Zeitschrift zur Ethnologie* 37 (1905): 649–716.

* Russell, M., and M. R. Russell. *Afrikaners of the Kalahari: White Minority in a Black State.* Cambridge: Cambridge University Press, 1979.

Sandilands, A. "A Sengwato Wedding." *Tiger Kloof Magazine* 23 (1939): 16–29.

———. *Sexual Morality, British and Bechuana.* Vryburg: London Missionary Society, 1953.

Schapera, I. "Agnatic Marriage in Tswana Royal Families." In *Studies in Kinship and Marriage.* Edited by I. Schapera, 103–113. London: 1963.

———. "The Aspirations of Native School Children." *The Critic* 2 (1933/34): 152–162.

———. "The BaKxatla BaxaKxafela. Preliminary Report of Field Investigations." *Africa* 6, no. 4 (1933): 402–414.

———. *The Bantu-Speaking Tribes of South Africa: An Ethnographic Survey.* London: Routledge, 1937.

————. *Bogwera: Kgatla Initiation*. Mochudi: Phuthadikobo Museum, 1978.

————. "The Contributions of Western Civilization to Modern Kxatla Culture." *Transactions of the Royal Society of South Africa* 24 (1936): 221–251.

* ————. *The Ethnic Composition of Tswana Tribes*. London: London School of Economics, 1952.

————. "Ethnographical Texts in the Boloongwe Dialect of SeKgalagadi." *Bantu Studies* 12 (1938): 157–187.

————. *Government and Politics in Tribal Societies*. London: Watts, 1956.

————. "Herding Rites of the Bechuanaland BaKxatla." *American Anthropologist* 37 (1934): 561–584.

* ————. "Kinship and Marriage among the Tswana." In *African Systems of Kinship and Marriage*. Edited by A. R. Radcliffe-Brown and C. D. Forde, 140–165. London: International African Institute, 1950.

————. "The 'Little Rain' (Pulanyana) Ceremony of the Bechuanaland BaKxatla." *Bantu Studies* 4 (1930): 211–216.

————. "Marriage of Near Kin Among the Tswana." *Africa* 27, no. 2 (1957): 139–159.

————. *Mekgwa le Melao ya BaTswana*. Alice, South Africa: Lovedale Press, 1938.

————. "The Native as Letter-writer." *The Critic* 2 (1933): 20–18.

————. "Notes on Some Herero Genealogies." Cape Town: University of Cape Town School of African Studies Communications, 1945.

————. "Oral Sorcery among the Natives of Bechuanaland." In *Essays Presented to C. G. Seligman*. Edited by E. E. Evans-Pritchard et al, 293–305. London: Routledge, 1934.

* ————. "The Political Organization of the Ngwato in Bechuanaland Protectorate." In *African Political Systems*. Edited by F. Fortes and E. E. Evans-Pritchard, 36–82. London: International Institute of African Languages and Cultures, 1940.

————. "Present-day Life in the Native Reserves." In *Western Civilization and the Natives of South Africa*. Edited by I. Schapera, 39–62. London: Routledge, 1934.

* ————. *Rainmaking Rites of Tswana Tribes*. Leiden: Afrika-Studiecentrum, 1971.

————. "The Social Structure of the Tswana Ward." *Bantu Studies* 9 (1935): 203–224.

————. "Some Ethnographical Texts in SeKgatla." *Bantu Studies* 4 (1930): 73–93.

* ————. *The Tswana*. Ethnographic Survey of Africa, Southern Africa Part III. London: International African Institute, 1953. New Edition 1976.

————. "The Tswana Concept of Incest." In *Social Structure: Essays Presented to A. R. Radcliffe-Brown*. Edited by M. Fortes, 104–120. Oxford: Clarendon Press, 1949.

Schapera, I., and S. Roberts. "Rampedi Revisited: Another Look at a Kgatla Ward." *Africa* 45, no. 3 (1975), 258–279.

Schapera, I., and D. F. van der Merwe. *Notes on the Tribal Groupings, History, and Customs of the Bakgalagadi.* Cape Town: University of Cape Town School of African Studies Communications 13, 1945.

Sebina, A. M. "Makalaka." *African Studies* 6, no. 2 (June 1947): 82–96.

Solway, J. "Affines and Spouses, Friends and Lovers: The Passing of Polygyny in Botswana." *Journal of Anthropological Research.* 46 (1990): 41–66.

———. *Report on Dutlwe Village, Kweneng District.* Gaborone: Rural Sociology Unit Report 14, 1979.

———. *Socio-economic Effects of the Commercialization of the Cattle Industry in Western Kweneng.* Gaborone: Ministry of Agriculture Rural Sociology Unit Report, 1979.

van Tonder, L. L. *The Hambukushu of Okavangoland.* Port Elizabeth, South Africa: P.E. Bookbinders and Rulers, 1966.

Vivelo, F. R. *The Herero of Western Botswana.* St. Paul, Minnesota: West Publishing, 1977.

Wande, O. *Socio-economic Survey of the Barolong Farms.* Cape Town: University of Cape Town School of African Studies Communications, 1949.

Werbner, R. "Land, Movement and Status among Kalanga of Botswana." In *Essays in African Social Anthropology.* Edited by M. Fortes and S. Patterson, 95–120. London: Academic Press, 1975.

———. *Ritual Passage, Sacred Journey.* Washington, D.C.: Smithsonian Institution Press, 1989.

———. *Tears of the Dead: The Social Biography of an African Family.* Washington, D.C.: Smithsonian Institution Press, 1991.

Willoughby, W. C. "Notes on the Initiation Ceremonies of the Becwana." *Journal of the Royal Anthropological Institute* 39 (1909): 228–245.

———. *Race Problems in the New Africa.* Oxford: Clarendon Press, 1923.

Wilmsen, E. N., and R. Vossen. "Labour, Language and Power in the Construction of Ethnicity in Botswana." *Critique of Anthropology* 10, no. 1 (1990): 7–37.

2. Art, Music, and Crafts

Alnaes, K. "Living With the Past: The Songs of the Herero in Botswana." *Africa* 59, no. 3 (1989): 267–299.

Biesele, M. "Kalahari San Thumb Piano Music." *Botswana Notes and Records* 7 (1975): 171–188.

Botswana Live 1993—Exhibition of Art and Craftwork. Gaborone: The Botswana Society, 1993.

Brearley, J. "A Musical Tour of Botswana." *Botswana Notes and Records* 16 (1984): 45–57.

Byram, M. L. and R. Kidd. "The Performing Arts: Culture as a Tool for Development in Botswana." *Botswana Notes and Records* 10 (1978): 81–90.

Ebert, M. "Patterns of Manufacture and Use of Baskets among the Basarwa of the Nata River Region." *Botswana Notes and Records* 9 (1977): 69–83.

England, N. "Music among the Zu/'wa-si of South West Africa and Botswana." Ph.D. diss., Harvard University Department of Music, 1968.

Grant, S. and E. Grant. *Decorated Homes in Botswana.* Mochudi: Phuthadikobo Museum, 1995.

Johnston, T. F. "Aspects of Tswana Music." *Anthropos* 68 (1973): 889–896.

Kidd, R., and M. Byram. "Performing Arts and Community Education in Botswana." *Community Development* 49 (June 1978): 415–427.

Lambrecht, D. "Basketry in Ngamiland." *Botswana Notes and Records* 8 (1976): 179–187.

Larsson, A. "Traditional Tswana Housing." *Botswana Notes and Records* 17 (1985): 37–45.

Lewycky, D. *Tapestry: Report from Oodi Weavers.* Gaborone: National Institute for Research, 1977.

Nteta, D. "Decoration on Ostrich Eggshells." *Botswana Notes and Records* 7 (1975): 17–18.

Terry, E. "The Anatomy of an Ngamiland Basket." *Botswana Notes and Records* 18 (1986): 49–54.

Tracey, H. "Recording Tour of the Tswana Tribe, October–November 1959." *African Music* 2, no. 2 (1959): 62–68.

Wood, E. N. "Observing and Recording Village Music of the Kweneng." *Botswana Notes and Records* 12 (1980): 101–117.

———. "A Study of the Traditional Music of Mochudi." *Botswana Notes and Records* 8 (1976): 189–221.

———. "A Supplement to 'A Study of the Traditional Music of Mochudi.' " *Botswana Notes and Records* 10 (1978): 67–79.

Yoffe, M. L. "Botswana Basketry." *African Arts* 12, no. 1 (1978): 42–47.

3. Communications, Press, and Publications

Kgosidintsi, T., and N. Parsons. "Publishing in Botswana." *African Book Publishing Record* 15, no. 3 (1989): 171–172.

*Zaffiro, J. J. *From Police Network to the Station of the Nation: A Political History of Broadcasting in Botswana, 1927–1990.* Gaborone: The Botswana Society, 1992.

———. "From Revolutionary to Regime Radio: Three Decades of Nationalist Broadcasting in Southern Africa." *Africa Media Review* 8, no. 1 (1994): 1–24.

———. "Mass Media, Politics, and Society in Botswana: The 1990's and Beyond." *Africa Today* 40, no. 1 (1993): 7–25.

———. "Media Policy Development in Botswana: Patterns of Change and Continuity." *Ecquid Novi* 13, no. 2 (1993): 125–141.

———. "Regional Pressure and Erosion in Media Freedom in an African Democracy: The Case of Botswana." *Journal of Communication* 33, no. 3 (1988): 108–120.

Current popular periodicals and newspapers from Botswana include those published by
Botswana Daily News (weekdays), Botswana Government, Department of Information and Broadcasting, Private Bag 0060, Gaborone.
Botswana Guardian (weekly), Pula Printing and Publishing, Box 1641, Gaborone.
The Gazette (weekly), The Gazette, Box 1605, Gaborone.
Kutlwano (monthly), Botswana Government, Department of Information and Broadcasting, Private Bag 0060, Gaborone.
Marung (monthly), Air Botswana, Box 92, Gaborone.
Mmegi wa Dikgang (The Reporter) (weekly), Mmegi wa Dikgang, Private Bag BR50, Gaborone.
Motswana Woman (monthly), Gaborone.
Okavango Observer (weekly), Camp Fire Ventures, Box 448, Maun.
Phikwe Bugle (weekly), Private Bag 70, Selebi Phikwe.
Phuo Phaa (monthly), Botswana National Front, Private Bag B045, Gaborone.
The Sun (weekly), Pula Printing and Publishing, Box 1641, Gaborone.
The Voice (weekly), Francistown.

4. Dictionaries, Language, and Linguistics

Brown, J. T., comp. *Setswana Dictionary*. 3rd ed. Gaborone: Pula Press. Reprint, 1982.
Chebane, A. et al. Ngatikwaleni Ikalanga: A Manual for Writing Kalanga as Spoken in Botswana. Gaborone: The Botswana Society, 1995.
Cole, D. T. "Fredoux's Sketch of Tswana Grammar." *African Studies* 30, nos. 3–4 (1968): 191–211.
———. *An Introduction to Tswana Grammar*. 2nd ed. Cape Town: Longman, 1975.
———. "Notes on the Phonological Relationships of Tswana Vowels." *African Studies* 8 (1949): 109–131.
Cole, D. T. and D. M. Mokaila. *A Course in Tswana*. Johannesburg: Cole and Mokaila, 1962.
Crisp, W. *Notes on a Secoana Grammar*. 4th ed. London: Society for the Propagation of Christian Knowledge, 1905.
Dickens, P. "A Preliminary Report on Kgalagadi Vowels." *African Studies* 37, no. 1 (1978): 99–106.
Dornan, S. S. "The Masarwas and Their Language." *South African Journal of Science* 8 (1911): 218–225.
Dornan, S. W. "The Tati Busmen (Masarwas) and Their Language." *Journal of the Royal Anthropological Institute* 47 (1917): 37–112.
First Steps in Spoken Setswana. Rev. ed. Gaborone: Botswana Training Center, 1978.
Fisch, M. *Einführung in die Sprache der Mbukushu Ost-Kavango, Namibia*. Windhoek: S.W.A. Wissenschaftlichen Gesellschaft, 1977.
Janson, T., and J. Tsonope. *Birth of a National Language: The History of Setswana*. Gaborone: Heinemann Botswana and the National Institute of Development, Research and Documentation, 1991.

Jones, D. *The Tones of Sechuana Nouns*. London: International Institute of African Languages and Cultures, 1928.

Kgasa, M. *Thuto ke eng*. Alice, South Africa: Lovedale Press, 1939.

Kgasa, M. L. A. "The Development of Setswana." *Botswana Notes and Records* 4 (1972): 108–109.

Kohler, O. "Observations on the Central Khoisan Language Group." *Journal of African Languages* 2 (1963): 227–234.

Lestrade, G. P. "A Practical Orthography for Tswana." *Bantu Studies* 11 (1937): 137–148.

———. *Some Kgatla Animal Stories (with English Translations and Notes)*. Cape Town: University of Cape Town School of African Studies Communication N.S. 11, 1944.

Matumo, Z. *Setswana English Setswana Dictionary*. 4th ed. Gaborone: Macmillan Botswana and Botswana Book Centre, 1993.

Merriweather, A. *English-Setswana Phrasebook and Dictionary*. Gaborone: Pula Press, 1965.

Mothibatsela, N. "The Demonstrative: A Comparative Survey." *Botswana Notes and Records* 16 (1984): 37–43.

Raditladi, L. D. *Motswasele II*. Johannesburg: University of the Witwatersrand Press, 1945.

Sandilands, A. "The Ancestor of Tswana Grammars." *African Studies* 17, no. 4 (1958): 192–197.

———. *Introduction to Tswana*. Tiger Kloof: London Missionary Society, 1953.

Seaborn, B. N. *Bua Setswana: A Ten-Week Introduction to Speaking Setswana*. Gaborone: Botswana Orientation Centre, n.d.

Snyman, J. W. "Occlusivation and Fortisatian in Tsware." *Limi* 2, no. 1 (1974): 67–76.

South African Government, Department of Bantu Education. *Tswana: Terminology and Orthography*. Pretoria: Government Printers, 1962.

Tucker, A. N. *The Comparative Phonetics of the Suto-Chuana Group of Bantu Languages*. London: Longman, 1929.

van der Merwe, D. F., and I. Schapera. *A Comparative Study of Kgalagadi, Kwena, and other Sotho Dialects*. Cape Town: University of Cape Town School of African Studies Communications N. S. 9, 1943.

Vossen, R. "Khoe Linguistic Relationships Reconsidered." *Botswana Notes and Records* 20 (1988): 61–70.

———. "Studying the Linguistic and Ethno-History of the Khoe-speaking (Central Khoisan) Peoples of Botswana." *Botswana Notes and Records* 16 (1984): 19–35.

Westphal, E. O. J. "The Click Languages of Southern and Eastern Africa." In *Current Trends in Linguistics*. Edited by J. Berry and J. H. Greenberg, 367–420. Vol. 7 of *Linguistics in Sub-Saharan Africa*. The Hague: Mouton, 1971.

———. "The Linguistic Prehistory of Southern Africa: Bush, Kwadi, Hottentot, and Bantu Linguistics." *Africa* 33 (1963): 237–265.

———. "On Classifying Bushmen and Hottentot Languages." *African Language Studies* 3 (1962): 30–48.

――――. "The Reclassification of Southern African Non-Bantu Languages." *Journal of African Languages* 1 (1962): 1–8.

Wookey, A. J. *Secwana Grammar*. 2nd ed. Revised by J. T. Brown. Tiger Kloof: London Missionary Society, 1922.

5. Literature and Folklore

Campbell, A. C. "100 Tswana Proverbs." *Botswana Notes and Records* 4 (1972): 121–132.

Hahn, C. H. "Traditions of the Bayaye." *Folk-Lore Journal* 2, no. 2 (March 1880): 34–37.

Head, B. *A Bewitched Crossroad: An African Saga*. Craighall, South Africa: AD Donker, 1984.

――――. *The Collector of Treasures*. Portsmouth: Heinemann, 1977.

――――. *A Gesture of Belonging: Letters from Bessie Head, 1965–1979*. Edited by Randolph Vigne. Portsmouth: Heinemann, 1991.

* ――――. *Maru*. Portsmouth: Heinemann, 1972.

――――. *A Question of Power: A Novel*. Portsmouth: Heinemann, 1974.

――――. *Tales of Tenderness and Power*. Portsmouth: Heinemann, 1990.

* ――――. *When Rain Clouds Gather: A Novel*. Portsmouth: Heinemann, 1969.

――――. *A Woman Alone: Autobiographical Writings*. Portsmouth: Heinemann, 1990

Larson,T. J. *Bayeyi And Hambukushu Tales From the Okavango*. Gaborone: The Botswana Society, 1994.

Lestrade, G. P. *Some Kgatla Animal Stories (with English Translations and Notes)*. Cape Town: University of Cape Town School of African Studies Communication N.S. 11, 1944.

Meeuwsen, J. P. "Customs and Superstititons among the Betshuana." *Folk-Lore Journal* 1 (1879): 33–34.

Mitchison, N. *Mucking Around*. London: Victor Gollancz, 1981.

――――. *Return to the Fairy Hill*. London: Heinemann, 1966.

Moloto, D. P. *Mokwena*, Bloemfontein, South Africa: Nasionale Pers, 1948.

Pilane, A. K., and N. Mitchison. "Riddles of the Bakgatla." *Botswana Notes and Records* 6 (1974): 29–35.

Plaatje, S. T. *Dintshontsho tsa bo-Juliuse Kesara*. Edited and revised by G. P. Lestrade. Johannesburg: University of the Witwatersrand Press, 1937.

――――. *Diposho-phoso*. Morija, Lesotho: Printing Works, 1930.

――――. *Sechuana Proverbs with Literal Translations and Their European Equivalents*. London: Kegan Paul, 1916.

* Rush, N. *Mating*. New York: A. Knopf, 1991.

――――. *Whites*. New York: A. Knopf, 1986.

Schapera, I. "Kxatla Riddles and Their Significance." *Bantu Studies* 6 (1932): 215–231.

* ――――. *Praise Poems of Tswana Chiefs*. Oxford: Clarendon Press, 1965.

Seboni, B. *Thinking Allowed*. Gaborone: Morula Publishers, 1992.

Seboni, M. O. M. *Diane le Maele a Setswana*. Alice, South Africa: Lovedale Press, 1962.

———. *Kgosi Isang Pilane*. Johannesburg: The Bantu Publishing House, 1961.

———. *Kgosi Sebele II*. Pretoria: J.L. van Schaik, 1956.

———. *Rammone wa Kgalagadi*. Bloemfontein, South Africa: Nasionale Pers, 1947.

Swanepoel, S.A. "Imagery in the Praisepoem 'Motswasele I': A Structural and Functional Analysis." *South African Journal of African Languages* 1 (1984): 100–110.

van der Merwe, D. F. "Hurutshe Poems." *Bantu Studies* 15 (1941): 307–337.

Wookey, A. J. *Dinwao leha e le dipolelo kaga dico tsa Secwana*. 3rd ed. Tiger Kloof: London Missionary Society, 1929.

6. Demography, Migration, Populations, Settlement, Urbanization

Bell, M. "Rural-Urban Movement among Botswana's Skilled Manpower." *Botswana Notes and Records* 12 (1980): 175–176.

Best, A. G. "Gaborone: Problems and Prospects of a New Capital." *The Geographical Review* 60, no. 1 (January1970): 1–14.

Bryant, C., B. Stephens, and S. Macliver. "Rural-Urban Migration: Some Data from Botswana." *African Studies Review* 21, no. 2 (1978): 85–109.

Corlett, J. T., and M. M. Mokgwathi. "Sport in Botswana." In *Sport in Asia and Africa: A Comparative Handbook*. Edited by E. A. Wagner, 215–228. Westport, Conn.: Greenwood, 1989.

Izzard, W. "Migrants and Mothers: Case Studies from Botswana." *Journal of Southern African Studies* 11, no. 2 (April 1985): 258–280.

* Kerven, C. *National Migration Study: Guide to Research in the Social Sciences in Botswana—1970s*. Gaborone: Central Statistics Office, 1979.

Kocken, E., and G. Ehlenbeck. *Tlokweng—A Village near Town*. Leiden: Afrika Studiecentrum, 1980.

Kuczynski, R. R. *A Demographic Survey of the British Colonial Empire. Vol. II: South African High Commission Territories*. London: Oxford University Press, 1949.

Larsson, A. "Traditional Versus Modern Housing in Botswana—An Analysis From the User's Perspective." In *Dwellings, Settlements and Tradition: Cross-Cultural Perspectives*. Edited by J.-P. Bourdier, N. Alsayyad, 503–525. Lanham, Md.: University Press of America, 1989.

Larsson, A. and V. Larsson. *Traditional Tswana Housing: A Study of Four Villages in Eastern Botswana*. Stockholm: Swedish Council for Building Research, 1984.

Miller, H. M. and J. D. Traver. "The Future Population of Botswana." *Eastern Africa Economic Review*, n. s., 7, no. 1 (1991): 85–91.

Morton, B. "Pre-1904 Population Estimates of the Tswana." *Botswana Notes and Records* 25 (1993): 89–100.

Motshologave, S. R. "Influence of Urbanization on the Role and Status of Husband and Wife in the Tswana Family." *South African Journal of Sociology* 17 (1978): 83–90.

Norstrand, J. *Old Naledi: The Village Becomes a Town.* Toronto: Lorimer, 1982.

Nurse, G. T. "Population Movement around the Northern Kalahari." *African Studies* 42, no. 2 (1983): 153–163.

Pennington, R., and H. Harpending. "How Many Refugees Were There? History and Population Change Among the Herero and Mbanderu of Northwestern Botswana." *Botswana Notes and Records* 23 (1991): 209–224.

Silitshena, R. M. K. "Chiefly Authority and the Organization of Space in Botswana: Towards an Explanation of Nucleated Settlements among the Tswana." *Botswana Notes and Records* 11 (1979): 55–67.

* ———. *Inter-rural Migration and Settlement Changes in Botswana.* Leiden: Afrika Studiecentrum, 1983.

———. "Notes on Some Characteristics of Population that Has Migrated Permanently to the Lands in the Kweneng District." *Botswana Notes and Records* 10 (1978): 149–157.

———. "Village-Level Institutions and Popular Participation in Botswana." *Review of Rural and Urban Planning in Southern and Eastern Africa* 1 (1989): 43–62.

Stephens, B. "Urban Migration in Botswana: Gaborone, December, 1975." *Botswana Notes and Records* 9 (1977): 91–100.

Traver, J. D., and H. M. Miller. "Rural-Urban Migration in a Developing Country Botswana, Africa." *African Quarterly* 24, no. 1/2 : 22–23.

Vander Post, C. "Fertility in Botswana: A District Perspective." *Botswana Notes and Records* 22 (1990): 99–104.

———. "The 1991 Census and Botswana's Population Problem." *Botswana Notes and Records* 24 (1992): 39–48.

7. Education

Bermingham, J. "Perspectives on Colonial Education in Botswana." In *Independence without Freedom: The Political Economy of Colonial Education in Southern Africa.* Edited by A.T. Mugomba and N. Nyaggah, 176–178. Santa Barbara, California.: ABC Clio Press, 1981.

Brothers, S. C. "The Development of Botswana's National Library Service." *Botswana Notes and Records* 23 (1991): 69–82.

Brown, B. "Girls' Achievement in School in Botswana." *Botswana Notes and Records* 12 (1980): 35–41.

Chernichovsky, D. "Socioeconomic and Demographic Aspects of School Enrollment and Attendance in Rural Botswana." *Economic Development and Cultural Change* 33 (January 1985): 319–322.

Clegg, A., and W. Duncan. "Girls and Science in Botswana." *Botswana Notes and Records* 17 (1985): 111–115.

Clegg, A., and M. J. Kahn, ed. *Science Education in Botswana*. Gaborone: Botswana Science Association, 1980.

* Crowder, M., ed. *Education for Development: Proceedings of a Symposium held by the Botswana Society at the National Museum and Art Gallery, Gaborone, 15–19 August, 1983*. Gaborone: Botswana Society/Macmillan Botswana, 1984.

Kann, U. "The Relationship between Socio-Economic Background and School Achievement in Botswana." Stockholm: University of Stockholm Institute of International Education Working Paper Series 2, 1978.

Kann, U., and D. C. Taylor. "Adult Literacy Rate in Botswana." *Botswana Notes and Records* 20 (1988): 135–142.

Lea, H. "Traditional Mathematics in Botswana." *Botswana Notes and Records* 20 (1988): 143–148.

Mgadla, P. T. *Missionaries and Western Education in the Bechuanaland Protectorate 1859–1904: The Case of the Bangwato*. Gaborone: Department of History and Department of Theology and Religious Studies, University of Botswana, 1989.

———. "Notes on the Foundation of the Moffat Institution and its Impact on the Bangwato 1872–1892." *Botswana Notes and Records* 25 (1993): 73–78.

Setidisho, N. O. H. et al. *Education for Kagisano: Report of the National Commission on Education*. 2 vols. Gaborone: Ministry of Education, 1977.

Thema, B. "Moeng College—A Product of 'Self-Help.' " *Botswana Notes and Records* 2 (1970): 71–74.

Thema, B. C. "The Church and Education in Botswana During the 19th Century." *Botswana Notes and Records* 1 (1969): 1–4.

Tlou, J. et al. "The Role of Primary Teacher Education in Botswana's National Development." *Rural Africana* 28–29 (1987): 83–93.

Ulin, R. O. "The Future of Setswana in the Schools." *Botswana Notes and Records* 7 (1975): 67–71.

Weeks, S. G. "Reforming the Reform: Education in Botswana." *Africa Today* 40, no. 1 (1993): 49–60.

Willoughby, W. C. *Tiger Kloof, the London Missionary Society's Native Institution in South Africa*. London: London Missionary Society, 1912.

8. Women

Bond, C. *Women's Involvement in Agriculture in Botswana*. Gaborone: Government Printer, 1974.

Brown, B. "Impact of Male Labor Migration on Women in Botswana." *African Affairs* 82 (July 1983): 367–388.

———. *Women's Role in Development in the Kgatleng District in Botswana*. Gaborone: Ministry of Agriculture, 1978.

Fortman, L. "Economic Status and Women's Participation in Agriculture: A Botswana Case Study." *Rural Sociology* 49 (Fall 1984): 452–464.

Griffiths, A. "Support for Women With Dependent Children Under the Customary System: The BaKwena and the Roman-Dutch Common and Statutory Law of Botswana." *Journal of Legal Pluralism* 22 (1984): 1–15.

Izzard, W. "Migrants and Mothers: Case-studies From Botswana." *Journal of Southern African Studies* 11, no. 22 (1985): 257–285.

——. "Rural-Urban Migration in a Developing Country: The Case of Women Migrants in Botswana." Ph.D. diss., Oxford University, 1982.

* Kerven, C. "Academics, Practitioners and All Kinds of Women in Development: A Reply to Peters." *Journal of Southern African Studies* 10, no. 2 (April 1984): 259–268.

Kossoudji, S., and E. Mueller. "Economic and Demographic Status of Female-Headed Households in Rural Botswana." *Economic Development and Cultural Change* 31 (July 1983): 831–859.

* Peters, P. "Gender, Developmental Cycles and Historical Process: A Critique of Recent Research on Women in Botswana." *Journal of Southern African Studies* 10, no.1 (October 1983): 100–122.

* ——. "Women in Botswana." *Journal of Southern African Studies* 11, no. 1 (October 1984): 150–153.

Pfotenhauer, L. "Interview With Unity Dow." *Botswana Notes and Records* 23 (1991): 101–106.

Procek, E., ed. *Changing Roles of Women in Botswana.* Gaborone: Botswana Society on behalf of Supa-Ngwao Museum Society, Francistown, 1993.

Rizika, J. "After the Decade." *Africa Report* 30 (September/October 1985): 75–81.

* Schapera, I. *Married Life in an African Tribe.* London: Faber, 1940.

Solway, J. S. "Affines and Spouses, Friends and Lovers: The Passing of Polygyny in Botswana." *Journal of Anthropological Research* 46, no. 1(1990): 41–66.

Syson, L. *Unmarried Mothers: A Report of Clinic and Hospital Patients in Selected Centers in Southern Botswana.* Gaborone: United Nations Development Programme Technical Note 1, 1972.

9. Religion

Amanze, J. N. *Botswana Handbook of Churches.* Gaborone: Pula Press, 1994.

Bruetz, P. -L. "Sotho-Tswana Celestial Concepts." In *Ethnological and Linguistic Studies in Honour of N. J. van Warmelo*, 199–210. Pretoria: Department of Bantu Administration Ethnological Publications no. 52, 1969.

Campbell, A. C. "Some Notes on Ngwaketse Divination." *Botswana Notes and Records* 1 (1968): 9–14.

Comaroff, J. "Barolong Cosmology: A Study of Religious Pluralism in a Tswana Town." Ph.D. diss., University of London, 1974.

Daneel, M. L. *Old and New in Southern Shona Churches.* 2 vols. The Hague: Mouton, 1971.

deJagar, E. J., and M. O. M Seboni. "Bone-divination amongst the Kwena of the Molepolole District, Bechuanaland Protectorate." *Afrika und Übersee* 48, no. 1 (1964): 2–16.

Feddema, J. P. "Tswana Ritual Concerning Rain." *African Studies* 25 (1966): 181–195.

Gulbrandsen, O. "Missionaries and Northern Tswana Rulers: Who Used Them?" *Journal of Religion in Africa* 23, no. 1 (1993): 44–83.

Landau, P. S. "Preacher, Chief, and Prophetess: Moruti Seakgano in the Ngwato Kingdom, East-Central Botswana." *Journal of Southern African Studies* 17, no. 1 (1991): 1–22.

Parratt, S. N. "Muslims in Botswana." *African Studies* 48, no. 1 (1989): 71–82.

Parsons, Q. N. "Independency and Ethiopianism among the Tswana in the late 19th and early 20th centuries." In *The Societies of Southern African in the Nineteenth and Twentieth Centuries. Volume One.* London: University of London Institute of Commonwealth Studies, 56–71, 1971.

Pauw, B. A. *Religion in a Tswana Chiefdom.* London: Oxford University Press, 1960.

Price, R. "The Ceremony of Dipheku." *Folk-Lore Journal* 1, no. 2 (March 1879): 35–36.

Proske, W. "The Political Significance of the Early Hermannsburg Mission in Botswana: An Assessment of its Role Among Batswana, the British and the Boers." *Botswana Notes and Records* 22 (1990): 43–50.

Richards, J. B. "The Mlimo Belief and Practice of Kalanga." *Native Affairs Department Annual* 19 (1942): 51–55.

Schapera, I. "Christianity and the Tswana." *Journal of the Royal Anthropological Institute* 83, no.1 (1958): 1–9.

———. "The Crime of Sorcery." *Proceedings of the Royal Anthropological Institute* (1969): 15–23.

* ———. *Rainmaking Rites in Tswana Tribes.* Leiden: Afrika Studiecentrum, 1971.

———. "Some Aspects of Kgatla Magic." In *Ethnological and Linguistic Studies in Honor of N.J. van Warmelo.* Pretoria: Department of Bantu Administration, Ethnological Publications no. 52, 1969.

———. "Sorcery and Witchcraft in Bechuanaland." *African Affairs* 51 (1952): 41–50.

Setiloane, G. M. *The Image of God Among the Sotho-Tswana.* Leiden: Balkema, 1975.

* Sundkler, B. *Bantu Prophets in South Africa.* London: Oxford University Press, 1970.

University of Botswana, Department of Theology and Religious Studies. Paper series on religion.

Werbner, R. P. "Atonement Ritual and Guardian Spirit Possession among Kalanga." *Africa* 34 (1964): 206–233.

* ———. "Continuity and Policy in Southern Africa's High God Cult." In *Regional Cults.* Edited by R. P. Werbner, 178–218. London: Academic Press, 1977.

————. "Sin, Blame and Ritual Mediation." In *The Allocation of Responsibility*. Edited by M. Gluckman, 226–255. Manchester: Manchester University Press, 1972.

————. "The Superabundance of Understanding: Kalanga Rhetoric and Domestic Divination." *American Anthropologist* 75 (1973): 1414–1440.

Willoughby, W. C. *Nature-worship and Taboo*. Hartford, Conn.: Hartford Seminary Press, 1932.

————. *The Soul of the Bantu*. London: Student Christian Movement, 1928.

B. Economics

1. General

* Colclough, C., and S. McCarthy. *The Political Economy of Botswana*. New York: Oxford University Press, 1980.

Great Britain. *An Economic Survey of the Colonial Territories, 1951. Volume I. The Central African and High Commission Territories*. London: H. M. S. O., 1952, 75–88.

————. *The Development of the Bechuanaland Economy: Report of the Ministry of Overseas Development Economic Survey*. Gaborone: Government Printer, 1965.

Hartland-Thunberg, P. *Botswana: An African Growth Economy*. Boulder, Colo.: Westview Press, 1978.

* Harvey, C., ed. *Papers on the Economy of Botswana*. London: Heinemann, 1981.

Hudson, D. J. "Booms and Busts in Botswana." *Botswana Notes and Records* 23 (1991): 47–68.

Isaksen, J. *Macro-economic Management and Bureaucracy: The Case of Botswana*. Uppsala, Sweden: Scandinavian Institute of African Studies, 1981.

Jackson, D. "Income Differentials and Unbalanced Planning—The Case of Botswana." *Journal of Modern African Studies* 8, no. 4 (1970): 553–562.

Mhozya, X. *The Specification and Estimation of a Macroeconomic Model for Botswana*. Addis Ababa: Organization for Social Science Research in Eastern Africa, 1991.

Murray, A., and N. Parsons. "The Modern Economic History of Botswana." In *Studies in the Economic History of Southern Africa*. Edited by Z. A. Konczacki et al., 159–199. London & Savage, Maryland: Cass, 1990.

* Oommen, M. A., F. K. Nganji, and L. D. Ngcongco, ed. *Botswana's Economy Since Independence*. New Delhi: Tata-McGraw Hill, 1983.

Saerbeck, R. *National Economic Parameters for Botswana*. Bradford, England: Development and Project Planning Centre, University of Bradford, 1989.

Schapera, I. "Economic Conditions in a Bechuanaland Native Reserve." *South African Journal of Science* 30 (1933): 633–655.
Stedman, S., ed. *Botswana: The Political Economy of Democratic Development*. Boulder, Colo.: Westview, 1992.

2. Agriculture

Alverson, H. "Arable Agriculture in Botswana: Some Contributions of the Traditional Social Formation." *Rural Africana* 4–5 (1979).
———. "The Wisdom of Tradition in the Development of Dry-Land Farming: Botswana." *Human Organization* 43 (Spring 1984): 1–8.
Ansell, D. *Cattle Marketing in Botswana*. Reading: University of Reading Development Studies No. 8, 1971.
Bond, C. A. *Women's Involvement in Agriculture in Botswana*. Gaborone: Government Printer, 1974.
Botswana Government, Ministry of Agriculture. *A Study of Constraints on Agricultural Development in the Republic of Botswana*. Gaborone: Government Printer, 1974.
Botswana Notes and Records, 14 (1982), 26–79. Various articles.
Cathie, J., and H. Dick. *Food Security and Macroeconomic Stabilization: A Case Study in Botswana 1965–1984*. Tubingen: J. C. B. Mohr, 1987.
Curtis, D. "The Social Organization of Ploughing." *Botswana Notes and Records* 4 (1972): 67–80.
Dahl, H.-E. *Rural Production in Botswana 1974–1975: A National Accounts Analysis of the Rural Incomes Distribution Survey, I*. Bergen: University of Bergen Institute of Economics, 1978.
Givetti, L. E. "Geographical Location, Climate, Weather, and Magic: Aspects of Agricultural Success in the Eastern Kalahari, Botswana." *Social Science Information* 20, no. 3 (1981): 509–536.
Gulbrandsen, O. *Agro-Pastoral Production and Communal Land Use*. Gaborone: Ministry of Agriculture, 1980.
Hitchcock, R. K. "Sandveld Agriculture in Botswana." *Botswana Notes and Records* 18 (1986): 91–105.
Hubbard, M. *Agricultural Exports and Economic Growth: A Study of Botswana's Growth Industry*. London: Routledge and Kegan Paul, 1986.
Hudson, D. J. "Rural Incomes in Botswana." *Botswana Notes and Records* 9 (1977): 101–108.
Kloppenburs, J. R. "Group Development in Botswana: The Principles of Collective Farmer Action." *Research in Economic Anthropology* 5 (1983): 311–333
Lischauer, J. G., and W. F. Kelly. *Traditional Versus Commercial Agriculture in Botswana*. Gaborone: Ministry of Agriculture, 1981.
Mazonde, I. N. "Vorsters and Clarks: Alternative Models of European Farmer in the Tuli Block of Botswana." *Journal of Southern African Studies* 17, no. 3 (1991): 443–471.
Odell, M. L. *Planning for Agriculture in Botswana: A Report on the*

Arable Lands Survey. Gaborone: Institute of Development Management, with the Planning and Statistics Division, Ministry of Agriculture, 1980.

Oland, K. "Agricultural Research in Botswana." In *Strengthening National Agricultural Research: Report from a SAREC Workshop, September 10–17, 1979. Part I: Background Documents.* Edited by B. Bengston and G. Tedia. Stockholm: Swedish Agency for Research Cooperation with Developing Countries, 1980.

Peters, P. E. "Household Management in Botswana: Cattle, Crops, and Wage Labor." In *Understanding Africa's Rural Households and Farming Systems.* Edited by J. L. Moock, 133–154. Boulder, Colo.: Westview, 1986.

Picard, L. A. "Self-Sufficiency, Delinkage, and Food Production: Limits on Agricultural Development in Africa." *Policy Studies Review* 4, no. 2 (November 1984): 311–319.

Roe, E. *The Development of Livestock, Agriculture and Water Supplies in Eastern Botswana Before Independence: A Short History and Policy Analysis.* Ithaca, N.Y.: Center for International Studies, Cornell University, 1980.

Roe, E. M. "Who Brews Traditional Beer in Rural Botswana? A Review of the Literature and Policy Analysis." *Botswana Notes and Records* 13 (1981): 45–53.

Watanabe, B., and E. Mueller. "A Poverty Profile for Rural Botswana." *World Development* 12, no. 2 (1984):115–127.

White, R. *Livestock Development and Pastoral Production on Communal Rangeland in Botswana.* Gaborone: The Botswana Society, 1993.

3. Commerce and Industry

Behrman, J. R. "Shadow Prices and Subsidies in Botswana." *Journal of Development Economics* 22 (July/August: 1986): 351–392.

Bell, M. "Transition to Urban Life: The Role of Indigenous Enterprise in Naledi, Botswana." *Geography* 66 (January 1981): 63–65.

Doing Business in Botswana. New York: Price Waterhouse World Firm Limited, 1990.

Kaplinsky, R. "Industrialization in Botswana: How Getting the Prices Right Helped the Wrong People." In *States or Markets? . . .* Edited by C. Colclough, 148–172. Oxford: Clarendon, 1991.

Lewis, S. R., and J. Sharpley. *Botswana's Industrialisation.* Brighton, England: Institute of Development Studies, University of Sussex, 1988.

Matsebula, M. S. "Tax Incentives in Bots, Les and Swa." *Journal of Southern African Affairs* 4, no. 1 (1979): 99–106.

Silitshena, R. M. K. and T. D. Gwebu. "Shopping Centres and Shopping Behaviour in Gaborone: Survey Results." *Botswana Notes and Records* 18 (1986): 123–131.

Stahl, C. W. "A Commercial Strategy in the Labor Export Market with Reference to Botswana, Lesotho and Swaziland." *Botswana Notes and Records* 7 (1975): 89–93.

4. Development

Alverson, H. "Peace Corps Volunteers in Rural Botswana." *Human Organization* 36, no. 3 (1977): 274–281.

Boehm, U. "Botswana—An Example for Successful Development in Southern Africa?" *African Development Perspectives Yearbook* (Berlin) (1989): 383–394.

Botswana Government
The National Development Plan. I. 1968–1973.
The National Development Plan. II. 1970–1975.
The National Development Plan. III. 1973–1978.
The National Development Plan. IV. 1976–1981.
The National Development Plan. V. 1979–1987.
The National Development Plan. VI. 1986–1991.
The National Development Plan. VII. 1991–1997.
The National Policy on Tribal Grazing Land. Government Paper No. 2, 1975.

Browne, A. W. "Rural Development in Botswana—The Role of Small-Scale Industries." *Geography* 67 (July 1982): 255–258.

Chambers, R. *Botswana's Accelerated Rural Development Programme, 1973–1976: Experience and Lessons.* Gaborone: Government Printing Press, 1977.

Chambers, R., and D. Feldman. *Report on Rural Development.* Gaborone: Ministry of Finance and Development Planning, 1973.

Chernichovsky, D. et al. *The Household Economy of Rural Botswana.* Washington, D.C.: World Bank, 1985.

Copperman, J. *The Impact of Water Supplies in Botswana: A Study of Four Villages.* Gaborone: Swedish International Development Authority, 1978.

Egner, E. B. *District Development in Botswana.* Gaborone: Swedish International Development Agency, 1978.

* ———. *Review of Socio-Economic Development in Botswana, 1966–1979.* Gaborone: Swedish International Development Agency, 1979.

Egner, E. B., and A. -L. Klausen. "Poverty in Botswana." Gaborone: National Institute of Research Working Paper No. 29, 1980.

Fortman, L. "Do the Poor Benefit from Publicly Provided Water in the Rural Areas?" *Botswana Notes and Records* 13 (1981): 55–59.

Gilmore, K. S. "An Investigation into the Decline of the Yambezi Fisherman's Co-operative Society." *Botswana Notes and Records* 11 (1979): 97–102.

Gracff. J. F. "The Brigades of Botswana." *Social Dynamics* 6, no. 1(1980): 23–35.

Grant, S. "The Non-Government Contribution to Development in Botswana, 1962–1980." *Botswana Notes and Records* 12 (1980): 41–47.

Harvey, C., and S. R. Lewis, Jr. *Policy Choice and Development Performance in Botswana.* London: Macmillan in association with the OECD Development Centre, 1990.

Hesselberg, J. *Third World in Transition: The Case of the Peasantry in Botswana.* Uppsala, Sweden: Scandinavian Institute of African Studies, 1984.

* Holm, J. D. "Liberal Democracy and Rural Development in Botswana." *African Studies Review* 25, no. 1 (March 1982): 83–102.

Jansen, R. H. F., and P. J. M. Van Hoff. "Regional Development Planning for Rural Development in Botswana." In *Third World Regional Development: A Reappraisal.* Edited by D. Simon, 190–209. London: Paul Chapman, 1990.

Mayende, G. P. "Bureaucrats, Peasants, and Rural Development Policy in Botswana." *Africa Development/Afrique et Developpement* (Dakar) 18, no. 4 (1993): 57–78.

Molomo, M. "Government Policy in Land and Housing Development in Gaborone, 1966–1986." Ph.D. diss. Boston University, 1988.

Molutsi, P. P. "Social Stratification and Inequality in Botswana: Issues in Development, 1950–1985." Ph.D. diss., Oxford University, 1985.

Mueller, B. "The Value and Allocation of Time in Rural Botswana." *Journal of Development Economics* 15 (May/August 1984): 329–360.

Mushonga, B. L. B. "Lentswe la Oodi Weavers: Bold Steps in Rural Development." *Botswana Notes and Records* 9 (1977): 119–122.

Narayan-Parker, D. "Motshelo: Implications for Stimulating Small Scale Production in Botswana." *Botswana Notes and Records* 13 (1981): 61–65.

Parson, J. D. "The Trajectory of Class and State in Dependent Development: The Consequences of New Wealth for Botswana." *Journal of Commonwealth and Comparative Politics* 21, no. 3 (November 1983): 38–60.

* Picard, L. A. *The Politics of Development in Botswana: A Model for Success?* Boulder, Colo.: Lynne Rienner, 1987.

Silitshena, R. "Mining and Development Strategy in Botswana." In *Natural Resources and National Welfare: The Case of Copper.* Edited by A. Seidman, 398–408. New York: Praeger, 1976.

Steenkamp, P. " 'Cinderella of the Empire': Development Policy in Bechuanaland in the 1930's." *Journal of Southern African Studies* 17, no. 2 (1991): 292–308.

van Rensburg, H. J. "Range Management in Botswana." *Botswana Notes and Records* 3 (1971): 112–130.

———. "Technical Notes," 2, 18, and 16. Gaborone: United Nations Development Program, FAO/UNDP/SF, 1971–1972.

van Rensburg, P. *Looking Forward from Serowe.* Gaborone: Foundation for Education with Production, n.d.

* ———. *Report from Swaneng Hill: Education and Employment in an African Country.* Stockholm: Africa Institute, 1974.

Vengroff, R. *Botswana: Rural Development in the Shadow of Apartheid.* Rutherford, N.J.: Fairleigh Dickinson University Press, 1977.

Watanabe, B., and E. Mueller. "A Poverty Profile for Rural Botswana." *World Development* 12 (Fall, 1984): 115–127.

Weimer, B. "Botswana-African Economic Miracle or Dependent South African Quasi-Homeland?" *African Development Perspectives Yearbook* (Berlin) (1989): 395–419.

5. External Relations

Cathie, J., and R. Herrmann. "The Southern African Customs Union, Cereal Price Policy in South Africa, and Food Security in Botswana." *Journal of Development Studies* 24, no. 3 (1988): 393–414.

Clark, L. J. "The Static Welfare Economics of a Small Developing County's Membership in a Customs Union: Botswana in the Southern African Customs Union." *World Development* 20, no. 7 (1992): 1021–1028.

Dale, R. "The Functional Web of Interdependence between Pre-independent Botswana and South Africa: A Preliminary Study." *Botswana Notes and Records* 6 (1974): 117–132.

* Hanlon, J. *Beggar Your Neighbors: Apartheid Power in Southern Africa*. London: Catholic Institute for International Relations/James Currey/Indiana Press, 1987.

———. *SADCC: Progress, Projects and Prospects*. London: Economist Intelligence Unit, 1985.

Hudson, D. J. "Brief Chronology of Customs Agreements in Southern Africa, 1855–1979." *Botswana Notes and Records* 11 (1979): 89–95.

Mosley, P. "The Southern African Customs Union: A Reappraisal." *World Development* 6, no. 1 (1978).

Niemann, M. "Diamonds are a State's Best Friend: Botswana's Foreign Policy in Southern Africa." *Africa Today* 40, no. 1 (1993): 27–47.

Robson, P. "Economic Integration in Southern Africa." *Journal of Modern African Studies* 5 (1967): 469–490.

6. Finance, Banking

Collings, F. d'A. et al. "Rand and the Monetary Systems of Botswana, Lesotho, and Swaziland." *Journal of Modern African Studies* 16 (March 1978): 97–121.

Hermans, Q. "Towards Budgetary Independence: A Review of Botswana's Financial History, 1900–1973." *Botswana Notes and Records* 6 (1974): 89–106.

Hudson, D. J. "The Establishment of Botswana's Central Bank and the Introduction of the New Currency." *Botswana Notes and Records* 10 (1978): 119–135.

Jones, K. F. "Britain's Contribution to Botswana's Public Debt, 1956–1976." *Botswana Notes and Records* 9 (1977): 109–117.

Makgetla, N. S. "Finance and Development: The Case of Botswana." *Journal of Modern African Studies* 20, no. 1 (January 1982): 69–86.

7. Labor, Unions, Employment

Bell, M. "Modern Sector Employment and Urban Social Change: A Case Study from Gaborone, Botswana." *Canadian Journal of African Studies* 15, no. 2 (1981): 259–176.

Conlin, R. "Employment Creation and Development in Kanye." *Botswana Notes and Records* 11 (1979): 77–88.

Cooper, D. "An Interpretation of the Emergent Urban Class Structure in Botswana: A Case Study of Selebi-Phikwe Miners." Ph.D. diss., University of Birmingham, 1982.

———. "The State, Mineworkers, and Multinationals: The Selebi-Phikwe Strike, Botswana, 1975." In *African Labor History*. Edited by P. C. W. Gutkind, R. Cohen, and J. Copans, 244–277. Beverly Hills, Calif.: Sage Publications, 1978.

———. "Unions in Botswana: Comparisons With Lesotho." *South African Labour Bulletin* 10, no. 8 (1985): 103–114.

Curry, R. L. "Poverty and Mass Unemployment in Mineral-Rich Botswana." *American Journal of Economics and Sociology* 46 (January 1987): 71–87.

Hansen, J. R. "Brigades Controversy." *Africa Report*. 27 (November/December 1982): 54–56.

Lipton, M. *Employment and Labor Use in Botswana*. 2 vols. Gaborone: Government Printer, 1978.

Martin, A. *Report on the Brigades in Botswana*. Gaborone: Government Printer, 1974.

Massey, D. "The Changing Political Economy of Migrant Labor in Botswana." *South African Labor Bulletin* 5, no. 5 (1980): 4–26.

* Parsons, Q. N. *Report on Botswana Brigades, 1965–1983*. Gaborone: National Institute for Research, 1983.

Pfau, R. H. "The Culture of the Workplace in Botswana." *Botswana Notes and Records* 23 (1991): 1–10.

* Schapera, I. *Migrant Labor and Tribal Life: A Study of Conditions in the Bechuanaland Protectorate*. London: Oxford University Press, 1947.

South African Team for Employment Promotion. "Minimum Wage Fixing in Botswana: Implications for Employment and Income Distribution." In *Assessing the Impact of Statutory Minimum Wages in Developing Countries*, 1–54. Geneva: International Labour Office, 1988.

Taylor, J. "Mine Labor Recruitment in the Bechuanaland Protectorate." *Botswana Notes and Records*, 10 (1978): 99–112.

———. "Some Consequences of Recent Reductions in Mine Labour Recruitment in Botswana." *Geography* 71, no. 1 (1986): 34–46.

* van Rensburg, P. *The Serowe Brigades*. London: Macmillan, 1978.

8. Land, Environment

Abucar, M. H., and P. Molutsi. "Environmental Policy in Botswana: A Critique." *Africa Today* 40, no. 1 (1993): 61–73.

Arntzen, J. "Land Shortage: The Need for Comprehensive Land Use Planning." *Botswana Notes and Records* 18 (1986): 133–137.

Arntzen, J. W. "Crop Production, Cattle Rearing and Land Use in Kgatleng District, Botswana." *Norwegian Geographical Journal* 38, no. 1 (1984): 95–108.

Botswana Government. *Report on Land Use Planning in Botswana*. Gaborone: Communal Area Research Group, 1984.

Campbell, A. C. *The Nature of Botswana: A Guide to Conversation and Development*. Gland, Switzerland: Field Operations Division, International Union for Conservation of Nature and Natural Resources, 1990.

Gulbrandsen, O. *Access to Agricultural Land and Communal Land Management in Eastern Botswana*. Gaborone: Ministry of Local Government and Lands Applied Research Unit, 1984.

Hitchcock, R. K. "Tradition, Social Justice, and Land Reform in Central Botswana." *Journal of African Law* 24 (1980): 1–34.

Kowet, D. *Land, Labor Migration and Politics in Southern Africa: Botswana, Lesotho and Swaziland*. Uppsala, Sweden: Scandinavian Institute of African Studies, 1978.

Molutsi, P. P. "The State, Environment and Peasant Consciousness in Botswana." *Review of African Political Economy* 42 (1988): 40–47.

Opschoor, J. B. *Environmental Resource Utilization in Communal Botswana*. Gaborone: National Institute of Research Working Paper 38, 1981.

Perrings, C. *Natural Resource Accounts for Botswana: Environmental Accounting for a Natural Resource–Based Economy*. London: London Environmental Economics Centre, 1989.

Peters, P. E. "The Ideology and Practice of Tswana Borehole Syndicates: Co-operative or Corporation?" In *Who Shares?: Co-operatives and Rural Development*. Edited by D.W. Attwood, B.S. Baviskar, 32–45. Delhi: Oxford University Press, 1988.

Picard, L. A. "Bureaucrats, Cattle, and Public Policy: Land Tenure in Botswana." *Comparative Political Studies* 13, no. 3 (October 1980): 313–356.

Schapera, I. *Native Land Tenure in the Bechuanaland Protectorate*. Alice, South Africa: Lovedale Press, 1943.

———. "Report and Recommendations Submitted to the Bechuanaland Protectorate Administration on the Native Land Problem in the Tati District, 1943." *Botswana Notes and Records* 3 (1971): 219–268.

———. "The System of Land Tenure on the Barolong Farms (Bechuanaland Protectorate): Report and Recommendations Submitted to the B. P. Administration, June 1943." *Botswana Notes and Records* 15 (1983): 15–37.

* Werbner, R. P., ed. *Land Reform in the Making: Tradition, Public Policy and Ideology in Botswana*. London: Rex Collings, 1982.

9. Mining

Lewis, D. "Direct Foreign Investment and Linkages in a Less Developed Country." *Botswana Notes and Records* 7 (1975): 81–88.

Lewis, D. "The Theory and Practice of Direct Foreign Investment in Less Developed Countries—a Study of Copper–Nickel Mining in Botswana." M. A. diss., University of Cape Town, 1974.

10. Veterinary

Barker, J. F. "A Preliminary Study of the Distribution of Acridoidea in Relation to Overgrazing in Botswana." *Botswana Notes and Records* 14 (1981): 1–10.

Bond, G. *A Report on Livestock Marketing.* Gaborone: Ministry of Agriculture, 1976.

Botswana Government. *An Integrated Programme of Beef Cattle and Range Research in Botswana, 1970–1976.* Gaborone: Ministry of Agriculture Animal Production Unit, 1976.

———. *Lefatshe la Rona—Our Land: The Report on the Botswana Government's Public Consultation and its Policy Proposals on Tribal Grazing Land.* Gaborone: Ministry of Local Government and Lands, 1977.

Botswana Meat Commission. *Annual Reports.* 1966–.

Greenhow, T. "The Tribal Grazing Land Policy and Integrated Land-Use Planning: A District View." *Botswana Notes and Records* 10 (1978): 159–168.

* Hitchcock, R. K. *Kalahari Cattle Posts: A Regional Study of Hunter-Gatherers, Pastoralists, and Agriculturalists in the Western Sandveld Region, Central District.* Gaborone: Ministry of Local Government and Lands, 1978.

———. "Water, Land, and Livestock: The Evolution of Tenure and Administration Pattern in the Grazing Areas of Botswana. [With Special Reference to the Ngwato(Bamangwato)]." In *The World of Pastoralism.* Edited by J. G. Galaty, D. L. Johnson, 216–254. New York: Guilford Press, 1990.

Hudson, D. "The Taxation of Income from Cattle Farming." *Botswana Notes and Records* 12 (1980): 49–65.

Jerve, A. M. *Cattle and Inequality: A Study in Rural Economic Differentiation from Southern Kgalagadi in Botswana.* Bergen, Norway: Michaelson Institute Department of Social Science and Development DERAP Publication 143, 1982.

McDonald, I. *A Report on Cattle Marketing in Botswana.* Gaborone: Ministry of Agriculture, 1979.

Mazonde, I. "Ranching in the Tuli Block." *Botswana Notes and Records* 17 (1985): 179–180.

Mazonde, I.N. "Agricultural Policy Flawed." *Mmegi/The Reporter* 10, no. 16 (1993): 25.

———. Review of *Livestock Development and Pastoral Production on Communal Rangeland in Botswana* by R. White. *Botswana Notes and Records* 25 (1993): 179–186.

Ndzinge, L. O. et al. "Herd Inventory and Slaughter Supply Response on Botswana Beef Cattle Producers." *Journal of Botswana Cultural Economics* 35, no. 1 (1984): 97–107.

Odell, J. M. "Socio-Economic Monitoring of the Tribal Land Grazing Policy." Seminar Report. Gaborone: Ministry of Agriculture Rural Sociology Section, 1977.

Peters, P. E. "Struggles over Water, Struggles over Meaning: Cattle, Water and the State in Botswana." *Africa* 54, no. 3 (1984): 29–49.

Ringrose, S., W. Matheson, and F. Tempest, "Procedural Considerations and Results of Landsat Multi-Temporal Analyses Concerned with Range Degradation (1972–1987) in Botswana." *Botswana Notes and Records* 24 (1992): 205–217.

Solway, J. S. *People, Cattle and Drought in the Western Kweneng District.* Gaborone: Ministry of Agriculture Rural Sociology Report 16, 1980.

Wilsen, E. "Antecedents of Contemporary Pastoralism in Western Ngamiland." *Botswana Notes and Records* 20 (1988): 29–40.

C. History

1. Archaeology, Rock Art

Brooks, A. "A Note on the Late Stone Age Features at /Gi: Analogies from Historic San Hunting Practices." *Botswana Notes and Records* 10 (1978): 1–3.

Brooks, A., and J. E. Yellen. "Archaeological Excavations at /Gi: A Preliminary Report on the First Two Field Seasons." *Botswana Notes and Records* 9 (1977): 21–30.

Campbell, A. "Notes on Some Rock Paintings at Savuti." *Botswana Notes and Records* 2 (1970): 15–23.

———. "A Record of Rock Art at Maredi." *Botswana Notes and Records* 18 (1986): 15–17.

Campbell, A., R. Hitchcock, and M. Bryan. "Rock Art at Tsodilo." *South African Journal of Science* 76, no. 10 (1980): 476–478.

Cohen, G. "The Ancient Workings at Gakgale." *Botswana Notes and Records* 9 (1977): 17–19.

———. "Stone Age Artifacts from Orapa Diamond Mine, Central Botswana." *Botswana Notes and Records* 6 (1974): 1–4.

Cooke, C. K. "The Stone Age in Botswana: A Preliminary Survey." *Arnoldia* 8, no. 27 (1979): 1–32.

Denbow, J., and J. Denbow. *Uncovering Botswana's Past.* Gaborone: The Botswana Society, 1989.

Denbow, J. R. "Broadhurst—A 14th Century A.D. Expression of the Early Iron Age in Southeastern Botswana." *South African Archaeological Bulletin* 36 (1981): 66–74.

———. "Cenchrus Ciliaris: An Ecological Indicator of Iron Age Middens Using Aerial Photography in Eastern Botswana." *South African Journal of Science* 75 (1979): 405–408.

———. "Congo to Kalahari: Data and Hypotheses About the Political Economy of the Western Stream of the Early Iron Age." *African Archaeological Review* 8 (1990): 139–175.

* ———. "Cows and Kings: A Spatial and Economic Analysis of a Hierarchical Early Iron Age Settlement System in Eastern Botswana." In *Frontiers: Southern African Archaeology Today.* Edited by M. Hall et al, 24–39. Oxford: British Archaeological Reports International Series 207, 1984.

———. "Early Iron Age Remains from the Tsodilo Hills, Northwestern Botswana." *South African Journal of Science* 76, no. 10 (1980): 474–475.

———. "Iron Age Economics: Herding, Wealth, and Politics along the

Fringes of the Kalahari Desert during the Early Iron Age." Ph.D. diss., University of Indiana, 1983.

———. "A New Look at the Later Prehistory of the Kalahari." *Journal of African History* 27, no. 1 (1986): 3–28.

———. "Patterns and Processes: A New Look at the Later Prehistory of the Kalahari." *Journal of African History* 27 (1984): 3–28.

* ———. "Prehistoric Herders and Foragers of the Kalahari: The Evidence for 1500 Years of Interaction." In *Past and Present in Hunter-Gatherer Studies.* Edited by C. Schrire, 175–193. New York: Academic Press, 1984.

* Denbow, J. R. and E. N. Wilmsen. "The Advent and Course of Pastoralism in the Kalahari." *Science* 234 (1986): 1509–1515.

———. *Class, Cattle, and Beads: An Iron Age Study in Botswana.* Chicago: University of Chicago Press, forthcoming.

Gautier, A. and C. van Waarden. "The Subsistence Patterns at Leeukop Site, Eastern Tuli Block." *Botswana Notes and Records* 13 (1981): 1–11.

Helgren, D. M. and A. S. Brooks. "Geoarchaeology at Gi, a Middle Stone Age and Late Stone Age Site in the Northwest Kalahari." *Journal of Archaeological Science* 10 (1983): 181–197.

* Kennedy, R. F., comp. *Catalogue of Pictures in the Africana Museum.* 5 vols. Johannesburg: Africana Museum, 1966–1968.

Lepionka, L. "Excavations at Tautswemogala." *Botswana Notes and Records* 9 (1977): 1–16.

Maggs, T. "Bilobial Dwellings: A Persistent Feature of Southern Tswana Settlements." *Goodwin Series No. 1*, South African Archaeological Society, 1972.

———. "Iron Age Patterns and Sotho History on the Southern Highveld: South Africa." *World Archaeology* 7, 3 (1976): 318–332.

———. "The Iron Age South of the Zambezi." In *Southern African Prehistory and Palaeoenvironments.* Edited by R. G. Klein, 329–360. Rotterdam: Balkema, 1984.

Malan, F. "A Wilton Site at Kai Kai, Bechuanaland Protectorate." *South African Archaeological Bulletin* 5 (1950): 140–142.

Mason, R. " 'Oori' or 'Moloko'? The Origins of the Sotho-Tswana on the Evidence of the Iron Age of the Transvaal." *South African Journal of Science* 79, no. 7 (1983): 261.

Pahl, R. H. "Samples of Iron Age Pottery in South-East Botswana." *Botswana Notes and Records* 6 (1974): 5–18.

Robins, L. H. "Archaeology in Southeastern Botswana." *Current Anthropology* 25 (April 1984): 229.

———. "Recent Archaeological Research in Southeastern Botswana: The Thamaga Site." *Botswana Notes and Records* 18 (1986): 1–13.

———. "Toteng, a Late Stone Age Site along the Nchabe River." *Botswana Notes and Records* 16 (1984): 1–6.

Tamplin, M. J. *Preliminary Report on an Archaeological Survey of the Republic of Botswana.* Peterborough, Ontario, Canada: Trent University Department of Anthropology, 1977.

van Waarden, C. "Archaeological Investigation of Leeukop: A Functional Approach." *Botswana Notes and Records* 11 (1979): 1–13; 12 (1980): 151–164.

————. "Leeukop: A Functional Analysis of a Refuge Period Settlement in Eastern Botswana." M. A. thesis, University of Trent Department of Anthropology, 1980.

Welbourne, R. G. "Tautswe Iron Age Site: Its Yield of Bones." *Botswana Notes and Records* 7 (1975): 1–16.

Wilmsen, E. M. "The Antecedents of Contemporary Pastoralism in Western Ngamiland." *Botswana Notes and Records* 20 (1988): 29–39.

Yellen, J. E. *Archaeological Approaches to the Present: Models for Reconstructing the Past*. New York: Academic Press, 1977.

————. "The Integration of Herding into Prehistoric Hunting and Gathering Economies." In *Frontiers: Southern African Archaeology Today*. Edited by M. Hall et al, 53–64. Oxford: British Archaeological Reports International Series 207, 1984.

Yellen, J. E. and A. S. Brooks. "The Late Stone Age Archaeology of the !Kangwa—?Xai?Xai Valleys, Ngamiland." *Botswana Notes and Records* 20 (1988): 5–28.

2. Primary Sources

a. Nineteenth Century

Agar-Hamilton, J. A. I., ed. "Dr. Livingstone and the Voortrekkers: Andries Hendrik Potgieter's Letter to the Rev. William Ross, 1849." *Quarterly Bulletin of the South Africa Library* 28, no. 2 (1973): 31–41.

Anderson, A.A. *Twenty-Five Years in a Waggon: Sport and Travel in South Africa*. Cape Town: C. Struik, reprint, 1974.

Andersson, K.J. "Explorations in South Africa with the Route From Walfisch Bay to Lake Ngami." *Journal of the Royal Geographical Society*, 25 (1855): 79–107.

————. *Lake Ngami, or Explorations and Discoveries in the Wilds of Southern Africa*. New York: Dix, Edwards, 1856.

Arkwright, R. *Sport and Service in South Africa*. Cape Town: A. A. Balkema, reprint, 1971.

Baines, T. *Explorations in Southwest Africa*. London: Longmans, Green, 1864.

Baldwin, W. C. *African Hunting from the Natal of the Zambesi from 1852 to 1860*. Cape Town: C. Struik, reprint, 1967.

Bent, J. T. *The Ruins of Mashonaland*. Freeport, N.Y.: Books for Libraries Press, reprint, 1971.

Billmore, P. *The Great Thirstland*. London: Cassell, Peter and Galpin, 1878.

Bradshaw, B. "Notes on the Chobe River, South Central Africa." *Proceedings of the Royal Geographical Society* 3, no. 4 (April 1881): 208–213.

Brown, W. H. *On the South African Frontier.* New York: Negro Universities Press, reprint, 1970.

Bryden, H. A. "A Friend of Livingstone." *Chamber's Journal* 7 July 1894: 420–421.

————. *Gun and Camera in Southern Africa: A Year of Wanderings in Bechuanaland, the Kalahari Desert, and the Lake River Country, Ngamiland.* London: Edward Stanford, 1893.

Burchell, W.J. *Travels in the Interior of South Africa.* 2 vols. New York: Johnson Reprint Corporation, reprint, 1967.

* Chapman, J. *Travels in the Interior of South Africa.* 2 vols. Edited by E.C. Tabler. Cape Town: A. A. Balkema, 1971.

Cumming, R. G. *A Hunter's Life in South Africa.* London: John Murray, 1850. 1904 edition: *The Lion Hunter of South Africa.*

Dachs, A., ed. *Papers of John Mackenzie.* Johannesburg: University of the Witwatersrand Press, 1975.

Decle, L. *Three Years in Savage Africa.* Bulawayo: Books of Rhodesia, reprint, 1974.

Dolman, A. *In the Footsteps of Livingstone.* London: John Lane, 1924.

Farini, G. A. *Through the Kalahari Desert.* Cape Town: C. Struik, reprint, 1973.

Finaughty, W. *The Recollections of an Elephant Hunter, 1864–1875.* Bulawayo: Books of Rhodesia, reprint, 1973.

Gibbons, A. *Africa from South to North.* 2 vols. London: John Lane, 1904.

Harris, W. C. *Portraits of the Game and Wild Animals of Southern Africa.* Mazoe: Frank Read Press, reprint, 1967.

* Hepburn, J. D. *Twenty Years in Khama's Country.* London: Frank Cass, reprint, 1970.

Hole, H. M. *The Jameson Raid.* Bulawayo: Books of Rhodesia, reprint, 1973.

Holub, E. "From Gazungula (Kazungula) to Schoschong (Shoshong) Our Stay in Schoschong." *Botswana Notes and Records* 7 (1975): 35–47.

————. "Journey through Central South Africa from the Diamond Fields to the Upper Zambezi." *Proceedings of the Royal Geographical Society* 2 (1880): 166–182.

* ————. *Seven Years in South Africa.* 2 vols. Johannesburg: Africana Book Society, reprint, 1976.

————. "The Past, Present, and Future Trade of the Cape Colonies with Central Africa." *Proceedings of the Royal Colonial Institute* 11 (1879–1880): 59–60.

Johnson, F. *Great Days.* Bulawayo: Books of Rhodesia, reprint, 1972.

Kirby, P. R., ed. *The Diary of Dr. Andrew Smith, 1834–1836.* Cape Town: van Riebeeck Society Publications 20 and 21, 1939, 1940.

Knight–Bruce, G. W. H. *The Story of an African Chief: A Short History of the Life of Khama.* London: Kegan Paul, 1893.

Leyland, J. *Adventures in the Far Interior of South Africa, Including a Journey to Lake Ngami and Rambles to Honduras.* Cape Town: C. Struik, reprint, 1972.

Lister, M. H., ed. *Journals of Andrew Geddes Bain.* Cape Town: van Riebeeck Society, 1949.

Livingstone, D. "Explorations into the Interior of Africa." *Journal of the Royal Geographical Society* 24 (1854): 291–306.

———. "Extract of Letters from the Reverend David Livingstone in Kolobeng." *Journal of the Royal Geographical Society* 20 (1850): 138–142.

* ———. *Missionary Travels and Researches in South Africa.* London: John Murray, 1872.

Lloyd, E. *Three Great African Chiefs: Khame, Sebele, and Bathoeng.* London: T. Fisher Unwin, 1895.

* Long, Una, ed. *The Journals of Elizabeth Lees Price.* London: Edwin Arnold, 1956.

McCabe, J. "Journal Kept During a Tour in the Interior of South Africa to Lake Ngami." In *History of the Colony of Natal, South Africa.* Edited by W. C. Holden, 413–436. Cape Town: C. Struik, 1855.

Mackenzie, J. *Austral Africa, Losing It or Ruling It.* 2 vols. New York: Negro Universities Press, reprint, 1969.

———. *Ten Years North of the Orange River.* Edinburgh: Edmonston and Douglas, 1871.

Mackenzie, W. D. *John Mackenzie: South African Missionary and Statesman.* London: Hodder and Stoughton, 1902.

Mathers, E. P. *Zambezia.* London: King, Sell and Railton, 1891.

Moffat, J. S. *The Lives of Robert and Mary Moffat.* London: T. Fisher Unwin, 1885.

Moffat, R. *Missionary Labors and Scenes in Southern Africa.* London: Snow, 1842.

Neethling, W. *Zendeling to Mochuli.* Neerbosch: Stoom-Snelpersdruk der Weesinrichtig, n.d. [1898].

Oates, F. *Matabeleland and the Victoria Falls.* Salisbury: Pioneer Head, 1971.

Oswell, W. E. *William Cotton Oswell, Hunter and Explorer.* 2 vols. London: W. Heinemann, 1900.

Patterson, R. R. "On the Bamangwato Country." *Proceedings of the Royal Geographical Society* 1 (1879): 241.

Pinto, A. deS. *How I Crossed Africa.* Vol. 2. London: Sampson, Low, Marsten, Searle and Rivington, 1881.

Reid, P. C. "Journeys in the Linyanti Region." *Geographical Journal* 17, no. 4 (June 1901): 573–588.

Schapera, I., ed. *Apprenticeship at Kuruman: Journals and Letters of Robert and Mary Moffat, 1820–1828.* London: Chatto and Windus, 1951.

* ———. *David Livingstone: Family Letters, 1841–1856.* 2 vols. London: Chatto and Windus, 1959.

* ———. *Livingstone's Missionary Correspondence, 1841–1856.* London: Chatto and Windus, 1961.

* ———. *Livingstone's Private Journals, 1851–1853.* London: Chatto and Windus, 1960.

Selous, F. C. *Travel and Adventure in South–East Africa.* Bulawayo: Books of Rhodesia, 1972.

Shippard, S. G. A. *Bechuanaland.* British Africa Series, volume 2. Edited by J. Scott Keltie. London: Kegan Paul, Trench, Trubner, 1899.

Smith, A. *A Report of the Expedition for Exploring Central Africa.* Cape Town: van Riebeeck Society, reprint, 1940.

van Waarden, C. *Oral Traditions of the Bakalanga and Bakhurutshe.* Gaborone: The Botswana Society, 1988.

Wallis, J. P. R., ed. *The Matabele Journals of Robert Moffat, 1829–1860.* 2 vols. London: Chatto and Windus, 1945.

————. *The Northern Goldfields Diaries of Thomas Baines.* 3 vols. London: Chatto and Windus, 1946.

Williams, R. *The British Lion in Bechuanaland.* London, 1885.

b. Twentieth Century

Barnes, L. *The New Boer War.* London: Hogarth Press, Leonard and Virginia Woolf, 1932.

Blackbeard, S. "Memoirs of Samuel Blackbeard." *Botswana Notes and Records* 17 (1985): 187–191.

* Brown, J. T. *Among the Bantu Nomads: A Record of Forty Years Spent among the Bechuana.* London: Seeley Service, 1926.

————. "Circumcision Rites of the Becwana Tribes." *Journal of the Royal Anthropological Institute* 51 (1921): 419–427.

Clifford, B. E. H. "A Journey by Motor Lorry from Mahalapye through the Kalahari Desert." *Geographical Journal* 73 (1929): 342–358.

————. "A Reconnaissance of the Great Makarikari Lake." *Geographical Journal* 75 (1930): 16–26.

* Comaroff, J. L. *The Boer War Diary of Sol. T. Plaatje, an African at Mafeking.* London: Macmillan, 1973.

Cooke, J. *One White Man in Black Africa: From Kilimanjaro to the Kalahari, 1951–1991.* Thornhill, Scotland: Tyron Press, 1991.

* Crowder, M., and Q. N. Parsons, ed. *Monarch of All I Survey: The Diaries of Sir Charles F. Rey.* Gaborone: Botswana Society, 1988.

Dingake, Michael. *My Fight Against Apartheid.* London: Kliptown Books, 1987.

* Duggan-Cronin, A. M. *The Bantu Tribes of South Africa.* Gaborone: Friends of the National Museum and Art Gallery, reprint, 1984.

Fawcus, Sir Peter. "Botswana Revisited. [A Personal Review of Political and Economic Developments 1965–1986]." *Botswana Notes and Records* 19 (1987): 157–171.

Flavin, M. *Black and White, From the Cape to the Congo.* New York: Harper, 1950.

Gluckmann, E. *The Tragedy of the Ababirwas and Some Reflections on Sir Herbert Sloley's Report.* Johannesburg: Central News Agency, 1922.

Haccius, G. *Hannoyersche Missionsgeschichte: Sweiter Teil.* Hermannsburg, 1910.

Hailey, Lord. *An African Survey, Revised 1956: A Study of Problems Arising in Africa South of the Sahara*. London: Oxford University Press, 1957.

* ———. *Native Administration in the British African Territories, Part V: The High Commission Territories*. London: HMSO, 1953.

Harragin, W. "Report of the Judicial Enquiry re Seretse Khama of the Bamangwato Tribe." *Botswana Notes and Records* 17 (1985): 53–64.

Head, B. *Serowe: The Village of the Rain-Wind*. Portsmouth: Heinemann, 1981.

Hodgson, M. L., and W. G. Ballinger. *Britain in South Africa (No. 2): Bechuanaland Protectorate*. Alice, South Africa: Lovedale Press, 1933.

Hodson, A. W. *Trekking the Great Thirst: Sport and Travel in the Kalahari Desert*. London: T. Fisher Unwin, 1912.

Hole, H. M. *The Passing of the Black Kings*. London: P. Allen, 1932.

Khama, Tshekedi. *Bechuanaland, a General Survey*. Johannesburg: Institute of Race Relations, 1957.

———. *Bechuanaland and South Africa*. London: African Bureau, 1956.

———. "Chieftainship under Indirect Rule." *Journal of the Royal African Society* 25 (1936): 251–261.

———. *Political Change in African Society*. London: African Bureau, 1956.

Mbuya, T. "The Horror of Apartheid." *MMEGI/The Reporter* 7, no. 9 (1990): 16.

Perham, M., and L. Curtis. *The Protectorates of South Africa: The Question of Their Transfer to the Union*. London: Oxford University Press, 1935.

Pilane, I. "Native Standpoints. In Favor of Transfer." *Race Relations* (Johannesburg) 2 (1935): 149–152.

Pim, A. W. *Financial and Economic Position of the Bechuanaland Protectorate*. Cmd. 4368. London: HMSO, 1933.

Pole Evans, I. B. *A Reconnaissance Trip through the Eastern Portion of the Bechuanaland Protectorate, April 1931, and an Expedition to Ngamiland, June–July, 1937*. Botanical Survey of South Africa Memoir 21. Pretoria: Government Printer, 1948.

Reyneke, J. "Mochudi: Lets uit die oue doos." *De Koningsbode Kerstnummer*. (December 1923): 41–43.

———. "A Remarkable Tribe." *Native Affairs Department Annual* (Salisbury) 2 (Dec. 1924): 91–94.

Sargent, E. G. *Report on Native Education in South Africa. Part III: Education in the Protectorates*. London: Longman, 1908.

Schapera, I. "A Native Lion Hunt in the Kalahari Desert." *Man* 32 (1932): 278–282.

Schapera, I., ed. *Ditirafalo tsa Merafe ya Batswana ba Lefatshe la Tshireletso*. Alice, South Africa: Lovedale Press, 1940.

Stigand, G. A. "Ngamiland." *Geographical Journal* 62, no. 4 (December 1923): 401–419.

———. "Notes on Ngamiland." *Geographical Journal* 39, no. 4 (April 1912): 376–379.

Stow, G. W. *The Native Races of Southern Africa.* Cape Town: C. Struik, reprint, 1964.

Tabler, E. C., ed. *Zambesia and Matabeleland in the Seventies.* London: Chatto and Windus, 1960.

van Rensburg, P. *Guilty Land: A Semi-Autobiography.* London: Jonathan Cape, 1962.

van Waarden, C., ed. *Kalanga Retrospect and Prospect.* Gaborone: The Botswana Society, 1991.

Williams, H. "The Passing of Bathoen Gaseitsiwe." *LMS Chronicle* n.s., 18 (1910): 153–154.

Williams, R. *How I Became a Governor.* London: John Murray, 1913.

Willoughby, W. C. "Khama: A Bantu Reformer." *International Review of Missions* 13 (1924): 74–83.

———. *Native Life on the Transvaal Border.* Private publication, 1900.

———. "Notes on the Totemism of the Becwana." *Journal of the Royal Anthropological Institute* 35 (1905): 295–314.

Wilmsen, E. N. "Conversations with Mr. Tommy Kays of Maun." *Botswana Notes and Records* 17 (1985): 175–178.

Wookey, A. J. "Missionary Work in Bechuanaland: Interesting Historical Reminiscences." *Diamond Fields Advertiser* (11 February 1907): 7.

3. Secondary Sources

* Agar-Hamilton, J. A. I. *The Road to the North.* London: Longmans, Green, 1937.

Ashton, H. "The High Commission Territories." In *Handbook on Race Relations in South Africa.* Edited by E. Hellman, 706–741. New York: Octagon Books, 1975.

Beach, D. N. *The Shona and Zimbabwe, 900–1850.* London: Heinemann, 1980.

Benson, M. *Tshekedi Khama.* London: Faber and Faber, 1960.

Bent, R. A. R. *Ten Thousand Men of Africa. The Story of the Bechuanaland Pioneers and Gunners, 1941–1946.* London: HMSO, 1952.

Best, A. "General Trading in Botswana, 1890–1968." *Economic Geography* 46, no. 4 (1970): 598–611.

Bhila, H. K. "The Impact of the Second World War on the Development of Peasant Agriculture in Botswana, 1939–1956." *Botswana Notes and Records* 16 (1984): 63–71.

Booth, A. R. "Lord Selborne and the British Protectorates, 1908–1910." *Journal of African History* 10, no. 1 (1969): 133–148.

Botha, H. J. "Die moord op Derdepoort, 25 November 1899. Nieblankes in oorlogsdiens." *Militaria*, 1, no. 2 (1969): 3–98.

Breutz, P. -L. "An Ancient People in the Kalahari Desert." *Africa und Übersee* 42, no. 42 (1958): 49–68.

———. *History of the Batswana.* Ramsgate: P. -L. Breutz, 1991.

Cashdan, E. "Trade and its Origins on the Botletli River, Botswana." *Journal of Anthropological Research* 43, no. 2 (1987): 121–138.

Chirenje, J. M. *Chief Kgama and His Times. The Story of a Southern African Ruler.* London: Rex Collings, 1978.

* ———. *A History of Northern Botswana, 1850–1919*. Cranbury, N.J.: Associated University Presses, 1977.

Crowder, M. "Botswana and the Survival of Liberal Democracy in Africa." In *African Independence: The Origins and Consequences of the Transfer of Power*. Edited by P. Gifford and W. R. Louis. New Haven: Yale University Press, 1988.

* ———. *The Flogging of Phinehas McIntosh: A Tale of Colonial Folly and Injustice, Bechuanaland, 1933*. New Haven: Yale University Press, 1988.

———. "Professor Macmillan Goes on Safari: The British Government Observer Team and the Crisis over the Seretse Khama Marriage, 1951." In *Africa and Empire: W. M. Macmillan, Historian and Social Critic*. Edited by H. Macmillan and S. Marks. London: Institute of Commonwealth Studies, 1988.

———. "The Regent of Bangwato's Market Gardens: Chadibe and Moeng 1936–41." *Botswana Notes and Records* 20 (1988): 51–60.

———. "Tshekedi Khama and Mining in Botswana, 1929–1959." In *Organization and Economic Change. Southern African Studies*. Edited by A. Mabin. vol. 5. Johannesburg: Ravan Press, 1989.

———. "Tshekedi Khama and Opposition to the British Administration of the Bechuanaland Protectorate, 1926–1935." *Journal of African History* 26, nos. 2–3 (1985): 193–214.

———. "Tshekedi Khama, Smuts, and South West Africa." *Journal of Modern African Studies* 265, no. 1 (1987): 25–42.

Dachs, A. J. *Khama of Botswana*. London: Heinemann, 1971.

———. "Missionary Imperialism—the Case of Bechuanaland." *Journal of African History* 13 (1972): 647–658.

———. "Rhodes's Grasp for Bechuanaland, 1889–1896." *Rhodesian History* 2 (1971): 1–9.

Dennis, C. "The Role of Dingaka tsa Setswana from the 19th Century to the Present." *Botswana Notes and Records* 10 (1978): 53–66.

Douglas-Home, C. *Evelyn Baring: The Last Proconsul*. London: William Collins, 1978.

Duggan, W. *A History of Agricultural Development in Southern Africa*. New York: Sage, 1985.

Dundas, C., and H. Ashton. *Problem Territories of Southern Africa*. Johannesburg: South African Institute for International Affairs, 1952.

Dutfield, M. *A Marriage of Inconvenience: The Persecution of Seretse and Ruth Khama*. New York: Oxford University Press, 1989.

Eilersen, G.S. *Bessie Head "Thunder Behind My Ears." A Biography*. Portsmouth, New Hampshire: Heinemann, 1996.

Eley, D. M. "The Early Days of the Post Office." *Botswana Notes and Records* 9 (1977): 37–40.

Ellenberger, J. "The Bechuanaland Protectorate and the Boer War, 1899–1902." *Rhodesiana* 11 (1964): 1–26.

Ellenberger, V. F. "History of the Ba-ga-Malete of Ramoutsa (Bechuanaland Protectorate)." *Transactions of the Royal Society of South Africa* 25, no. 4 (1937): 1–72.

————. "History of the BaTlokwa of Gaberones (Bechuanaland Protectorate)." *Bantu Studies* 13 (1939): 165–198 and diagrams.

Ettinger, S. J. "The Bechuanaland Protectorate's Participation in pre-1910 Customs Unions." *Botswana Notes and Records* 7 (1975): 49–52.

Gabatshwane, S. M. *Introduction to the Bechuanaland Protectorate History and Administration*. Kanye: Privately published, 1957.

————. *Seretse Khama and Botswana*. Gaborone: Bechuanaland Press, 1966.

————. *Tshekedi Khama of Bechuanaland: Great Statesman and Politician*. London: Oxford University Press, 1961.

Gadibolae, M. N. "Serfdom (bolata) in the Nata Area, 1926–1960." *Botswana Notes and Records* 17 (1985): 25–32.

Galbraith, J. S. *Crown and Charter: The Early Years of the British South Africa Company*. Berkeley: University of California Press, 1974.

Grant, S. "A Chronological Career Summary: Chief Linchwe II Kgafela." *Botswana Notes and Records* 17 (1985): 47–52.

————. "A Very Remarkable School." *Botswana Notes and Records* 8 (1976): 87–96.

Haacke, W. D. "The Kalahari Expedition March 1908, The Forgotten Story of the Final Battle of the Nama War." *Botswana Notes and Records* 24 (1992): 1–18.

Halpern, J. *South Africa's Hostages: Basutoland, Bechuanaland, and Swaziland*. Harmondsworth: Penguin, 1965.

Hickman, A. S. "Journey in Search of History." *Botswana Notes and Records* 2 (1970): 106–108.

————. *Rhodesia Served the Queen: Rhodesian Forces in the Boer War, 1899–1902*. 2 vols. Salisbury: Government Printer, 1970, 1975.

Hitchcock, R. K. "Socioeconomic Change among the Basarwa in Botswana: An Ethnohistorical Analysis." *Ethnohistory* 34, no. 3 (Summer 1987): 219–255.

Hudson, H., reviewer of D. Wylie, *The Little God: The Twilight of Patriarchy in a Southern African Chiefdom. Botswana Notes and Records* (1992) vol. 24: 225–229. Johannesburg: Witwatersrand University Press, 1991.

Hyam, R. *The Failure of South African Expansion, 1908–1948*. London: Macmillan, 1972.

————. "The Political Consequences of Seretse Khama: Britain, the Bangwato and South Africa, 1948-1952." *Historical Journal* 29, 4 (1986): 921–947.

Jones, J.D. "Mahoko a Becwana—the Second Setswana Newspaper." *Botswana Notes and Records* 4 (1972): 111–120.

Kebonang, B.B. "The History of the Herero in Mahalapye, Central District: 1922–1984." *Botswana Notes and Records* 21 (1989): 43–60.

Kiyaga-Mulindwa, D. "The Bechuanaland Protectorate and the Second World War." *Journal of Imperial and Commonwealth History* 12, no. 3 (May 1984): 33–53.

Knober, L. "The History of Sechele." *Botswana Notes and Records* 1 (1969): 51–64.

Kuper, A. "The Kgalagadi in the Nineteenth Century." *Botswana Notes and Records* 2 (1970): 45–51.

———. "A Note of Ruling Generations and Historical Time in Botswana." *Botswana Notes and Records* 3 (1971): 111.

* Landau, P. S. *The Realm of the Word: Language, Gender, and Christianity in the Southern African Kingdom.* Portsmouth, N.H.: Heinemann, 1995.

Landau, P. S. "When Rain Falls: Rainmaking and Community in a Tswana Village c.1870 to Recent Times." *International Journal of African Historical Studies* 26, no. 1 (1993): 1–30.

Leepile, M. "The Impact of Migrant Labor on the Economy of Kweneng, 1940–1980." *Botswana Notes and Records* 13 (1981): 33–43.

Legassick, M. "The Sotho-Tswana Peoples before 1800." In *African Societies in Southern Africa.* Edited by L. Thompson, 86–125. London: Heinemann, 1969.

Lye, W. F. "The Ndebele Kingdom South of the Limpopo." *Journal of African History* 10, no. 1 (1969): 88–93.

Main, E. *Man of Mafeking: The Bechuanaland Years of Sir Hamilton Goold-Adams 1884–1901.* Gaborone: The Botswana Society, 1996.

Maree, W. L. *Uit Duisternis Geroep die Sendingwerk von die Nederduitse Gereformeerde Kerk onder die Bakgatla von Wes-Transvaal en Betsjoenaland.* Johannesburg: N.G. Kerk Boekhandel, 1966.

Massey, D. "A Case of Colonial Collaboration: The Hut Tax and Migrant Labor." *Botswana Notes and Records* 10 (1978): 95–98.

Matthews, Z. K. "A Short History of the Tshidi Barolong." *Fort Hare Papers* 1 (1945): 9–28.

Mautle, G. "Bakgalagadi-Bakwena Relationship: A Case of Slavery, c. 1840–c. 1930." *Botswana Notes and Records* 18 (1986): 19–31.

Maylam, P. R. "The Making of the Kimberley-Bulawayo Railway: A Study in the Operation of the British South Africa Company." *Rhodesian History* 8 (1977): 13–33.

*———. *Rhodes, the Tswana, and the British: Colonialism, Collaboration, and Conflict in the Bechuanaland Protectorate, 1885–1899.* Westport, Connecticut: Greenwood, 1980.

Miers, S. and M. Crowder, "The Politics of Slavery in Bechuanaland: Struggles and the Plight of the Basarwa in the Bamangwato Reserve, 1926–1940." In *The End of Slavery in Africa.* Edited by S. Miers and R. Roberts, 172–200. Madison: University of Wisconsin Press, 1988.

Mockford, J. *Seretse Khama and the Bamangwato.* London: Staples Press, 1950.

Mokopakgosi, B. "The Socio-Economic and Political Impact of the Second World War on the Bakwena, 1939–1950." In *Africa and the Second World War.* Edited by R. Rathbone and D. Killingray, 160–180. London: Macmillan, 1986.

Molema, S. F. *The Bantu, Past and Present.* Edinburgh: Green, 1920.

Morton, B. C. *A Social and Economic History of a Southern African Native Reserve: Ngamiland, 1890–1966.* Ph. D. diss. Indiana University, 1996.

Morton, F., A. Murray, and J. Ramsay. *Historical Dictionary of Botswana*. Metuchen, New Jersey: Scarecrow Press, 2nd Edition, 1989.

Morton, R. F. "Chiefs and Ethnic Unity in Two Colonial Worlds: The Bakgatla baga Kgafela of the Bechuanaland Protectorate and the Transvaal, 1872–1966." In *Partitioned Africans: Ethnic Relations across Africa's International Boundaries, 1881–1984*. Edited by A. I. Asiwaju, 127–154. London: C. Hurst, 1985.

———. "Linchwe I and the Kgatla Campaign in the South African War, 1899–1902." *Journal of African History* 26, nos. 2–3 (1985): 169–191.

* Morton, R. F., and J. Ramsay, ed. *Birth of Botswana: A History of the Bechuanaland Protectorate from 1910 to 1966*. Gaborone: Longman Botswana, 1987.

Mpotokwane, J. "A Short History of the Bahurutse of King Motebele, Senior Son of King Mohrutse." *Botswana Notes and Records* 6 (1974): 37–45.

Muzorewa, B. C. "The Role of Local Treasuries in the Under-Development of Botswana: 1938–1953." *Botswana Notes and Records* 10 (1978): 113–118.

Nangati, F. "Constraints on a Precolonial Economy: The Bakwena State, c. 1820–1885." *Pula: Botswana Journal of African Studies* 2, no. 1 (February 1980): 125–138.

Ndai-Paulos, I. "Agricultural Production and Exchange: The Case of Central District, Bukalanga Area, c. 1890–1940." *Pula: Botswana Journal of African Studies* (1983).

Nettelton, G. E. "History of the Ngamiland Tribes to 1926." *Bantu Studies* 8 (1934): 343–360.

Ngwenya, B. N. "The Development of Transport Infrastructure in the Bechuanaland Protectorate, 1885–1966." *Botswana Notes and Records* 16 (1984): 73–84.

Okihiro, G. Y. "Hunters, Herders, Cultivators, and Traders: Interaction and Change in the Kgalagadi, Nineteenth Century." Ph.D. diss., University of California, Los Angeles, 1976.

———. "Resistance and Accommodation; BaKwena-baga-Sechele, 1842–1852." *Botswana Notes and Records* 5 (1973): 104–116.

Parsons, Q. N. "Colonel Rey and the Colonial Rulers of Botswana: Mercenary and Missionary Traditions in Administration, 1884–1955." In *Peoples and Empires in African History: Essays in Memory of Michael Crowder*. Edited by J. F. Ade Ajayi and J. D. Y. Peel, 197–215. London: Longman, 1992.

———. "Frantz or Klikko, the Wild Dancing Bushman: A Case Study of Khoisan Stereotyping." *Botswana Notes and Records* 20 (1988): 71–76.

———. "The 'Image' of Khama the Great—1868 to 1970." *Botswana Notes and Records* 3 (1973): 41–58.

———. " 'Khama & Co.' and the Jousse Trouble, 1910–1916." *Journal of African History* 16 (1975): 383–408.

* ———. "Khama III, the Bamangwato, and the British, with Special Reference to 1895–1923." Ph.D. thesis, University of Edinburgh, 1973.

*———. *New History of Southern Africa*. London: Macmillan Education, 1982.

———. "On the Origins of the Bamangwato." *Botswana Notes and Records* 5 (1973): 82–103.

———. "Shots for a Black Republic?: Simon Ratshosa and Botswana Nationalism." *African Affairs*, 73 (1974): 449–458.

*———. "The Economic History of Khama's Country in Botswana, 1844–1930." In *The Roots of Rural Poverty in Central and Southern Africa*. Edited by R. Palmer and N. Parsons, 113–143. Berkeley: University of California Press, 1977.

———."The Tswana Press—An Outline of Its History Since 1856." *Kutlwano*, 8, no. 8 (August 1968): 48–52.

———. *The Word of Khama*. Lusaka: Historical Association of Zambia Pamphlet 2, 1972.

Picard, L. A. "Administrative Reorganization—A Substitute for Policy? The District Administration and Local Government in the Bechuanaland Protectorate, 1949–1966." *Botswana Notes and Records* 16 (1984): 85–95.

Pilane, A. K. "A Note on Episodes from the Boer War." *Botswana Notes and Records* 5 (1973): 131.

———. "A Note on Traditional Courtesy between Chiefs." *Botswana Notes and Records* 9 (1977):160.

Ramage, R. *Report on the Structure of the Public Services in Basutoland, Bechuanaland and Swaziland, 1961*. Cape Town: Cape Times, 1962.

Ramokate, Chief. "Notes on the Khurutshe." *Botswana Notes and Records* 2 (1970): 14.

Ramsay, J. "The Botswana-Boer War of 1852–53: How the Batswana Achieved Victory." *Botswana Notes and Records* 23 (1991): 193–208.

*———. "The Rise and Fall of the Bakwena Dynasty of South-Central Botswana, 1820–1940." 2 vols. Ph.D. diss., Boston University, 1991.

———. "Some Notes on the Colonial Era History of the Central Kalahari Game Reserve Region." *Botswana Notes and Records* 20 (1988): 91–94.

Redfern, J. *Ruth and Seretse, "A Very Disreputable Transaction."* London: Victor Gollancz, 1955.

Robertson, H. H. "From Protectorate to Republic: The Political History of Botswana, 1926–1966." Ph.D. thesis, Dalhousie University, 1979.

Robins, E. *White Queen in Africa*. London: Robert Hale, 1967.

Schapera, Isaac. *A Short History of the Bakgatla-baga-Kgafela*. Cape Town: University of Cape Town School of African Studies Communications no. 3, N.S, 1942.

———."A Short History of the Bangwaketse." *African Studies*, 1 (1942): 1–26.

*———. *Ditirafalo tsa Merafe ya Batswana*. Alice, South Africa: Lovedale Press, 1940.

———. "The Early History of the Khurutshe." *Botswana Notes and Records* 2 (1970): 1–5.

———. "Kinship and Politics in Tswana History." *Journal of the Royal Anthropological Institute* 93, no. 2 (1963): 159–173.

———. "Notes on the Early History of the Kwena (BakwenabagaSechele)." *Botswana Notes and Records* 12 (1980): 83–87.

———. "Notes on the History of the Kaa." *African Studies* 4, no. 3 (1945): 109–121.

* ———. *Tribal Innovators: Tswana Chiefs and Social Change, 1795–1940*. London: Athlone Press, 1970.

Selolwane, O. "Colonization by Concession: Capitalist Expansion in the Bechuanaland Protectorate, 1885–1950." *Pula: Botswana Journal of African Studies* 2, no. 1 (February 1980): 75–124.

Shamukuni, D.M. "The Basubiya." *Botswana Notes and Records* 4 (1972): 161–184.

Shillington, K. *The Colonisation of the Southern Tswana, 1870–1900*. Braamfontein, South Africa: Ravan Press, 1985.

Silitshena, R. M. K. "Notes on the Origins of Some Settlements in the Kweneng District." *Botswana Notes and Records* 8 (1976): 97–103.

Sillery, Anthony. *The Bechuanaland Protectorate*. Cape Town: Oxford University Press, 1952.

———. *Botswana: A Short Political History*. London: Methuen, 1974.

* ———. *Founding a Protectorate: History of Bechuanaland, 1885–1895*. The Hague: Mouton, 1965.

———. *John Mackenzie of Bechuanaland: A Study in Humanitarian Imperialism 1835–1899*. Cape Town: Balkema, 1971.

———. *Sechele: The Story of an African Chief*. Oxford: G. Ronald, 1964.

Smith, E. W. *Great Lion of Bechuanaland: The Life and Times of Roger Price, Missionary*. London: LMS, 1957.

———. "Sebetwane and the Makololo." *African Studies* 15, no. 2 (1956): 49–74.

Spears, J.V. "An Epidemic among the Kgatla: The Influenza of 1918." *Botswana Notes and Records* 11 (1979): 69–76.

Spence, J. E. "British Policy Towards the High Commission Territories." *Journal of Modern African Studies* 2, no. 2 (1964): 221–246.

Tabler, E. C. *The Far Interior*. Cape Town: Balkema, 1955.

———. *Pioneers of Rhodesia*. Cape Town: C. Struik, 1966.

Tlou, T. "Documents on Botswana History: How Rhodes Tried to Seize Ngamiland." *Botswana Notes and Records* 7 (1975): 61–65.

———. "The History of Botswana Through Oral Traditions." *Botswana Notes and Records* 3 (1971): 79–110.

* ———. *A History of Ngamiland, 1750–1906: The Formation of an African State*. Gaborone: Macmillan Botswana, 1985.

———. "Khama III—Great Reformer and Innovator." *Botswana Notes and Records* 2 (1970): 98–105.

———. "Melao yaga Kgama: Transformation in the Nineteenth Century Ngwato State." M.A. thesis, University of Wisconsin, Madison, 1968.

———. "The Nature of Batswana States: Towards a Theory of Batswana Traditional Government—The Batawana Case." *Botswana Notes and Records* 6 (1974): 57–75.

———. "Servility and Political Control: Botlhanka among the Batawana of Northwestern Botswana, c. 1730–1906." In *Slavery in Africa: Historical and Anthropological Perspectives*. Edited by S. Miers and I. Kopytoff, 367–390. Madison: University of Wisconsin Press, 1977.

* Tlou, T. and A. Campbell. *History of Botswana*. Gaborone: Macmillan Botswana, 1984.

Truschel, L. W. "Accommodation Under Imperial Rule: The Tswana of the Bechuanaland Protectorate, 1895–1920." Ph.D. diss., Northwestern University, 1970.

———. "The Tawana and the Ngamiland Trek." *Botswana Notes and Records* 6 (1974): 47–55.

Tylden, G. "The Bechuanaland Border Police, 1885–1895." *Journal of the Society for Army Historical Research* 19 (1940).

van Onselen, C. "Reactions to Rinderpest in Southern Africa, 1896–1897." *Journal of African History* 13 (1972): 473–488.

Werbner, R. P. "Land and Chiefship in the Tati Concession." *Botswana Notes and Records* 2 (1970): 6–13.

———. "Local Adaptation and the Transformation of an Imperial Concession in Northeastern Botswana." *Africa* 41, no. 1 (1971): 32–41.

Westphal, E. O. J. "Notes on the Babirwa." *Botswana Notes and Records* 7 (1975): 191–194.

Will, D., and F. Dent. "The Boer War as Seen from Gaborone." *Botswana Notes and Records* 4 (1972): 195–210.

Williams, W. W. *The Life of Sir Charles Warren*. Oxford: Basil Blackwell, 1941.

* Wilmsen, E. N. *Land Filled With Flies: A Political Economy of the Kalahari*. Chicago: Chicago University Press, 1989.

Wylie, D. *A Little God: The Twilight of Patriarchy in a Southern African Chiefdom*. Hanover, New Hampshire: Wesleyan University Press, 1990.

Zaffiro, J. J. "Twin Births: African Nationalism and Government Information Policy in the Bechuanaland Protectorate, 1957–66." *International Journal of African Historical Studies* 22, no. 1 (1989): 1–26.

D. Political Science

1. General

* Colclough, C., and S. McCarthy. *The Political Economy of Botswana: A Study of Growth and Distribution*. London: Oxford University Press, 1980.

Holm, J. D. "Botswana: A Paternalistic Democracy." In *Democracy in Developing Countries, vol. 2: Africa*. Edited by L. Diamond et al., 179–215. Boulder, Colorado: Lynne Rienner, 1988.

———. *Dimension of Mass Involvement in Botswana Politics: A Test of Alternative Theories*. Beverly Hills, California: Sage Publications, 1974.

——. "Liberal Democracy and Rural Development in Botswana." *African Studies Review* 25, no. 1 (March 1982): 83–102.

Holm, J. and P. Molutsi, eds. *Democracy in Botswana*. The Proceedings of a Symposium held in Gaborone, 1–5 August 1988. Athens, Ohio. Ohio University Press, 1989.

Legum, C., ed. *Africa Contemporary Record*, 1 (1968–1969)+, c.v. "Botswana."

Molomo, M. G. and B. T. Mokopakgosi, ed. *Multi-party Democracy in Botswana*. Harare: SAPES Books, 1991.

*Molutsi, P. P. and J. D. Holm. "Developing Democracy When Civil Society is Weak: The Case of Botswana." *African Affairs* 89, no. 356(1990): 323–340.

Morgan, E. P. "Botswana: Development, Democracy, and Vulnerability." In *Southern Africa: The Continuing Crisis*. Edited by G. M. Carter and P. O'Meara, 228–248. London: Macmillan, 1979.

Munger, F. S. *Bechuanaland: Pan-African Outpost or Bantu Homeland?* London: Oxford University Press, 1965.

* Parson, J. *Botswana: Liberal Democracy and the Labor Reserve in Southern Africa*. Boulder: Westview Press, 1984.

——. "Cattle, Class, and the State in Rural Botswana." *Journal of Southern African Studies* 7, no. 2 (April 1981): 236–255.

——. "The Peasantariat and Politics: Migration, Wage Labor, and Agriculture in Botswana." *Africa Today* 31, no. 4 (1984): 5–25.

——. "Political Culture in Rural Botswana: A Survey Result." *Journal of Modern African Studies* 15 (1977): 639–650.

* Picard, L. A. *The Politics of Development in Botswana: A Model for Success?* Boulder, Colorado: Lynne Rienner, 1987.

Picard, L. A., ed. *The Evolution of Modern Botswana*. London: Rex Collings, 1985.

Stevens, R. P. *Lesotho, Botswana and Swaziland*. London: Pall Mall Press, 1967.

Wiseman, J. A. *Botswana*. Oxford: Clio Press, 1992.

2. Administration and Government

Bouman, M. "A Note on Chiefly and National Policing in Botswana." *Journal of Legal Pluralism and Unofficial Law* 25/26 (1987): 275–300.

Charlton, R. "Bureaucrats and Politicians in Botswana's Policy-making Process: A Re-interpretation." *Journal of Commonwealth and Comparative Politics* 29, no. 3 (1991): 265–282.

Egner, B. *The District Councils and Decentralization*. Gaborone: Economic Consultancies, 1987.

Fosbrooke, H. A. "An Assessment of the Importance of Institutions and Institutional Framework in Development." *Botswana Notes and Records* 5 (1973): 26–34.

Frimpong, K. "The Administration of Tribal Lands in Botswana." *Journal of African Law* 30, no. 1 (1986): 51–74.

Gillett, S. "Survival of Chieftaincy in Botswana." *African Affairs* 72, no. 287 (April 1973): 179–185.

Gontse, I. "Botswana National Assembly." *Parliamentarian* 60, no. 1 (1979): 21–28.

Gossett, C. "The Civil Service in Botswana." Ph.D. diss., Stanford University, 1986.

Griffiths, J. E. S. "A Note on the History and Functions of Local Government in Botswana." *Journal of Administration Overseas* 10 (1971): 127–133.

———. "A Note on Local Government in Botswana." *Botswana Notes and Records*, 2 (1970): 64–70.

———. "Notes on the History and Functions of Local Government in Botswana." *Journal of Administration Overseas* 10, no. 2 (April 1971): 127–133.

* Hailey, L. *The Republic of South Africa and the High Commission Territories*. London: Oxford University Press, 1963.

Hitchcock, R. and J. D. Holm. "Bureaucratic Domination of Hunter-Gatherer Societies: A Study of the San in Botswana." *Development and Change* 24, no. 2 (1993): 305–338.

Holm, J. D. and R. G. Morgan. "Coping with Drought in Botswana: An African Success." *Journal of Modern African Studies* 23, no. 3 (September 1985): 463–482.

Jeppe, W. J. O. "Local Government in Botswana." In *Local Government in Southern Africa*. Edited by W. B. Vosloo, D. A. Kotze, and W. J. O. Jeppe. Pretoria: Academica, 1974.

Jones, D. S. "Traditional Authority and State Administration in Botswana." *Journal of Modern African Studies* 21 (March 1983): 133–139.

Luke, T. C. *Report on Localization and Training*. Gaborone: Government Printer, 1966.

Maluwa, T. "The Concept of Asylum and the Protection of Refugees in Botswana: Some Legal and Political Aspects." *International Journal of Refugee Law* 2, no. 4 (1990): 587–610.

Mentz, J. C. N. "Evaluation of the Role of the Presidential Commission on Localization and Training in Implementing the Policy of Localization in Botswana." *Botswana Notes and Records* 17 (1985): 65–75.

Picard, L. A. "Bureaucrats, Cattle and Public Policy: Land Tenure Changes in Botswana." *Comparative Political Studies* 13, no. 3 (October 1980): 313–356.

———. "Development Administration Revisited: Administrative Attitudes in Tanzania and Botswana." *Journal of Contemporary African Studies* 2, no. 1 (October 1982): 31–58.

———. *District Administration Training in Botswana*. Gaborone: Ministry of Local Government and Lands, 1984.

———. "District Councils in Botswana: A Remnant of Local Autonomy." *Journal of Modern African Studies* 17, no. 2 (1979): 285–308.

———. "Independent Botswana: The District Administration and Political Control." *Journal of African Studies* 8, no. 3 (Fall 1981): 98–110.

———. "Rural Development in Botswana: Administrative Structures and Public Policy." *Journal of Developing Areas* 13, no. 3 (April 1979): 283–300.

Raphaeli, M., J. Roumaniand, and A.C. MacKellar. *Public Sector Management in Botswana*. Washington, D.C.: World Bank, 1984.

Reilly, W. "Decentralization in Botswana—Myth or Reality?" In *Local Government in the Third World: The Experience of Tropical Africa*. Edited by P. Mawhood, 141–176. Chichester: John Wiley and Sons, 1983.

Shuttleworth, G. "The Real Earnings of Civil Servants in Central Government Since Independence." *Botswana Notes and Records* 13 (1981): 25–32.

Simmons, C. and S. Lyons. "Rhetoric and Reality: The Management of Botswana's 1982–1988 Drought Relief Programme." *Journal of International Development* 4, no. 6 (1992): 607–631.

Tordoff, W. "Local Administration in Botswana." *Journal of Administration Overseas* 12, no. 4 (October 1973): 172–183; 13, 1 (January 1974): 293–304.

——. "Local Administration in Botswana." *Public Administration and Development*, 8, no. 2 (1988): 183–202.

Vengroff, R. "Traditional Political Structures in the Contemporary Context: The Chieftaincy in the Kweneng." *African Studies*, 34, no. 1 (1975): 39–58.

Watson, D. A. *Report on a Study of Local Government and District Administration Training*. Gaborone: Government Printer, 1978.

Zaffiro, J. J. "Facing Up to a Crisis: The Politics of AIDS Policy in Botswana." *Scandinavian Journal of Development Alternatives* 13, no. 1 (1994): 79–111.

3. Constitutional Development, Law

Brewer, I. G. "A Note on the Botswana Customary Courts (Amendment) Act of 1972." *Comparative and International Law Journal of Southern Africa* 6 (1973): 282–286.

——. "The Sources of Criminal Law of Botswana." *Journal of African Law* 18, no. 1 (1974): 24–36.

Campbell, A. C., S. A. Roberts, and J. M. Walker. *A Restatement of the Malete Law of Family Relations, Land, and Succession to Property*. Gaborone: Government Printer, 1971.

* Comaroff, J. L., and S. A. Roberts. *Rules and Processes: The Cultural Logic of Dispute in an African Context*. Chicago: University of Chicago Press, 1981.

——. "Marriage and Extra-Marital Sexuality: The Dialectics of Legal Change Among the Kgatla." *Journal of African Law* 21, no. 1 (1977).

Edwards, R. H. "Political and Constitutional Changes in the Bechuanaland Protectorate." In *Boston University Papers on Africa: Transition in African Politics*. Edited by J. A. Butler and A. A. Castagno, 135–165. New York: Praeger, 1967.

Forster, B. "Introduction to the History of the Administration of Justice of the Republic of Botswana." *Botswana Notes and Records* 13 (1981): 89–100.

Grant, S. " 'Reduced to Nothing?' Chieftaincy and a Traditional Town: The Case of Linchwe II Kgafela and Mochudi." *Botswana Notes and Records* 12 (1980): 89–100.

Groff, D. "Tswana Government and Law in the Time of Seepapitso, 1910–1916." In *Law in Colonial Africa.* Edited by K. Mann and R. Roberts. Portsmouth, New Hampshire: Heinemann, 1991.

Himsworth, C. M. G. "The Botswana Customary Law Act, 1969." *Journal of African Law* 16 (1972): 4–18.

Kiggundu, J. "Company Law: Some Interesting Aspects in Botswana." *Commonwealth Law Bulletin* 15, no. 4 (1989): 1524–1532.

Kuper, A. "The Work of Customary Courts: Some Facts and Speculations." *African Studies* 28, no. 1 (1969): 37–48.

Love, C. "Court Sentencing in Botswana: A Role for Probation?" *Journal of Social Development in Africa* 7, no. 2 (1992): 5–17.

Molokomme, A. "Marriage: What Every Woman Wants or a Declaration of Civil Death? Some Legal Aspects of the Status of Married Women in Botswana." *Pula: Botswana Journal of African Studies* (1984): 70–79.

———. "The Reception and Development of Roman-Dutch Law in Botswana." *Lesotho Law Journal* 1 (1985): 121–134.

Otlhogile, B. "Juvenile Delinquency in Botswana and the 1981 Children's Act." *Comparative and International Law Journal of Southern Africa* 18, no. 3 (1985): 396–403.

Pain, J. H. "The Reception of English and Roman-Dutch Law in Africa with reference to Botswana, Lesotho, and Swaziland." *Comparative and International Law Journal of South Africa* 11, no. 2 (1978): 137–167.

Palley, C. *The Constitutional History and Law of Southern Rhodesia.* Oxford: Clarendon Press, 1966.

Proctor, J. H. "The House of Chiefs and the Political Development of Botswana." *Journal of Modern African Studies* 6, no. 1 (1968): 59–79.

Roberts, S. "Kgatla Law and Social Change." *Botswana Notes and Records* 2 (1970): 56–61.

———. "Marriage and Extra-marital Sexuality—The Dialectics of Legal Change among the Kgatla." *Journal of African Law* 21 (1977): 97–123.

———. "The Recording of Customary Law—Some Problems of Method." *Botswana Notes and Records* 3 (1971): 12–21.

———. *A Restatement of the Kgatla Law of Domestic Relations.* Gaborone: Government Printer, 1970.

———. *A Restatement of the Kgatla Law of Succession to Property.* Gaborone: Government Printer, 1970.

———. *A Restatement of the Kgatla Law Relating to Land and Natural Resources.* Gaborone: Government Printer, 1970.

———. "The Settlement of Family Disputes in the Kgatla Customary Courts." *Journal of African Law* 15 (1971): 60–76.

———. "Tradition and Change at Mochudi." *African Law Studies* 17 (1979): 37–51.

———. *Tswana Family Law.* London: Sweet and Maxwell, 1972.

———. "The Tswana Polity and 'Tswana Law and Custom' Reconsidered." *Journal of Southern African Studies* 12, no. 1 (October 1985): 75–87.

Roberts, S., and J. Comaroff. "Chief's Decision and the Devolution of Property in a Tswana Chiefdom." In *Politics in Leadership: A Comparative Perspective.* Edited by W. A. Shack and P. S. Cohen, 115–138. Oxford: Clarendon Press, 1979.

Saunders, A. J. G. M. "Chieftainship and Western Democracy in Botswana." *Journal of Contemporary African Studies* 2 (1983): 365–379.

———. "Constitutionalism in Botswana—A Valiant Attempt at Judicial Activism." *Comparative and International Law Journal of Southern Africa* 16 (1983): 350–373; 17 (1984): 49–64.

———. "The Internal Conflict of Laws in Botswana." *Botswana Notes and Records* 17 (1985): 77–88.

———. "Legal Dualism in Lesotho, Botswana and Swaziland." *Lesotho Law Journal* 1 (1985): 47–67.

Schapera, I. "Contract in Tswana Case Law." *Journal of African Law* 9, no. 3 (Fall, 1963): 142–153.

———. "Contract in Tswana Law." In *Ideas and Procedures in African Customary Law.* Edited by M. Gluckman, 318–332. London: Oxford University Press, 1969.

———. "Early European Influences on Tswana Law." *Journal of African Law* 31, no. 1/2 (1987): 151–160.

* ———. *A Handbook of Tswana Law and Custom.* London: Frank Cass, reprint, 1977.

———. *Mekgwa le Melao ya Batswana.* Alice, South Africa: Lovedale Press, 1938.

———. *The Political Annals of a Tswana Tribe.* Cape Town: University of Cape Town School of African Studies Communication N.S. 18, 1947.

———. "Some Notes on Tswana Bogadi." *Journal of African Law* 22, no. 2 (1978): 112–124.

———. "The Sources of Law in Tswana Tribal Courts: Legislation and Precedent." *Journal of African Law* 1, no. 3 (Fall 1957): 150–162.

———. *Tribal Legislation Among the Tswana of the Bechuanaland Protectorate.* London: London School of Economics, 1943.

———. "Tswana Legal Maxims." *Africa* 36, no. 2 (April 1966): 121–134.

———. "The Work of Tribal Courts in the Bechuanaland Protectorate." *African Studies* 2 (1943): 27–40.

van Niekerk, B. J. "Notes on the Administration of Justice Among the Kwena." *African Studies* 25, no. 1 (1966): 37–45.

Werbner, R. "Small Man Politics and the Rule of Law: Centre-Periphery Relations in East-Central Botswana." *Journal of African Law* 21 (1977): 24–39.

4. Elections, Political Parties

Cohen, D. L. "The Botswana Political Elite: Evidence from the 1974 General Election." *Journal of Southern African Affairs* 4, no. 3 (1979): 347–370.

Holm, J. D. "Elections in Botswana: Institutionalization of a New System of Legitimacy." In *Elections in Africa*. Edited by F. Hayward, 121–148. Boulder, Colorado: Westview Press, 1986.

McCartney, W. J. A. "Botswana Goes to the Polls." *Africa Report* 14, no. 8 (December 1969): 28–32.

Nengwekhulu, R. "Some Findings on the Origins of Political Parties in Botswana." *Pula: Botswana Journal of African Studies* 1, no. 2 (June 1979): 47–76.

Parson, J. "A Note on the 1974 General Election in Botswana and the UBLS Election Study." *Botswana Notes and Records* 7 (1975): 73–80.

———. "Political Culture in Rural Botswana: A Survey Result." *Journal of Modern African Studies* 15 (1977): 639–656.

Polhemus, J. H. "Botswana Votes: Parties and Elections in an African Democracy." *Journal of Modern African Studies* 21, no. 3 (September 1983): 397–430.

Ramsay, J. "The 1962 BPP Split." *Botswana Notes and Records* 25 (1993): 9–88.

Stevens, C., and J. Speed. "Multi-Partyism in Africa: The Case of Botswana Revisited." *African Affairs* 77, no. 304 (January 1978): 381–387.

Weiseman, J. A. "Multi-Partyism in Africa: The Case of Botswana." *African Affairs* 76, no. 302 (1977): 70–79.

Zaffiro, J. J. "The Press and Political Opposition in Botswana." *Journal of Commonwealth and Comparative Politics* 27, no. 1 (1989): 51–73.

5. External Relations

Bodenmuller, R. *Botswana, Lesotho and Swaziland: Their External Relations and Policy Towards South Africa*. Pretoria: Africa Institute of South Africa, 1973.

* Carter, M., and E.P. Morgan, ed. *From the Frontline: Speeches of Sir Seretse Khama*. London: Rex Collings, 1980.

Dale, R. "Botswana." In *Southern Africa in Perspective: Essays in Regional Politics*. Edited by C. P. Potholm and R. Dale, 110–124. New York: Free Press, 1972.

———. "Botswana's Relations With Bophuthatswana: The Politics of Ethnicity, Legitimacy, and Propinquity in Southern Africa." *Journal for Contemporary History/Joernaal Vir Eietydse Geskiedenis* 17, no. 2 (1992): 1–19.

———. "The Loosening Connection in Anglophone Southern Africa: Botswana and the Rhodesian Regime, 1965–1980." *Journal of Contemporary African Studies* 2, no. 2 (1983): 257–285.

———. "Not Always So Placid a Place: Botswana under Attack." *African Affairs* 86 (January 1987), 73–91.

———. "The Politics of National Security in Botswana: 1900–1990." *Journal of Contemporary African Studies* 12, no. 1 (1993): 40–56.

Halpern, J. *South Africa's Hostages*. Harmondsworth: Penguin, 1965.

Landell-Mills, P.M. "The 1969 Southern African Customs Union Agreement." *Journal of Modern African Studies* 9, no. 2 (1971): 263–282.

Maluwa, T. "The Concept of Asylum and the Protection of Refugees in Botswana: Some Legal and Political Aspects." *International Journal of Refugee Law* 2, no. 4 (1990): 587–610.

Mangope, L. "Will Bophuthatswana Join Botswana?" *Munger Africana Library Notes* 20 (1973): 1–40.

Nyelele, L., and E. Drake. *The Raid on Gaborone: June 14, 1985. A Memorial.* Gaborone: Nyelele and Drake, 1986.

Polhemus, J. M. "The Refugee Factor in Botswana." *Immigrants and Minorities* 4, no. 1 (1985): 28–45.

Southall, R. "Botswana as a Host Country for Refugees." *Journal of Commonwealth and Comparative Politics* 22, no. 2 (1984): 151–179.

* Thompson, C. *The Frontline States in the Liberation of Zimbabwe.* Boulder, Colorado: Westview Press, 1985.

Zaffiro, J.J. "African Legislatures and Foreign Policy: The Botswana Case." *Botswana Notes and Records* 25 (1993): 39–58.

———. "Botswana's Foreign Policy in the Post-Cold War Era." In *African Foreign Policies.* Edited by Stephen Wright. Boulder, Colorado: Westview, 1995.

———. "Foreign Policy-Making in Botswana: Structure and Process." In *The Political Economy in Botswana.* Edited by Steven Stedman, 139–160. Boulder, Colorado: Lynne Reinner, 1993.

———. "U.S. Relations With Botswana: 1966–1989." *TransAfrica Forum* 9, no. 3 (Fall 1992): 57–74.

Zealey, L. "Carnage in Botswana." *Africa* 167 (July 1985): 181.

Zetterqvist, J. *Refugees in Botswana, in the Light of International Law.* Uppsala, Sweden: Scandinavian Institute of African Studies, Research Report No. 87, 1990.

E. Science

1. Climate

Andersson, R. "Climatic Factors in Botswana." *Botswana Notes and Records* 2 (1970): 75–78.

Andringa, J. "Clear Skies and Cloudy Days in Botswana." *Botswana Notes and Records* 18 (1986): 115–121.

———. "The Climate of Botswana in Histograms." *Botswana Notes and Records* 16 (1984): 117–125.

Brown, R. C. "Climate and Climatic Trends in the Ghanzi District." *Botswana Notes and Records* 6 (1974): 133–146.

Cooke, H. J. "The Evidence from Northern Botswana of Late Quaternary Climatic Change." In *Proceedings of the International Symposium on Late Cenozoic Palaeoclimates of the Southern Hemisphere.* 265–278. Rotterdam: A. A. Balkema, 1984.

Devitt, P. "Coping with Drought in the Kalahari." In *Drought in Africa 2.* Edited by D. Dalby, R. J. Harrison Church, and F. Bezzaz, 186–200. London: International African Institute, 1977.

Grove, A. T. "Landforms and Climatic Change in the Kalahari and Ngamiland." *The Geographical Journal* 135 (1969): 191–212.

Mazor, E. "Rain Recharge in the Kalahari: A Note on Some Approaches to the Problem." *Journal of Hydrology* 55, no. 1 (February 1982): 137–144.

Vierich, H. *Drought 1979: Socio-economic Survey of Drought Impact in Kweneng.* Gaborone: Ministry of Agriculture Division of Planning and Statistics, 1979.

Vierich, H., and C. Sheppard. *Drought in Botswana: Socioeconomic Impact and Government Policy.* Gaborone: Rural Sociology Unit, 1980.

Wayland, E. J. "Past Climates and Present Groundwater Supplies in the Bechuanaland Protectorate." *Botswana Notes and Records* 13 (1981): 13–18.

2. Diet, Medicine, and Health

Alnaes, K. "Living With the Past: The Songs of the Herero in Botswana." *Africa* 59, no. 3 (1989): 267–299.

Barber, E. L. "Biomedical Resistance to Ethnomedicine in Botswana." *Social Science and Medicine* 22, no. 1 (1986): 75–80.

Corlett, J. R. "Health Related Physical Fitness of Young Tswana Adults." *Botswana Notes and Records* 16 (1984): 59–61.

Grivetti, L., and F. Mogome. "A Survey of Food Availability among the BaTlokwa-ba-Moshaweng of Tlokweng, Southeast District, Republic of Botswana." In *Occasional Reports on Food and Diet.* Gaborone: Ministry of Health Director of Medical Services, 1974.

Haram, L. "Tswana Medicine in Interaction With Biomedicine." *Social Science and Medicine* 33, no. 2 (1991): 167–175.

Hogh, B., and E. Petersen. "The Basic Health Care System in Botswana: A Study of the Distribution and Cost in the Period 1973–1979." *Social Science and Medicine* 19, no. 8 (1984): 783–792.

Ingstad, B. "The Cultural Construction of AIDS and its Consequences for Prevention in Botswana." *Medical Anthropology Quarterly* 4, no. 1 (1990): 28–40.

Larson, T. J. "The Ethno-Medicine of the Hambukushu in 1950." *Botswana Notes and Records* 18 (1986): 39–47.

Merriweather, A. *Desert Doctor: Medicine and Evangelism in the Kalahari Desert.* Lutterworth, 1974.

Molefi, R. K. K. *A Medical History of Botswana 1885–1966.* Forthcoming.

Nurse, G. T. and T. Jenkins. *Health and the Hunter-Gatherer.* Basel, Switzerland: S. Karger AG, 1977.

Otzen, W. et al. *Integrated Rural Development Planning with Emphasis on Nutritional Basic Needs for Serowe District/Botswana.* Berlin: German Development Institute, 1979.

Selelo-Kupe, S. *An Uneasy Walk to Quality: The Evolution of Black Nursing Education.* W.K. Kellogg Foundation, 1993.

Squires, B. T. *The Feeding and Health of African School Children: Report on the Kanye Nutrition Experiment.* Cape Town: University of Cape Town School of African Studies Communications 20, 1949.

——. "Malnutrition Amongst Tswana Children." *African Studies*, 2 (1943): 210–214.

Staugard, F. *Traditional Healers: Traditional Medicine in Botswana.* Broadhurst, Botswana: Ipelegeng Publishers, 1985.

——. *Traditional Medicine in a Transitional Society: Botswana Moving Towards the Year 2000.* Broadhurst, Botswana: Ipelegeng Publishers, 1989.

Teichler, G. H. "Notes on the Botswana Pharmacopoeia." *Botswana Notes and Records* 3 (1971): 8–11.

Ulin, P. R. "The Traditional Healer of Botswana in a Changing Society." *Botswana Notes and Records* 7 (1975): 95–102.

Zaffiro, J. J. "Aids in Botswana." In *Health Care in Sub-Saharan Africa.* Edited by E. Kalipeni and P. Thiuri. Forthcoming.

3. Geography, Geology

Baillieul, T. A. "A Reconnaissance Survey of the Cover Sands in the Republic of Botswana." *Journal of Sedimentology and Petrology*, 45 (1975): 494–503.

Baldock, J. W. *Resources Inventory of Botswana: Metallic Minerals, Mineral Fuels and Diamonds.* Gaborone: Geological Survey of Botswana Mineral Resources Report 4, 1977.

Boocock, C., and O. J. van Straten. "Notes on the Geology and Hydrogeology of the Central Kalahari Region, Bechuanaland Protectorate." *Transactions of the Geological Society of South Africa* 65, no. 1 (1962): 125–170.

Clarke-Lowe, D. D., and A. K. Yeats. *The Hydrocarbon Prospects of Botswana.* Gaborone: Shell Coal Botswana Report to Botswana Government, 1977.

Cooke, H. J. "The Origin of the Makgadikgadi Pans." *Botswana Notes and Records* 11 (1979): 37–42.

Cooke, H. J., and T. A. Baillieul. "The Caves of Ngamiland: An Interim Report on Explorations and Fieldwork 1972–1974." *Botswana Notes and Records* 6 (1974): 147–156.

Ebert, J. and R.K. Hitchcock. "Ancient Lake Makgadikgadi, Botswana: Mapping, Measurement and Palaeoclimatic Significance." *Palaeo-Ecology of Africa* 10/11 (1978): 47–56.

Evans, M. E. "A Palaeomagnetic Study of the Gaborones Granite of Botswana." *Geophysics Journal of the Royal Astronomical Society* 12 (1967): 491–498.

Geological Survey of Botswana, Lobatse. *Bulletin*, 1+ (1966+); reports, maps.

Green, D., R.M. Crockett and M.T. Jones. "Tectonic Control of Karoo Sedimentation in Mid-Eastern Botswana." *Transactions of the Geological Society of South Africa* 83 (1980): 213–219.

Grey, D. R. C., and H. J. Cooke. "Some Problems in the Quaternary Evolution of the Landforms of Northern Botswana." *Catena* 4 (1977): 123–133.

Helgren, D. M. "Historical Geomorphology and Geoarchaeology in the Southwestern Makgadikgadi Basin, Botswana." *Annals of the Association of American Geographers* 74 (June 1984): 298–307.

Jones, C. R. "The Geology of the Kalahari." *Botswana Notes and Records* 12 (1980): 1–14.

Jones, C. R., and R.M. Key. "Botswana's Contribution to the International Geodynamics Project: A Review of a Second Two Years' Participation." *Botswana Notes and Records* 9 (1977): 123–127.

———. "Botswana's Contribution to the International Geodynamics Project: A Terminal Report." *Botswana Notes and Records* 11 (1979): 43–54.

Key, R. M. *The Geology of the Area Around Francistown and Phikwe, Northeast and Central Districts, Botswana.* Lobatse: Geological Survey, 1976.

Key, R. M., M. Litherland and J.V. Hepworth. "The Evolution of the Archaean Crust of Northeast Botswana." *Precambrian Research* 3 (1976): 375–413.

Key, R. M. and E.P. Wright. "The Genesis of the Gaborone Rapakivi Granite Complex in Southern Africa." *Journal of the Geological Society* 139 (1982): 109–126.

Lancaster, I. N. "Pans of the Southern Kalahari." *Botswana Notes and Records* 6 (1974): 157–169.

———. "The Pans of the Southern Kalahari, Botswana." *Geographical Journal* 144/145 (1978–1979): 81–98.

Litherland, M. "The Geodynamics Project Seminar: A Review of Two Years' Participation." *Botswana Notes and Records* 6 (1974): 171–178.

Mallick, D. I. J. *A Geological Interpretation of Landsat Imagery and Air Photography of Botswana.* London: HMSO, 1981.

Mallick, D. I. J., F. Habgood, and A. C. Skinner. "Geological Interpretation of Landsat Imagery and Air Photography of Botswana." *Overseas Geological and Mineral Resources* 56 (1981): 1–25.

McConnell, R. B. "Notes on the Geology and Geomorphology of the Bechuanaland Protectorate." In *Proceedings of the 20th International Geological Congress*, 175–186. Mexico City: IGC, 1959.

Morel, S. W. "The Age of the Gaborone Rapakivi Granite Complex." *Botswana Notes and Records* 17 (1985): 181–182.

Reeves, C. V. "Rafting in the Kalahari?" *Nature* 237 (1978): 222–223.

Rogers, A. W. "The Build of the Kalahari." *South African Geographical Journal* 17 (1934): 3–12.

———. "The Surface Geology of the Kalahari." *Transactions of the Royal Society of South Africa* 24 (1936): 57–80.

Silitshena, R. M. K., and G. McLeod. *Botswana: A Physical, Social and Economic Geography.* Gaborone: Longman Botswana, 1989.

Stansfield, G. *The Geology of the Area Around Dukwe and Tlalamabele, Central District, Botswana.* Gaborone: Geological Surveys Department, Minister of Mineral Resources and Water Affairs, 1973.

Vink, B. W. "Some Geological Features of the Central Mokgware Hills Central District, Botswana." *Botswana Notes and Records* 18 (1986): 63–70.

Watts, N. L. "Quaternary Pedogenic Calcretes from the Kalahari (Southern Africa): Mineralogy, Genesis and Diagenesis." *Sedimentology* 27 (1980): 661–686.

Wayland, E. J. "More about the Kalahari." *Geographical Journal* 119 (1953): 49–56.

Wright, E. B. "Geological Studies in the Northern Kalahari." *Geographical Journal* 144, no. 2 (1978): 235–250.

4. Land and Water Resources

Arntzen, J. W. "Economic Policies and Rangeland Degradation in Botswana." *Journal of International Development* 2, no. 4 (1990): 471–499.

Bawden, M. G. and A. R. Stobbs. *The Land Resources of Eastern Bechuanaland.* Tolworth, England: Directorate of Overseas Surveys Forestry and Land Use Section, 1968.

Cooke, J. "Environmental Conservation—The Road to Survival." *Botswana Notes and Records* 23 (1991): 83–100.

Cooke, H. J. "The Kalahari Today: A Case of Conflict Over Resource Use." *Geographical Journal* 151 (March 1985): 75–85.

———. "On the Conservation of Natural Resources, with Special Reference to the Kalahari in Botswana." *Botswana Notes and Records* 13 (1981): 141–143.

Debenham, F. *Report on the Water Resources of the Bechuanaland Protectorate, Northern Rhodesia, et al.* Colonial Research Publications 2. London: HMSO, 1948.

Jennings, C. M. H., et al. "Environmental Isotopes As Aid to Investigation of Ground Water Problems in Botswana." *Botswana Notes and Records* 5 (1973): 179–190.

McCarthy, T. S. "Physical and Biological Processes Controlling the Okavango Delta—A Review of Recent Research." *Botswana Notes and Records* 24 (1992): 57–86.

Mazor, E., et al. "Northern Kalahari Groundwaters: Hydrologic, Isotopic and Chemical Studies at Orapa, Botswana." *Journal of Hydrology* 34 (1977): 203–234.

Mitchell, A. J. B. *The Irrigation Potential of Soils Along the Main Rivers of Eastern Botswana—A Reconnaissance Assessment.* Surbiton, England: Land Resources Division, Overseas Development Ministry, 1976.

Pretorius, D. A. "The Contribution of the Aeromagnetic Interpretation to an Assessment of the Mineral Potential of Botswana." In *Reconnaissance Aeromagnetic Survey of Botswana, 1975–1977.* Lobatse: Geological Survey, n.d., A14–50.

Schwartz, E. H. L. *The Kalahari or Thirstland Redemption.* Cape Town: T. M. Miller, 1928.

Shaw, P. "The Desiccation of Lake Ngami: A Historical Perspective." *Geographical Journal* 151, no. 3 (1985): 318–326
———. "A Historical Note on the Outflows of the Okavango Delta System." *Botswana Notes and Records* 16 (1984): 127–130.
———. "The Okavango Research Centre." *Botswana Notes and Records* 23 (1991): 296.
Thomas, D. S. G., and P. Shaw. *The Kalahari Environment.* New York: Cambridge University Press, 1991.
Woto, T., Jr. "Solar Desalination for the Provision of Drinking Water to Small Settlements in the Kgalagadi Desert—Botswana." *Botswana Notes and Records* 21 (1989): 43–60.

5. Vegetation

Allen, A. "A Preliminary Reconnaissance of the Vegetation of Orapa and Environs." *Botswana Notes and Records* 10 (1978): 169–185.
Campbell, A., and R. Hitchcock. "Some Setswana Names of Woody Plants." *Botswana Notes and Records* 17 (1985): 117–129.
Cole, M. M. "The Vegetation of the Ghanzi Area of Western Botswana." *Journal of Biography* 3, no. 3 (1976): 169–196.
Labovitch, L. "Traditional and New Methods of Dealing with Arable Weeds in Botswana." *Botswana Notes and Records* 10 (1978): 187–197.
Leistner, O. A. *The Plant Ecology of the Southern Kalahari.* Pretoria: South African Department of Agricultural and Technical Services Botanical Survey Memoir 38, 1967.
Miller, O. B. "Addenda and Corrigenda to the Woody Plants of the Bechuanaland Protectorate." *Journal of South African Botany* 19 (1953): 177–182.
———. "The Woody Plants of the Bechuanaland Protectorate." *Journal of South African Botany* 18 (1952): 1–100.
Reavell, P. E. "A Discussion of Factors Limiting Plant Plankton Growth in the Water of the Okavango Delta." *Botswana Notes and Records* 9 (1977): 129–137.
Ringrose, S., and W. Matheson. "Characterization of Woody Vegetation Cover in the South-East Botswana Kalahari." *Global Ecology and Biogeography Letters* 1, no. 6 (1991): 176–181.
Timberlake, J. *Handbook of Botswana Acacias.* Gaborone: Ministry of Agriculture Divison of Land Utilization, 1980.
Van Voorthuizen, E. G. "The Mopane Tree." *Botswana Notes and Records* 8 (1976): 227–230.
Weare, P. R., and A. Yalala. "Provisional Vegetation Map of Botswana." *Botswana Notes and Records* 3 (1971): 131–147.

6. Wildlife

Archer, A. L. "Results of the Winifred T. Carter Expedition 1975 to Botswana, Mammals—Chiroptera." *Botswana Notes and Records* 9 (1977): 145–155.

Auerbach, R. *The Amphibians and Reptiles of Botswana.* Gaborone: Mokwepa Consultants, 1988.

———. "First Steps in Setswana Herpetology." *Botswana Notes and Records* 18 (1986): 71–90.

———. *The Reptiles of Gaborone.* Gaborone: Botswana Book Centre, 1985.

The Babbler. Newsletter of the Botswana Bird Club. Gaborone: Botswana Society, 1981 +.

Barker, J. F. "The Distribution of Acridoidea (Grasshoppers) in Relation to Overgrazing." *Botswana Notes and Records* 17 (1985): 141–148.

———. "A Preliminary Study of the Distribution of Acridoidea in Relation to Overgrazing in Botswana." *Botswana Notes and Records* 14 (1982): 1–10.

———. "Towards a Biogeography of the Kalahari: Part 1, To Which Region Does the Kalahari Belong?" *Botswana Notes and Records* 15 (1983): 85–91.

Busse, C. "Leopard and Lion Predation Upon Chacma Baboons Living in the Moremi Wildlife Reserve." *Botswana Notes and Records* 12 (1980): 15–21.

Campbell, A. "A Comment on Kalahari Wildlife and the Khukhe Fence." *Botswana Notes and Records* 13 (1981): 111–118.

Child, G. *An Ecological Survey of Northeastern Botswana.* No. TA 2563. Rome: FAO, 1968.

Child, G., and J. D. Le Riche. "Recent Springbok Treks (Mass Movements in South Western Botswana." *Mammalia* 33 (1969): 499–504.

Dawson, J. L. "The Birds of the Kutse Game Reserve." *Botswana Notes and Records* 7 (1975): 141–150.

DeGraff, G. "Notes on the Southern African Black-Tailed Tree Rat (Thallomys Paedulcus) and its Occurrence in the Kalahari Gemsbok National Park." *Koedoe* 21 (1978): 181–190.

———. "On the Mole Rat (Cryptomys Hottentotus Damarensis) (Rhodentia) in the Kalahari Gemsbok National Park." *Koedoe* 15 (1972): 25–35.

Eagle, V. "A Survey of the Spider Fauna of Botswana: Project Report, June 1984." *Botswana Notes and Records* 17 (1985): 131–139.

Eloff, F. C. "Cub Mortality in the Kalahari Lion." *Koedoe* 23 (1980): 163–170.

———. "Water Use by the Kalahari Lion." *Koedoe* 16 (1973): 149–154.

Forchhammer, P. "Seasonal and Daily Variations in Activity of Antlife Flower Beetles (Anthicidae) collected in Serowe, Botswana." *Botswana Notes and Records* 17 (1985): 163–174.

Haacke, W. D. "A New Gecko (Sauria Geckonidae) from Bechuanaland." *Arnoldia* 2, no. 25 (July 21, 1966): 1–7.

Hewitt, J. "Scientific Results of the Vernay-Lang Kalahari Expedition, March to September, 1930: The Trap-Door Spiders, Scorpions and Solifuges." *Annals of the Transvaal Museum* 16, no. 3 (1935): 459–479, plus plates 22–25.

Hey, R. B., et al. "Ecological Shifts in Sympathy: Kalahari Fossorial Lizards (Typhlosaurus)." *Ecology* 55 (1974): 304–316.

Hodgeson, M. "Note: The Formation of the Botswana Bird Club." *Botswana Notes and Records* 13 (1980): 178–179.

Houston, J. F. T. "Grasshoppers of South-east Botswana." *Botswana Notes and Records* 9 (1977): 139–143.

Lamoral, B. H. " 'Paraoecobius Wilmotae,' a New Genus and Species of Spider from the Okavango Delta, Botswana." *Annals of the Natal Museum* 24, no. 2 (1981): 507–512.

Lawrence, R. F. "Scientific Results of the Vernay-Lang Kalahari Expedition, March–September 1930, Spiders." *Annals of the Transvaal Museum* 17, no. 2 (1936): 145–158.

Martin, E. B. "The Ivory Industry in Botswana." *African Elephant and Rhino Group Newsletter* 3 (June 1984): 5–7.

McBride, C. J. "Age and Size Categories of Lion Prey in Chobe National Park, Botswana." *Botswana Notes and Records* 16 (1984): 139–143.

Mills, M. G. L. "Ecology and Behaviour of the Brown Hyaena in the Kalahari." In *Proceedings of a Symposium on Endangered Wildlife in Southern Africa*. Johannesburg: Endangered Wildlife Trust, 1976.

Nchunga, M.L. *A Study of the Potential for Commercial Use of Wildlife, in the North Eastern Tuli Block*. Gaborone: Department of Wildlife, 1978.

Nel, J. A. J., and I. L. Rautenback. "Body Temperatures of Some Kalahari Rodents." *Annals of the Transvaal Museum* 30, no. 17 (August 1977): 207–210.

Owens, M., and D. Owens. *Cry of the Kalahari: An American Couple's Seven Years in Africa's Last Great Wilderness*. Boston: Houghton Mifflin, 1984.

Parris, R. "Important Role of the Kalahari Pans." *African Wildlife* 24 (1970): 234–237.

Parry, D. C., and B. M. Campbell. "Wildlife Management Areas in Botswana." *Botswana Notes and Records* 22 (1990): 65–78.

Pinaka, E. R. "Lizard Species Density in the Kalahari Desert." *Ecology* 52, no. 6 (1971): 1024–1029.

Pinaka, E. R., and R. B. Huey. "Comparative Ecology, Resource Utilization and Niche Segregation Among Gekkonid Lizards in the Southern Kalahari." *Copeia* 4 (1978): 691–701.

Pinhey, E. "Check List of the Butterflies (Lepidoptera Rhopalocera) of Botswana, Part 3." *Botswana Notes and Records* 6 (1974): 197–214.

Raseroka, B. H. "Past and Present Distribution of Buffalo in Botswana." *Botswana Notes and Records* 7 (1975): 131–140.

Simon, C. D. "Food Studies on the Chobe Bushbuck, Tragelaphus Scriptus Ornatus Bocock 1900." *Arnoldia* 6, no. 32 (June 28, 1974): 1–9.

Smithers, R. H. N. *A Checklist of the Birds of Bechuanaland Protectorate and Caprivi Strip*. Salisbury: Trustees of the National Museum of Rhodesia, 1964.

———. *The Mammals of Botswana*. Salisbury: Trustees of the National Museum of Rhodesia Museum Memoir 4, 1971.

Sommerlatte, M. W. L. "A Preliminary Report on the Number, Distribution and Movement of Elephants in the Chobe Park with Notes on Browse Utilization." *Botswana Notes and Records* 7 (1975): 121–129.

Spickett, A. M. "Kalahari's Sand Tampan, a Remarkable Creature." *Bustos* 13, no. 4 (July 1984): 39–41.

Spinage, C. *History and Evolution of the Fauna Conservation Laws of Botswana*. Gaborone: The Botswana Society, 1991.

Taylor, C. R. "Ranching Arid Areas: Physiology of Wild and Domestic Ungulates in the Desert." *Botswana Notes and Records* 1 (1969): 89–95.

Turton, L. *Some Flowering Plants of South Eastern Botswana*. Illustrated by V. Ermatinger-Blomberg. Gaborone: The Botswana Society, 1988.

van Hille, J. C. "Anthicidae (Coleoptera Hetsesoma) Collected in Botswana 1982–1983." *Botswana Notes and Records* 17 (1985): 149–162.

von Richter, W. "Black and Square-Lipped Rhinoceroses in Botswana." *Biological Conservation* 5 (1973): 59–60.

———. "Wildlife and Rural Economy in S.W. Botswana." *Botswana Notes and Records* 2 (1970): 85–94.

von Richter, W., and J. Passineau. "Endangered Wildlife Species in Botswana." *Botswana Notes and Records* 11 (1979): 121–125.

Williamson, D. T. "The Status of Red Lechwe in the Linyati Swamp." *Botswana Notes and Records* 13 (1981): 101–105.

Williamson, D. T., and J. E. Williamson. "An Assessment of the Impact of Fences on Large Herbivore Biomass in the Kalahari." *Botswana Notes and Records* 13 (1981): 107–110.

About the Authors

Jeff Ramsay (B.A., University of Pennsylvania; M.A., Ph.D., Boston University) is now the head of the social sciences department at Legae Academy in Gaborone, Botswana, where he teaches history. After completing his Ph.D. on the Kweneng District, he moved to Botswana in 1992. His long-running weekly column "Back to the Future" in the national press has made him the best-known historian in the country. He has also served as a consultant for government committees mediating boundary disputes with neighboring countries. Ramsay has coedited *The Birth of Botswana: A History of the Bechuanaland Protectorate from 1910 to 1966* (Longman Botswana: 1987) with Fred Morton and has written two forthcoming books with Barry Morton.

Barry Morton (A.B., Ohio University; M.A., Ph.D., Indiana University) wrote his dissertation on the colonial history of Ngamiland District. He grew up in Botswana in the 1970s and 1980s and is the author of *Pre-Colonial Botswana: An Annotated Bibliography and Guide to the Sources* (Botswana Society: 1994). In addition, he and Ramsay have coauthored *The Making of a President: A Biography of Sir Ketumile Masire* (Pula Press: forthcoming) and, with Themba Mgadla, *Building a Nation: A History of Botswana to 1910* (Longman: forthcoming).

Fred Morton (B.A., Ohio Northern University; M.A., Ohio State University; Ph.D., Syracuse University) is professor of history at Loras College, Iowa. Between 1976 and 1987 he lectured at the University of Botswana. He has written extensively on East Africa and southern African slavery and recently coedited *Slavery in South Africa: Captive Labor on the Dutch Frontier* (Westview: 1994) with Elizabeth Eldredge. He has a long-standing interest in the Kgafela Kgatla of southeast Botswana and has written several articles about their history.